Tatya
OPERATION 1

Tatya Tope's
OPERATION RED LOTUS

The Topé family presents the story of Tatya
and the Anglo-Indian War of 1857

Parag Topé

Rupa & Co

Published 2010 by

Rupa & Co

7/16, Ansari Road, Daryaganj,
New Delhi 110 002

Sales Centres:

Allahabad Bangalooru Chandigarh Chennai
Hyderabad Jaipur Kathmandu
Kolkata Mumbai

Typeset by
Mindways Design
1410 Chiranjiv Tower
43 Nehru Place
New Delhi 110 019

Printed in India by
Rekha Printers Pvt Ltd.
A-102/1, Okhla Industrial Area, Phase-II,
New Delhi-110 020

CONTENTS

PREFACE

History is always written with an agenda. There are times when the agenda is benign, but far too often it is not. Dig deeper, put the context in perspective, and very often a dark underbelly reveals itself. In that darkness exist, many real stories that were not only covered up or buried, but also distorted and destroyed.

So what was *our* agenda? To resolve a long standing dichotomy between stories passed down in the family about Tatya Topé and coming to terms with a history written by aliens, and to uncover and reconstruct the *real* story of 1857.

Understandably, English historians had a biased view on this subject. A common thread running through most English narratives is to either trivialise facts, prejudice the reader by giving an unsightly physical description of 'natives', or pass off undecipherable events as religious rituals! What about Indian historians? Did they simply lack the will or the ability to synthesise facts? Were they more concerned with pleasing those who controlled their purse strings?

As much as academic historians – either English or Indian, claim to be objective about history, the question remains whether it is really possible. In the introduction to *1857 in India*, Ainslee T. Embree of Columbia University writes in reference to various narratives on the subject, 'the writers have proclaimed their freedom from prejudice and their intention of treating their materials with objectivity, yet their biases are strikingly evident in both the selection of the evidence and in the value judgments they apply to it'. In many cases when certain subjective evidence is available, historians have two options – one, accept that it is authentic or two, say it is questionable and therefore reject it. When objective criteria to assess the veracity of that piece of information are lacking – it is often the prerogative of the historians to make that interpretation.

In making that interpretation, *context* is everything.

In our quest to unravel the real story of Tatya Topé, we stumbled upon the 'hidden history' of 1857. Tucked away in the archives and the libraries, is a plethora of information, either overlooked, side-stepped or misrepresented. Add to these, the original and never before translated letters written in Urdu, the letters in Bundeli, eye-witness accounts in Marathi, English reports viewed from a different context, and we have a dramatically different story. Within the new context, these nuggets of information became the missing pieces in the mosaic of the war of 1857. While the red lotus flower has a symbolic meaning representing Indic ideas and ideals, this book demonstrates that the red lotus represented something far more specific during the war of 1857.

While this book is the most detailed account yet of Tatya Topé's contribution to 1857, presenting nearly all his movements and battles during his incredibly long campaign, it is certainly not definitive. At a minimum, it enforces the argument that Indian history, particular that of 1857, needs significant reassessment. We hope that this makes a case and, encourages Indian academics to relinquish their revisionist outlook, and take a fresh look at Indian history.

Illustrations are an integral part of the narrative and they have been used to represent the complicated troop movements in the various phases of the war as well as schematically describe the battles; all of which the English claim to have won. The base map was created electronically from publicly available information. All troop movements and analysis was overlaid on the base map, based on the various sources as cited in the text. No modern political boundaries are represented, because they are not relevant to the topic.

In the context of spellings for the names of towns, our primary goal was effective communication. The approach to the spellings of Indian words was premised on overcoming the inability of the Roman script to represent Indian sounds. We have used spellings generally based on phonetic conventions that have evolved in a post-British India. Many maps have been annotated with information from various reports showing the English spelling of the places used in the communication during that period. For example, a map showing the town of Deohati is annotated as, 'November 29, 1858: Tatya Tope at Dewhuttee'. This attempts to bridge the gap between the narratives of 1857 and the modern spellings of various towns. In many cases, decoding the English spellings and studying the maps was like solving a puzzle that involved guessing what the original Indian name would be, based on how the English were likely to have pronounced it, and then locating it on the map. While words like Raatghur for Rahatgarh were easy, Saltol for Sarthal were frustrating. Poonah for Pahoona were confusing, and Sooseneer for Susner were amusing. And of course, we have an entire chapter dedicated to 'Cawnpore'.

A significant amount of effort went into compiling the movement of the troops in the early part of the war. The troop movement table is a compilation of the main infantry and cavalry regiments of the Bengal and the Gwalior armies. It summarises where each of the regiments were stationed, the date when they overpowered the local English army, and more importantly, their destination. This table summarises the initial theater of the war and most of the action in the early stages of the war. Our focus on the subsequent phases of the war was on Tatya Tope's movements. The many battles fought in other parts of India, are referred to only when the context demanded it.

We have referred to the War of 1857 as an Anglo-Indian War. Regardless of the ethnic identities of the soldiers who fought the battles, there were clearly two sides in this war. Tatya Tope and other Indian leaders were fighting to rid India of the English. The English, on the other hand, were willing to pay anyone and everyone who would allow them to continue their plunder of India. While many earlier narratives have used the words British, European or White as being more representative of the personnel that were involved, they camouflage something very important. Whether the soldiers were Irish, Scottish or mercenaries of other ethnic identities, they all were being paid by their English masters. They were fighting a war that represented English interests and the English empire, where the Irish, the Scottish and others were amongst those oppressed. Therefore, we have often used the word English to represent what many other narratives have chosen to use the word British.

Divij Joshi, Rajesh Tope, Rupa Tope-Joshi, Dhananjay Joshi, Parag Tope, Monisha Tope
Naoise Tope (on lap), Nandita Saini-Tope, Prabhakar Tope, Eira Tope, Saoirse Tope

December 2008, Pune

Figure I

We, the contributors, are graduates and post-graduates in disciplines as diverse as psychology, computer science, engineering, medicine, military history, business and finance from universities in India, Ireland and the United States. Research skills from our respective subject areas were now applied to the context of history.

We spent more than two years in and out of various archives and libraries, poring over volumes of source material, translating original letters, picking-up the threads of a scattered Tatya Topé family, and in deciphering the tiresome English lexicon used for what was a massive cover-up operation, presented as 'history'.

While Parag Topé is the author and architect of this work, this project was the brainchild of Rupa Topé-Joshi. It was her challenge to Parag to fill the lacunae in this period of Indic history. With his incisive analysis and an ability to alter the context, the author created a new dimension to view the events of 1857 and Tatya Topé's campaigns.

Sourcing some of this information from various libraries and archives was the responsibility of Nandita. She has a secret source of energy, which she taps into when dividing her time between battling kilometres of Delhi roads and in caring for her little children. Nandita's early finding from her trips to various archives and libraries gave the project a strong momentum.

Painstakingly poring over mounds of paper, making meticulous notes and following-up with translations were Rupa and Dr Rajesh Topé. In fact, so unwavering was Rajesh's focus that we had a bizarre instance of him flitting in and out of the operation theatre in his surgical mask, spending time with our Urdu translator, confined in the anaesthetists' office in the hospital. Rupa was always a constant source of encouragement.

Dhananjay is the wordsmith who was not only critical in the editing process, but was also responsible for contributing to half a dozen sections in the book.* He is an alumnus of the Defence Services Staff College at Wellington and spent the better part of his youth in service to India. He now teaches at an international school in Mumbai.

Prabhakar Topé, Baba to all of us, is the senior patriarch. His razor sharp memory that spans more than eighty-five years, makes portions of this narrative personal. While visiting Parag in San Diego, Baba spent many hours a day for several months, painstakingly going over books and maps and providing valuable inputs to Parag. From his childhood in the trying times of Yeola, to the run-up of the fateful events that took place in 1946 and 1947, he has had a ringside seat to these events that shaped today's India. As a practising architect, Baba always encouraged his children to use illustrations to visually express ideas. The several dozen maps in the books that illustrate various troop movements, and reconstruct historical events, were a result of Baba's training.

We owe this work to the next generation, our children: Abhineet, Divij, Eira, Saoirse and Naoise, and, we dedicate this work to Aai, who introduced us as children, to what freedom really means. Aai is no longer with us, but we know that we make her proud. We bow to her using the words of Sri Aurobindo who translated Bankimchandra's beautiful poem.

---

*Some sections from the *Prologue, The Freedom Foundation, The Operation* and *Deconstructing Cawnpore*.

Laughing low and sweet!
Mother I kiss thy feet,
Speaker sweet and low!
Mother, to thee I bow

Divij Joshi, Parag Tope, Prabhakar Tope, Dhananjay Joshi, Rajesh Tope, Saoirse Tope
Eira Tope, Monisha Tope, Rupa Tope-Joshi, Naoise Tope (on lap), Nandita Saini-Tope

December 2008, Pune

Figure II

ACKNOWLEDGMENTS

The Tope family was invited for a special gathering in April 2007, in Shivpuri, Madhya Pradesh, to observe the 150th anniversary of 1857. The size of the gathering and the hospitality of the people of Shivpuri truly moved us. We owe a special thanks to the people of Shivpuri, who welcomed us with deference and genuine warmth.

It was at Shivpuri that the scattered extended family of Tatya Tope had congregated. Topes from Pune, Mumbai, Delhi, Nasik, Bhopal, Gwalior, Bithur and San Diego, California had all gathered for a special occasion. The instant connection with our distant cousins, and the anecdotes exchanged, kept the excitement of writing this book alive. The person instrumental in coordinating the Shivpuri meet was Mr Vashisht, a serious Tatya Tope aficionado. Our thanks to him for helping us unearth the Urdu and Bundeli letters used in our analysis. Thanks also to Mr S.R. Neekhra for translating the letters in Bundeli.

It is always the ordinary people who keep the extraordinary stories of our ancestors alive by narrating them to successive generations. We met people in Jhansi, Bhopal, Gwalior and other places in Central India who carried the stories of 1857 down generations with the fervour that 1857 truly deserves. We want to acknowledge the people of these cities. During the course of the last few years we met the descendants of several heroes of 1857 who have also kept the stories alive in their families. Amongst them were the descendants of the Nawab of Banda, Rani Lakshmibai's personal bodyguard as well as those of Emperor Bahadur Shah and Raja Man Singh.

My discussions with Prof Devendra Swarup on the subject provided the fodder for a critical understanding of the historiography of 1857. Prof Harish Trivedi was always a source of positive energy that encouraged us to stay on-course. We sincerely appreciate their support. Thanks also to Dr Gautam Chakravarty, who invited us to present our research at the University of Delhi in November 2007. A special thanks to Anant Darwatkar and Maj. Mukund Joshi (retd). Our discussions during my visit to Pune, on the history of the Marathas created a better context on the subject.

We would like to thank Prof S.M. Azizuddin Husain of Jamia Millia Islamia in meeting with us several times and supporting our effort. The Urdu letters were written in Khat-e-shikhasta and needed an expert who could read them with precision. Prof Azizuddin helped us find Mohamed Aminullah, a Ph.D. student and an expert at reading Khat-e-shikhasta. We would like to acknowledge Mr Aminullah's efforts and thank him for doing a thorough job, working as a team with Dr Rajesh Tope in translating the Urdu letters.

Dr Rajesh Tope himself found support in his colleagues at the Indraprastha Apollo Hospital, New Delhi, especially Dr Murali, Dr Raju Vaishya, Dr Anil Jain, Dr Ajay Kumar and Dr Shaktibhan Khanna. It was Dr Raju Vaishya who urged us to visit Shivpuri and Gwalior and meet with Mr Suresh Atre, a descendant of the family that served the Scindias (Shinde's) during 1857.

Archives and libraries provided us much research materials. We owe a big thanks to the well informed and extremely helpful staff at the National Archives in Delhi, Bhopal and Mumbai as well as the friendly staff at the Mumbai Marathi Granth Sangrahalaya at Dadar. The staff of the various libraries in Delhi, Mumbai as well as the University of California Libraries in San Diego and Los Angeles, were always helpful in locating the hardest to find materials.

I wish to thank my Vistarus team for their help with the scans of the Urdu letters. I appreciate their patience as well as that of my business partner Niral Patel, while I was distracted with this book. Thanks to my 'sparring partners' Prashant Rao and Anuraag Sanghi, who helped with the editing, and to bring better clarity to the complex arguments presented in the book.

We are genuinely appreciative of the internationally acclaimed artist and a true friend, Mr Balbir Bodh, for putting his heart and soul into the work of art that forms the captivating cover of *Operation Red Lotus*.

A special note of appreciation for Manjari Chaturvedi, who has been a part of this journey from the very beginning, and has indeed become a part of the family Thanks, Manjari!

I wish to thank my wife Monisha for her support and encouragement, and my daughter Eira who had to forego her favourite stories, to hear only of the stories of Tatya and 1857. Eira eventually started to suspect that her dad was perhaps Tatya in a previous birth.

INTRODUCTION

'Forty thousand men are ready to take on the real Tantia Topee and five thousand of his sepoys', was the summary of a letter from Major General G.S.P. Lawrence to the secretary to the Government of India.

This letter would have been otherwise routine fare during the War of 1857, however, this was written on 29 June 1863, four years after the War was over![1] Such was the panic the name Tatya Tope struck in the hearts of the English, even years after he was allegedly executed by the English themselves. Tatya's campaigns had become legendary during the war.

Generations later, the legend lives on. The name of Tatya Tope remains in the hearts and minds of the people of India, Central India in particular, even today. In 2007 a newborn baby, in a village near Shivpuri (in Madhya Pradesh), was named after Tatya Tope in honour of the hero.

'Tatya used to store ammunition here...,' someone whispered, as the author and his family peered down the dark tunnel leading to the basement of an old house. The place was Yeola, in northern Maharashtra, about thirty-five kilometres from Shirdi. The legend was alive in the family as well. It was this small house, where the author's father, Prabhakar Tope, spent his childhood years. Tatya Tope, the Tope family's ancestor*, also spent his childhood in Yeola in a house nearby, before moving to Bithur (near Kanpur) with his family.

Tatya Tope was not just one of the important leaders of the War of 1857; but as this book demonstrates, a central figure. During his times, he was a

---

*See family tree.

strategist whose electrifying marches very nearly reversed the outcome of the war; and later a legend admired by subsequent generations. Tatya's later campaigns, in 1858 indeed brought him to northern Maharashtra; however, Tatya was never near Yeola to have stored any ammunition in this ancestral home. Family folklore had that, Tatya once visited this house, disguised as a sadhu, several months after he was 'executed' by the English. Then, there were stories of Tatya receiving messages in lotuses and sending messages in chapatis shortly before the war started. While many of these stories were largely myths, buried within these myths were nuggets of information that helped the author unravel a couple of puzzles that had remained unsolved for over 150 years.

The author learnt about the 'Sepoy Mutiny' of 1857 in his history lessons during secondary school. While Tatya Tope's name stood out in history books, Tatya's real role in the war, and the story of 1857, remained muddled in the presentation.

The historiography of 1857, first penned by the victors of the war, presented an obvious Anglo-centric bias. Although challenged in 1908, most subsequent narratives remained largely loyal to the Victorian presentations. There were minor semantic changes, and the role of the civilians was amplified to synchronise with political views; yet, the historiography remained largely revisionist in its outlook. Recent attempts to challenge this biased history, have been attacked as 'rebelling against history', by entrenched academics, who have made a career defending this 'history'.

The author is of the opinion that the real historiography of 1857 remains blurred with these revisionist lenses, and what is required to bring clarity, is not just a 'rebellion', but a 'war' on the 'history' of 1857. The continuation of a 'war' that was first declared over a hundred years ago.

THE WAR ON 'HISTORY'

Vinayak Damodar Savarkar was the first person to challenge the historiography of 1857 when he published *The Indian War of Independence-1857*.[2]

Writing in 1908, Savarkar was not attempting to be an academic in search of coveted scholarships, or to win accolades and laurels. Neither was he hankering for the label of a great historian nor looking to earn fellowships in England. His goal was simply to liberate India, and the book was written to inspire Indians to rise against the English. Referring to the Indian nation, Savarkar wrote:

> ...within her heart, whose treasure is all-forbearing calmness, besides concealed, the terrible power of vengeance, too... Hast thou ever beheld a volcano! Apparently it is clothed with soft green vegetation; but let it once open its jaws, and then all sides will begin to pour forth boiling lava...[3]

As a later chapter in the book discusses, this volcano erupted on 18 February 1946 and changed India's history forever.

Beyond the inspirational elements of his book, Savarkar viewed 1857 in a completely different context. Considering that he was only twenty-four when he wrote this book, Savarkar showed an extraordinary insight into understanding the potency of the events of 1857. He challenged the premise of 1857 as a 'Sepoy Mutiny', and urged his readers to view the 'real history' of 1857 writing:

> ...to write a full history of a revolution means necessarily the tracing of all the events of that revolution back to their source – the motive, the innermost desire of those who brought it about. This is the telescope which will show clearly the lights and shadows obscured by the blurred presentation of partial and prejudiced historians. When a beginning is made in this manner, order appears in the apparent chaos of inconsistent facts, crooked lines become straight, and straight lines appear crooked, light appears where darkness is, and darkness spreads over light, what appeared ugly becomes fair, and what looked beautiful is seen to be deformed. And expectedly or unexpectedly, but in a clear form, the Revolution comes into the light of real history.[4]

Savarkar had only scratched the surface when he demonstrated that a significant reassessment of 1857 was required for a more complete understanding of the events of 1857. His job, relative to the historiography of 1857 remains unfinished, thanks to the continuation of 'partial and prejudiced historians' and academics who chose not to further study Savarkar's underlying thesis. Regardless of Savarkar's rigour and objectivity in writing, 1857 is indeed a very difficult subject, particularly from an Indian perspective. John Kay, a Victorian historian, who wrote three volumes of the 'history' of 1857, commented in his preface about the difficulty of the task, writing, '...truth lies very far below the surface. It is a long and laborious task to exhume it'.[5] Despite their obvious biases, the task for the Victorian historians, was therefore of exhuming what was buried beneath the surface.

For the Indians, however, history was literally, and figuratively, cremated when India lost the war. What survived and was published as 'history' is highly biased accounts, which were largely rubber stamped by later Indian academics and 'official' historians on the subject. The task today, of finding the truth, therefore, is not simply about exhumation of history, but that of reconstructing it.

History was cremated, because most of the communication between the Indian leaders of the war was destroyed.[6] So was objectivity. Amongst what has survived, of any communication with any Indian leaders of the war, are over a hundred letters in Urdu written to Tatya Tope. Tatya Tope was a mentor to Nana Saheb Peshwa, who was amongst the main leaders of the War. These previously unpublished letters, mostly written over a three-week period in early 1858 give us an insight into the government of Nana Saheb Peshwa that was established in Bundelkhand in 1857 until the fall of Jhansi and Kalpi in 1858.

In the last chapter of his book, Savarkar underscores the advanced planning that took place prior to the war, and follows up with a question:

Then, why was there a defeat?

Answering his own question, Savarkar opines that:

...the chief reason appears to be this. Though the plan of the destructive part of the Revolution was complete, its creative part was not attractive enough. Nobody was against destroying the English rule, but what about the future?[7]

As the present book argues, India lost the War for reasons far less abstract than Savarkar's conclusions. Considering his motivations in 1908, it is not difficult to see that Savarkar was projecting his personal experiences that he needed to address, to what happened in 1857. As a twenty-four-year-old revolutionary, Savarkar faced the paradox of destructive versus the creative elements of a revolution, which he attributes to 1857. Savarkar's thrust was to inspire other Indians for an armed revolt against the English. His challenge, as he attempted to inspire people around him, was indeed 'what about the future?' This book demonstrates the existence of both, the 'destructive' and the 'creative' elements of 1857. Therefore, the challenges of 1857, were very different than 1908.

The 125 Urdu letters represent only a small fraction of the communication that was taking place. As a later chapter in this book discusses, Tatya Tope, as the representative for an independent Indian government, demonstrated remarkable ability to manage multiple civil and military functions simultaneously. Savarkar was not privy to this 'creative' side of 1857 when he ascribed India's defeat on that particular point.

Undoubtedly, new source materials such as these provide an important insight into the events of 1857. Yet, a real wealth of information stares us in the face in what is already published. This treasure can be uncovered by simply analysing and assessing the information from another context.

There are a few critical elements essential in understanding the history of any war, more so that of 1857. These include the study of troop movements, their logistics and most importantly, their supply lines. Despite the large body of work that has been published on this subject, one finds precious little information on the aforementioned topics, especially the troop movements. Thousands upon thousands of Indian soldiers marched millions of man-miles in the period, which remains largely ignored. A study of Tatya Tope's movements after June 1858 uncovers a dramatic story that has never been told. *Operation Red Lotus* is an attempt to view the events of the War of 1857 from a vantage point that is vastly different from what has been presented so far.

Most narratives describe the battles based on reports filed by English officers and generals. These narratives have an obvious bias: Indian strengths are exaggerated, defeats are presented as victories and pages upon pages are dedicated to British 'courage and bravery'. However, a study of the troop movements before, and after the battles, often exposes English mendacity in the accounts. The analysis in this book focuses primarily on the movement of the troops and other events, rather than accepting English narratives at face value, to reconstruct the reality of 1857.

A few months before the war started, red lotus flowers mysteriously began to appear in the garrisons where Indian soldiers were stationed. This was followed by a chain of 'chapatis' that were travelling from village to village. Savarkar beautifully expresses the symbolism of the red lotuses that were making the rounds of the garrisons prior to the war, that were carrying an inspirational message.

> A Lotus flower! The symbol, the poet-appointed symbol of purity, victory, light! And its colour red, vivid red! ...What a tumult of thoughts must be raging in the mind of every sepoy when he touched the red flower! That courage which it would have been impossible for the eloquence of orators to inspire was imparted in those warlike fellows by the dumb lotus flower and by mute eloquence of its red, red color. [8]

While Savarkar accurately recognised the symbolism of the red lotus, these red lotuses were not mute. They actually carried an important numerical message, and 'spoke back', to their senders. This book attempts to 'hear' what these 'mute' flowers relayed and to solve the 150-year-old puzzle of the red lotuses and the mysterious chapatis. As this book demonstrates, there was a direct link between the red lotuses, the chapatis and the *real* cause of India's defeat.

As the significant events of 18 February 1946 unfolded, Savarkar's primary goal of liberating the country was achieved; however, the history of 1857 remains incomplete. Savarkar declared a war on 'history' when he successfully published his book despite being proscribed by the English in many countries. At the centennial year of Savarkar's groundbreaking book on 1857, the Tope family is attempting to carry forward Savarkar's task when he wrote *The Indian War of Independence-1857* with a focus on Tatya Tope's role in the War.

Many Indian historians have difficulty in understanding the real history of 1857, primarily because they use yardsticks defined by the English. Obviously, these criteria betray an Anglo-centric point of view. By changing the vantage point, the same information yields dramatically different results.

A renowned Indian 'historian' on the subject insisted that 1857 was not a 'war' but 'purely a mutiny of the sepoys', primarily because the existence of a nation was a prerequisite for a 'war'. The Indian nation, in his opinion, never existed until the twentieth century. The biases in the history of 1857 emerge from a foundation that is built on a fundamentally flawed axiom. The foundation of the Anglo-Indian War of 1857 is rooted in how one views India the country and India the nation.

THE FOREVER NATION

European polity has dominated modern discourse in recent times. Western notions of a nation evolved from their tribal roots, where linguistic and cultural identities eventually defined their political units as nations. Influences of the three Semitic religions during varying periods reinforced this rigidity. These religions derive their own identity from books, each considered as the 'final' word from God, therefore unique and superior to others. Tribal identities, and later religious dogmas eventually emerged as the glue that bound these European tribes. Europe evolved from a large collection of warring tribes to a smaller collection of warring states that had distinct individual identities. This became Europe's definition of a nation-state. Recently there has been an attempt in Europe to reassess the impliability of these attributes. Since the late twentieth century, Europe is making an attempt to politically unite these disparate nations.

Indic polity, however, is in complete contrast to these western experiments in nation building. Western ideas of a nation can therefore, never apply to India. In India's history, not a single major empire ever was limited to one language group or a sectarian association. While hundreds of sects have existed within the framework of Indic thought, one's existence was never considered a threat by others. From Emperor Ashoka to the times of the Marathas and Mughals, empires enlarged and shrunk, but language and sects were never a primary criteria in their identity – neither the Vijayanagar Empire, nor the Marathas. For the English and other European intellectuals, in their own sense of logic, the Indian identity was too nebulous to be considered a nation. The same applied to faiths that have originated in India, the world's 'thought factory'.

Unfortunately, historians like R.C. Majumdar and many others, who viciously refute the existence of the Indian nation during 1857, view India from these European lenses.

The words 'nation' and 'country' are often used interchangeably; however, there is an important distinction between the two. Geographical boundaries only define a *country* as a political unit. The Indian *nation,* however, is defined by a few core attributes, such as traditions, stories that are narrated across generations and the faiths that have originated on its soil.

Unlike many modern nations that came into prominence in the second millennium CE, the political boundaries of ancient nations such as India, or China, spanned across their diverse cultures and languages. The current process of the attempted unification of Europe was, in many ways, already mature in nations such as India and China a few thousand years ago. Whether empires in India shrank or expanded, or their names changed with time, the concept of a common polity, which we describe as a *nation*, was always well recognised, both within and outside.

India as a *nation* has an unique place in world history: it is the *only* nation in the world that has successfully defended the *continuity* of the core attributes that define it. India is the only *living* ancient civilisation in the world. India's continuity in its history, culture and polity is unmatched by many other great nations. Not China, Japan or Egypt. Not Greece or Rome; neither Mesopotamia, Sumeria nor Europe. Not any nation in the Americas, Africa or Southeast Asia.[9]

To be able to successfully defend the nation and its core beliefs, in addition to military prowess, economic freedom and more importantly, political freedom, is a prerequisite.

Despite a few hiccups, India to its credit has had the longest winning streak in its ability to remain both, a free nation and a free country; five thousand years as a nation and nearly four thousand years as a country. This is not to suggest that everything in India is five thousand years old, but that the continuous evolution of ideas, stories, faiths and philosophies from ancient times until today, continued on its own terms, and even thrived, despite the advent of foreign political and religious influences.

As a free country, if one measures the continuity of political freedom, India's winning streak spans from its beginnings which predated 3000 BCE until significant parts of northern India fell to invaders around 900 CE. No other nation in the world has ever successfully defended itself militarily for this long.[10] There has to be something about its people that makes India unique. Unfortunately, too many historians are unwilling to recognise this fact.

Even after 900 CE, while northern India kept up its spirited resistance against the invaders, southern India flourished, and in fact, continued to dominate the oceans. Southern India, via its large seaboard was the primary channel for a very large export market of textiles, spices and other goods. The empire of Vijayanagar was thriving even as the northern states came under foreign political rule all the way until the 1500s.

This was no easy achievement.

Ocean trade was disrupted when state-sanctioned European piracy that started in the sixteenth century shortly after India was 'discovered', strengthened in the seventeenth century. This had a significant impact on India's ability to control the supply chain of the products it exported. There was a large-scale trade diversion primarily by means of force in the seventeenth and the eighteenth centuries. This shifted significant profits and surplus away from India to Europe. Rapid erosion in this profitability had an ominous impact on its domestic socio-economic conditions.

This period from the 1500s to 1818 was perhaps the most dramatic transition for India than any other nation. Even as the socio-economic conditions rapidly declined, and the odds were heavily stacked against India, its people put up an incredible resistance. All the way from the North to the South and along a coastline that extends to more than 7600 kilometres, they defended every port, protected their trade and markets and, most significantly, their way of life.

Trade along the southern half of India's West Coast was protected by the Samuthiris (Anglicised as Zamorins). The Marathas, under Shivaji, defended the northern half of the West Coast. Shivaji rebuilt the navy, first, to protect its ports and second, to protect trade routes. He encouraged innovation in the ship-building industry and oversaw the building of smaller and more navigable ships to replace the much larger but sluggish cargo ships, to outrun the European pirates in the open seas. As different ports fell to the Europeans, he would reconquer them, right from Surat and all along the Konkan Coast. Shivaji did not limit himself to the West. Shivaji's last major campaign was in the South as he engaged the French near Puducherry (earlier Pondicherry).

As the Mughals crumbled in the eighteenth century, the Marathas ruled over this empire with a proxy government that paid the emperor of Delhi an annual pension of Rs. 13 lakhs (1.3 million). It controlled large parts of India from Orissa in the East to the Indus in the West and put up a spirited resistance to defend this young empire under the leadership of Mahadji Shinde. This period of expansion of the Maratha Empire in the late eighteenth century is very relevant to the events of 1857, especially in the context of the Mughal-Maratha relations and will be discussed in detail later. After a near half century of controlling an area that was nearly the size of Ashoka's empire, the Marathas finally fell in the early nineteenth century.

The nineteenth century saw a complete loss of political and economic freedom. For the first time in India's history, the core attributes that defined India as a *nation* were also challenged in a substantive way by the policies enforced after William Bentinck's proclamation on Indian education (discussed later). In addition to plundering India's wealth and causing long-term damage to its economy, the English unleashed a systematic policy to unravel India's education system, its culture, its history, its faiths and its traditions.

This was a period of transition when the last of a major Indian resistance was defeated and English rule was taking hold. However, it was not that this transition went unchallenged. Scores of battles were fought all over India even after the fall of the Marathas in the period that spanned from 1818 to 1857. These battles continued, until something significant happened again in the 1840s. The wars in the Punjab, the second one in particular at Chillianwala (1848-9), demonstrated that the British were vulnerable. Taking a cue from Chillianwala, events were set in motion to challenge the enemy once again, but on a much larger scale.

What started in 1857 was the continuation of India's obsession to be free.

India's defeat in this War meant that India as a political unit remained under the tyranny of the English, until the events of 1946. However, Tatya's dramatic resurgence in the October of 1858 forced the English to make an important concession. They rolled back their policies to subvert India as a nation. England backed off from its attempts to destroy the core attributes that have defined India for the longest of times. As a *country*, India remained in chains, but as a *nation*, India survived.

There were many heroes who shared this obsession. An obsession to protect India's traditions, its stories, its languages, its faiths, its markets, and its economy. India has had many heroes who laid down their lives for this freedom. This book attempts to analyse and narrate the stories of Tatya and his times, the War between the English and the Indians from 1857-9, which inspired the events of 1946 and re-established India's unique place in the world and history. This book is a tribute to the heroes of 1857 who inspired the unnamed leaders of 1946. Thanks to them, India remains today, the forever nation.

EIGHTEEN FIFTY-SEVEN AND THE TRIAD OF FREEDOM

The Indian leaders of the War of 1857 including Tatya Tope, Nana Saheb Peshwa as well as Bahadur Shah Zafar, the emperor of Delhi, under whose name the War was fought, made various proclamations during the War. One such proclamation was made by the forces that liberated Azamgarh, sixty miles north of Varanasi, by Bahadur Shah's grandson.[11] The proclamation was made with a specific purpose of encouraging the Indian population in this cause of freedom and seeking their support during difficult times. The following is a summary of the key points made in the five sections of the proclamation.

'The people of India are keenly aware of the tyranny and oppression of the English. I, the grandson of Bahadur Shah, have come here to declare that we will rid India of the English and will liberate the poor people who are groaning under their iron rule. I present this proclamation, to all the people of India, so that they can understand the policies that the Badshahi Government will enact. This will bring reform and freedom to the people in the following five key areas.

1. Taxation

India has been reeling from the heavy taxation the British have imposed on all the landed people of India, who in return tax the rest. I commit to lower the taxes, to preserve the dignity and honor of the people.

2. Trade and Commerce

The English government has monopolized the trade of all the fine and valuable goods that India manufactures. Products such as textiles, indigo and other articles that India has exported in the past are now a complete monopoly of the English. This leaves only the trade of trifles to the people, and even in this, they are not without their share of profits by means of high customs, stamps, and bureaucracy that is entrenched in limiting freedom in trade.

My government will abolish these fraudulent practices and open the trade of every article, without exception, both by land and water, to all Indian merchants. The government will support this trade with steam-vessels and steam-carriages for their merchandise. Merchants with little or no capital of their own shall have access to capital at lower costs with the assistance of the government treasury as necessary.

3. Public Servants

Today, Indian officials in the British Government have a limited scope for growth – the highest level they can reach is that of a Subhedar with a salary of no more than Rs 60 or Rs 70 per month. All the Officers under my government will have starting salaries of Rs 200 to Rs 300 per month with the promise of reaching higher levels in public service. Understandably, if they cannot publicly proclaim their support to my government today – I ask them help my government indirectly and help assist us to free India from the British.

4. Industry

The British economic policies have thrown India's skilled workforce into a life of poverty. From weavers to cotton dressers, from carpenters to blacksmiths to shoemakers have all lost their livelihood under this oppressive rule of the British. Support us in this effort and help us to enjoy the fruits of our labor and economic freedom for eternal prosperity.

5. Personal Freedom

The British have imposed and forced Christianity upon us – Hindus and the Muslims alike. I urge the guardians of both faiths to join me in this effort to rid India of the British and to create a nation that freely practises its faiths and its culture'.

At the core of this proclamation was the message, that can be paraphrased as, 'help us gain *political* freedom, so you can enjoy *economic* and *personal* freedom'. This simple message is the summary of the manifesto presented by the leaders of 1857. With this, the leaders displayed an understanding of the 'triad' of freedom discussed below and the government's role in ensuring freedom for its subjects. They specifically indicted the English for the state's interference in these areas.

European historians invented the concept of the 'Oriental Despot' from who they were 'saving the natives'. A proclamation made in 1857 demonstrates that, far from being 'despots', Indian rulers were very aware of the importance of governing principles that ensured political and personal freedom for economic prosperity.

The leaders of 1857 demonstrated that they understood the foundations of the Indian nation. A foundation that existed in the form of an implicit charter that governed organised society.

The charter that has historically existed in Indic polity for many millennia is not only the least understood of all Indian history, but also perhaps the most misunderstood. While India remains the only nation in the world, which had evolved ideas and maintained a cultural continuity for the longest of times, many ideas that allowed India to be a prosperous and free nation in the past have dramatically dimmed during the last millennium. Although these ideas were embedded in tradition, they were either lost or dismantled over a long period of foreign political rule.

The foundation of Indic polity displays a fundamental understanding of what freedom really means. Freedom in one sense comprises three mutually exclusive, but interdependent, attributes: political, economic and personal. In any organised society, these attributes correspond to some core functions that exist in society. They correspond to administrative and military functions, commercial and financial functions, and theological and philological functions respectively.

At the root of Indic polity were embedded rules that would limit the privileges of these functions. Historically, without these limits, these positions have lent themselves to abuse and misappropriation of power. While representatives in each of these three functional categories have a potential to misuse their power, the abuse gets worse when two or more of these groups connive under the pretext of collaboration. Historically in India, traditions and precedence served as a broad charter that would restrict their powers at many levels. This implicitly served as the Indic Constitution.

Western history is replete with examples of one or more of these functions grossly abusing their powers. At one point, the Roman Catholic church not only had its own army, it also connived with mercantile interests.

This represented the conglomeration of all three sources of power in the hands of a few. Protestantism emerged as a form of rejecting papal authority and doctrine.

Learning from these lessons, the founders of the United States of America, separated the powers of the church and the state in the American Constitution. While this concept was an important first step for Western civilisation, Indic thought was not only rooted in these ideals, it had additional limits on powers of the state, reflected even in the Proclamation of 1857. Not only was the Indian leadership demanding the withdrawal of religious dogma as a state policy, they specifically censured the interference of the state in economic affairs as well. In fact, three of the five sections have an emphasis on economic freedom. This message was potent and has been at the foundation of the Indian nation for the longest of times. The leaders of 1857 demonstrated a definitive understanding of Indian polity.

Despite celebrating ideals of democracy, western societies have been unable to separate economic power from the state's jurisdiction. While the Constitution of the United States set out to limit the power of the government, the creation of the Federal Reserve in 1913 went against the spirit of the US Constitution.[12] Many other nations followed and all powerful central banks became the central authority in defining monetary policies. In continuation of their mercantile history, trade and monetary policies today remain to be the cornerstone of political power in the West. Although these principles are in complete contradiction to India's long history, 'modern' India embraced these principles, under the pretext of a 'benevolent' government.

Of the three primary goals of the War of 1857 as presented in the manifesto of 25 August 1857, Tatya Tope achieved one monumental goal on 1 November 1858. As a later chapter discusses, India succeeded in taking one important step towards freedom. The next step was taken on 18 February 1946. However, in view of the triad of freedom, Tatya's task remains unfinished. The book later discusses some important additional steps India must take to achieve complete freedom in this context.

Understanding 1857 is critical for India to build on its current system, to allow its people to live their lives freely and enjoy the fruits of their labour; to create a government that, neither abuses its powers, nor interferes in economic and personal freedom of its subjects.

Only with this understanding can India truly celebrate its unbroken streak as the world's only ancient living civilisation, and the world's only Forever Nation.

PROLOGUE

FRESH AIR: PART 1

Medieval government buildings in their distinctive buff sandstone flanked either sides of the Bazaar Gate Street of Bombay. A few horse carriages and black government cars moved about silently ferrying their important passengers. The Bazaar Gate Street crossed the Mint Road at right angles and where, as the name suggests, the government mint was located. Beyond it to the left, were the military barracks for the English, and beyond that was the Arabian Sea.

Six steps led up to the tall Reserve Bank of India building with its imposing entrance. Neat rows of seesam tables were arranged on either side of a dimly lit passageway that led to the controller of account's office at the rear. Precariously suspended from the ceiling, fans stirred the warm humid air around. The controller had recently sanctioned ceiling fans – a rare luxury in government offices those days. Right next to the controller's office was a flight of rickety wooden stairs that led to the records department and from there to the terrace door. A lonely earthen pot of drinking water adorned the space below the staircase, which was zealously guarded by an office peon in a starched turban. It was a Monday morning on 18 February 1946, and, the account clerks were immersed in their precious papers when the impatient growl of a Triumph motorcycle broke their serenity.

An English officer in a sparkling white naval uniform arrived in obvious hurry at the Commissariat building. Struggling to park his heavy motorcycle, his folder of important papers spilt open. A few passers-by helped him with his scattered papers and his motorcycle, which was still running. Trusting the motorcycle to his unexpected helpers, the officer took the steps two at a time while the leather straps of his Admiralty binoculars dangled in his hand.

'Where are the stairs to the terrace?' he bellowed at no one in particular at the entrance. The clerks detached themselves from their papers and peered over their glasses, sizing up the officer silently. A few inquisitive locals had followed the officer and, now stood puzzled watching the scene. The officer repeated his question and someone pointed to the rear of the office. He spun around on his boot heels and bumped into the peon fetching him a glass of water. Skirting the well-intentioned peon, he ran towards the rear as the now puzzled clerks rose slowly. There was more commotion at the door as the curious crowd swelled, their eyes on the officer now clattering up the stairs.

Suddenly there was a crashing sound followed by silence.

The clerks rushed behind the peon to the terrace. The English officer lay sprawled at an ungainly angle; his arms and legs still flailing in their final throes as first the peon and then clerks reached him. The shattered lenses of his binoculars shone in the glare of the mid-morning sun. As the puzzled group hovered over him, a dark wet circle began expanding on the chest of his white tunic. Some clerks speculated the origin of the shot in muted whispers as, others knelt to inspect the wound. Someone from the crowd generously splashed water on the officer's face as life ebbed out of his now vacant eyes. His breath came in rasping bubbles as his punctured lungs deflated with every breath. His limbs thrashed the air feebly and, with a final shudder that racked his entire being, his body went limp. As the controller of accounts made his way through the crowd, the officer was dead from the single shot that had found its mark.

That day – 18 February 1946 – the accounts office had an unexpected half-day, as did many other government offices. Government employees went home puzzled as the air hung heavy with anticipation.[1]

The English naval officer's death symbolised a new beginning for an old nation. The events forced an important announcement to be made over four thousand miles away the following day, which paved the way for India's eventual freedom in 1947. The air of anticipation and uncertainty lasted another couple of days.

On 20 February 1946, a young man of twenty-two attended a large gathering at Chaupati. In a significant speech, an important Indian leader reaffirmed the rumours floating around. He announced, 'आजादी तो चंद दिनों की बात है।' *Azaadi toh chand dino ki baat hai (independence is just a few days away)*.[2] India truly was going to be free. As the relevance of this momentous gathering sank in, memories of his childhood in Yeola, his birthplace and that of his ancestor, Tatya Tope[3] flooded this young man.

DEPARTING YEOLA—AT A CROSSROADS

The *anarsa* is a wicked delicacy made entirely from rice, jaggery and ghee, and its fragrance hedonistically wafts through the house. It is circular and about the size of the palm. When made to perfection, it is crunchy to bite into and soft inside. The *anarsa* has been enticing fickle minds in Maharashtra for generations.

As Prabhakar Tope stood at the footsteps of his house in Yeola, he was a victim to the *anarsa* as well. The year was 1932; Prabhakar was all of nine years and the fragrance unmistakable. Perhaps his mother, Kaki as she was called, had made them for the important guests that were visiting later in the afternoon. Following his nose, he arrived at the *baithak* (living room) part of the house, where Kaki had struck an unusually tetchy note. Standing before her was Kashinath, sheepishly clutching a plateful of *anarsas* neatly covered in a translucent cloth.

'Kashya...where did you get the money for the *anarsas*?' Kaki enquired in Marathi, rather stiffly. Times were tough and ghee was expensive. Then she turned her ire towards Prabhakar. 'What are you standing and staring at? Go call Pandit from the *akhada*. Remind him that we have guests coming this afternoon.'

Kashya or Kashinath, was a weaver who lived in a single rented room in Kaki's house. He stood before her, shifting uneasily from one foot to the other, his eyes firmly on the dung-thatched floor. It had been quite some time since even Prabhakar had had *anarsas*. Kaki was upset with Kashinath because she suspected that he had taken to brewing and peddling liquor. Young Prabhakar never ate the *anarsas* that day.

'But, it wasn't always like this,' reminisced Kashinath to young Prabhakar as they walked out of the house. 'My grandfather used to weave hundreds of yards of fine cotton, which he would then dye with Indigo. Merchants would come from far-off places and give advances to him. Today, I can't even afford the *zari* (gold thread) to make the only thing that can earn us a living – the silk *Paithani*.' Kashinath attempted to explain to young Prabhakar.

Prabhakar ran towards Raghuji's *akhada* (roughly equivalent of a gymnasium) to fetch his older brother. Pandit was a teenager then and took pride in developing his chest and biceps. At the *akhada*, he was learning what had survived of the ancient Indian martial arts and would often return home splattered in the red *akhada* mud. The remnants of the ancient *Shastra Vidya* had survived as Kalari Payattu in Kerala, Gatka in Punjab and Thang-Ta in Manipur. In Maharashtra, most of the more complex forms of martial arts were extinct by the late 1800s because of the strict English laws prohibiting their practice and teaching. Pandit was practising the *lathi-kathi*, a form of martial arts that had survived, which combined strength with agility. Prabhakar was curious about the guests who were arriving this afternoon, but still thinking of Kashinath's explanation, Prabhakar asked Pandit about the Paithani sari.

'The Paithani sari is very expensive and only the wealthy wear it. Yeola and the Paithani sari go hand in hand; one is incomplete without the other,' Pandit explained. What Pandit, as many others did not know was that the Paithani sari was more of an aberration than a representation of the state of weavers in Yeola. Yeola was part of the Indian textile industry that dominated the world with its fine cotton textiles. Silk clothing like the Paithani was only secondary to the Indian economy.

'Who is visiting this afternoon?' asked Prabhakar, changing the subject, not exactly sure, how Kashinath, whose saris were worn by wealthy people, was himself so poor. Pandit replied, 'Gajanan Tope, from Vadodara. He is one of our uncles, and is also a descendant of Tatya Tope. Our grandfathers grew up together here in Yeola over a hundred years ago.'

There was a lot happening around the 1800s in the bustling weaver town of Yeola. Living at a stone's throw away from the same house that Prabhakar grew up in, but over a hundred years earlier was Prabhakar's great grandfather Sadashiv and his brother Pandurang, sons of Tryumbak Tope. Contrary to what is indicated in most books related to Tatya Tope, the Tope last name actually predated Tatya.[4]

Bhau Vaizapurkar, Kamalabai Tope, Mrs. Tope (Vadodara), Ambu Tope Kulkarni (Child Shriram), Sindhu Tope, Mrs. Ramakant Dhande (Child), Mr. Dhande
Gajanan Tope, Tope (Vadodara), Kusum Kulkarni (Ambu Tope's Child), Kaki, Tope Aai, Ramakant Dhande
Trimbak Tope, Prabhakar Tope, Narahari Tope, Vaman Dhande or Gotya

Photograph by Ambades (Ambunana) Charne - Friend

Figure 1: Tope Family Reunion of 1932

Pandurang became a well-known scholar of Sanskrit and an expert in the ancient Indian texts and literature. His knowledge and subject expertise spread as far as Pune (erstwhile Poona or Poonah) and right into the court of Peshwa Baji Rao II. His expertise included the ancient text categories of both of *shruti* (what is heard) and *smriti* (what is remembered). These sophisticated texts are unique to Indic philosophy, wherein the religious and the secular elements are distinct yet complementary in their presentations. While the shruti elements included the Vedic literature, a basis for the religious expression of Indic philosophy, the smriti elements were represented by the epics such as the *Ramayana* and the *Mahabharata*. These epics presented ideas that were designed to provoke debate. Fundamental to these stories was an analysis of choices and their consequences and discussions on action and inaction. These epics told the stories of a war that politically united India and the stories of a civil war that nearly tore it apart; stories of love, courage, freedom and the bedrocks of Indic polity, on the backdrop of negotiations in a war and the politics of power. Implicitly embedded in these debates were the roles of a ruler and guidelines for good governance.

Like many other Indian kings, respecting these Indic traditions was a part of the Maratha leadership as well. The Peshwas continued the traditions rejuvenated by Shivaji and respected the ancient wisdom passed on in these texts. Impressed with Pandurang Tope, Bajirao Peshwa II invited him to Pune and made available all resources required for these scholarly studies. From then on, Pandurang became a part of all proceedings, ceremonies and events at the courts of the Peshwa.

Born to Pandurang and Rukhmadevi Tope in 1814 was Ramchandra. He became Tatya (elder brother) with the birth of his little brother Gangadhar. Having a father who understood the quintessential nature of India as a nation would have had a substantial influence on a young Tatya. A nation that was, in front of his very eyes, withering. By the time Tatya was born, Yeola was still shielded from foreboding events unfolding in other parts of the country. Yeola in 1814, still free, had not witnessed English state intrusion into the lives of ordinary citizens. The Tope family home was adjacent to the areas where textiles were manufactured. Weavers in Yeola in the early 1800s were well off and independent. Tatya spent his childhood in this well-to-do neighbourhood of weavers – very different from Prabhakar's in the 1900s when weavers were reduced to a life not very different from that of Kashinath.

Tatya was four in 1818 when Bajirao II was defeated in Pune in what is described as the third Anglo-Maratha War. The terms of the treaty forced Bajirao II into exile. Bajirao II chose Brahmavarta (Bithur), a beautiful and ancient town near Kanpur. He shifted his court from Pune to Bithur. Pandurang Tope, too, left with Bajirao II in 1819. His wife and his children – Tatya and Gangadhar – joined him a few years later.

In the years to come, Tatya was witness to one of the most dramatic collapses of an economy that any nation has witnessed.

The Yeola that Tatya left behind was soon to change. The economic freedom that manufacturers had under Indian rulers was now gone with the defeat of the Marathas in 1818. Pandurang's brother and Tatya's uncle, Sadashiv's descendants, continued to live in Yeola right up to the 1930s.

Baburao Tope, who was visiting from Vadodara, was from the Tope side of the family that had left Yeola in the 1820s.[5]

Yeola was a far different place in the twentieth century in comparison to when Tatya left it. Economic opportunities were limited and poverty was rampant. India had de-industrialised and Yeola had transformed from a manufacturing hub to an agrarian little town without even a dependable source of water. The Paithani sari was what was left of Yeola from the days of its prosperous past.

Standing balefully with his plate of delicious but uneaten *anarsas* was Kashya, a victim of the wave of economic devastation that had engulfed millions of Indian weavers and other skilled workforce; but how was Kaki to understand all of this?

Kaki and the Tope family had economic difficulties of their own, though far less significant than those of Kashinath. She was a widow raising eight children. A few years earlier, Prabhakar's oldest brother was sent to Bombay to work as an assistant accountant for a merchant in Yeola who had operations in Bombay. He was only thirteen when he left home. He promptly took the economic responsibility of his family after the death of his father in 1925. In the next few years, Prabhakar's other older brothers also left for Bombay. Eventually, in 1935, the rest of the family moved to Bombay as well, in search of opportunities and the promise of a better life. The Topes were leaving Yeola, that prosperous place of the 1800s, which after a century of decline had little to offer to its residents.

Chapter 1

FLICKERING FLAME

INDIA AND THE KING

Students in India learn that the English came to India in ships to 'trade'. Conceivably, 'trade' is a reasonable euphemism for what the English were really doing for over two hundred years on the open seas—which was old-fashioned piracy. Perhaps the historians who author these textbooks want to shield the students from the grim reality.

At the root of this 'trade' were some products that India had to offer to these 'merchants'. Regardless of the methods that the English employed or the implicit price that the English paid, export of manufactured goods out of India played a central role in Anglo-Indian relations. As the proclamation of 1857 indicates, it was the deterioration of this relationship, which culminated in the War of 1857. Therefore, understanding India's economic history is a prerequisite for understanding the history of 1857.

Shortly before the Civil War in the United States, the southern colonies in their negotiations with the north declared: 'Cotton is King'. Cotton was King, not only in North America but it was the King of global trade. Cotton was at the centre of global economy. The textile industry in India was the backbone of the Indian economy as well.

A study of the Indian textile industry and the associated political and military dynamics provides an insight into the interaction between India and Europe in general and England in particular.

The urban centres that originated over five thousand years ago in the vast areas near the Sindhu and surrounding rivers were rooted in this industry. Block printing originated in India and had already evolved into a complex process during that period. Excavations in Mohen-jo-daro have revealed textiles dating from as early as 3000 BCE. A woven and madder-dyed cotton fragment wrapped round a silver pot, figures draped with patterned cloth, as well as cotton spindles were discovered from this period.[1] The technology for block printing cotton spread from India to Egypt and Greece 2000 to 500 BCE. Wax resist and gold thread chintz were produced in India and then introduced to west Asia and Rome from 300 BCE to 300 CE.[2]

The supply chain that starts with cotton to the finished products was fairly extensive, complicated and employed millions of people. Collectively, India 'owned' this *entire* supply chain from the agricultural aspects of growing the raw materials such as cotton and dyes including indigo, all the way to manufacturing, and even the ships that would carry these finished goods to far-off ports.

Weavers in a free India were the backbone of the economy. Even during the eighteenth century, despite the disruptions of the trade supply chains, they fared relatively well. It was common practice for weavers 'to employ their own capital in manufacturing goods, which they sold freely on their own accounts'. In fact, the markets were significantly free from oligopolistic practice that, 'an English merchant in the older days could secure 800 pieces of muslin one morning at Dacca without the interference of any dealers, pykars or gumastas (middlemen employed by the English)'.[3]

The process of starting from the cotton plant to producing even the thread was complex. This included picking, ginning and then spinning the thread.[4] Europeans who were more familiar with wool were complete strangers to cotton even in the second millennium. In Europe, the cotton plant was also the source of one of the more persistent fables of the European Middle Ages. In fact, unfamiliar with the plant that produced the fluffy fibre, many Europeans called it the 'Vegetable Lamb'. A supposed animal-plant combination that came from somewhere from the East, it was described as a shrub with a heart, with a mouth and a soft fibrous coat. There are illustrations of this plant from the European medieval period which include a specimen looking not unlike a warthog perched on top of a pole in the Garden of Eden.[5] Understandable, perhaps, since the only fluffy fibre the Europeans were familiar with in the Middle Ages was wool.

In 1728, Daniel Defoe, an English writer and journalist, in *A Plan for English Commerce*, noted that countries such as India and China had, 'the most extended Manufacture, and the greatest variety in the World; and their Manufactures push themselves upon the World, by the mere Stress of their Cheapness'.[6] In fact, India's efficiency in manufacturing derived from better agricultural practices that had traditionally existed. In many markets, Indian cloth had a far-reaching impact. Indian clothes were lighter and more elegant than their European counterparts were. In England, as a mark of quality, English cloth was falsely marketed as Indian.[7] India, a global leader in manufacturing in 1750, accounted for a full quarter of the world's manufacturing output.[8]

In India's long history, the coastal states dominated the seas in terms of both trade and military strength. India's traditional seafaring merchants travelled large distances to export its industrial output including various textiles, calicoes, chintz, silk, indigo, spices, medicines and other items.[9] These were sold in East Africa, the Guinea coast, Myanmar, Pegu, Thailand, the Indian archipelago, Southeast Asia including the ports of Aceh, Japan, Persia and Western Asia. The total annual export of Indian textiles alone in the seventeenth century is estimated to be fifty million square yards. India's military prowess made a strong mark on these countries as well. Southeast Asian countries in the early part of the second millennium came under military and political control of the Indian states.[10]

The sixteenth century witnessed the Mughals establish a firm grip on Delhi. Despite some oppressive policies of the Mughals, during this period, India remained a vibrant nation, maintaining its strong trading traditions and controlling nearly 25 per cent of the world GDP.[11]

Continuing into the early 1800s, Indians had substantial freedom in areas that were not directly under English control. For example, India had a privately managed education system, with no government restriction or promotion that created a society that had literacy rates that were higher than contemporary England. India's education system included *pathshalas**

---

*School

and *gurukuls** from India's ancient times and the *madarsas*† amongst the Muslim population. India's economy was based on the foundation of a strong educational system that had evolved over a long period. This is evident in a statement made by Thomas Munro (later the governor of Madras) in the early nineteenth century to the British House of Commons. He said, if, '*civilization* is to become an article of *trade*', England 'will *gain* by the *import* cargo [Emphasis added]'. Munro was explicitly recognising that India had more to offer to England in terms of 'civilisation'. In evidence, he referred to India's 'schools established in every village for teaching reading, writing and arithmetic'.[12] Even English surveys of the Indian education in the early 1800s reveal that the educational system had high participation of children from very varied socio-economic backgrounds.[13]

With a barrage of attacks on India's exports and economy, India was going to face periods of alternating light and darkness, where two emerging political powers would be competing with the Mughals for the control of India.

The War of 1857 was a continuation of the same contest.

COMPANY OF *VRIJBUITERS*

The naval supremacy of the southern Indian states prevented the Indian coast from facing any serious threat until the sixteenth century, shortly after India was 'discovered' by the Europeans.[14] To describe the English, Portuguese, Dutch and other Europeans who came to India and surrounding areas in the sixteenth and seventeenth centuries as merchants is to euphemise all the words that describe old-fashioned piracy.

In India's long history of maritime trading, the ships built for transportation were large; meant primarily to carry cargo. They were much larger than the European ships, and were strongly and capaciously built. However, because of their size they lacked the manoeuvrability and were easy prey to the European pirates.[15]

---

*A Gurukula (Guru–Teacher; Kula–domain or extended family) is a form of a 'boarding' school where students live away from their homes in the proximity of the teacher. In addition to education, the students participate in doing the mundane chores of the teacher including washing clothes, cooking, etc.
†Islamic school

Soon after the English and the Dutch East India companies were set up, Indian exports were impacted. This simple form of trade diversion was a direct result of Indian cargo being attacked and looted in the open oceans. In 1602, it was reported that about eighteen Indian ships a year laden with textiles arrived at Aceh, but in the 1630s, only three Indian ships a year arrived there.[16] For European 'merchants', trade and war were near synonymous words. In 1614, Jan Coen, a Dutch 'merchant' wrote home to his bosses in the Dutch East India Company:

We can't trade without war, nor make war without trade.[17]

This one sentence reflects the reality of what the Europeans represented. 'Merchants' like Coen and others, would simply intercept Indian cargo ships laden with goods meant for export and raid the contents and then these 'traders' would sell these goods in far-off ports.

In 1685, 'the EEIC sought the permission of James II, to fit out and send one fleet to cruise off Surat and take, plunder and destroy all Indian ships and vessels, and another fleet with troops to Bengal to act *vigorously* in that quarter'.[18] Piracy was openly practised by the English on both coasts of the Indian peninsula.

The culture of large-scale piracy and looting each others' ships was rampant in sixteenth century Europe, as the American continent was being plundered. The ships sailing back from the Americas with their booty were raided by other ships to get the cargo for 'free'. Thus, the word freebooter (from the Dutch vrijbuiter) originated around 1560 to mean a pirate or a plunderer.[19] A letter written in 1647 gave specific instructions to the East India Company at Surat to 'intercept all Indian cargo ships that were 'bound thither'.[20] A 1658 East India Company letter said the following:

In a postscript dealing with a Madras letter just received it was laid down that for the future none but the Company's (East India Company) ships were to be allowed to trade to Achin, Bantam or elsewhere. You suffering (allow) no private man's ships of our nation whatsoever to voyage to and from neither to the ports of the Honorable Company trade not unto, as well as where they do; nay, not suffer (allow) Banias or Moors vessels to trade at the ports the Company does, to the prejudice.

The Dutch do not any, why we? It is our practice here, and it will be the getter for our Master's profit that you do it there also.[21]

When negotiations were not in favour of the Europeans, true to the 'spirit of trade' they would resort to violence. In the same 'spirit', Coen in 1621 massacred the inhabitants of one group of islands in Indonesia.[22] William Bolts, in 1772 'Considerations on Indian Affairs' notes the following:

The fleet on the Malabar coast made immense booty at sea from indiscriminately plundering all Indian merchant ships; whilst the troops in Bengal, under the command of Mr Job Charnock, the Company chief factor at Hoogly, experienced many changes of fortune.[23]

This pattern of piracy and looting continued for decades into the seventeenth century, and soon the Indian merchants were going to need an armed navy for the protection of their cargo. Although, both the coasts were being attacked, the Mughal Empire of the north and the Deccan Sultanates to the south did little as the Indian economy started to take a beating.

The situation was about to change as another nascent empire along the West Coast would emerge to protect India's long history of export and trade.

A SPARK OF LIGHT

India's economic status quo was fundamentally altered when Indian merchant ships along coastal India was being plundered by European pirates. There was a dramatic decline in the control of India's export value chain. This affected trade along both the coasts. The southern half of India's West Coast was protected by the Samoothiris (Anglicised as Zamorins). This included not only the Malabar Coast, but also the entire coast including coastal regions of modern day Kerala and Karnataka. This resistance continued even in the eighteenth century in varying degrees. Marthanda Varma, the king of Thiruvithaamkoor (later Anglicised as Travancore) successfully repelled an attack by the Dutch fleet led by Captain D'lennoy in 1741. The Dutch were vanquished in a battle fought off the coast of Kanyakumari. Capt D'lennoy was captured. Instead of executing the vanquished captain, the pragmatic

Varma hired him instead. D'lennoy went on to serve Travancore for another thirty years. His tomb today lies in the fort of Udaygiri.[24]

While the Samoothiris defended the southern half of the West Coast, the northern half remained largely defenceless in the sixteenth century. The Europeans continued to plunder the northern half of the West Coast, with the Mughals and their protectorates doing little to rein the scourge of piracy, creating massive disturbances to the regions as well as India's economy. It was this shift in the economic status quo, which necessitated the rise of a leader who would take on these new enemies of free trade.

During the early seventeeth century, the Vijayanagara Empire of the south and the Bahamani Sultanates had given way to the many Deccan Sultanates. One of them was the Ahmednagar Sultanate. During 1633 and 1636, when the Nizam was still a child, a man named Shahaji administered his sultanate as his proxy.[25] In the following years Shahaji negotiated a strong position in the Bijapur Sultanate, while personally maintaining control over significant 'jagirs' of the kingdom, even as he transferred his services. As a general in the Bijapur Sultanate, Shahaji commanded an army of over 12,000.[26] As a continued act of demonstrating his autonomy, Shahaji appointed his twelve-year-old son, Shivaji as the king of the areas that were under his direct control.[27]

As Shivaji exerted control over the region, he began the process of creating a state that would take the Europeans head on. The long coastline and the Ghats inland were the lands he controlled. Shivaji needed an armed navy to protect the coast, and an infantry and a cavalry for the land. This needed capital. The areas along the Western Ghats became his base, where the population would now pay the 'chauth' or taxes, to Shivaji instead.

Shivaji's assertiveness and autonomy was to the annoyance of Deccan Sultanates and the Mughals to the north. Shivaji's new and independent state received the land revenue that these empires had historically claimed as theirs. Shivaji created this independent state while fighting on three distinct fronts – the ocean, the coast and inland. He built the navy for the first two fronts – protecting the merchant ships in the ocean from European piracy; and the infantry and the cavalry to fight inland against the Mughal protectorates who saw their empire coming under threat. Under the leadership of his Admiral Kanhoji Angre, his navy also defended the ports from seaborne attacks from both the Europeans and the Siddis.[28] The third front was represented by the battles with Deccan Sultanates and the Mughals.

In the 1650s, Shivaji specifically created a naval policy to protect seafaring merchants from European piracy. The larger cargo ships were being easily captured and looted by the European pirates along India's western coast. Shivaji encouraged the building of smaller, more navigable ships (*gharabs* and *galbats*) to replace the large cargo ships. English records indicate that his fleet consisted of 'small ships and vessels'[29] which was a direct result of his 'shrink or sink' policy. European travellers to India witnessed the extensive shipbuilding during this period in the seventeenth century. They write extensively about the existence of 'master shipbuilders' who could 'ingeniously perform all sorts of iron works—manufacturing spikes, bolts, anchors and more'.[30] This was also a period when Shivaji created a fundamental shift from the bulky and unmanoeuvrable ships that had become easy prey to European pirates. His armed fleet consisted of what the Europeans called as *Sanguiceis* (singular Sanguicel, possibly derived from the place Sangameshwar where they were manufactured) that could hold up to twenty armed sailors.[31]

Shivaji liberated many ports along the coast where he created passageways for merchant ships to travel to Persia, Basra, Mocha and other places. The West Coast of India, now under direct protection of a nascent but growing empire under Shivaji to the north and the Samoothiris to the south, was therefore hard to penetrate. Many battles were fought between Shivaji and the English over Surat and other ports. Following Shivaji's orders, his Admiral Kanhoji Angre engaged many such European fleets. These 'vrijbuiters' frustrated by Angre's successful protection of India's West Coast, described him as a 'pirate'.[32] Obviously, in the spirit of a famous Hindi adage, *'ulta chor kotwal ko daante'*, roughly translated as 'the wrongdoer admonishing the law-keeper'.

Shivaji's ability to protect his people and the trade, while growing this empire against multiple enemies; facing them in the oceans, in the plains and in the mountains, was a remarkable achievement. He leveraged his ability to be nimble and flexible to win battles when the odds were heavily stacked against him. Shivaji was a hero to many, including all later Marathas. Tatya Tope's nimble marches, his flexible war strategies, and his undiminished spirit in the face of adversity are often compared to those of Shivaji.

In 1664, Shivaji gathered his fleet of eighty-five ships and mounted his Basrur campaign along the Konkan coast.[33] This campaign was meant to send across the message to the population that the coast was now under his protection and to encourage merchants to take to the oceans again, and to boost the economy by resurrecting exports and trade, which were under a cloud of European piracy. Despite the macabre and barbaric attacks by Europeans on civilian merchant ships, Shivaji was able to protect trade and major ports of the West Coast against this new and growing infestation. At the peak of his empire, Shivaji was said to have over two hundred ships in his fleet.[34]

Shivaji was immensely successful in carving out an empire, which started out of nothing. New research is revealing that the Mughal-Maratha relations during the times of Shivaji and Aurangzeb were more complex than presented earlier. In fact after Shivaji's coronation, Shivaji's focus was more on the south than the north. Shivaji consolidated his power in the south to protect India from the menace of European piracy and plunder.[35]

The success of the Marathas was largely due to the secular nature of their military combined with a strong culture of discipline. This allowed them to rule most of India in less than hundred years after Shivaji's coronation in 1674. The English, unable to expand in the West Coast, were forced to find other weaker areas within India. They found a weakness in the east. The company of pirates finally found solid ground.

Chapter 2

PENUMBRA

BUFO CLIVEUS AND THE ENGLISH
EVOLUTION—AMPHIBIAN PIRACY

The English started controlling the ocean trade through forceful subjugation; therefore, the supply chain of products and goods that reached India's former trading partners as well as the new was disrupted. After meeting with stiff resistance from the western and southern coasts of India, the English with Clive at the head were finally able to penetrate the coast into inland Bengal. Lord Clive can be described as someone who graduated summa cum laude in the class of the English 'merchants' who went from piracy on the open seas and ports, to looting the land.

They began in Bengal.

On June 23, 1757, one of the richest provinces of Asia lay before him defenseless, ripe for plunder. Eight hundred thousand pounds were sent down the Hooghly to Calcutta, in one shipment; Clive himself too received between two and three hundred thousand pounds.[1]

Thomas Macaulay who was also considered to be a historical authority on plundering of India said the following of this famous Clive:

We may safely affirm that no Englishman who started with nothing has ever, in any line of life, created such a fortune at the early age of thirty-four.[2]

But the takings of Clive, either for himself or for the government, were trifling compared to the wholesale robbery and spoilation which followed his departure, when Bengal was surrendered to a helpless prey to a myriad of greedy officials. These officials were absolute, irresponsible, and rapacious, and they emptied the private hoards. Their only thought was to wring some hundreds of thousands of pounds out of the natives as quickly as possible, and hurry home to display their wealth. Enormous fortunes were thus rapidly accumulated at Calcutta, while thirty millions of human beings were reduced to the extremity of wretchedness... the savings of long years of toil were exhausted, and when, in 1770, a drought brought famine, the resources of the people failed, and they perished by the millions: the very streets of Calcutta were blocked up by the dying and the dead.[3]

This sight was again common in the 1940s. However, what Adams was referring to, was the infamous Bengal Famine of the 1770s where over ten million people, nearly a third of Bengal, was wiped out.[4] That the English policy was that of pillage and plunder was common knowledge even in England.

In reference to the English East India Company (EEIC) that was eventually dissolved in 1858, it was said:

...that there was something in the first frame and constitution of the company, which extended the sordid principles of their origin over all their successive operations; connecting with their civil policy, and even with their boldest achievements, the meanness of a pedlar, and the profligacy of pirates.[5]

Even the directors of the East India Company admitted that their vast fortunes acquired in the inland trade were obtained by 'tyrannical and oppressive' conduct. The methods for setting prices were enforced on the pain of 'flogging and confinement'.[6]

The English were able to create barriers in the trading process. As the calicoes, muslins and silks form the innumerable weaving centres and manufacturing hubs of India were pouring into the Asian, African and European markets, the English were restricting the weaver's even indirect access to these markets, old and new, that they monopolised.[7]

As Bengal came under the political control of the English, they forcefully destroyed the existence of free marketplaces for rice, bamboo, fish, ginger, tobacco, salt, betelnut, ghee and employed their own servants in the trade—disrupting the entire economic infrastructure that existed at that time.[8] In fact, 'they forcibly took away the goods of ryots and merchants for a fourth part of their value and obliged the ryots to give five rupees for articles which were not worth one'.[9] Any attempts to access alternative markets resulted in physical punishment in the lands that the English had political control. Fines, imprisonments, floggings and other methods unknown to the skilled workforce that comprised the basis of Indian manufacturing were utilised to enforce their monopoly.

> Various and innumerable are the methods of oppressing the weavers, which are daily practised by the Company's agents and gomastahs in the country; such as by fines, imprisonments, floggings, forcing bonds from them, by which the number of weavers in the country has been greatly decreased.[10]

The position of weavers had become precarious as their access to markets was choked off by the English.

However, there were more causes to the decline in the Indian textile industry than simply the old-fashioned looting and barbaric methods of price control practised by the English. During the years that the English were destroying market access for Indian manufacturers, new competitors were emerging. India's largest competitors for the entire cotton value chain were the North American colonies. However, there was a fundamental asymmetry in this competition between India and the United States, since the weavers, the spinners and cotton pickers in India were independent workers; however, their primary competition were the unpaid slaves in the Americas. Between 1784 and 1861 there was an eight-fold increase in the number of African slaves in America—most of them brought in to work in the boundless new acres of the cotton plant.[11]

In this period of darkness, India's markets and the value chains for cotton and other industries that had thrived in India for centuries were destroyed.

The irony was that despite these monopolistic trade practices and oppressive governance, the English presented themselves as the bearers of free markets. A dissimulation, that stands unchallenged, even today.

There are other 'contributions' to the world of trade that England made during this 'golden period' of plunder. One such key 'contribution', was the introduction, institutionalisation, transportation and large-scale global trade of an important substance. A contribution for which, England richly deserves *high* grades.

A TIME BEFORE 'CALI'

The 'Cartel de Cali' was a Colombian drug cartel founded in the 1970s around the city of Cali. At its zenith, the Cali Cartel controlled over three quarters of the cocaine exports from Colombia to the United States.[12] In 2006, Colombia produced about half the world's cocaine output. Gilberto Rodríguez Orejuela along with his brother Miguel Rodríguez Orejuela founded the Cali Cartel. As founders of an elaborate drug running operation, they made an important mark on history.

The 'Cali' Cartel was in good company. The EEIC also ran a drug cartel for about two hundred years, although much larger than the Cali Cartel could ever wish to be.

There are important differences between the Cali Cartel and the EEIC drug running businesses. First, a cartel by definition is a group of people or companies, therefore, technically speaking what the EEIC operated cannot be described as a cartel, it was actually a state sanctioned *monopoly* for drug trafficking. England became a cartel for drug running only in 1834, when other English merchants vying to profit from this trade had the King's authority. Second, while the British were trafficking opium, which is in the heroin family, the Cali Cartel focused on cocaine, a drug originating from the coca plant. Third, the Cali Cartel could benefit from the advances in drug refinement and could traffic drugs in the more concentrated form of cocaine. The English had to transport much larger volumes of the drugs, which they did brilliantly. Thousands of ships ran across the world trafficking drugs. The English were the pioneers in setting standards in the practices and processes of drug trafficking. The Cali Cartel could never really achieve a goal of surpassing the heights scaled by the English, in terms of the volume of drugs traded.

The opium trade picked up steam in the eighteenth century. The nineteenth century saw a huge growth for the English as they started trafficking drugs in significant numbers to China. China lost to the British in what is called the First Opium War in 1830 when it tried to defend itself. At its peak, British India had more than 600,000 acres of land that was growing opium (See Figure 2).

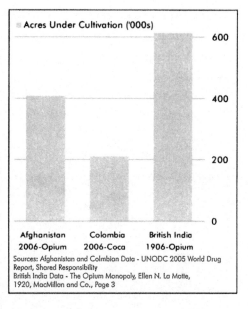

In comparison, the English were cultivating opium on more acres of land than Afghanistan, which produced 92 per cent of the world's heroin in 2004 and Colombia, which produced 50 per cent of the world's cocaine in 2004, *combined*.[13]

Figure 2

The EEIC also directly and indirectly controlled opium cultivation in India; starting from the seedling, to packaging, distribution and sale of the finished product auctioned in Calcutta. The Company disengaged itself officially from the opium trade by leaving its distribution to country ships, which sailed under the Company's licence. In the licence, a clause required such ships to *carry* the company's opium but in the sailing order, there was always a statement of prohibition *against* carrying opium—lest the company be implicated. Thus, the Company perfected the technique of growing opium cheaply and abundantly in India, while piously disowning it in China.[14]

Large swathes of land in northern and Central India was under opium production. Tatya Tope's town of birth Yeola, as well as his adopted hometown of Bithur near Kanpur, was impacted by these policies. Growing opium meant that in many cases it affected cotton production. This not only affected the revenue of farmers, but also killed the skilled workforce related to the cotton industry as well.

In the nineteenth century, opium was exported from India to various countries. These included primarily China and Southeast Asia. They were packaged in what were called 'chests', each weighing 133 to 160 pounds.

Most of the opium that was produced in India was exported. The average annual production in the period of 1854-9 was more than 70,000 chests of opium. A large part of the opium produced in India was exported to China (See Figure 3).

The English in India produced two primary types of opium, the Patna (Bengal opium) and the Malwa (Central Indian opium). A chest of Patna opium weighed 160 lb and Malwa opium weighed 133.33 lb. When sold in Macao, a chest of Patna opium fetched $2,075 in 1821.[15]

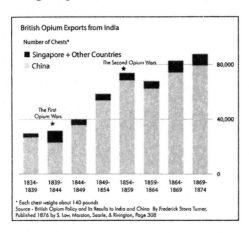

Figure 3: Drugging the Dragon

Then something important happened in 1834 that caused the price of Patna opium to drop to $744 per chest in 1835 although the demand in China had remained strong. The reason was the loss of the EEIC's monopoly. After persistent lobbying, other English companies were finally allowed to compete with the EEIC. The monopoly of the EEIC had now become the English cartel. One such firm was Jardine Matheson and Company that used to trade thousands of chests. However, their volumes were insignificant in comparison with the Honourable Company. Jardine Matheson described the EEIC as, 'the father of all smuggling and smugglers'.[16]

Needless to say that the lessons of English piracy in India, first at sea and then on land were not lost on the Chinese, or the Japanese. The Japanese had a hundred-year head start to learn and adapt to techniques and to protect themselves from this global infestation of European piracy. This head start allowed Japan to retain better control over their trade, markets, and their economy.

The Chinese were not as fortunate. Although, observing the methods of the English, which could hardly be described as trading, the Chinese decided to completely shut off any relations. After the Chinese refusal to have extended relations with them, the English started smuggling opium into China. In March 1839, the Chinese Emperor's special emissary, Lin Ze-xu, arrested the smugglers and confiscated 11,000 pounds of opium. In June, another 20,000 chests of opium were confiscated and then burnt publicly. The port of Canton was closed to all smugglers.[17]

What the English had done successfully in India, they did so in China as well. The English navy, highly experienced at raiding and looting many ports in India and other places in the seventeenth and eighteenth century, was able to win yet another decisive war in China, known as the First centuries 'Opium War'. The Second Opium War started in 1856, when many British troops were deployed to China from India. In fact, Indian leaders took advantage of the troop deployment to set the timing of the War in 1857.

After having won the War of 1857 in India and the Second Opium War, Britain was practically unstoppable in its opium trade, which peaked near the beginning of the twentieth century.[18] The success of the English opium trade and the tainted wealth it brought to England is unparalleled in world history. No other country before the English, and even later, were ever able to achieve this high.

As the English began to control eastern parts of the withering Mughal Empire, the Marathas attacked this once mighty Empire from the south. It was only a question of time before the Marathas and the English would battle for the control of Delhi and for India. They did so in three long and hard fought wars described by the historians as the Anglo-Maratha wars. The first was fought for a few years starting 1778 and led by Mahadji Shinde.

MAHADJI'S MIGHTY MARATHAS

In 1789, the pension of the Mughal Emperor, Shah Alam II of Delhi, was set at thirteen lakh rupees (Rs 1.3 million) per year and the Mughal Empire was only symbolically under his control.[19]

The real power lay elsewhere. It was not with the English, yet, but with the Marathas. Under Mahadji Shinde, the Marathas implicitly controlled one of India's largest empires.

The English were routed in the battle of Vadagaon in 1778 and the treaty of Salbai in 1782 returned all the territories west of the Yamuna to Mahadji Shinde. At the end of what were later called the first Anglo-Maratha wars, the Marathas controlled a very large part of India. The end of these wars defined the Marathas as the supreme power in India, surpassing their peak before the setback at Panipat in 1761. Eventually in 1803, during the series of the Second Anglo-Maratha wars, the Marathas lost Delhi and additional territories to the English. The EEIC resumed the emperors' allowance, but on paper, the EEIC was subservient to the emperor, just as Mahadji Shinde on paper, was only the emperor's minister. Obviously in both cases, the emperor was just a figurehead, first for the Marathas and then for the English. The idea was to extend power over the Empire without overtly declaring themselves the masters. That was a pragmatic decision by the Marathas that the English elected to continue. Other than the title, Mahadji Shinde was India's last *real* emperor.

Grandiose volumes of history books skip rather easily from the Mughal Empire to the British Raj, implying that the Mughals controlled India from 1526 until 1857 and then the British imperial rule took over in 1858. Their focus is more on continuity rather than content.

Randolf G.S. Cooper asks the pertinent question in the introduction of *The Anglo-Maratha Campaigns and the Contest for India*. If modern India, 'had grown out of a seamless transition of imperial power, why had the British fought such a long series of wars there?'[20] With the Marathas alone the British had three large series of important wars. The Marathas dominated the entire eighteenth century and was the last major Indian empire before the English took control.[21]

The events of 1857 are a direct consequence of the power triangle that existed in the eighteenth century between the English, the Mughals and the Marathas. The battle for India meant the battle for the ancient city of Hastinapur or modern Delhi. Countless battles were fought for the city that Indra once ruled. The Anglo-Indian War of 1857 has its roots in important wars that were fought for Delhi in the hundred preceding years.

In 1857, Bahadur Shah represented the once powerful Mughals and Nana Saheb Peshwa represented the last Indian empire that once ruled Delhi and controlled a large part of India.[22] The Marathas conquered Delhi from the Mughals in the eighteenth century but then lost it to the British in the nineteenth.

The foundations of the Maratha military culture are aptly portrayed in stone carvings at Bavda and Akluj. Bavda is about forty kilometres west of Kolhapur, and Akluj is roughly halfway between Pune and Solapur—in

Maharashtra. The elaborate carvings show local forts under siege and the disciplined ranks of well-drilled troops moving in tactical linear formations.[23]

India's long military heritage has innumerable descriptions of highly thought out and complex operations. These include the ancient vedic wars between the *sur* and the *asur* fought for the control of the hundreds of vedic cities along the 'sapta-saindhwa' region (seven Sindhu or Indus rivers); and the *Mahabharata*, describes each day of the eighteen-day-long climactic battle with full descriptions of the military formations on both sides.[24] India's long military traditions continued during various times in the second millennium not only by the Marathas but also by the Rajputs, Sikhs, Bengalis, Malayalis, Cholas, Pandyas, Vijayanagar and many other states.

The Marathas developed elaborate systems to, both, extend their rule into the imploding Mughal Empire, and defend this nascent Indian empire against the invading English. At the peak of the power in the 1780s, the Marathas had some seventy thousand trained and disciplined infantrymen in three armies. The army under the command of Daulat Rao Shinde, Mahadji's successor, was considered the best contemporary Indian army.[25]

MILITARY LABOUR MARKET

Eighteenth century warfare in India, particularly in the second half was dominated by economic issues as the contest to control India intensified. With small and large wars being fought every year or two, the military culture degenerated into a mercenary nature. A significantly higher proportion of the population now began to enlist in the military, as conflicts became a dominant part of life. Personal loyalty took a backseat as soldiers weighed their options financially and, were able to differentiate between their affiliations and their salary. This marked the infusion of mercenaries into the armies of India.

Despite this growing trend, Mahadji was able to maintain a strong grip over the empire. Mahadji derived his strength from two important areas. First, his pragmatism in dominating the military labour market that extended in northern India by leveraging his credit line, which was widely respected. His ability to pay soldiers based on the receivables of his large empire lowered the implicit cost of maintaining a large army. Second, he had the ability to call on the private militia in the form of the Pindaris.[26]

The EEIC, on the other hand, had to put upfront cash to recruit soldiers. As the mercenary culture dominated warfare; over time, the EEIC who also dominated the ocean trade of Indian exports, were able to afford more soldiers. The economic advantage that the Marathas had over the English was reflected in the large portions of India that they controlled. However, the EEIC with their ability to leverage their monopolies on the export had an upper hand. The Marathas tried to keep up with the military labour market by raising taxes on their new acquisitions, in attempts to keep up with the British. In the 1780s, Mahadji Shinde hired a Frenchman in the Maratha forces. This was Benoît de Boigne, the son of a French fur merchant employed by the French East India Company in 1784. Impressed by his military skills, Mahadji hired him as a mercenary and he first trained and later led two battalions for the Marathas. In 1788 after the Battle of Agra, the Marathas controlled most of India. He was given the command of a brigade with ten battalions of infantry. With more victories in 1790 at Patan and Mera he was given command of two additional brigades. He was eventually made commander-in-chief of Shinde's army in 1793. De Boigne's failing health coincided with Mahadji's death in 1794. He retired from the armed forces in 1795.[27]

Thus, the military labour market in the late 1700s started favouring the English and over time, the Marathas were simply not able to compete with the English plundering machine. The *chauthai* or the taxes collected by the Marathas, although already high were no match for the high collections of the EEIC. The English were collecting from the Indian economy a combination of high taxes as well as the economic 'surplus' generated with the help of their trade monopolies.

The transformation of India's military culture into that of a mercenary one was now complete. Despite every effort by the likes of Daulat Rao Shinde, the economics of India in the late 1700s meant that the Marathas had strategically lost the War to the English even before the actual battles of 1802 and 1818 had started. The rivalries and the battles for succession that ensued within the Maratha leadership after Mahadji Shinde died in 1794 were symptomatic of these broader issues than the *cause* of the decline.

The defeat of the Marathas in the Second Anglo-Maratha War was a result of the economic disintegration of India and the inability of the Marathas to keep up with the military labour market that had fallen into the hands of the English. While the regions of India that were under English control had already seen long periods of darkness, the fall of Marathas brought all of India under this iron rule.

Chapter 3

THE RULE OF DARKNESS

FROM THE GOLD SINK TO QUICKSAND

India had massive export earnings until the seventeenth century, which it exchanged regularly for gold. This had earned India the epithet of the 'Gold Sink'. The roots of India's real economic decline were in the early seventeenth century when India lost direct access to its markets via the naval route and were forced to sell their products at a fraction to pirates masquerading as merchants. However, the precipitous fall in Indian economic conditions happened during the nineteenth century when *all* of India was politically and economically under British control. In these hundred or so years, India's share of the world GDP fell from twenty-five per cent to around sixteen per cent. In the same period, Britain's share of world GDP nearly doubled (see Figure 4).

Economists explain away the relative increase in British GDP because of England's industrialisation. They argue that as the western economies entered the global market, India and China were not able to compete effectively. While compelling on the surface, this argument has very little basis.

With little or no industry, England's contribution to the world GDP during the first half of the second millennium was minuscule.[1] Britain and other European countries were late participants in the industrialisation process, in which countries such as India and China were pioneers. Although a late bloomer, Britain finally did achieve industrialisation in the seventeenth century, which would explain the rise in their GDP.

This, to an extent, can also explain a *relative* decrease in India's portion of the world GDP. However, this argument is not sufficient to explain India's absolute *reduction* in per capita GDP in the same period. If India's per capita production expanded in the first half of the second millennium, why did it *shrink* during a period when global trade was significantly up? (see Figure 5)

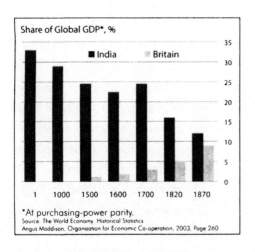

Admittedly, the market forces *did* have an impact. For example, the cost of producing cotton yarn, a labour-intensive process, was much lower in the United States than in India. This was because in the United States, slave workers performed this job. To the owners of these slaves, the slaves represented a 'capital' or 'fixed' cost. This was a clear economic advantage to the cotton producing southern colonies in the US to have little 'variable' costs since the workers were not paid any wages.[2] Indian weavers paid higher for yarn in real terms. While this did make India less 'competitive', to an extent, this factor was relatively small in comparison to the much larger damage caused by the loss of the direct access to markets because of the trading monopoly of the EEIC.

Most economists would agree that trade, in general, creates benefits, although to varying degrees, for *all* its participants. Trade is not supposed to be a zero sum game, *unless* it is a direct result of *forced* trade diversion or a direct transfer of wealth and production. In lay English that would translate as 'looting'. India's economic decline was not simply the result of the 'market forces' working against India, but in fact, because the EEIC, which also politically ruled India, restricted India's access to the global market. Indian manufacturing declined as the market access to India's products and technology was controlled by government interference thereby destroying the supply chain.[3]

Figure 4: Share of GDP – Relative Decline

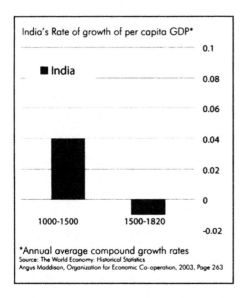

India's Rate of growth of per capita GDP*

■ India

0.1
0.08
0.06
0.04
0.02
0
-0.02

1000-1500   1500-1820

*Annual average compound growth rates
Source: The World Economy: Historical Statistics
Angus Maddison, Organization for Economic Co-operation, 2003, Page 263

Figure 5: Absolute Decline

England's industrialisation was a direct result of access to very low cost capital. In fact, the only 'cost' of capital was the military effort put to plunder India.

As India succumbed militarily to the English, so did India's economic and social fabric. India was entering a period of darkness, where economic conditions were tearing at the enlightened values that once embedded Indic thought. The fundamentally flexible and uplifting teachings in Indian faiths were giving way to dogma and rigidity in social norms.

Without economic and political freedom, India was falling into an abyss of ignorance akin to Europe in their dark ages.

DARKNESS SHINES—THE BOVVER BOYS

'Lord Macaulay was a statesman, a jurist, and a brilliant ornament of society, at a time when to shine in society was a distinction', wrote Macaulay's nephew George Trevelyan eulogising his uncle in 1876.[4] There are many like Trevelyan, admirers of Thomas Macaulay, including a section of the English-speaking Indian elite who metaphorically prostrate before Lord Macaulay and demonstrate this servile complaisance. Macaulay represented a so-called 'new' thinking in England in the early nineteenth century that influenced England's policies in India that continue to affect India even in the twenty-first century.

Macaulay attempted to influence India in three distinct ways. His minute on India's education from 1834 that led to Bentinck's Proclamation of 1835 is probably the most well known. However, the two additional facets to the Macaulay persona are rarely discussed. Macaulay was also an expert on

English history in India during the period when the English were plundering Bengal. In 1895, Brooks Adams, an American historian (grandson of John Quincy Adams, US president from 1825 to 1829) wrote the following about Macaulay's contribution to historiography:

> Upon the plundering of India there can be no better authority than Macaulay, who held high office at Calcutta when the administration of Hastings was still remembered; who less than any of the writer have followed him was a mouth-piece of the official class.
>
> Macaulay's essays have been the subject of much recent adverse criticism; but in regard to the plundering of Hindoostan, nothing of consequence has been brought forward against him. All recent historical work relating to India must be taken with suspicion. The whole official influence has been turned to distorting evidence in order to make a case for the government.[5]

Obviously, historians ignored Adams' warning – since much of India's history of the period remains consistent with what Macaulay's 'authority' had concluded.

However, Macaulay's most dominant profligacy was his obsession to convert India to Christianity. He was born in 1800 and brought up in a family of Christian preachers and army personnel who had fought battles in India. Influenced by the people around him, he had started making plans for conversions in India when he was quite young.[6] Though Thomas did not become a preacher himself, the idea of spreading Christianity continued to be on his mind. In 1813, he wrote a letter to his father from Shelford saying he was 'very much pleased that the nation (England) seems to take such interest in the introduction of Christianity into India'.[7]

Shortly after Bentinck's policies were in place, he wrote to his father from Calcutta on 12 October 1836, about his 'success' in English schools that were 'flourishing' in India:

> The effect of this (English) education on the Hindoos is prodigious. No Hindoo, who has received an English education, ever remains sincerely attached to his religion. Some continue to profess it as a matter of policy; but many profess themselves pure Deists, and some embrace

Christianity. It is my firm belief that, if our plans of education are followed up, there will not be a single idolater (Hindu) among the respectable classes in Bengal thirty years hence.[8]

Macaulay made a significant mark on India. While a section of Indian intellectuals continues to honour his 'contributions', there is a growing voice of people who criticise his policies. However, too often, the voices that criticise Macaulay attribute him with statements he never made or essays he never wrote, often mistaking his implicit goals paraphrased by someone else, with his explicit statements and writing. On the other hand, those who defend Macaulay suggest that Macaulay's goals were to 'uplift' India from the social and cultural issues it was facing.

Macaulay wrote to his sister Margaret in 1834, while in India and expressed his 'distaste for Indian literature'.[9] This distaste was evident as policy in his famous minute on Indian Education. Admitting that he possessed no knowledge of Sanskrit, he made a claim that demonstrated his obvious bias, 'A single shelf of a good European library was worth the whole native literature of India and Arabia'.[10]

Macaulay was very clear in the goal he set forth in his proposal to 'reform' Indian education. He wanted to create 'a class of persons, Indian in blood and colour, but English in taste, in opinions, in morals....'.[11]

In his 1899 book, *Education in India*, William Chamberlain acknowledges that this Minute of Macaulay, contained a 'prejudiced estimate' of Sanskrit literature, yet it was accepted as a model for a policy on controlling Indian education.[12] Macaulay's 'prejudiced estimates' eventually became English policy and were endorsed by Bentinck, who issued a Proclamation that paved the way for the destruction of the foundations of traditional Indic education. Two of the resolutions of this proclamation stand out in particular:

- The chief aim of the education policy of the government should be to promote knowledge of European literature and science.
- The printing of Oriental books should at once cease.[13]

This policy was devastating for India. Hundreds of thousands of *pathshalas* shut down in the next two decades, and literacy rates dropped dramatically. The state of India's education before Macaulay's policies set in is a subject of controversy.

The phrase, 'the beautiful tree' was used by Mahatma Gandhi in a speech he gave in London in 1931, as a metaphor for an India, and particularly the educational system, that had perished under the English rule.[14] He stated, what was well known to Indians, that India's literacy in the 1930s was much lower than hundred years before.[15] The English set out on a mission to alter India's educational system and assigned William Adam to 'survey' the schools in Bengal during 1836-8.[16]

Adam came to India as a Baptist missionary in 1818, but changed his profession later. Like Macaulay and many other missionaries who arrived in India during this period, Adam's attitude towards India's private education was hardly objective.[17] After an extensive survey of many districts in the Bengal and Bihar area, Adam reached an important—conclusion every village has at least one school, and Bengal and Bihar had 150,748 villages. Adam arbitrarily downsized the number to say that these areas have at least 100,000 schools.[18]

However, prior to these 'reforms' unleashed by Bentinck, the English had already surveyed the schools on the Madras Presidency during the 1820s.

Contradicting much of Adam's conclusions, the hard data from these surveys reveal some important facets of India's pre-British educational system. Indic education was private, where each student paid a typical schoolteacher (in southern India during the 1820s) 4-8 annas.[19] About a third of the students went to a local *pathshala* while the majority of students, both boys and girls, were educated by a private tutor or were homeschooled.[20] As economic conditions eroded in India in the eighteenth century, education decayed as well. Despite this damage, Indian schooling remained extensive and prolonged.[21]

Primary education typically started at age five and was offered from seven to twelve years, based on the school district.[22] After primary education, students could choose to go to institutes with higher learning. While primary education focused on reading and mathematics, higher education offered more variety, with colleges offering specialisations in medical sciences, astronomy, law, ethics and advanced mathematics. Some colleges offered advanced curriculum in the study of Vedas.

These surveys shatter an important modern myth that Indian traditional education was 'elitist'. This narrative of India's 'elitist past', was carefully crafted by England's liberals, justifying government intervention in India's private education, once Macaulay's 'reforms' had successfully destroyed the traditional educational system. This was later rubber-stamped by their 'Macaulayan' followers, in addition to the Marxists who view India's 'pathshala' and 'gurukula' education system with jaundiced eyes.

It is difficult to estimate at which point in the second millennium India's dynamic economic specialisations transformed into the rigid social hierarchies that became prevalent from the eighteenth century onward. While interesting, this topic goes beyond the scope of this book. However, Adam's survey revealed something very important: *Despite economic stagnation, India's modern social hierarchy played little or no role in school participation in primary education.*[23]

However, many modern intellectuals who represent Macaulay's 'liberal' thinking suggest that these new centralised policies actually brought 'progress' to India. They considered these *pathshalas* as 'vernacular' schools that offered little more than knowledge they considered either irrelevant or decadent. This collapse in literacy was considered an unfortunate but a necessary step in the right direction—of 'progress'. They concluded that the Indians' social decadence needed to be addressed by centralised government policies, and Macaulay's educations 'reforms', they claimed, tried to achieve this goal. This inference is not only contrived, but it is also fallacious.

Earlier chapters have argued that India's economy was groaning under England's iron rule. This was clearly articulated in the Proclamation of Freedom of 25 August 1857. England's economic policies were destroying the markets and were deindustrialising India—creating unemployment amongst millions of its skilled workforce. That Indian society was in a shambles in the nineteenth century is hardly a matter of debate. India's social structure was capitulating to the downward economic spiral that India was facing. The social issues that were tearing away India's social fabric were the *result* of India's economic decline and the massive unemployment in the country. Political and economic freedom was a prerequisite to India's reversion to a stable and equitable society that it once was.

Obviously, the English, including Macaulay, did not want to admit that India's 'problems' were not a result of the rigid state controls that England imposed on India's markets and its economy. They chose to lay the blame on its Indic traditions. Their idea of a solution was Christianity, which they claimed was going to take India, out of its 'darkness'. Macaulay's education 'reforms' were thus, designed to replace India's strong, private, and decentralised education system that had allowed high literacy rates and a strong educational foundation during India's prosperous past. Macaulay's policies were going to replace it with a centralised structure, a concept that was completely alien to India.

The idea was simple: the English were using the power of state to enforce a foreign language and Christianity to 'detach' Indians from their personal choices of language and faith to weaken the Indian 'nation'. In the ultimate form of state intrusion into matters of faith, England was intimidating India towards Christianity. Unlike modern missionaries who target the poor, the target of the nineteenth century missionaries was the 'respectable classes' that were chosen in this quest.

The intellectual inheritors of these English educated elite, who recently have been labelled as 'Macaulay's children' find it difficult to relate to a period when the seemingly secular rule of the English was ever any different. Most Indian history books reveal nothing of the period when the English systematically attempted to destroy Indic traditions.

These same 'children', who represented Macaulay's 'class of people Indian in blood and color, but English in tastes, morals and opinion', though influential, remains quite small today. Not all who were educated in these fine educational institutes fell for Macaulay's trap. If it were not for the events of 1857, his policies and institutions could have succeeded in their goals. Although he did not completely succeed, a small percentage of Indians continued to subscribe to the thoughts he intended to propagate. Some salute the English for bringing 'progress' to an otherwise 'decadent' nation, by bringing 'innovations' such as the railways. This display of reverence typically starts with the famous 'choo-choo' salute.[24]

Standing behind the façade of 'progress' were policymakers, like Macaulay, who were attempting to bully India out of its traditions. This was a dark period for India. Economic conditions were rapidly declining and as a result, the societal structures were coming undone. The time was ripe and England wanted to strike at the core of the Indian nation. Christianity was unleashed with a zeal never before seen in India.

SHADOWY CHARLATANS AND THEIR 'GRAND WORK'

Macaulay's policies were bearing fruit for the English. Destruction of Indic education had created a void that was filled with 'new' and 'reformed' systems. Christian missionaries were proclaiming victory in their efforts. In the February of 1857, *The Friend of India*, wrote:

> ...the greatest hope of all remains in this. Our schools and colleges amongst the thousands they turn out may yet produce a Native Apostle. He will ring the knell of Hindooism...[25]

Many Indian 'children' of Macaulay and many western sympathisers of his policies attempt to distance him from this type of rhetoric, celebrations and other overt attempts to subvert the ethos of the world's oldest living civilisation. Macaulay's intentions, as an individual, are less relevant if you consider that he was part of an official English policy to dissociate Indians from their culture and traditions. It was direct interference of the state and an assault on personal choices.

These policies continued in the years leading up to 1857. The Act 21 of 1850 was specifically created for this purpose. Syed Ahmad Khan, despite the knighthood that was bestowed on him was critical in his description of this act, calling it 'to have been passed with the view of cozening men to Christianity'. In fact, the government and missionary nexus was so strong, that 'the missionaries were actually attended by policemen from the station'.[26]

Continuing with the successes of destroying the Indic identity, the English were in the state of launching the next phase of attacks on Indic thoughts and polity. Many pages from Edward Rupert Humphreys' 'Manual for the British Government in India' published in 1857, read like a strategy paper on ruling India. Here are some excerpts:

On the lack of success in converting Indians to Christianity:

> Towards the conversion of the Hindus much laudable energy and perseverance have been devoted; but they are not a people easily converted. The Hindus have in the original (Sanscrit) language their Vedas and Shastras...in which the existence of one Supreme God

is inculcated, and they consider an appeal to the authority of these writings a sufficient answer to all argument. The prevailing superstitions engrafted, in the course of time, upon what was originally a system of pure Deism, are that of the ancient Hindu Trinity, or the religion of Brahma, whose allegorical types of the Creator, Preserver, and Destroyer, found their way, in some ante-historic period, into the older mythology of the Greeks, under the names and forms of the Chimaera, Briareus, Argus, Minotaur...[27]

On the role the government and Christianity had to play:

Applying this theory to India, and remembering that the moral influence of a Government, by which alone it can be permanently upheld, is exclusively derived from a conviction on the part of its subjects that they are benefited by their subjection, we must perceive that, *by identifying the interests of the natives with our own, by extending to them such mental illumination as shall enable them to appreciate, and participate in, our administration, and above all, by exhibiting to them the practical superiority of Christianity in its social influences,*(sic–italicised in the original) we shall most effectually perpetuate our dominion and fulfil the legitimate functions of a Government.[28]

Humphreys argues for a large-scale settlement of the English in India, saying, unless England was to 'really colonize India, and raise up an (sic) European element in the population, we shall be regarded merely as slave-holders and tax-gatherers.'[29]

In 1858, Reverend M.A. Sherring, in his book in titled, *The Indian Church During the Great Rebellion* wrote:

The Grand Scheme of Missions to the heathen is being acted on... This country of 200 millions of men has been claimed by the Church, which has sent thither its ministers, to proclaim throughout its length and breadth the way of redemption through Christ... The whole land has been shaken by missions to its innermost centre. The Hindu trembles for his religion and the Mohammedan for his...

Early in 1857 the chair of directors of the English East India Company, Mr Mangles said in the House of Commons:

> Providence has entrusted the extensive empire of Hindustan to England, in order that the banner of Christ should wave triumphant from one end of India to the other. Everyone must exert all his strength that there may be no dilatoriness on any account in continuing in the country the *grand work* of making India Christian. [Emphasis added] [30]

The 'vrijbuiters' who once proudly and openly plundered India, now had established methods to do it more surreptitiously. The English were packaging their retrograde policies under the guise of 'progress'. The goal was to, culturally denationalise India, and to motivate the missionaries to convert people for this 'grand scheme'.

Tatya Tope and the War of 1857 succeeded in preventing this 'grand work' from coming to fruition.

WEAVING A TRAGEDY

Indian's economic collapse had the biggest impact on all the producers of India's textile industry and the weavers in particular. The breakdown was not because of new competition or the so-called 'industrialisation' of the western nations, but primarily because of English interference in India's free markets. In the early 1800s, in parts of India where the English rule was entrenched, the situation of Indian manufacturing was already declining. English policies were interfering in the trade and limiting the access of the weavers with merchants. Weavers, in parts of India that were under direct or indirect political control of the English held violent protests against the EEIC, as 'the powerful merchants came to be arrayed against weak producers'.[31]

Tatya's birthplace, Yeola, southern India as well as the north—were all participants in the textile manufacturing based economy. Prior to this intrusion in other parts of India, and in Yeola, skilled workers in general, and weavers in particular, enjoyed tremendous freedom in trade and a degree of power. Prasannan Parthasarathi, in *Rethinking Wages and Competitiveness in the Eighteenth Century: Britain and South India*, makes a case that in many respects, the position of Indian weavers before English control, was superior to that of their counterparts in England.[32]

Weaving was often a family tradition. It is likely that young Tatya's friends would come home from school to a personal lesson in the techniques of weaving, from their fathers.

The boys were trained in the art of weaving within the household and family. The first step was to assist in the preparation of yarn. Preparing bobbins was especially valuable as it was an opportunity for a young child to learn how to reconnect the yarn when it broke. From here, the boy would have progressed to more difficult tasks, culminating with weaving itself. Teenage boys developed their skills by weaving turbans. The narrow width of turbans may have been ideal cloths on which to learn.[33]

Indian weavers derived their security and power from the economic arrangement that they had with traders. Traders would forward them an advance against which the weaver bought yarn and other requirements. 'By entering into such a relationship, weavers forced merchants to bear some of the risk associated with cloth production. These risks included uncertainties in the prices of yarn and cloth. A merchant had to share the burden of losses resulting from economic fluctuations and this gave the weavers an enormous measure of security'.[34] As a result, the weavers were financially stable with much needed financial liquidity. Typically, weavers in southern India who produced ordinary varieties of cloth earned enough to purchase about 250 pounds of rice a month. The weavers always had at hand, a minimum advance of two months, but sometimes even more.[35]

Weavers in free India enjoyed tremendous economic power that came from their ability to cancel their contracts. 'Weavers could cancel a contract by simply selling their cloth on the open market and returning their advance'.[36] This shielded them from market fluctuations in their costs as well as the prices they could fetch in the marketplace.

Tatya was four in 1818 when Bajirao II was defeated in Pune in what is known as the Third Anglo-Maratha War. The terms of the treaty forced Bajirao II into exile. Bajirao II chose Brahmavarta (Bithur) a beautiful and ancient town near Kanpur. He shifted his court from Pune to Bithur. Pandurang Tope, too, left with Bajirao II in 1819. His wife and his children, Tatya and Gangadhar, joined him a few years later.

The circumstances in Brahmavarta were far worse than Yeola, since this region had been firmly in English hands for decades. Here, not only had cotton manufacturing dramatically declined, but even worse, the cotton farms were replaced by the forced cultivation of opium. In the 1820s, Tatya saw a different India in the north as compared to the south. Yeola, free until 1818, had not seen the dramatic economic decline that northern and eastern India had witnessed by this period already. Long standing equations of free trade were not just upset, but turned on their head by the EEIC, through the forceful integration of political and economic power in the areas they ruled. The first step was to take away the weaver's power to negotiate with the trader. They did this by introducing methods that were tried and tested in England.

An age-old Hindi adage represents this exact principle: '*Raja bane vyapari, praja bane bhikhari*'. (If a king became a merchant, the population would become beggars). India had a long tradition where government administrative functions did not interfere with these markets. Western experiments in free markets have generally failed because the power quickly shifted from the producer to the merchant-trader. In the textile industry in England, for example, during the 1700s, the weavers became employees of the merchants. Indic polity implicitly protected the producer by restricting the traders from integrating vertically and attempting to control the manufacturing supply chain.

India's free markets were soon replaced by the English version where rich merchants, the monarchy and the parliament controlled the capital. This was India's introduction to the world of crony capitalism, which the English packaged under the name of 'free trade'.

ENGLAND'S EXPORTS—CRONY CAPITALISM

Unlike India, many weavers in England were 'employees' of the merchants rather than independent manufacturers. These 'merchant employers' acting in concert, lobbied the English parliament and facilitated the passage of legislation to discipline workers and reduce their powers of resistance. These include the Bugging Act of 1749, the Worsted Act of 1777 and the Combination Acts of 1799 and 1800. These Acts shortened the amount of time that home workers were given to complete their work. Insubordinate workers were held up as examples through public whippings and even hangings. Comparable legal interventions were unknown in India during the same period.[37]

These English practices were introduced in India as well. The EEIC used their political power to tilt the negotiating power in favour of the merchant who now represented the EEIC. Thus, that balance that allowed free trade to exist was eliminated by the use of political force and intervention. The weavers lost their power to cancel their contracts with merchants by returning the advances, often forcing the weavers to be indebted to the merchants. The EEIC assisted merchants in collecting debts and limited migration by workers. Thus, for the first time in India's history with its legacy of free trade in India, there was large-scale state interference in textile manufacturing. 'For several centuries, the English state had been intervening actively in the lives of labourers and in the operation of the labour market. Some interventions were to protect the labour, but more often, their purpose was to discipline and weaken producers. In India, by contrast, there was no such tradition of state interference by the kings'.[38]

Tatya was witness to this dramatic collapse of India at many levels. Tatya's early childhood in Yeola, followed by his later years in Bithur, in all likelihood, were important influences on his life. As a young man in the 1830s Tatya had probably recognised that a political alignment was a prerequisite for India's freedom. An alignment whose precedence was initiated by Mahadji Shinde.

Chapter 4

THE FREEDOM FOUNDATION

VEXATIOUS VIRTUES

Historian Amar Farooqui, in his essay on Baija Bai Shinde, emphasises that 'Tatya Tope, Nana Saheb or Laxmibai did not wake up to the reality of British rule just on the eve of 1857; they were products of a strong anti-British tradition that continued even after the fall of Marathas in 1818'.[1]

During the decline of the Maratha Empire, the central power of the Marathas had weakened and the structure had become decentralised. The Shindes, the Holkars, the Gaekwads and the Peshwas were now the remnants of a once powerful empire, each coming to terms with the English as the new centralised ruler of India.

The role of Jiyaji Rao Shinde (spelt varyingly as Sindia, Scindia or Sindhia by the English) during 1857 is an important part of history and is presented in later chapters. Another Shinde whose role has not been adequately chronicled, but was pivotal, is Baija Bai. During that dark period of history, the enigmatic persona of Baija Bai, perhaps, was the spark that inspired people like Tatya Tope and Nana Saheb Peshwa.

Mahadji Shinde died without an heir in 1794. Daulat Rao Shinde, who was Mahadji's nephew,[2] took over the reins of an empire at the tender age of fifteen. Baija Bai, the daughter of Sarje Rao Ghatge was married to Daulat Rao Shinde in 1798, just before the Second Anglo-Maratha war.

She was a first-hand witness to the dogged resistance being put up by her young husband, despite worsening economic conditions.

Baija Bai was an extremely astute 'hands on' queen, keenly interested in matters of administering the state. Not unusual to tradition, the young queen played a decisive advisory role to Daulat Rao. She even accompanied him in some of his campaigns, including the Anglo-Maratha wars, at the battle of Assaye in 1803.[3]

Surendra Nath Roy in his *A History of the Native States of India*, written in 1888, uses many adjectives to describe Baija Bai. He borrows heavily from G.B. Malleson's book titled *An Historical Sketch of the Native States of India in Subsidiary Alliance with the British Government*, published in 1875, including many creatively derisive phrases to describe this brave woman. Malleson's demonisation of Baija Bai is expectedly in the spirit of a true English historian, churning out volumes of history to fill the proverbial Macaulayan bookshelf. However, the epithets get more colourful in Roy's book. Baija Bai was the daughter of Sarje Rao Ghatge.[4] The first attack on her is calling her a daughter of an 'infamous father'. Many pages of English history books are dedicated to Ghatge, using words and phrases that are positively impudent. The 'loyal subject', Roy, predictably succeeds in transferring the alleged slurs on her father to Baija Bai. Roy attacks the character of this brave woman, calling her 'unscrupulous' as she negotiated a strong position with the English as Regent of Gwalior, after the death of her husband.[5] These attacks get personal when Roy uses epithets such as 'petty' and 'vexatious', and describes her as a woman who was 'naturally violent and overbearing in her temper'. This is evidence to the lengths which loyalists went to, to prove their loyalty!

It is exactly these large-scale character demonisations by the English or their Macaulayan faithfuls, which are pointers to obfuscation. They reveal more than the attempt to hide. Such pointers can be often fruitful to visit. Baija Bai's story reveals a rather interesting chapter in the history of Maratha power—even during this period of decline. Amar Farooqui in his essay titled 'From Baiza Bai to Lakshmi Bai' does due justice to the *real* story of Baija Bai.[6]

Baija Bai's early influences were indeed from this same 'infamous' father, who was fiercely opposed to the English rule—the father who taught her to be a skilful horsewoman and to use both a spear and a sword. Sarje Rao Ghatge was a part of Daulat Rao's court. However, Sarje Rao wanted more independence from the English meddling in Gwalior affairs. The English had, in fact, demanded his ejection from the Gwalior court, so that they could get on without much bother.[7] The affairs of Gwalior worsened and Ghatge was eventually assassinated in 1809.[8] These early lessons in diabolical diplomacy could not have been lost on Baija Bai.

In 1818 as the Maratha Empire was facing the third assault from the English, Baji Rao II was fighting the English in the Third Anglo-Maratha war. The once mighty Maratha Empire was now considerably weakened. The Shindes, the Holkars, the Gaekwads, and the Peshwas were now operating more autonomously. When the news of the English campaign against Baji Rao II reached Gwalior, there were two opinions within Gwalior—one to support Baji Rao II and the second to stay neutral. Despite the recent divergence amongst the Marathas after their defeat in the Second Anglo-Maratha war, Baija Bai insisted upon sending the Gwalior army to engage the English.[9] She had in fact commenced marching in the direction of the Deccan to join Baji Rao II. The English Resident in the court of the Shindes later observed that Baija Bai did all in her power to uphold Baji Rao II.[10] Though lost on modern historians, this expression of Maratha solidarity could not have been lost on Nana Saheb Peshwa, Baji Rao II's heir in the 1850s.

Shortly before his death, Daulat Rao decided to adopt an heir to the throne and sent for sons of his relatives from the Deccan. Five children were selected and were sent to Gwalior, but Daulat Rao died before they arrived.[11] The boy who was selected was eleven-year-old Mugat Rao and was adopted in June 1827. Baija Bai chose a title of Jankoji Rao Shinde, naming him after the great Jankoji who helped expand the Maratha Empire in the 1750s. Naming her son after a great hero symbolised Baija Bai's respect for Maratha power. She maintained the title of Regent for herself, to continue her involvement in matters of the state.

Baija Bai's independence had a direct impact on the Gwalior-English relations during this period. Despite the defeat of the Marathas, the position of the English *vakil* or 'resident' in the Gwalior court was largely the same as vakils of other states. The death of Daulat Rao created an opportunity for the English to demonstrate their politicking in Gwalior matters. In one of the attempts to limit Baija Bai's power, the English championed the cause of the adopted maharaja. The governor general sent a letter to the regent in October 1829 asking her to accord proper respect to the maharaja.[12] Baija Bai indicated her displeasure of this English interference and did not take note of this communication for several months.[13] She eventually did respond after persistent reminders, and continued to maintain diplomatic relationship with the EEIC, while asserting her independence.[14]

As the diplomatic gamesmanship was going on, the English raised the stakes. The EEIC asked for a 'loan' of Rs 1 crore (10 million) from Baija Bai. The English often depended on such local credit for its military and commercial activities in India. Implicit in this borrowing was the pre-condition to recognise her as a Regent of Gwalior. Yet to find her footing, Baija Bai 'thought it politic to accede to a request so earnestly pressed upon her'.[15] She recognised that the English were indirectly extorting her. The terms of repayment were designed to be deliberately vague, which signalled the English intentions. Thus, the woman who was 'naturally violent and overbearing in her temper' outplayed the English, in whittling down the amount to Rs 80 lakh (8 million).

Knowing that the English were treating this as a 'soft loan' with no intention of paying it back, Baija Bai remained tough. Once Baija Bai was firmly in power, she insisted on a formal acknowledgement, specifically stating the principal and the interest that were due.

The English tried every trick in the book to subvert repayment of the loan. One such attempt demanded her to prove that the funds were her personal wealth, and not from the Gwalior treasury.[16] English attempts to back out repayment of the loan were unfruitful as this 'Sindhia' woman persisted until the English agreed. Baija Bai made sure that the amount was paid into her banking firm in Varanasi, not into the treasury at Gwalior, which the English were slowly attempting to control.[17]

The Company was not pleased, neither were their loyal historians. Baija Bai was going to be more trouble than what the English were hoping. This explains the fond usage of the term 'petty' in Malleson, and later Roy's, narrative on the 'Bai'.

For the English, Baija Bai was becoming more than simply petty. She upped the ante, and tried to cut off the finances to the English by using her influence on the large bankers that operated in the prosperous Malwa region.[18] Baija Bai herself owned a large network of banking firms which operated under various names, from Varanasi to Ujjain. In Ujjain, she was reportedly at the head of the banking firms Nathji Kishan Das and Nathji Bhagwan Das.[19]

Baija Bai was able to keep the English from getting control of Gwalior despite her husband's death. However, Jankoji II, her adopted son, was going to be more trouble than Baija Bai anticipated.

As he grew older, Jankoji II started leaning towards developing an understanding with the English, possibly recognising personal gains[20] much to his adopted mother's disapproval. Her goal was to maintain power and the relative independence that Daulat Rao had created despite the defeat of the Marathas. Ignoring his 'new' mother's advice, Jankoji II desired to expand his relationship with the English. Even after many attempts to stop him, the weak son took refuge with the English in October of 1832.[21] Soon it was official, the son, the 'King' Jankoji and the mother, the 'Regent' Baija Bai were at odds. Baija Bai, in an attempt to bring sanity to this situation caused by the inanely weak behaviour of her son, reconciled. Although he returned to the palace, seven months later he took refuge with the English once again. With the possible encouragement of the English, he urged the army to rise against their regent, his mother. Facing the threat of a civil war, Baija Bai left the palace at Gwalior. The coup of July 1833 was bloodless, but possibly altered the course of history.

The English made sure that she never returned to Gwalior. Baija Bai changed residences frequently in the years to come. She proceeded to Dholpur, then to Agra, Mathura and Fatehgarh.[22] In 1840, she moved to Nasik and stayed there for about eight years. Subsequently she *did* return to Gwalior at a time that could not be accidental. Most historians close the chapter on her by indicating that this 'vexatious' woman caused no further trouble to the English until her death in 1862.

They are mistaken.

After she stepped away from her political position, she was looking beyond the petty rivalries and weaknesses of her adopted son, who was more interested in extracting favours from the English. Baija Bai indeed retired from active interest in matters of Gwalior, however, she was now thinking beyond Gwalior. While in Nasik and Ujjain, she reached out to rally other like-minded people. Using an emissary named Krishna Shastri, Baija Bai opened a channel of communication with the Holkars. Around 1838, Holkar made a visit to the north, including Delhi, Agra and Bithur, Satara and Kolhapur to the south in an attempt to gauge the strength of each of the collaborators. Each represented the leftovers of a once massive empire. This was meant to evaluate the possibility of overthrowing the English nationally.[23] In 1838, Bajirao II was still alive and was not the same person who could confront the English anymore. Nana Saheb, despite the influences of Tatya Tope, was too young and powerless to send a favourable reply to Baija Bai.

Baija Bai had done her job and set a sequence of events in motion. Things changed after Bajirao II died in 1851, and Nana Saheb saw an opportunity to act on the goal that was presented to the Indians who wanted freedom by Baija Bai. Baija Bai got the reply she was expecting from Bithur, thirteen years after her first communiqué to Baji Rao II in 1838. Sometime in 1851, Nana Saheb sent his trusted priest to Baija Bai, who at that time was in Ujjain. Baija Bai was ready, and she responded with her ideas and a plan was in place.[24] Nana Saheb began communicating with various Indian leaders and financiers. Amongst the first to respond was Baija Bai's personal banker from Mathura, Lakshmichand.[25]

Baija Bai's name is strangely absent from any English narrative related to 1857. We suspect there is a reason why Baija Bai's name was eliminated from the narratives and will be discussed in a later chapter. However, her name does come up in a few, but important, communiqués. In addition, one of the few Indian accounts of 1857 is narrated by Vishnubhat Godse in his memoirs of 1857, titled, माझा प्रवास (*My Journey*). What made this young man travel from a small town of Varsai, in Maharashtra to the north? He was travelling on the invitation of the same Baija Bai Shinde who had arranged a *sarvatomukhah yajnya*, in Mathura.

Baija Bai Shinde, described as the 'vexatious Scindhia woman' by historians, was very possibly the seed for the brave attempt to 'vex' the English rule in 1857. Baija Bai had left Gwalior after the coup of 1833 and did not return for a long time. Where was Baija Bai when the War of 1857 started? Right there in Gwalior. She had returned in 1856 and sent invitations to priests all over India for the yajnya.

A very vexatious woman, indeed.

NANA SAHEB'S KITCHEN—RECIPE FOR FREEDOM

Growing up under the guidance of a father who was a scholar of Sanskrit, Tatya was in all likelihood well versed with India's polity. The passion for protecting India's freedom that he demonstrated during the War was possibly an inspiration from his early influences. These influences were a combination of his father's knowledge, the *kirtans*,* the education in the schools, and the affiliation with the section of the Maratha dynasty that had once ruled India. These influences intersected with the reality of an India that was collapsing. Tatya's journey from Yeola to Bithur not only exposed the economic difference between these two places, but the causality of these differences, as well as the English presence in nearby Kanpur.

In 1838, when Tatya and Nana was twenty-four and fourteen respectively, were they aware of a letter that Bajirao II had chosen to ignore? It was an invitation, a call to arms, to overthrow the English. Baija Bai Shinde from Gwalior attempted to communicate with the erstwhile Maratha leaders in 1838 to overthrow the English rule.[26] And in 1849, when Tatya and Nana were adults, were they aware that Bajirao had allowed the English to use his infantry and cavalry against the Punjabis who were then fighting the English?

Although these answers will never be known, Nana's actions that followed Bajirao II's death on 28 January 1851 indicate a clear change of a mindset. As someone who Nana respected, trusted and considered a mentor, Tatya was a major influence on young Nana. Sharing Baija Bai's resolve of freedom, Nana Saheb, under the guidance of Tatya Tope, initiated contact with Baija Bai sometime in 1851 through a priest named Dassa Bawa.[27]

While Tatya's role as mentor and guide to Nana Saheb Peshwa was known in the family, many English narratives are flummoxed over the sudden emergence of Tatya on the scene and his sustained resistance. English narratives describe Tatya Tope as Nana Saheb Peshwa's aide-de-camp (Tatya's purported testimony), his *darogha* or his 'superintendant in the kitchen'.[28] In the many letters that were found addressed to Tatya Tope, his role as a chief revenue officer is also evident. Why this disparity in the various functions and roles? Do they necessarily contradict each other?

There is one function that often existed in the courts of some Indian kings that was sometimes described as a *diwan*. While this Persian word

---

*Kirtankars were expert narrators who visited towns and villages and narrated listorical events or stories from India's past. A *kirtan* would often comprise a *poorna ranga* (a philosophical preface and introduction) and an *uttar ranga*, an analysis and narration of an event or events that related to *poorna ranga*.

can be loosely translated as 'minister', the role of a diwan varies with the context of time and place. As a nineteenth century Maratha king, as Nana Saheb's 'diwan', Tatya would be responsible for managing not only the accounts, but also many of the protocols in interactions with dignitaries.[29] In addition to these duties, the diwan also was responsible for many household activities. These, for example, would include, managing the jewellery for the women in the house, a significant responsibility, as well as something much more personal, such as overseeing the kitchen. Tatya was the primary point of contact for all personal activities of a king, in addition to his official responsibilities. From managing personal affairs to later planning military strategy, Nana Saheb trusted Tatya completely.

Tatya was about ten years older than Nana and his mentor during his early years, a guide, and a friend as Nana grew. Tatya was a mentor not only to Nana Saheb but also to another youngster, who would look up to Tatya with respect and admiration in her childhood as well as in her short adult life. Her name was Manikarnika Tambe.

Manikarnika was the daughter of Moropant Tambe and his wife Bhagirathi. Tambe was in the court of Bajirao II's brother, who had also left Pune for Bithur following the terms of exile.[30] Manikarnika was born in 1828.[31]

Manikarnika was growing up in the company of Nana, his brothers and Tatya, all of whom were destined to play a defining role in the years ahead. A quick comparison of their ages, in say 1840, makes Nana sixteen, Manikarnika twelve years and Tatya twenty-six years. Tatya, who was the oldest, was a mentor and coach and an important role model.[32] Having grown up listening to narratives of the heroic Marathas,[33] and playing war games with friends, the memories of an India lost to the English were too fresh to be dimmed. To revive India's freedom must have been one of their collective youthful dreams.[34] These formative years shaped the queen-to-be not only as doughty and ambitious but also influenced by events common with Nana and Tatya.

Manikarnika or Manu as she was called, became Rani Lakshmibai after her marriage to Gangadhar Rao, the King of Jhansi in May 1842. Their only child died as an infant in 1851. They adopted Damodar Rao, a child of around five, from the same family tree, on 20 November 1853. Gangadhar Rao died immediately thereafter on 21 November 1853.[35]

The Rani was fully equipped to run the affairs of Jhansi after her husband's death. She would wake at about 4 am, and begin with her fitness regime, which included speed and strengthening exercises as well as an hour or more of hard riding. Usually, she would be dressed in breeches, a purple sleeveless jacket, a man's headgear, and would nearly always have a sword at her waist. On return, she would begin her daily bath; private prayers followed by a community gathering attended by more than 150 people. She would make it a point to check in on anyone who was missing in that daily gathering. She would then tend to state matters in full attendance with her ministers.[36]

After the death of her husband, the Rani of Jhansi demonstrated that she was perfectly capable to run matters of states. She was a woman who in a matter of few years would demonstrate her ability to take on the English along with Nana Saheb and Tatya.

After Bajirao II died and Nana Saheb inherited the mantle, Nana Saheb made some important changes to the court. In addition to Tatya's role as the first point of contact for personal and many official duties, he included some additional people in his court. Amongst them was Jwala Prasad, who during Baji Rao II's rule was simply a soldier with a salary of Rs 6 per month. Jwala Prasad was clearly a person of ability, as he demonstrated later during the war. Nana Saheb recognised this, and after Baji Rao II's death, promoted him to a *risaldar* or the head of a cavalry unit. During the War, he also acted as a commanding officer for the Indian army.

In addition to Tatya Tope and Jwala Prasad, there was another young man who was taken on board shortly after Baji Rao II's death. His name was Azimullah Khan. Nana Saheb, Tatya Tope, Jwala Prasad, Azimullah Khan were at the core of the team that responded to Baija Bai Shinde's call to arms. The popped seeds of the lotus that were placed in the chapatis were symbolically part of a plan – a recipe for freedom that would take the English head on. The ingenuity of this plan was in its ability to inspire the soldiers to take up arms against the English, brilliance in communicating the troop movement and the sheer simplicity in addressing the logistics of war.

Nana and his trusted advisers were developing a plan for the overthrow of the English Empire. It is likely that it was Tatya's influences on Nana Saheb as his mentor, which had initiated this spark for freedom, which led to the War of 1857.

FOUNDATIONS OF A GRAND ALIGNMENT

When Delhi came under the rule of Mahadji Shinde in 1771, there was apprehension amongst some segments of society about a new ruler controlling Delhi. The Mughals had offered a stable rule that had lasted until the Marathas finally overran this two-hundred-year-old Mughal Empire. Mahadji Shinde allayed these insecurities by maintaining Shah Alam II as the Emperor. The 'Shah was still revered as the source of power and the fountain of honor in the whole of India', however, it was Mahadji Shinde 'who wielded most of the real power of the empire'.[37]

While the Mughal emperor was to continue as the supreme leader, and receive a pension, the Marathas were the actual rulers, keeping most rights to tax collection. Mahadji made himself only a minister in the Mughal court, although he wielded the 'real power' of India. He pragmatically 'participated in the reverence' as the figurehead emperor.[38] Mahadji's pragmatism allowed this continuity without disrupting the status quo that existed. This act could not have been lost on the minds of the Muslim leadership and the Muslim population. Mahadji's actions demonstrated that the plausible fears of a 'Hindu backlash' were unfounded.

Unfortunately, although not surprisingly, Mahadji's pragmatic actions were lost on modern historians; who neither saw Mahadji Shinde's rule over Delhi as complete, since a Maratha was not sitting at the throne, nor gave him credit for forging a pan Indian empire with a Mughal as the figurehead emperor.

However, Mahadji Shinde's ability to bridge this gap between the Marathas and Mughals was the basis for alignment amongst the leaders of 1857. Nana Saheb, Tatya Tope and Azimullah Khan, represented the once mighty Maratha Empire and Bahadur Shah of Delhi and the Nawab of Awadh and Begum Hazrat Mahal represented the remnants of the Mughal Empire. Nana Saheb's alignment with the Nawab of Awadh and the Emperor of Delhi, labelled as 'intrigues' by English historians, were founded on the principles laid out by Mahadji Shinde.

Hundreds of letters written in Urdu addressed to Tatya Tope analysed during the course of researching this book indicate that the logistics was well coordinated between Tatya Tope and Muslim leadership. Amaresh Misra dedicates his book *Mangal Pandey: The True Story of an Indian Revolutionary* to 'The 1857 Hindu-Muslim Solidarity'.[39] While this Hindu-Muslim solidarity is indeed evident during 1857, these coordinated movements between the political leadership signify something much more than the symbolic Hindu-Muslim 'civilian' unity. During the War of 1857, the relevance of this coordinated front was not only about civilians and their faiths, but also about the political alignment of two of the most powerful rivals that fought for control of India, against the third.

The War of 1857 was about the Mughals and the Marathas as a combined front against the English. The entire preceding century was witness to this three-way contest for Delhi and for India. Nana Saheb Peshwa's 'intrigues' with Bahadur Shah and the Nawab of Awadh were one of the grandest alignments in India's history of military rivals to secure political, economic, and personal freedom for the nation.

Chapter 5

THE PLANNED WAR

PIECES OF THE PUZZLE

Tatya's legendary campaigns during the War of 1857 inspired generations of people in India – especially Central India. His campaign was a source of many myths as well. One such myth was that Tatya Tope had received a *vardaan* (granted a wish) that he would be *immortal* during the daytime. This innocent exaggeration is indicative of the awe Tatya inspires in Central India, 150 years after his death. Amongst the narratives heard about Tatya in the family, some relate to his visit to Yeola. A visit, it was rumoured, in which ammunition was stored in the basement of the house where the author's father grew up. Another story had Tatya visiting Yeola, disguised as a *sadhu*. These stories would often be more interesting than hearing information about Tatya sending messages in chapatis and receiving them in lotuses. Considering that the English were using telegraphs to send messages, stories of messages in chapatis and lotuses sounded intriguing but primitive.

Legends could often be exaggerations, as stories could be incorrectly retold. Yet sometimes, hidden in these stories are nuggets of information that could help solve intriguing puzzles.

What is well-known is Tatya Tope's ability to reorganise and restrategise his actions as the situation changed. What is also known is that Tatya Tope was the last major resistance and the War was largely over when Tatya died.

What is *not* much known is, how early was Tatya's involvement in the War. In most narratives, and in his own purported testimony, Tatya's role did not begin until the 2nd Light Cavalry 'mutinied' in Kanpur and 'forced' Nana Saheb and Tatya Tope to be their leaders. Tatya was technically Nana Saheb's aide-de-camp, but in reality, he was a friend, a trusted advisor. Were Nana Saheb and Tatya really the reluctant leaders as is claimed?

While the story of the messages in the chapatis and red lotuses was intriguing, the only thing this indicated on the surface was that these 'primitive' methods were used for sending something along the lines of secret messages because Indians did not have access to the telegraph lines. Was it that simple?

Historians such as Surendra Nath Sen were not able to (or perhaps did not intend to) figure out this puzzle—dismissively writing, '*A conspiracy is not conducted through such an unintelligible and uncertain medium of communication*'. Since the messages themselves were never known or passed on in the family, the story in itself was a dead end for generations.

Was this story incomplete without the message? Was this to be a puzzle that was meant to remain unsolved? Perhaps the answer was always staring at us for a 150 years, waiting to be discovered!

Decoding these events leading up to the War of 1857 is like putting together torn pieces of a paper that had an elaborate plan written on it. However, because a coherent story has not been told, what was presented as history were incomplete interpretations. So, what did the red lotuses and chapatis have to do with the War?

1857 - The Whole Story?

Soldiers   Leadership

Greased Cartridges   Pension and Other
Grievances   Grievances

Historians would have us believe that there were only two major factors that mattered, the soldiers' emotions over greased cartridges and the leadership's emotions over their pension and other grievances. However, this assumes that it was indeed a mutiny that expanded into a civil rebellion, not a war with leaders who had an advanced plan.

However, if the premise of a *mutiny* is abandoned, the relevance of the red lotuses and chapatis suddenly gain significance. Therefore, 'official' historians, such as Surendra Nath Sen were unable to explain the relevance of the chapatis and the red lotuses.

These stories of the chapatis and the red lotuses have baffled historians for 150 years. There has been a mystery about the events that took place starting late 1856 and continued into 1857 in parallel to the more visible resentment about the greased cartridges. In addition to these, there are stories about Nana Saheb's ambassador Azimullah Khan's visit to England.

This mosaic of seemingly uncorrelated events synthesises itself into an elaborate plan. The first piece in this puzzle are the travelling chapatis. The chapatis that 'Tatya sent messages in....'

TRAVELLING CHAPATIS AND FLOWER RITUALS

Consider these events from an English context. They have extensively documented the 'strange' events of the mysterious chapatis doing the rounds, although it is apparent that the narrators were baffled by their presence, and struggled to explain it. The story starts with the appearance of a 'mysterious token in the shape of one those flat cakes' called 'Chupatties'. It was also apparently known that a messenger from outside arrived in a village and gave the 'cake' to the headman, with a request for onward dispatch to the next village. Soon, the travelling chapatis were reported in many parts of India. As the intrigue grew in proportion, so did the range of explanations for it. They ranged from the 'chupatties' being a common superstition to something indicating that their means of subsistence would be taken away. The issue was not completely ignored however. During the March of 1857 the lieutenant governor of the north-western provinces, Mr Corvin, issued circulars to all the local officers of the district to keep an eye on events.[1]

Lord Canning, the governor general of India, was intrigued about the strange story he heard in April 1857 from the north-west, which even the 'most experienced men were incompetent to explain'.[2] The confusion about the magnitude of this strange phenomenon and its association with 'native' beliefs and superstitions was enormous. In a manual published during 1857, these chapatis were called 'sacred cakes' comparing them to the burning of incense sticks. The British remained clueless about 'native' superstitions and beliefs even after decades of interaction with Indians.[3] The confusion related to the chapatis was endemic.

Even the terminology kept varying—some even called the chapatis 'griddle-cakes'. The story about their transmission from one village to the other also varied. A messenger would come to a village, seek out the headman or village elder, give him six chapatis and say: 'These six cakes are sent to you; you will make six others and send them on to the next village.' The headman accepted the six cakes and punctually sent these forward as he had been 'directed'. These chapati incidents were common across the entire region that would eventually go to war against the English, 'from the North-West to all the way to Bengal and Oude (Awadh)'.[4]

The mystery of the travelling chapatis became common knowledge to the English in India; 'then we heard of a mysterious affair about some chupatties. It seemed that a chowkedar of Cawnpore gave to a chowkedar of Futtehghur two chupatties, with an order to make ten more and give two to each of the nearest chowkedar to distribute in a like manner'.[5]

The chapatis crossed religious lines; they travelled from village to village regardless of religion. There were reports of Muslim villages singing nationalistic songs.[6] The number of chapatis seemed to vary—but all were brought by runners or informers.

Not only were these chapatis travelling in the Gangetic plain, they had travelled to many areas, including Sagar and other towns in Central India.

John William Kaye writes:

So far back as January, 1857, 'small wheaten cakes (chupatties) were passed in a most mysterious manner from village to village in most of the districts, and, although all took it as a signal that something was coming, nobody in the division, I believe, knew what it portended, or whence it came, and it appeared to have been little thought about except that in the money-market of Saugor it is said to have had some slight effect in bill transactions....[7]

People

Chapati Messages

The earliest references to the chapatis seem to go as early as 1856 after the annexation of Awadh, and also in late 1856 when there was an outbreak of cholera. At the early stages the only explanation that the British had was that somehow these chapatis (or bannocks) had something to do with speeding away the plague.[8]

The last of these chapati 'chains' occurred in February 1857.

The commissioner of the Agra division was on tour in the Mainpuri district when his attention was drawn to a mysterious distribution of chapatis being made with astonishing rapidity. Nothing could be elicited from the bearers who appeared to know no more of the purport of the symbols than of the fact that on the receipt of a cake, five more were to be prepared and forwarded without delay to villages further in advance along the line of the Grand Trunk road where they could be called for. In this manner the cakes travelled often over 160 to 200 miles in a night. He saw some more which had that morning been delivered on the Etawah side of Mainpuri. On the following day the commissioner heard of them at the extremity of Etah and Aligarh.[9]

Were these mysterious chapati movements arbitrary? Was their number fixed? Were their destinations predecided or was there a pattern to it? There are some hints in history books about this. One fact alone conclusively proves that the chapati signal given had a special reference to English rule in India. In *no* instance were these chapatis distributed outside of the areas where the English had direct control. They were sent only among the villages over which English rule extended.[10]

Indian women even offered their spindles (wooden cylinders to roll chapatis) to the river—along all the villages adjacent to the Ganga—as if uniting in some form of a prayer. Some imagine that it was a 'sacrifice'. The extent of bewilderment was so high that some British thought that this superstition was invented by the manufacturers of spindles.[11]

The chapati mystery has some common elements. First, they all came from messengers or runners outside the village. Second, they approached either the sentry or the village chief and passed on the message. Third, the number of chapatis were not identical, varying from two to six. Fourth, a large part of the population was involved, including women. Fifth, the chapatis travelled in only specific well-defined locations. Sixth, the critical piece of information is that the message was to send the chapatis to the next *village*—in singular—not *villages*.

By July of 1857, the mystery of the chapati was discussed widely. Benjamin Disraeli, the leader of the opposition in the British Parliament, who went onto become the prime minister of Britain in the 1860s asked the British Parliament, rather sarcastically:

> Suppose the Emperor of Russia were told—'*Sire, there is a very remarkable circumstance going on in your territory; from village to village, men are passing who leave the tail of an ermine or pot of caviar, with a message to someone to perform the same ceremony. Strange to say this has been going on in some ten thousand villages and we cannot make head or tail of it.*' I think the Emperor of Russia would say: '*I do not know whether you can make head or tail of it, but I am quite certain there is something wrong, and that we must take some precautions; because, where the people are not usually indiscreet and troublesome, they do not make secret communication unless it is opposed to the government. This is a secret communication, and therefore a communication dangerous to the government.*'[12]

Disraeli continued to debate the subject of the chapatis in the Parliament, suggesting that these events were an evidence of a 'conspiracy' to overthrow English rule in India.

> The annexation of Oude took place in 1856. This is only the middle of 1857. Is it true that in the interval there has been no evidence of combination and conspiracy in India? There may have been evidence which the Government has not understood. There may have been symbols which have perplexed them. There may have been conduct, the motives of which they could not penetrate. But, that there is no evidence of combination for the last twelve months, especially in Bengal,

seems to me a position which cannot be for a moment maintained. The House has heard of the circulation of the mysterious cakes in India or, if not, allow me to tell them what has taken place, and was taking place in India many months ago. This took place. A messenger comes to the headman of a village, and brings him six pancakes-chupatties, such as the Native make of wheaten flour and he says, 'These six pancakes are sent to you; distribute them among as many villages, and make six others, and send them on with the same message to another headman.' The headman obeys, accepts the six cakes, makes six others, and sends them on to the headman of the next village with the same message.... How did it begin? It is a mystery.[13]

There have been some attempts to solve this mystery. Amaresh Misra in his book *Mangal Pandey: The True Story of an Indian Revolutionary*, indicates that the path in which these chapatis travelled represented a triangle that had a symbolic meaning. Nevertheless, were these chapatis only symbolic? Was this only a metaphorical ritual that the 'natives' were following? Was this behaviour symbolic only at some abstract level, using shapes and maps, or was Tatya Tope, as someone who would be commanding a large army, trying to send a message that was clear, focused and relevant to the War? The answers to these questions become obvious when these 'chapati messages' are viewed in a broader context to include some other 'strange' events that took place shortly before and after the chapati incidents.

The journey of the chapatis was preceded by another significant one. This was the journey of red lotuses that were making rounds of the garrisons where the Indian soldiers were stationed.

Starting in late 1856, red lotus flowers began to appear in nearly all the military stations where the Bengal Army was stationed.

Soldiers

Red Lotuses

This story is echoed in many accounts. What is consistent is that the *subhedar*, who commanded a platoon, would line up his soldiers, and hand the first soldier a red lotus flower. These soldiers then held this lotus flower, and then passed them on to the soldier immediately behind. This was repeated until the lotus reached the last person, who would leave the station with the flower.[14-15]

What could be the mystery behind these flowers? Was the lotus only a sort of an inspirational ritual or was there something more to it?

However, what is important to note is that the chapatis were sent *only* to the villages and the lotuses *only* to the soldiers.[16]

Were the lotuses the 'message without number' that is referenced in some accounts?

Messages and letters without number(s) were sent to every regiment; agents and emissaries were travelling to and fro; and nightly meetings were held without much disguise of concealment in the lines of every station.[17]

Indian historians, to their credit, are less 'bewildered' about the chapatis and the red lotuses, knowing that these had clearly nothing to do with 'native' superstition. Were they then only 'symbols of the projected revolution?'[18-19]

Complementary to the stories of the red lotus flowers making the rounds of the garrison is another story that has been largely glossed over by most historians. It is the story of a 'puja' that Nana Saheb had arranged a few months before the war broke out. This puja involved taking the 'makhana' (popped seeds of the lotus) and adding it to the dough to make chapatis.[20] There is an embedded clue in the Sanskrit name of the red lotus flower. The red lotus in Sanskrit is *kokanadam rakta-kamal*, which literally translates as 'the blood-coloured lotus'. What was that message in the blood-coloured lotus? What was Tatya Tope doing with these lotuses? As we will see in a later analysis that these seemingly unrelated events form a coherent plan.

To this date, the stories of the chapatis and the red lotuses remain very popular amongst Indians as a symbol of war. After India's freedom, the state government of Uttar Pradesh installed a stone with the lotus and the chapati carved on it.

TENSES IN RED—MAPS, BLOOD OR FLOWERS?

In addition, we have the two Hindi sentences, which were being commonly spoken by the Indian soldier starting in late 1856 and early 1857. Not in secrecy either. When the red lotus flowers would arrive at the garrisons, the soldiers would say with a nod *Sab lal ho jayega* (Everything will become red).[21-22] A few months later, in January, in the midst of the chapati and red lotus incidents, the slogan changed and the loud cries of *Sab lal ho gaya hai* (Everything is red)[23] were common. The English soldiers would hear these loud cries in many garrisons, some of them fearing the meaning. In February of 1857, a few months before the War started, a satirical poem appeared in a Calcutta journal, intended to ridicule these fears. The last passage goes as follows:

I heard a giant voice again proclaim, Mid shouts of murder, mutiny and blood, 'SAB LAL HO GAYA HAI,' and I awoke.[24]

Which Red?

There are two possible explanations that historians have given in reference to the word 'lal' or the colour red. First, the possibility of red symbolising hostilities, and therefore *Sab lal ho jayega* (Everything will become red) could symbolise 'there *will* be blood everywhere'. Similarly *Sab lal ho gaya hai* (everything is red) could mean 'there *is* blood everywhere'.

Second, the possibility that many historians propose, is that it symbolised the geographical area of India that the British controlled on a map. They have this statement possibly confused with a statement that Maharaja Ranjeet Singh had made in 1838. Referring to a map of India that showed the portions under English control as Red, Maharaja Ranjeet Singh had once commented, *'Kisi din ye bhi lal ho jayega'* (Some day this too will become red).[25-26] This was in reference to Punjab. Therefore, many historians make a similar conclusion that the statement 'Everything has become red' symbolised the annexation of Awadh.

Neither of the two explanations is logically complete. It is unlikely that the colour red symbolised immediate action, because between the two *tenses*, '*will* become red' and '*has* become red', nothing had overtly changed. There were no hostilities and there were no redrawing of the boundaries.

In that case, could it really have represented the areas that the English controlled?

Some historians claim that the annexation of Awadh caused people to say, 'Everything has become red'—meaning, 'All of India is now red—under British control'. This explanation is also logically incomplete since there were no changes to the map between '*will* become red and *has* become red (since Awadh was *already* annexed)'. It is unlikely that the colour red symbolised either British controlled parts of the map—whether or not they were annexed.

If both the plausible alternatives do not fit the information that is available, the explanation has to be outside these boundaries. What could an alternate explanation be? Was the colour red linked to the colour of the lotus flowers that were making the round? If so, what was the symbolic nature of *ho jayega* or 'will' and *ho gaya hai* or 'has'?

Most attempts to address the mystery surrounding the chapatis and the red lotuses never really get beyond the basic premise of 'native superstition'. Surendra Nath Sen, who wrote the 'official' history of 1857, is quick in dismissing its relevance. However, recently, Amaresh Misra[27] attempts to see something more than superstition in the lotuses suggesting that the lotus represents the Hindu call to arms and the chapati being a Muslim symbol denoting the earth. Were the red lotuses and the chapatis purely symbolic in their appearance just prior to the War?

Tatya Tope was a hands-on general and led his army into many combats. Was Tatya Tope simply looking at the metaphorical attributes of these two symbols? On the other hand, was there something beyond the abstractness, which a general of an army might be of far more interest? Were sending messages in the chapatis somehow linked with receiving messages in the red lotuses?

Let us consider some critical elements that relate to any planning that involved war.

TRAVELLING STOMACHS—THAT ELUSIVE SUPPLY LINE

Napoleon once said, 'An army travels on its stomach'. By this, he meant that the problem of keeping an army supplied is the prerequisite for the very existence of the force.

????

Food and Supply Line Logistics

Any large-scale military engagement with the British, who at that time were at the peak of their military power, was nearly impossible to do without their knowledge. Any early warning could possibly derail their plan. Very little is analysed or discussed about the logistics, the supply line, and the economics of waging a war. It is well known that the cost of fighting the war against the British was enormous. While the military logistics of acquiring and maintaining weapons and ammunition is important to the understanding of how the Indian fought this war, the critical piece is the mystery of the supply line.

> Troop movement in the 1850s in India was a long and arduous process and the logistics involved was enormous. Three to five camp followers accompanied each soldier. With this calculation, when two divisions of troops were on the move, the total number of human beings marching exceeded 20,000. In addition there were thousands (of) horses, camels, elephants, mules, and bullocks. The elephants would drag the cannons. The bullock carts would transport the soldiers. The camels would be needed to carry the supply of grain for the cavalry and artillery horses. The supply for one day for 8,000 horses would require 200 camels for its conveyance. More camels would be needed to transporting the hospital stores, wines, medicines, quilts, beds, pots, pans of all sorts and sizes. In addition, 'troop stores' were also transported. These included horse clothing, head and heel ropes, pickets, nose bags and spare shoes. In addition, there was the private baggage for the soldiers and the tents for officers.[28]

As this indicates, the critical part of waging a successful war is to have an elaborate logistics for food for the soldiers and the horses and elephants, if any. In addition, as mentioned above, each soldier was followed by three to five camp followers just to manage the needs of the soldiers including food.

While there are many little things including horses, clothing and medicine supplies, the primary need for troops on the move is food, critical for the success on the battlefield. A marching army required provisions not just for the soldiers, but feed also for the horses, elephants, bullocks and camels. We have estimated that an average soldier on the move would need about 1 kg of grain equivalents per day assuming a plain diet like daal-roti. (details in notes)[29]

Before waging a war against the English, the Indian soldiers, as employees of the East India Company, had access to the full spectrum of support and a functional supply line. Once the Indian soldiers 'mutinied', they no longer had access to that infrastructure. All basic needs, including food and other logistics had to be managed. Did they travel with their rations? Did they have access to the camels that would be carrying the rations? For each soldier there were three camp followers who would take care of the essentials. Did the 'rebel' soldiers have any camp followers? What about pots, pans and cooks? Who cooked the food? Did they get access to any of the camp equipment before they mutinied, including pots and pans?

A soldier fights a war based on the assumption that the basic things such as food, water and a camp to sleep are taken care of.

Here is a glimpse into the scale of the problem that has been glossed over by most historians. Over 50,000 Indian troops fought in this war. Just for one month, they would have needed nearly 1,500 tons of grains, not including the feed for horses and elephants. Where did the grains come from and more importantly who cooked the food for the soldiers? The EEIC's army had three camp followers for every soldier. Did the camp followers mutiny as well? How did they carry their grains? Did they have supply lines as elaborate as the English did?

Food was a critical element of this War for the Indian soldiers and this was another very important piece that has been missing in history books. Tatya Tope demonstrated the use of fully functional supply lines in the later phases of the War. However, in the initial phase, planning for a fully functional logistics would have impossible task to achieve *covertly*. Was Tatya able to invent an alternate and fully functional supply lines for his soldiers? Who accounted for that critical piece of supply line logistics?

All these answers are in the chapatis, the red lotuses and the slogans of the colour red, as presented in the next chapter.

Chapter 6

THE PLANNED WAR
Logical Inferences

THE LOGIC OF LOGISTICS

If only the English historians then or their followers later had studied the mystery of the red lotuses and the chapatis, they would have seen beyond a 'mutiny' or a 'civil rebellion'. Unfortunately, many historians have dismissed this intrigue, which is why it continues to be just that—an intrigue. In order to understand the meaning behind these red lotuses and chapati messages, first, let us reconstruct the arrival of a red lotus flower at a 'native' infantry camp.

Consider the 'ritual' that the soldiers followed when red lotuses arrived at the garrison gate through a runner. Some references describe that the senior Indian soldier (*subhedar*) would line up his soldiers. The subhedar handed over the complete lotus flower to the first soldier who would pluck a petal for himself before passing it on to the next soldier who repeated the 'ritual'. The red lotus *kokanadam rakta-kamal* has about twenty-five to thirty petals and, if each soldier plucked one, the last soldier in the platoon would be left with the stalk of the lotus. Observers say that the last soldier went away and then returned—indicating that he could have possibly delivered the stalk of the lotus to someone, very possibly the messenger, who delivered the lotuses in the first place. If the delivered lotuses carried an embedded message, what was that message and how was it relevant?

Consider what a typical Native Infantry (NI) regiment looked like in 1857.

A regiment comprised 700-1,000 men, with a platoon being its smallest unit. The platoon comprised twenty-five to thirty soldiers commanded by a *subhedar*. The British did not allow any Indians to lead a group, larger than the size of a platoon. Four platoons comprised a company, which would have a hundred-odd soldiers, and, ten companies formed a regiment. The significance of the number of petals in a red lotus to the number of men in a platoon is telling.

As mentioned earlier, the last soldier would return the lotus stalk to the messenger. Who would the messenger in turn return the reeds to? Of the several 'testimonies' in the historiography of 1857, there are some important statements that Sitaram Baba* made that indicate

---

Symbolising Life and Blood
The Kokanadam Rakta-Kamal

There are three main variants of the Indian lotus. The blue lotus called 'Indivara' in Sanskrit, the white 'Pundarika' and the Red Lotus is called 'kokanadam rakta-kamala'. As explained before, Rakta translates as blood.

The lotus flower has had a continuous revered presence of 5,000 years or more in India as well as other Asian countries. One of the names of the blue lotus is 'Pushkaram', which also means the 'great void' or the 'universe' and is credited to be the source of the 'light of knowledge' and 'wisdom' and symbolises the origin of fire and light.

The lotus is extensively represented in most art forms from rock art in caves to music, dance and as motifs on clothes and in jewellery. The *Rig Veda* and *Atharva Veda* mentions the red lotus, and the *Yajur Veda*, garlands made of white lotuses. During the Indus days, the lotus became popular as a decorative motif and as a symbol. Pottery excavated from Mohenjo-daro in the Indus Valley is found painted with designs composed of lotus-petal-type leaf-patterns.

At Angkor Wat in Cambodia and at Java, the lotus has been used as part of the iconography of Lakshmi, Ganesh and various other deities. The lotus would then be, representative of the creator, Brahma, with full control of the elements of the cosmos, when he appeared yogi-like seated in a lotus, obviously because the lotus had emerged from the unfathomable depths of ocean, as creation did out of the non-form.

---

that the reed of the lotus was part of a *puja* that Nana Saheb performed. Which could mean it was Tatya Tope receiving the stalk of the lotuses.

---

*Sitaram Baba was Nana Saheb's priest. His statements that make up his 'testimony' are studied in more detail later.

This brings us to the all important question, why was the stalk of the lotus important? We reason that, the act of plucking a petal of the red lotus tacitly implied committing yourself to 'the cause'. The lotus stalks implicitly carried a very important number. It was a reasonably accurate count of the number of willing soldiers. A quick calculation shows that each reed approximately represented a platoon and four reeds a company. If this 'ritual' was carried out in all ten companies of a regiment—and let us say the messenger returned with thirty reeds—Tatya would know that the entire regiment had signed up for the cause.

This method of recruitment needed no paper messages to be sent to Tatya. The only information that was passed on was stalks and the embedded logic—a fact that was completely lost on the English while the red lotuses were making rounds of the garrisons. This would have been sufficient information for Tatya to plan the next step in the process, which was to arrange for supply lines for these regiments that had 'signed up'. Only in hindsight did the English possibly recognise that there could have been messages that were sent, and later observed: 'messages and letters without number(s) were sent to every regiment agents'.[1]

To summarise, the recruitment portion of the 'Operation Red Lotus' achieved certain landmark objectives. First, the recruitment method was purposeful and remained largely undetected, since it was confused as a 'strange *native* custom'. Second, an estimate of the number of soldiers who had committed was a crucial input in planning war logistics, and third, the symbolism of the red lotus itself in Indian tradition.

About 50,000 Indian soldiers participated in the early stages of this operation. We estimate that two to three thousand lotuses must have travelled to different garrisons and that a large number of stalks of the lotus flower were being returned back to Tatya Tope, for him to start planning the logistics.

MARCHING ON STOMACHS

As eloquent as the red lotuses and their embedded messages were, the next piece of the puzzle was the travelling chapatis. Here is a summary of key information associated with the chapati incidents from various historical accounts of the period:

- The chapatis arrived from the hands of messengers or runners, outside the village.
- They approached either the sentry (*chowkedar*) or the village chief (*mukhiya*) and passed on the chapati message.
- The number of chapatis varied by region, between the numbers two and six, but the 'message' to make the same number of chapatis was the same in each unique case.
- A large part of the population was involved including women.
- The chapatis travelled along specific well-defined routes and locations.
- The message was to send the chapatis to the next 'village'.

The significance of the chapatis that travelled these specific routes can best be explained by an example.

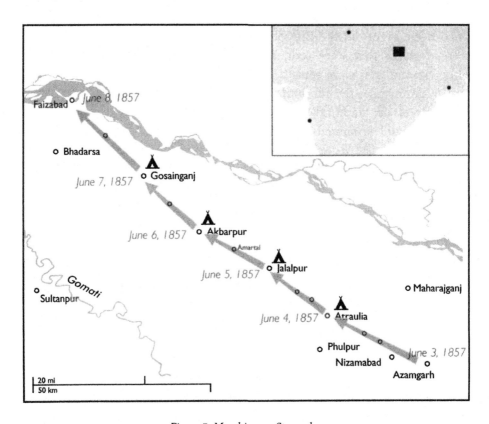

Figure 7: Marching on Stomachs

The 17th Native Infantry regiment was stationed at Azamgarh. Consider what the 17 NI did after they overpowered their garrison on 3 June 1857. The 17 NI started their march to Faizabad, where they helped the 22 NI overpower their local garrison and liberate the city. Faizabad is about eighty-five miles from Azamgarh. Considering that a well-trained infantry column covers about fifteen-twenty-five miles a day, the journey of eighty-five miles to Faizabad would have taken four-five days. Records corroborate that the 17 NI reached Faizabad on 8 June. The exact route that they travelled is not recorded, but a cursory look at the map makes it apparent that they are more than likely to have travelled through the following towns: Atraulia, Jalalpur, Akbarpur, Gosainganj and then on to Faizabad. The troops finally arrived at Faizabad on 8 June. It is likely that they camped near these towns on each of the nights of 4-7 June.

We have already discussed that once these soldiers rebelled, they were without logistical support that came with their regular army, no luxury of camp followers. They could have requisitioned bullock carts. However, how could an entire regiment be on the move for five days without provisioning for food?

Therefore the question: Who provided for them? The people in the villages did. Alexander Duff writes: 'In every instance where the troops have mutinied, they have been joined by the inhabitants, not only of the bazaars but also of the towns and villages adjacent'.[2] He goes on to write that the same pattern existed in many other places including north-west and Central India.

The march from Azamgarh to Faizabad passed through four towns and a dozen or so villages; and they probably had one meal in one town or village and reached the next town to camp for the night. It is worthwhile to note that in 1857, Atraulia, Jalapur, Akbarpur and Gosainganj were small towns, unlikely to be able to feed a thousand soldiers without any previous knowledge of their arrival. The village chief had to know to stock up in advance and the message was in the chapati.

The message did not have to be elaborate or be specific. The need was simply to stock-up on rations and be prepared. If we revisit the mysterious chapati that travelled from village to village in early 1857, it is easy to see that, the chapati was *the* message. The villages and their 'eating' the chapati was their 'commitment' to feed the soldiers when the time came. If we correlate this hypothesis with evidence from historical accounts, the fit is extremely satisfactory. The following table analyses each observation.

Observation	Inference
The chapatis came from messengers outside the village.	The route the soldiers were going to follow was known, as well as the villages that would come along the way.
They approached the sentry or the village chief.	The village chief would probably express his approval and then recruit different households to take on this commitment, based on the number of soldiers who needed to be supported. It would only be the village chief who would need to know the details.
A large part of the population was involved, including the women.	After all the planning, it was the women who would be cooking the food for the 'visitors'. They had already expressed their commitment to the cause.
The chapatis travelled in only specific and well defined locations.	This is a very important consideration, which confirms that there was no reason to involve villages where the troops were not going to pass through.
The message was sent to the next 'village' in singular, not villages.	These messages were not sent arbitrarily to all villages, they were sent to the villages that came along the way in this long march. So the messages followed a linear chain based on each regiment's troop movement.
The number of chapatis varied by region, but was consistent within a region.	It is very likely that the number of chapatis in the message correlated to the number of companies that would arrive. *One chapati for each company.* How was that number determined? From the information collected from the red lotuses of course. One reed of the lotus flower represented one platoon. Four reeds indicated one company. So if about thirty lotus reeds were collected from Azamgarh—eight chapatis were sent along the entire route from Azamgarh to Faizabad. It is important to note that the exact number was not critical to this logistical operation, but it was important for a *mukhiya* or village chief to know whether two hundred or two thousand soldiers would be arriving.

It is also possible that in addition to food, these villages also contributed in terms of other logistical support that these troops needed. From spare clothing, laundry, bullock carts, horse feed for the cavalry, eliminating the need for camels, feed for elephants and so on.

RECONNAISSANCE MAN

Using Savarkar's metaphor, these mute red lotuses had very eloquently passed the messages to Tatya. Knowing that information, Tatya was able to plan the movement of the troops and then give some kind of an advance warning to the villages using the chapati messages. Logistics and troop movements are tactical planning issues, and need attention a few months prior to D-day. However, implicit in any strategic planning is the necessity to get the big picture.

Strategic inputs were required, such as, where were other British troops deployed? What were the English vulnerabilities? The EEIC represented only one face of England. What was the perception of the people of England with respect to India during the period? Some answers are found in important events preceding the War through the travails of a fine young emissary.

The story of Azimullah Khan is one of the most fascinating stories in the history of the period. Even the most disapproving of British authors have acknowledged him and his contribution. Others have devoted dozens of pages in running him down. Why was so much space given to a 'retainer' of Nana Saheb, as most English authors would want their readers to believe? The stock story churned out follows a premeditated pattern, often recounting his humble origin, his popularity in Britain, his 'conquests' of British women and of course the 'failed mission' of restoring Nana Saheb's pension. This emissary in his twenties was in fact hobnobbing with the highest EEIC officials and socialites in an alien land and extracting their grudging approval.

The purpose of Azimullah Khan's visit, supposedly, was to impress upon the Company directors the merit of the case of re-instating the annual pension that was due to Nana Saheb, his pension plea having been already rejected in India. What was then the real purpose of spending close to thirty thousand pounds on an Azimullah visit? Some historians suggest that it was for bribery. However, another ambassador, Rango Bapoji[3] had attempted to negotiate with the EEIC for fourteen years on behalf of the raja of Satara, without success. Nana Saheb, who was in communication with the Raja, easily knew that the 'pension negotiations' were not going to be productive. If the outcome was already known, why did Nana Saheb *really* send Azimullah Khan?

Growing up as the son of Bajirao II, who enjoyed entertaining the English, Nana Saheb had cultivated quite a few British civil and military officers, often plying the ever-eager officials with expensive gifts. He put this to good use in planning Azimullah Khan's trip to Britain in January 1854. Letters were written to influential people to ensure that Azimullah and his companion, Mohammed Ali Khan, were well received and, met the 'right' people. Mohammed Ali Khan had been to Britain before with King Jung Bahadur of Nepal and was well versed with the English language and English etiquette.

On arrival in England, Azimullah Khan was settled in a suite at Hanover Square, and had *supposedly* hired a barrister named Frederick L. Biddle[4] to prepare a petition and lobby on his behalf at the East India House on Leadenhall Street. We say *'supposedly'* because there is no evidence of the existence of any lawyer named Frederick Biddle in 1854 in London. The only Biddles practising law at that time was William and Sydney. One worked out of Oxford and the other was not admitted to The Bar until 1856.[5] There is no reference ever to this mysterious Biddle again, *nor* are there any references to the petitions he may have filed with the Company Headquarters or their replies. Every other detail of Azimullah's visit has been extensively chronicled, including trivialities such as him attending an opera in the company of older women, or leaving his golden slippers at the doors of a place of worship.[6] However, other than Azimullah's stated intent, surprisingly, there is nothing that points as evidence to verify that Azimullah Khan's mission to England was to negotiate the lost pension.

Was Frederick L. Biddle a creation of Azimullah Khan's imagination, purely as a name to be used in conversations? No one would know that Biddle did not exist. That seems to be the only plausible explanation. Azimullah Khan's *overtly* projected mission was to reinstate Nana Saheb's pension, and he dutifully went through the motions of doing so. Perhaps, as John William suggests, Frederick L. Biddle never really existed and it was simply a part of Azimullah's smokescreen.

Azimullah Khan put his visit to good use in understanding the English and their way of life. Azimullah met Lady Lucie Duff Gordon through the Company's liaison officer John Stuart Mill. She was politically well connected since she was married to the then prime minister's cousin, Alexander Duff Gordon, who was an usher to the Queen. This proximity was also the reason that Lady Lucie Duff Gordon was also an influential socialite. She was so awed by the young Azimullah that she took it upon herself to champion him and Mohammed Ali Khan. Upon Lady Lucie's persistent requests, Azimullah finally did see the Queen. Unimpressed, Azimullah described her as 'a squat little woman in the sway of her German husband'.[7]

Days of war are heydays for political hangers-on, not so much for their views but for the crumbs thrown their way at cocktail circuses, which faithfully assembled most evenings in Lady Duff Gordon's house. Azimullah Khan gained first-hand knowledge of the bitterness with which the political establishment was divided. He heard of British military deployments in other parts of the world and their war reversals. The British had already lost Afghanistan and opened new fronts in Crimea. Azimullah Khan also satiated himself with books and articles on the socio-economic conditions of Britain. There are recorded instances of Azimullah Khan assimilating this type of information in his host's study. In one letter written by Lucie Duff Gordon, she says: 'You would be amused at the incessant questioning that goes on—I have gone through such a course of political economy and all social sciences day after day and had to get so many books for my pupil to devour that I feel quite solemn and pedantic....'[8] For all the graciousness and hospitality extended by the Lady, Nana Saheb had bestowed her with a gold and pearl necklace.

An important element of Azimullah Khan's mission to England was to get an accurate picture of English troop deployment around the world to provide a strategic input for Tatya. Some of this information was easily available, but the English were certainly not naïve to publicise the details. Spending time in elite circles, and having disarmed his hosts with his personality, Azimullah over a period of many months could have gathered the information that was critical to the planning of the War.

Azimullah Khan's task of studying English strengths and vulnerabilities from January 1854 to June 1855 was nearing completion. The exact date of his departure from Southampton in June 1855 is unknown, however, a series of curious episodes unfold in his return journey. This further strengthens the evidence that his trip to England was primarily for planning and assessment.

Historians write that once his mission (to renegotiate the pension) 'failed', he decided to return to India 'empty handed'. Some narratives suggest that his original plan was to return *directly* to India.[9] However, Azimullah followed a most interesting and indirect route to India. He was seen everywhere—in Crimea, Constantinople, Turkey, Baghdad, Egypt, and even in France.

W.H. Russell, in *My Diary in India* writes about his encounter with Azimullah Khan in Constantinople. Russell writes that Azimullah had made acquaintance of a Mr Doyne who was heading to Crimea as the head of Army Works Corps. Russell notes that Azimullah was looking forward to the visit and spoke of wanting to see the 'famous city, and those great Roostums and the Russians, who have beaten the French and the English, together'.[10] They parted company and a few weeks later, the English were defeated at Sebastopol on 18 June 1855. Russell had a reputation as a 'fearless' war correspondent and was fast developing a reputation as the ultimate 'man on the spot'. The 'hot spot' at that moment happened to be Sebastopol, and sure enough, Russell was there. Whom would the intrepid Russell meet in this 'war zone', but Azimullah Khan himself! In fact, Russell walked Azimullah to the General's hut to get a pass for him. Azimullah watched with careful interest the fire of the Russian guns.[11]

Was Azimullah inspired by the events at Crimea and 'sowed the seeds of war' in Nana Saheb's head after he returned from his 'failed mission', or was Azimullah in regular communication with Nana Saheb throughout his journey?

Azimullah Khan met the Turkish General Umar Pasha as well as Russian agents in Constantinople.[12] As a matter of protocol, it is highly unlikely that Azimullah Khan would have made these arrangements without the knowledge of Nana Saheb. In fact, what is most likely is that there was regular communication between Nana and Azimullah during many months of his return trip home. Azimullah Khan in all likelihood had been reporting his progress in England regularly to Nana Saheb, who in turn planned further meetings with General Pasha and the Russians. It was left to Azimullah to negotiate for their support, which he did. General Umar Pasha had 'mentioned that he would be glad of information as to the condition of

India'.[13] The Russians promised material support if a rebellion was stirred up. This was nothing new; in fact, *The Illustrated London News* of 21 January 1854 had stated: 'There is no room to doubt that, whenever disaffection has been excited against our rule on the Indian frontier, Russian emissaries have had something to do with it'.[14]

Azimullah left Southampton in June 1855 and arrived at Aden in October 1856. It took Azimullah Khan seventeen months to complete a journey that should have taken no longer than three. His journey was full of detours to Sebastopol and his meetings with many local leaders. Some accounts suggest that they even met the Sultan of Turkey and the powerful Khalif of Baghdad. Were these random flights of fancy of a political greenhorn or was it masterminded in India by Nana Saheb and his adviser Tatya Tope?

The strength of the Bengal Army's infantry was 71 Regiments— numbered between 50,000-70,000 troops.[15] Cavalry regiments added a few thousand more. These were the core of the Indian organised and trained resistance. The number of English troops deployed in India was 24,000. Azimullah Khan provided some important information. The English had an additional 75,000 English[16] troops that they could deploy and send to India.[17]

Knowing the English troop deployment and overall strength was critical information for Tatya. He had to consider not only the logistics of the regiments on the move; he had to consider the sequence in which the events should roll out. Assuming that about half of the NI regiments would accomplish overpowering their local English garrisons, this left Tatya with an important shortfall. Tatya had to recruit the local armies and irregulars in addition to the NI regiments to overcome the deficit. Later we will see how Tatya's focus was on mastering the complicated logistics – in secrecy.

Although the task was difficult, it was not impossible.

Azimullah's *overt* mission to renegotiate Nana Saheb's pension failed. There are no documents such as petitions filed in any courts, minutes of proceedings, or judgments passed to suggest that it was indeed his *real* mission. Even Biddle the lawyer mentioned in some accounts, who he had supposedly hired to petition, possibly did not exist. It seems, however, that his covert mission was extremely successful, as even before Azimullah's return, Nana Saheb and Tatya Tope began the process of communicating with other Indian leaders.

WHEN TITANS SHOOK HANDS

The Marathas and Mughals were rivals ever since Shivaji carved out an empire and expanded into Mughal-controlled territories in the seventeenth century. What came between the Marathas and Delhi was the warrior Aurangzeb who defended the Mughal Empire until his last breath in 1707. Shivaji's successors in the eighteenth century were able to expand this young empire, which finally conquered and ruled over Delhi.

However, Mahadji's pragmatism allowed the symbolism of the Mughal Empire to continue to exist. Although the Mughal Emperor Shah Alam II was under direct control of the Marathas, this arrangement helped in putting up a united front against the English. However, after Mahadji's death and suffering losses to the British in 1804 in the Second Anglo-Maratha war, Delhi was finally transferred from the Marathas to the English. The Mughal emperor received a raise in his pension from the new rulers.

Growing up hearing the stories of Mahadji, the last Maratha hero, Tatya Tope and Nana Saheb saw similar possibilities that had enabled Mahadji Shinde to keep the English at bay. Nana Saheb decided that Bahadur Shah should be approached and be made the same offer that was made to Shah Alam II. Sometime in late 1856, after Azimullah Khan's reconnaissance mission, Nana Saheb was 'intriguing with the King of Delhi' and with 'the Nawab of Oudh' and other leaders.[18] Although it was going to be a long shot, Nana Saheb also attempted to contact the Sultan of the Ottoman Empire, asking Azimullah Khan to take a detour to Istanbul after reviewing the conditions in Crimea in 1856.[19] He also approached the King of Burma, possibly to support if Calcutta could be liberated.

Nana Saheb opened lines of communications with like-minded Indians through a variety of channels. Some were through letters directly sent to various Indian kings.[20] Nana Saheb also hired a Frenchman named Lafont. Lafont, who was on the payroll of Nana Saheb (through Azimullah Khan) travelled at least to Benares, Chandannagore and Calcutta. Benares indicates the possible connection to the Nawab of Awadh. Chandannagar, thirty kilometres to the north of Calcutta (earlier called Chandernagore), was controlled by the French from 1673 (except for a few years in the interim) until India secured its freedom in 1947. Lafont in his letters promised positive results on the *'principales choses'* or 'principal things'. The letters by Lafont are reproduced along with their rough and direct English translation.[21] These letters were found in Nana Saheb's palace after Bithur was captured by the English in July 1857.[22]

In April 1857, Nana Saheb and Azimullah Khan arrived in Lucknow, the capital of Awadh and the home of Begum Hazratmal. Following their trip to Lucknow, they continued on to Delhi, the home of Bahadur Shah.[23] They arrived 'at this peculiar crisis to take a note of things there'. Their arrival during this stage, just weeks before the War started, was noticed as suspicious by Henry Lawrence.[24]

So far we have tried to take stock of the frenetic activity preceding the War, which is either conveniently glossed over by most narratives, or no attempt is made at an analysis. Could this be a deliberate attempt to divert attention from the issue of planning?

During the War, after Kalpi fell into the hands of the English, important documents were discovered by the English.

> A box has been found containing most important correspondence belonging to the Ranee of Jhansie which it is said will throw great light on the revolt and its principal authors.[25]

Neither the box nor the contents are available, most likely destroyed by the English to dismantle the role of Indian leaders in the War. However, the presences of such correspondence and that the War was 'authored' is critical in viewing the 1857 without the revisionist prism.

While these letters were destroyed, the analysis above is corroborated by a witness whose testimony has been marginalised by all 'reputable' historians.

COCK-AND-BULL STORIES

Royal priests in India enjoyed the king's confidence and were often privy to 'inside information' and acted as informal channels of confidential communication. Sitaram Baba was an important priest affiliated with the court of Nana Saheb Peshwa. In this period, it was not uncommon for priests to be invited for important pujas, and yajnyas, and therefore, their movement would not automatically raise suspicion.

Sitaram Baba was arrested in January of 1858 in Mysore, and was accused to be one of 'chief rebels', and a 'close associate' of Nana Saheb Peshwa. He was in constant communication with Nana Saheb and other 'collaborators' through 'agents' until his arrest. His testimony to H.B. Devereux, the judicial commissioner of Mysore in January 1858, combined with the evidence of the red lotus and chapati messages reveal some fascinating information about the operation.

Many historians have systematically rejected or undermined the authenticity of 'native' testimonies, especially those that suggest planning for the war. In a similar vein, Surendra Nath Sen, in his 'official' version of the history of 1857, dismisses Sitaram Baba's testimony as a cock-and-bull story. Was Sen overreacting, mistaken or deliberately attempting to undermine important evidence in the historiography of 1857? On the other hand, could it be that Sen himself was repackaging a cock-and bull story that was invented by the English?

Which of these two is the real cock-and-bull story, Sitaram Baba's testimony or Sen's 'history'?

Consider this.

Amar Farooqui's essay on Baiza Bai,[26] accurately points out that this testimony is that of a person who was extensively familiar with the politics of the nineteenth century. He revealed a 'fairly extensive knowledge of people and events in several parts of the country', including, the various phases of the life of Baija Bai Shinde. Farooqui also points out that several references in his testimony are startling in their accuracy relative to the context. For example, Sitaram Baba accurately mentions that a prominent financier of the War in the early phases was Seth Lakshmichand (spelt varyingly as Luchhmichund) of Mathura, who in turn was associated to the celebrated Mani Ram, the financier and merchant of Gwalior who was personally affiliated to the 'vexatious' Baija Bai Shinde.[27] If Sitaram Baba was telling a cock-and-bull story, he certainly was extremely accurate with the people, their aspirations and their past behaviours.

Sitaram Baba was arrested on 18 January 1858 and was interrogated for about a week. The commissioner of Mysore, J. Cunningham, sent a file to the secretary to the English government of India on January 1858, which included the questions that were asked to Sitaram Baba and the translations of his answers.[28] After the testimony, the English concluded that Sitaram Baba, was 'if not an actor', he was 'at any rate to have been in the confidence of the chief conspirators, and early initiated into their designs'. In addition, they concluded that Sitaram Baba appears 'remarkably clear and consistent in all his statements', and he was 'inclined to attach a considerable credit to them'.

On the first day of his arrest, 18 January, Sitaram Baba refused to answer any questions when asked about an 'incriminating' letter found on him.[29] He responded, 'I am quite willing to sacrifice myself, but I will not sacrifice others. I will not give any information. Many great men would suffer if I did.' The minutes from the testimony say that after refusing to speak to the judge 'he was sent back to the confinement' to be *persuaded*. We are not exactly sure what 'civilised methods of persuasion' the English used on the priest. This was a period when thousands of men, women, and children were being tortured, bayoneted, hanged, and burnt alive. Certainly, getting a priest to talk could not have been hard for the English using their 'civilised' methods.

By January of 1858, the brutality of the English during the War was widely known. Sitaram Baba himself had faced a day of English 'persuasion' with methods the letter has not cared to elaborate. Success came the following day. The priest started talking.

Sitaram Baba in his testimony reveals many facts and provides many opinions. In this analysis, we are more concerned about the facts that Sitaram Baba provides rather than his opinions, which were most likely clouded by his fears of was facing more 'persuasion' and possibly death.

The following are some excerpts from his testimony:

> The Baija Bhaiee (Bai) was the person who first commenced this conspiracy about twenty years ago, at the time she was taken from Gwalior and kept at Nassick. She continued plotting at Oojein to which place she was afterwards removed...[30]

Nana Saheb's priest Dassa Bawa was an important participant in the planning stages, including communication with other leaders.

> When Dassa Bawa went to Oojein the Baiza Bhaiee consulted with him on the subject of a rising. This happened about six years ago. She

told him all her plans, and he then went to the Nana, and advised him to join with her. This was the means by which the two plots became connected.[31]

In the above statement, Sitaram Baba is referring to the Raja of Satara's plans in 1838 to overthrow the English as the first plan that was connected to the plan by Baija Bai.

Sitaram Baba provides the timing for the Nana Saheb's plan.

This is the real beginning. Three years ago, or perhaps a month less...

Sitaram Baba was arrested in January of 1858. This places the tactical stages of the planned war around February of 1855. This is consistent with Azimullah Khan's detours in west Asia after he had left London.

All this was communicated by the Nana to Baiza Bhaiee and to all the other states—to Holkar, Scindia, to Kumroo (Assani or Purserani Khoond), the country of Brumha Rajah where gold sand is found (Burma), to Jeypoor, Jaudhpoor, Kota, Boonda, Jhalawur, Rewah, Baroda, Kutch Bhooj, Nagpore, to the Ghonds of Chanda and Subbulpore [this last doubtfully], to Hyderabad, Sorapoor, Kolapoor, Sattarah, Indore, also to Mysore, in fact he did not leave out any place where there was a Native Prince. He wrote to all....[32]

In reference to when and how the plan was communicated with the Regiments, Sitaram Baba replies:

Not before the annexation of Oude, but before the affair of the greased cartridges, which was a mere pretext....[33]

As regards to the 'how' question,

After that Maun Sing sent four or five Poorbeas to every Regiment in the service of the Company, and by their means all communications took place....[34]

These 'Poorbeas' were likely to be the runners who sent and collected the information. Raja Man Singh of Awadh probably aggregated the information and sent that information to Tatya Tope.

Sitaram Baba summarises the sequence of events after Nana Saheb sent the letters:

> The plot among the Sepoys first took place—then the discontent about the greased cartridges—then answers began to pour in.[35]

Sitaram Baba provides an interesting connection between the lotuses and the chapatis. This is in reference to a puja that Dassa Baba was performing:

> He then took the seed of the Lotus or Kumul called Mukhana, and made an idol of it. He then reduced the idol to very small pills and having made an immense number of cakes, he put a pill in each. As far as those cakes were carried so far the people would determine to throw off the Company Raj.[36]

Makhana are the popped seeds of the lotus flower. The priest, in his ceremony, was adding the makhana into the first round of chapatis that were sent to the villages.

The symbolism of the red lotus and the chapatis were entwined by the act of placing the popped lotus seeds inside the chapatis. Sitaram Baba's testimony is important, but not critical to this presentation. The analysis from different sources reaches independent conclusions, which are corroborated by Sitaram Baba. The complementary evidence and a factual premise support his testimony.

Nana Saheb may have been a religious person, but embedded in the symbolism of this religious ceremony was a potent plan to set India free.

A LUBRICATED PRETEXT

The English and many Western nations were searching for the causes of this 'mutiny' for decades following 1857. On 1 February 1902, more than forty years after the War ended, the *New York Times* reviewed a 'dramatic story' of the 'sepoy rebellion' written by W.H. Fitchett. The debate was still on about the causes of this 'mutiny'. Were the 'far-famed greased cartridges the immediate occasion if not the supreme producing cause of the outbreak?' W.H. Fitchett concludes otherwise and 'avers upon the authority of Kaye, that none of the guilty cartridges were actually issued to the men'.[37]

If the answer was simple and the cause of the so-called mutiny was indeed the 'greased cartridges', why was there still a debate about it forty years later? Why this continued confusion?

These contradictions are a result of the presumption that the events of 1857 were a *mutiny*. If this premise is abandoned, these illusory paradoxes disappear. Were the greased cartridges really the *cause* for conflict?

Consider the following timeline relative to the introduction of the Enfield rifle and the 'far-famed cartridges'.

Date	English Observations
1853	First Enfield cartridges sent to India for climatic testing.
1854	EEIC promised 3,000 new Enfield guns by the British govt. for the Bengal Presidency. Crimean war prevented first batch of 1,500 rifles reaching India.
1856	Spring of 1856, rifles reached India. Initially earmarked for Bengal troops. Finally issued to 60th British regiment.
4 February 1856	Troops at Barrackpore (2NI) shown ungreased cartridges and the paper used for making them at a parade.
May 1856	12,000 Enfield rifles arrive in Bengal. Only British 60th regiment issued the rifles. Rest in the armoury.
Early January 1857	Asked to send one detachment each to either Dum-Dum, Ambala or Sialkot for instructions in care and handling.
23 January 1857	Many Indian troops refuse to touch cartridges and request use of wax and oil instead.
27 January 1857	Col. Richard Birch, military secretary, orders all cartridges to be free from grease. Sepoys can use whatever mixture they want.
29 January 1857	Col. Abbott from ordnance, reports to Birch that a mixture of tallow and bee wax had been used. Troops allowed to use their own grease.
30 January 1857	2NI now objects to cartridge *paper* as being offensive.

Date	English Observations
30 January 1857	The lack of a genuine grievance prompts the speculation that some *guiding hand*—within or without the regiment—was trying to keep the cartridge controversy alive by switching attention from grease to paper. Canning suspects controversy and tells Vernon Smith that the mutinous spirit has 'not been roused by the cartridges alone'.

In the initial deployment of the Enfield rifle, only the 2nd Native Infantry was involved. The rifles were *not* deployed widely. The English were very quick to recognise that the possible use of animal fat in the cartridges was risky and quickly gave orders to switch to vegetable fat and wax. Cartridges with animal fat were not deployed to any regiments once their risk was understood. In fact, by 30 January all Indian soldiers of the 2nd Native Infantry were allowed to use their own grease, which could be vegetable fat and wax. At this point, when the soldiers started complaining about the paper, the English suspected that there was more to the 'mutinous' spirit than the greased cartridges.

In fact, the red lotuses were making rounds of various garrisons shortly before and during the deployment of the cartridges. As other evidence indicates, Nana Saheb and others were recruiting the soldiers, independently of the cartridge issue. The introduction of the cartridges was simply another opportunity that came along. The inspiration to overthrow English power in India symbolised by the red lotuses was complemented by the timely (or untimely if you are on the other side) introduction of the cartridges. The greased cartridges were nothing more than an opportunity that helped gather the momentum for a cause that was already well under way. Sitaram Baba is clear in his testimony about the sequence of events: 'Nana Saheb first sent the letters.... Then the plot among the Sepoys...then the discontent about the greased cartridges....'[38]

The greased cartridges were an opportunity that was used as a battle cry against the English. What the English were witness to was this rallying cry. The cartridges symbolised the socially oppressive policies that the English had unleashed starting 1835. The cartridge or the 'kartoos' symbolised English tyranny.

Indian soldiers were found reciting a couplet that represented this battle cry, a poem that represented the synecdoche for the War of 1857.

Na Iran ne kiya, na Shah Russ ne,
Angrez ko tabaa kiya, kartoos ne.[39]

(What neither Russia nor Iran were able to do, the English have been beaten by the cartridge.)

THE INVISIBLE LOTUS—THE PUZZLE OF 1857

While many historians reject Sitaram Baba's testimony, a most unlikely eyewitness to the events of 1857 corroborates the story. Vishnubhat Godse, a priest from a town called Varsai, was visiting Pune during the Mahashivratri[*] festival in February 1857. While in Pune, he heard about an invitation for priests to attend a very large sarvatomukhah yajnya.[†] While these yajnya invitations are not uncommon in India, the grandeur of this yajnya was unique. Additionally, there were three things worthy of consideration about this planned event: the who, the where and the when of this yajnya.[40]

The Who: the organiser was Baija Bai Shinde, who had suddenly re-emerged on the scene. Living in exile or away from Gwalior since 1832, Baija Bai made Gwalior her home in late 1856, just as the plan for the War was falling in place.

The Where: the location was Mathura. Although a little over a hundred miles from Gwalior, the location is significant. The first 'financiers' of the War was Seth Lakshmichand of Mathura. This becomes especially important since the amount of money that was to be spent on this yajnya alone was in excess of seven lakh rupees.[41]

The When: the timing interestingly was to be around the middle of 1857. The grandness of the planned yajna had hundreds of priests, like Vishnubhat Godse travelling from different locations towards the planned zones of War. *In this flurry of movements of priests, priestly messengers, carried secret messages, could travel undetected.*

---

[*]Mahashivratri translates as 'Great Night of Shiva' is a festival celebrated every year, in the eleventh month of the Luni-Solar Indian civil calendar, on the 13th night of the waning period of the moon. The festival is celebrated by offerings of Bael (Bilva) leaves to Lord Shiva, fasting and an all-night long vigil.
[†]Sarvatomukhah is in reference to Vishnu and translates as He Who can be approached from many paths or He Who has faces on all sides.

Surendra Nath Sen, who wrote the 'official' history 1857, accuses Sitaram Baba of inventing a 'cock-and-bull' story. If it indeed were such, it would be an enormous coincidence that the people, the place and the events, are independently corroborated in Vishnu Godse's memoirs.

Consider the story of 1857 that has largely been told thus far. For example, in the words of R.C. Majumdar, described by many as 'India's greatest historian', 1857 was 'purely a *mutiny* of the *sepoys*, joined at a later stage by some *discontented elements* as well as the *riff-raff* and other *disturbing elements* of society'. Figure 8 below, roughly approximates the Victorian spin on the story, as echoed by the likes of Majumdar and Sen.

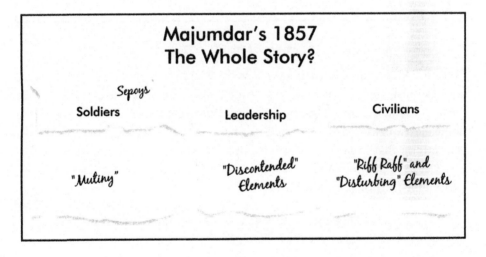

Figure 8: Majumdar's 1857

Unlike Majumdar, the Marxist historians do not view the people as the 'riff raff' or 'disturbing elements', but rather as the *real* heroes of the story and perhaps the only heroes. Leaders such as Tatya Tope and Rani of Jhansi, who came from 'ordinary' backgrounds, are by definition the representatives of the people, and therefore heroes as well. However, the leadership of Nana Saheb Peshwa and Bahadur Shah, the planning and the principles presented in the proclamation of freedom is largely marginalised.

The real story of 1857 is hidden behind the façade of semantic duplicity.

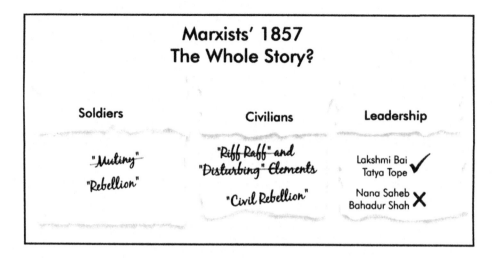

Figure 9: Marxists' 1857

Both the Victorian historians as well as the Marxists' view of 1857 is in reality a revisionist view of history, that is unable to reconcile the facts that have been presented earlier. Neither of these two revisionist views of 1857 can logically explain the events prior to May 1857. The whole story of 1857 is something that is profound in its simplicity, yet powerful in its execution.

On 28 September 1857, an American businessman named George Train, who later ran for president, asked:

> Was it not a ruling mind that waited for the breaking out of the Persian war before they struck their colours?
> Was it not a ruling mind that took advantage of England's attention in China before they raised the red flag of mutiny?
> Was it not a ruling mind that selected the centennial anniversary of the battle of Plassey for the general insurrection?
> Was it not a ruling mind that chose Delhi, the centre of the Mogul Empire, as a rendezvous hoarded throughout the Indian Empire, disarranging the exchanges of the West?
> Are all of these things the result of accident? [42]

While English explanations were being challenged by the Americans during the War, simply based on reasoning and facts, the English discourse was crafted and assimilated as 'History'. A history that was first challenged by Savarkar in 1908, but remained unchallenged in a free India.

THE LOTUS REVEALED

The advanced plan for the War of 1857 is what we describe as a planned military operation. We have chosen to dub this plan as 'Operation Red Lotus'. The plan was elaborate, but simple in its execution. Operation Red Lotus was a plan created by Tatya Tope. It was Nana Saheb, with the help of his court that took it to the next stage and coordinated with other leaders, such as Bahadur Shah and Begum Hazrat Mahal. These leaders worked the plan in secrecy and their overt behaviour prior to the War gave nothing away. Additionally there was Baija Bai Shinde, who also participated in the planning but did not overtly support the War but did everything to support it covertly. Rani Lakshmi Bai of Jhansi—postured against the Indians at the outset of the War, but her covert behaviour was always supportive of freedom.

The civilian villagers participated in the logistics of the operations, providing for the logistics for transportation and supplies. The civilian landlords and bankers such as Lakshmichand provided the capital. During the planning of the War, each of three groups displayed a covert behaviour that would not raise any suspicion. Only in hindsight did the likes of Benjamin Disraeli view the ingenuity in this plan. Of course, the English labelled it as a 'conspiracy'. Figure 10 summarises the story of the planning of the War of 1857.

The Operation Red Lotus plan: Nana Saheb was following Mahadji Shinde's policy of keeping Bahadur Shah as the figurehead Mughal ruler. He had full support from the Begum Hazrat Mahal of Lucknow. The idea was to liberate a few important cities, such as Delhi, Lucknow and Kanpur, and expand the rule under the name of the Badshah to other areas. Many proclamations, including those made by Nana Saheb and Lakshmi Bai and other participating leaders acknowledged the implicit authority of Bahadur Shah.[43]

The goal of Operation Red Lotus was to mobilise the Indian soldiers employed by the EEIC, to overrun their local garrisons and march to previously defined locations, to liberate a few primary cities in addition to all the surrounding villages. Following the liberation, the idea was to create an Indian government with roles and functions that would represent the real India. Some historians who accept that there was indeed a plan

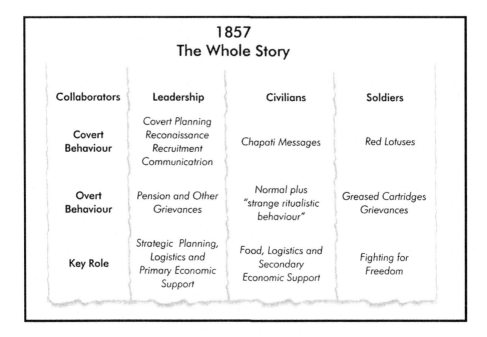

Figure 10: 1857, The Whole Story

indicate that there was a fixed date to start the war.[44] We argue later that a fixed date was not only unnecessary, but in fact would have complicated the logistics of the soldiers.

As the figure above indicates, the key elements of the planning were the logistics, transportation and provisions. Who amongst this group demonstrated the most leadership in these areas during the course of the War? The evidence points towards Tatya Tope.

Hundreds of Urdu and Bundeli letters written to Tatya Tope indicate that Tatya was keenly aware about, not only the military movements, but also the logistics and the provisions for the army. We believe that Operation Red Lotus was about Tatya receiving messages in red lotuses and sending messages in chapatis. Tatya Tope as a mentor encouraged Nana Saheb Peshwa to fight for India's freedom and Tatya himself died fighting for it.

Chapter 7

THE OPERATION
Trails to Freedom

Early during 1857, Nana Saheb who rarely travelled made three 'unusual' visits. First to Kalpi, then to Delhi, and then on 18 April, he visited Lucknow.[1] While Henry Lawrence, Lucknow's chief commissioner, thought it was strange, many others were unable to comprehend the relevance of these 'intrigues' with the Nawab of Awadh, the Begum Hazrat Mahal and Bahadur Shah Zafar of Delhi. Coincident with these visits was the 'mysterious yajnya' arranged by Baija Bai Shinde and Nana Saheb's covert discussions with this pragmatic patriot, who had made Gwalior her residence in late 1856. As discussed earlier, the early months of 1857 also saw the red lotus flowers doing the rounds of the garrisons followed by the 'chapati' messages. Mangal Pandey's outburst on 29 March 1857 represented the inflamed and an eager anticipation of Operation Red Lotus.

While these events were unfolding, the priest Vishnubhat Godse had begun his journey from Varsai near Pune to Gwalior, to attend the yajna organised by Baija Bai Shinde. His long and arduous journey to Gwalior and then his stay in Jhansi intersected with many important events of the War, offer an independent ringside view of the Indian troop movements.

Infantry regiments depended on bullock carts for transportation and ranged about ten to twenty miles per day. Cavalry was certainly faster;

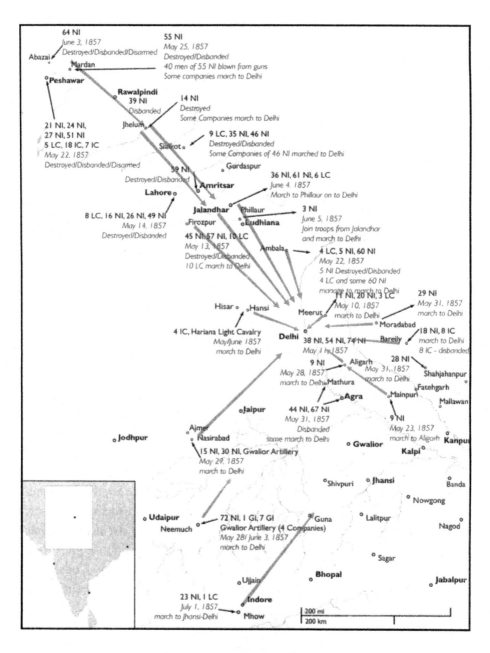

Figure 11: Trails to Delhi
Legend: NI – Native Infantry, LC – Light Cavalry, IC – Irregular Cavalry

however, it comprised only a fraction of the army. In the early months of the War, these soldiers marched hundreds of thousands of man-miles.

An analysis of the Indian troop movement indicates a high level of planning that went into the rationale behind the selection of the cities as well as the movement of the troops. Most historians wrongly assume that the initial theatre of war was merely the garrisons where the soldiers were stationed. There were dozens of places where the hundred-odd regiments of the Bengal Army were stationed, but each of them after overcoming resistance, marched to very well defined and specific destinations. Travelling mostly without camp followers, these soldiers depended heavily on the villages that came along the way for their transportation and rations. The complicated troop movements that were planned were in built into the chapati messages; each village playing host to the soldiers, as an embedded supply line, as they marched to their destination. The staggered troop movements helped in the sustainable support from the villages.

Operation Red Lotus unfolded on 10 May 1857 with the liberation of Delhi followed by Kanpur, Lucknow, Gwalior and Banda. As we will see later, the dates seem to be neatly staggered and in the form of a wave. The pattern was similar. Regiment after regiment stationed in dozens of towns and cities, first took up arms, defeated the local English soldiers, took control of their garrisons and then began marching to pre-arranged destinations.

Delhi came first.

INDRA SMILED—LIBERATION OF DELHI

Figure 11 indicates the various troops that marched into Delhi in the few weeks after the War started. However, the curtain raiser to the imminent liberation of Delhi was enacted in Meerut, a town thirty-eight miles to the north-east of Delhi. The large cantonment of Meerut comprised the 3rd Regiment Light Cavalry, 20th Regiment Native Infantry and 11th Regiment Native Infantry. The English were represented by a troop of Horse Artillery Battery, 60th Rifles and 6th Dragoon Guards.[2]

On Sunday, 10 May 1857, at about 5 pm, while several English officers of the 20th NI were at their commanding officer's house,[3] Indian soldiers gathered at the Gol Bhatta, a brick kiln just outside the city, to give the final touches to their action plan. By 6.30 pm, they were ready, and the men of the 20th NI began by taking control of the regimental magazine assisted by the local population of the Sadar Bazaar and the city.[4] Meanwhile, at the barracks of the 11th NI, the Indian troops overpowered their English officers and joined the 20th NI in capturing the magazine.[5] The task cut out for the cavalry was different. A troop of the 3rd LC galloped down to the new jail[6] to rescue eighty-five men of their regiment who had been recently sentenced by a court-martial.[7] Simultaneously, another troop of the 3rd LC thundered away for a far more important task, that of securing the road to Delhi. They were able to achieve this without any resistance.

Back at the jail, the 3rd LC had not only freed eighty-five of their men, but set free all the 1,200 Indian prisoners incarcerated there. Regrouping with the other regiments, they joined the local population, which was swelling with the arrival of men from nearby villages. By this time the entire cantonment and district police had also deserted their quarters, and the telegraph line to Delhi was severed.[8]

The stunned English officers debated their next step, after 'much delay', they decided to bring out troops of the 60th Rifles and 6th Dragoon Guards.[9]

The 6th Dragoons were apparently dispatched to the jail, but incredulously, the Dragoon Guards lost their way![10] The 60th Rifles fared no better. English euphemisms at their best could not disguise the rank confusion that prevailed that eventful night at Meerut: '...by the time we reached the Native Infantry Parade ground, it was too dark to act with efficiency. Consequently, the troops were retired to the north....'[11]

The night of the 10th passed with Indian troops in full control of the strategic southern part of Meerut cantonment. From here, led the road to Delhi, which at this time was under Indian control. The Indian troops already had control over the arms magazine and severed telegraph lines. The local police and people had joined the victorious regiments.

The 3rd LC had already sent an advance party towards Delhi, and was soon joined by the infantry of 20th and 11th NI. Delhi itself was fortified by 38th, 54th, 74th Regiment Native Infantry and a battery of Native Artillery with English officers under the command of Brigadier Graves.[12]

The following day, Graves received news of the build-up of Indian troops on the banks of the Hindon River, for the impending liberation of

Delhi. He immediately ordered civilian Englishmen to hide in the fortified Flagstaff Tower some distance away from the city. Rather than take control of the Hindon Bridge and engage the Meerut troops away from the city, Graves chose instead to defend the cantonment. Leading troops out from the Kashmiri Gate, he came upon the 250 outriders of the 3rd LC and several other infantrymen marching unflinchingly towards troops of the 38th, 54th and 74th that he led.

Viewed from a 'mutiny' prism, the events that followed, present a near tragicomic account of the 'battle' that ensued when the troops from Meerut reached Delhi. In the words of G.B. Malleson:

> Meanwhile the regiments were ordered out, the guns loaded, and every possible preparation made…. His brief, pithy address was received with cheers. The 54th, especially, seemed eager to exterminate the mutineers, and loudly demanded to be led against them. The Brigadier, responding to their seeming enthusiasm, put himself at their head, and led them out of the Cashmere Gate to meet the rebels, whose near approach had been announced. As they marched out in gallant order, to all appearance proud and confident, a tumultuous array appeared advancing from the Hindun. In front, and in full uniform, with medals on their breasts gained in fighting for British supremacy, confidence in their manner, and fury in their gestures, galloped on about two hundred and fifty troopers of the 3rd Calvary: behind them, at no great distance, and almost running in their efforts to reach the golden minarets of Delhi, appeared a vast mass of Infantry, their red coats soiled with dust, and their bayonets glittering in the sun. No hesitation was visible in all that advancing mass; they came on, as if confident of the result. Now the Cavalry approach nearer and nearer! At this headlong pace, they will soon be on the bayonets of the 54th. These latter are ordered to fire; the fate of India hangs on their reply. They do fire, but alas! into the air; not one saddle is emptied by that vain discharge. And now the Cavalry are amongst them; they fraternise with them….
>
> It was too true, indeed! The bold and confident bearing of the rebels was thus accounted for; the Delhi troops, too, had been corrupted.[13]

Firing in the air, signified celebration and an honourable welcome, and here on the battlefield, the 54th NI fired in the air to welcome the victorious Meerut troops. While Malleson appropriately presents the shock of Brigadier Graves, the extension of this narrative to the context of a 'spontaneous mutiny' is obviously invalid. The behaviour of the Delhi-based regiments was obviously not spontaneous, but clearly calculated.

The battle for the liberation of Delhi ended with Brigadier Graves and other English officers fleeing the battlefield. They decided to take refuge amongst non-combatants in Flagstaff Tower. Taking refuge amongst their women, children and non-combatants was a pattern that was to be routinely followed by the English in the months ahead.

The 3rd LC rode victoriously into Delhi and made straight for the palace of Emperor Bahadur Shah at Lal Qila. Although an octogenarian, Bahadur Shah was fully aware of these events and welcomed the arrival of the troops. The caricature of a 'reluctant Emperor' is thus an English invention, manufactured to fit the 'mutiny' narrative.

Nana Saheb had made a special visit to Delhi amongst other places earlier in 1857. For obvious reasons, Bahadur Shah's participation in this planned overthrow of an oppressive regime was not well received by the English or their spin doctors, who wrote most of the history on the subject. Malleson indignantly accuses Bahadur Shah of this 'conspiracy', which was 'hatched with the King of Oudh'.[14] R.C. Majumdar, a historian admired by some Indians and decorated by the English, added his own venom by calling this octogenarian King, a 'dotard'. Other narratives present Bahadur Shah varyingly, from malevolence, derision to caricature. The following is an example of the ridiculous trivialisation of what ensued at the palace. This, unfortunately, is an archetypal representation of the historiography of 1857:

...the first of them turned-up below the emperor's balcony at about seven o'clock the next morning, their horses lathered from the forty mile ride. 'Help O King!' they shouted up through the stone lattice that shielded the old emperor's apartments. 'We pray for assistance in our fight for the faith'. The Emperor of Delhi was a henpecked octogenarian named Bahadur Shah whose dominion had receded in stages from the walls of his fort to his staterooms. At the sight of the mutineers, he shrank back into his apartments and summoned Captain Douglas, the commander of his guard, who ordered the rebels to stop annoying His Royal Highness. Exhausted and confused, the rebels trotted around the walls of the fort and swarmed into the city...[15]

Captain Douglas the commandant of the palace guards and Commissioner Simon Fraser, were the face of the English rule. When the victorious troops rode into the palace, these men were hiding in the Angoori Bagh of the palace orchards. With the implicit knowledge or the explicit orders of Bahadur Shah, they were caught and executed.[16] The palace in Delhi was now free from the foreign 'guards' that in reality represented the chains of subjugation. Their execution symbolised a passage, and the possibility of a new beginning. Graves and the other civilians hiding at Flagstaff Tower are irrelevant to the monumental events at the palace and our narrative.

Over the next few weeks, dozens of infantry and cavalry regiments marched towards Delhi from places hundreds of miles away. From as far as Mardan, Rawalpindi, Lahore and Amritsar to the north, Neemuch, Mhow, Nasirabad to the south and Azamgarh and Mainpuri to the East. In garrisons where the English troop strengths were higher, thousands of Indian soldiers were executed in the most brutal manner. Yet, wave upon wave of Indian regiments made their way into Delhi to defend it. As Figure 11 shows, many regiments were 'destroyed' in the aftermath. Some were disbanded and disarmed.

Delhi was free and would remain so for another four months.

AWADH TASTES FREEDOM

In a well-documented meeting, Nana Saheb and Azimullah Khan had already conferred with Begum Hazrat Mahal and Mirza Bahadur Bakht, the grandson of Bahadur Shah Zafar on 18 April 1857 at Lucknow,[17] possibly to give shape to their final plans. After the liberation of Delhi, in quick succession on 4th, 5th and 6th June 1857, Azamgarh, Varanasi and Allahabad were liberated. With breathtaking speed, Faizabad, Dariabad/Barabanki, Salan, Sultanpur, Gonda were liberated by 11 June 1857. 'In less than a fortnight, British administration in Oudh had virtually ceased to exist'.[18] Meanwhile in Central India, in the same time period, Jhansi, Naugaon, Gursarai, Banpur and Orai were already in the throes of war, and English troops were holed up in some fortifications, sheltered by their human shields (discussed in a later chapter). Englishmen from the areas of Sitapur, Malan, Mahamadi, Sinkora, Gonda and Bahraich were fleeing in droves, some even pouring into Lucknow.[19] By mid-June, English rule in the area had shrunk to the confines of Lucknow city—the districts and outlying areas were completely under Indian control. Now for the liberation of Lucknow city itself!

The 17 NI was based in Azamgarh, which is about eighty miles south-east of Faizabad. Faizabad was headquarters of the 22 NI, a detachment of Irregular Cavalry and a battery of artillery. The 17 NI liberated Azamgarh on 3 June 1857 and started their march towards Delhi. They reached Faizabad on 8 June and assisted the 22 NI to liberate Faizabad.[20] Faizabad was liberated on 8 June 1857. After Faizabad was liberated, an important Maulvi named Ahmadullah Shah[21] who had coordinated the plan for the liberation was freed from jail to lead Indian forces gathered there for the imminent liberation of Lucknow.

The wave of local battles continued as regiment after regiment of Indian soldiers overpowered their English officers in Awadh. Starting in early June and continuing on to the middle of June, about nine regiments were in control of their garrisons. These included the regiments from Salan, Bahraich, Gonda, Barabanki, Faizabad, Sultanpur and Sitapur.

Each of these places is about sixty-eighty miles from Lucknow. These troops liberated their local cities and then marched about thirty miles to three locations approximately thirty miles from Lucknow by 15 June. They set up camps at Bari, thirty-five miles to the north of Lucknow, at Ramnagar, thirty-eight miles north-east of Lucknow and Haidergarh, thirty-two miles south-east of Lucknow.[22] English dispatches seem to indicate that a coordinated attack was imminent in the next few days. The battle finally did take place on 30 June at Chinhat.

What is important to note is that the movement of troops was not only coordinated, but had also taken into account soldier's provisions. Who supplied the soldiers with food once they had 'mutinied'? It had to be the nearby villages. However, the scope was tremendous, there were at least a few hundred soldiers in each regiment, and when they camped at the Bari, Haidergarh and Ramnagar, they were more than a thousand.

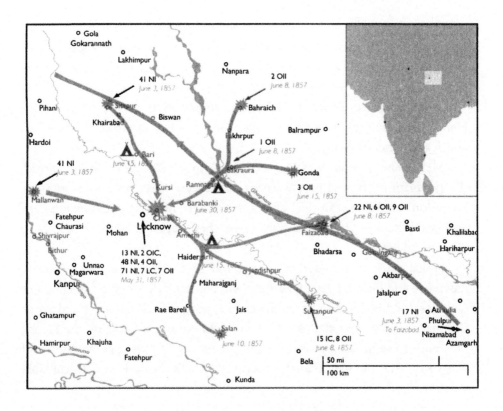

Figure 12: March to Lucknow
Legend: NI – Native Infantry, LC – Light Cavalry, OIC – Oudh Irregular Cavalry,
OII – Oudh Irregular Infantry

These towns were simply not capable of feeding over a thousand men without notice and planning. The travelling chapatis, as noted, were the key to a planned supply line.

Witnessing the massive mobilisation of the troops, the English were also preparing for battle under Henry Lawrence. He had identified the Residency and the Machi Bhavan of particular strategic importance. The Residency had a sprawling campus ensconced in a walled enclosure. It had several buildings and outhouses as well as a multitude of underground vaults and passages, more importantly, it was situated on a natural elevation, which was tactically important. Machi Bhavan was located closer to the River Gomti and had strong turreted defenses. As military targets, two important bridges cross the Gomti; one was a stone bridge near the Machi Bhavan and the other, an iron bridge closer to the Residency.

The magazine and supplies for English troops was shifted to Machi Bhavan and protected by positioning thirty guns. The treasury was shifted inside the Residency and guarded by six guns. Twenty guns protected the two bridges mentioned before.[23]

As Indian forces concentrated on the three towns outside of Lucknow, Henry Lawrence continued his fortifications, possibly aware of the build up and fearing Indian victories.

Meanwhile, Kanpur was liberated on 27 June 1857. As the news spread, the population erupted in a wave of jubilation. This contagious spirit of liberation caught up with the huge camps at Bari, Ramnagar and Haidergarh and with their established supply lines, they began the march down to liberate Lucknow.

Holed up in the sprawling compound of the Residency were Henry Lawrence and his followers. Lawrence was constantly goaded by an ebullient Gubbins for his inaction at intelligence reports of an enemy build-up at Chinhat. 'It is certain that Mr Gubbins was continually urging Sir Henry Lawrence to send out a force to meet the enemy. But what he certainly did was to ridicule the idea that the enemy were advancing in any formidable strength'.[24]

By 30 June, one regular NI and eight irregular regiments were deployed at Chinhat in anticipation of the final assault on Lucknow. Chinhat is located on the banks of a large water body and covered with thick vegetation, notably mangroves to its west. Indian troops had concealed themselves in these mangroves. An estimate of the Indian troops, which is based on the troops positioned in the province probably, comprised elements of the 22 NI from Faizabad, 2nd, 3rd, 5th, 6th, 8th, and the 9th Regiments of the Oudh Irregular Infantry and two regiments of the military police. In addition, there are estimates of a 500-strong cavalry and 12 pieces of artillery.[25]

Lucknow was now less than a day's march away, when opportunity trotted their way in the form of Henry Lawrence and his troops arriving onto the outskirts of Chinhat.

Lawrence had set out shortly before daybreak, crossed the Iron Bridge on the city's outskirts, and headed out towards the Kokrail Bridge over a small tributary of the Gomti. So far, there were no signs of the Indian troops, and the English troops were emboldened to move further up towards Chinhat, leaving the village of Ismailganj to their left.

The English had already made an important tactical error. Gubbins writes:

> So far the road was metalled. But beyond this it was a newly-raised embankment, constructed of loose and sandy soil, in which every now and then gaps occurred, indicating the positions of future bridges. After some halt, during which no refreshment was served out to the men, the force moved on along this heavy causeway.[26]

As a result, the cavalry was well ahead, while the artillery and infantry laboured up and down the embankments. This slow moving enemy was a tempting target for Indian troops waiting in the mangroves as well as the artillery lying in readiness at Ismailganj, and a first shot was fired into the English column from a distance of 1,400 yards with devastating effect. It was only after this shot that the English troops could pinpoint the location of Indian troops camouflaged in the thickets and began to move their artillery forward.[27]

A twenty-minute exchange of artillery fire is reported to have taken place when the English committed another tactical error. The main body of Indian troops had quickly split into two, and were moving to the right and left flanks of the English troops. English commanders incorrectly read this outflanking movement as that of retreat.[28] Now in addition to being outflanked, the Indians had a stronghold in the village of Ismailganj to the left of the enemy. From here, heavy firing was poured onto enemy ranks, this time from the flanks. 'With more than a third of their number killed or wounded, the English 32nd fell back. The guns were almost out of ammunition, the situation hopeless, when Sir Henry Lawrence gave the order to retreat'.[29] However, it was already too late. Indian cavalry had galloped to the rear and cut-off the retreat route by consolidating at the Kokrail Bridge, which had been surprisingly left unguarded by the English during their advance.

In the thick of retreat, caught between two crucial bridges, the Kokrail and the Iron Bridge, the English forces suffered enormous casualties. Eyewitness accounts report: 'dead bodies were heaped, one over the other'.[30] The slow retreat continued into the buildings of the Residency and the Machi Bhavan with Indian forces in hot pursuit well into the city, where they were now joined by local police at the Imambara. 'The defeat, the pursuit, and the investment of our posts had been so rapid and unexpected, that there was all confusion at the Residency'.[31] The siege of the Residency continued with continuous pounding by Indian artillery and Henry Lawrence was killed on 4 July.

Amongst widespread jubilation, a victory salute was fired with the booming of guns from Mitauli on 5 July 1857, signalling the coronation of the young Birjis Qadr, the adopted son of Wajid Ali Shah. Begum Hazrat Mahal ruled in his name and an administration was set in place.[32]

Lucknow and the surrounding areas were now free.

Let us now address another question. The villages surrounding Lucknow had already been strained in terms of food and other provisions during the liberation of Lucknow. If additional troops repeatedly passed through these villages, it would have been impossible to support them. This logic weakens the theory that a 'simultaneous' date for the 'rebellion' was planned, but could not be executed.

GWALIOR, KANPUR AND BANDA

Lucknow lies on the shores of the Gomti river—a river much smaller than the Ganga. Kanpur was a strategic centre because it was accessible by steamboats from Calcutta as well as by the Grand Trunk Road. Kanpur was an important city to liberate and defend and so was Gwalior.

Nana Saheb and Tatya Tope were the centre of the plan to overthrow the English. However, by the end of May, the English had yet to know the real power centre behind these troop movements. While the troops were being 'mutinous' when they overpowered their English officers, their subsequent marches had to be clearly coordinated. Nana Saheb overtly portrayed himself as a helpless victim of these 'mutinous' soldiers who placed Nana Saheb and Tatya Tope under arrest. Obviously, there is no evidence of Nana Saheb or Tatya Tope being arrested. However, unless Kanpur was secure, there was no real necessity for Nana Saheb to expose himself as the leader of the War.

The events in Kanpur unfolded on 4 June, when the 2nd Light Cavalry and the 1st, 53rd and the 56th NI took over the collector's office and confiscated the treasury. The events after 4 June get a little difficult because a set of events that took place for the next five weeks are complicated by highly biased narratives on the subject.

For all practical purposes, Kanpur was free. Kanpur's liberation and its fall a few weeks later and the 'Story of Cawnpore' are discussed in later chapters.

The Nawab of Banda, Ali Bahadur, played an active role during the War and well into late 1858. Banda became a magnet for the troops in August and September, as a countermove to England's dramatic response to the War. Banda became a strategic centre to help launch Kalpi as a new capital for the rebellion at a point when India had nearly lost the War.

The events of Gwalior are also complicated by a plethora of hyperbole about the role of Jiyaji Rao Shinde. Baija Bai Shinde, as discussed earlier was a key figure in inspiring Nana Saheb and Tatya Tope. The adopted heir, Jiyaji Rao Shinde, or Scindia as he was called by the English, also overtly portrayed a pro-English stance. His behaviour and the narrative of Gwalior in later months are discussed later. However, the events that transpired in early June of 1857 in Central India followed a pattern similar to the marches of various troops in Delhi and Lucknow.

Gwalior had a different arrangement of its army under the treaties that were signed after the Anglo-Maratha wars. A large body of troops with seven infantry regiments and two cavalry regiments were called the Gwalior Contingent and was not administered under the Bengal Army as most of the other participating regiments were. Regardless of their technical differences, most of the Gwalior Contingent, in June, marched from their various locations into Gwalior to secure it in a planned manner.

In a coordinated move, some Gwalior regiments were ordered to march to other locations. The 6th Gwalior Infantry Regiment, stationed at Lalitpur marched to Kanpur. The Gwalior artillery in Nasirabad and Neemuch marched to Delhi.[33] The Gwalior Horse stationed at Hathras also marched to Delhi on 24 May 1857. However, on 14 June 1857 the 2nd Gwalior Infantry and the 3rd Gwalior Infantry Regiments took over the cantonment in Gwalior (see Figure 13). Other regiments of the Gwalior Contingent from Agar, Guna and Etahawah marched into Gwalior as well.

By the middle of June 1857, Gwalior was also free.

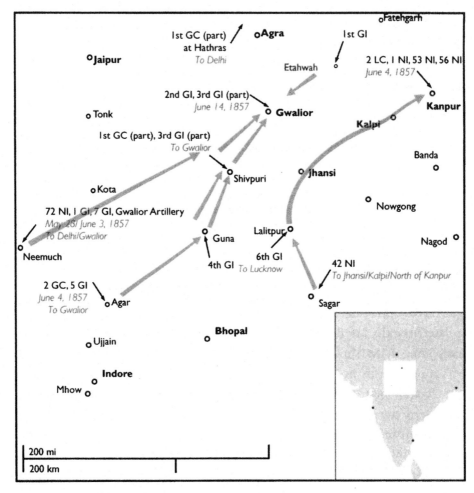

Figure 13: March to Gwalior
Legend: NI–Native Infantry, LC–Light Cavalry, GI–Gwalior Infantry, GC–Gwalior Cavalry

The towns and villages in the areas that the soldiers had overpowered their local English officers were now under Indian control. Large portions of northern India were now free.

Chapter 8

THE FLAME OF LIBERTY

TRANSITORY FREEDOM

By July 1857, Operation Red Lotus was largely a success. The goal of Operation Red Lotus was to establish Indian rule over the areas that were liberated. Most of the areas surrounding Delhi, Lucknow, Kanpur, Gwalior and parts of Central India were free. Lucknow and Delhi continued to hold out against the English.

Nana Saheb's leadership is evident in the protocol and the welcome he received in the court of Wajid Ali, the Nawab of Lucknow and Begum Hazrat Mahal, on 1 August 1857, *despite* the loss of Kanpur discussed later. The collector of Lucknow, Jay Lal Singh, went to Fatehpur Chaurasi to welcome Nana Saheb to Lucknow. He went with twelve camels, twenty-nine bullock-carts, ten carriages, and over twenty elephants. Nana Saheb came out of the 'Chaudhary ki Garhi' with his family and marched towards Lucknow.

For his reception, Nusrat Jang went out with 200 sowars, two elephants caparisoned with silver howdahs and two camel drivers. As he entered the town, eleven rounds of cannon fire greeted him. Nana Saheb was to reside at the Sheesh Mahal, which was furnished with ten *shatranji*, ten *chandni*, ten cots, several chairs, glasswares and paintings. Wajid Ali enquired about his welfare and Begum Hazrat Mahal presented a *khilat* (robe) to Nana

Saheb. In addition, Nana was honoured with a *nazrana* (offering) that was personally approved by the Begum herself. It included a golden *qaba* (gown), a sword and shield, *mala* (beads) of pearls, *dhuk-dhuki* saddled with jewels, *kantha* made of pearls, jewelled *navratanan dast-band* made of pearls, *doshala*, *roomal*, embroidered cloak, *kamar-bandi* shawl, horse with a silver saddle and an elephant with a silver howdah (*ambaryi*).[1]

Besides the pageantry and wealth, the welcome accorded signifies something extremely important. Despite the loss of Kanpur, the king and queen of Awadh were honouring Nana Saheb a welcome accorded to royalty. Nana Saheb was more than simply a Maratha 'Raja' of Bithur. It was an acceptance as the de facto leader of a free India under the name of the Badshah.

Shortly before arriving for his reception at Lucknow, Nana Saheb had sent Bala Rao, who served in Nana Saheb's court, to Delhi and Tatya Tope to Gwalior. Tatya's visit to Gwalior is of huge significance, as we shall later see.

Parts of India were now liberated and an Indian government was in place under the name of Bahadur Shah Zafar. A proclamation was drafted sometime in the second week of August that was eventually presented to the people on 25 August 1857 (referred in the Introduction of the book). The grandson of Bahadur Shah read it out. However, he did not read this out in Delhi, but in Azamgarh, which is closer to Lucknow. It is possible that Nana Saheb himself authoured this articulate proclamation like many other Urdu proclamations he made during the period.

Over the next few months, the English offensive was able to recapture the cities. While the battle for the cities continued, the government under the leadership of Nana Saheb continued to rule in many parts of north and Central India until about May of 1858, nearly one year, with its headquarters at Kalpi.

LETTERS TO TATYA

A descendant of the Diwan of Orchha recently found over a hundred Urdu and 125 Bundeli letters. Most of these letters were written during the first quarter of 1858 in a three-week period from late January to early February of 1858. The communication in these letters represents the affairs of the government of Nana Saheb Peshwa. Obviously, the letters represent only a small portion of the overall communication that had taken place.

These include letters written by Peshwa Nana Saheb's office, his high civilian officials, officers in the army, soldiers, spies at the battlefront and reporters (*harkaras* and *akhbarnaveez*) and revenue officials. These letters are addressed either to Tatya Tope himself or to Syyed Mohammed Isaakh, who forwarded them to Tatya Tope for his information and approval. Syyed Mohammed Isaakh is referred to as mir munshi or chief secretary or chief accountant. He assisted Tatya Tope in coordinating various activities when Tatya Tope's headquarters were in Kalpi.

These are amongst the few documents representing the Indian side that have survived deliberate destruction of Indian documents. There has been some previously published work related to the free governments established in the Delhi and Awadh area, however, little has been published about the establishment of an Indian government in Bundelkhand. The letters reveal not only the structure of civilian and military administration, but also the planning process of the battles themselves. The analysis that ensues gives us an idea of the administration in place for that brief period of transitory freedom; freedom from the time Nana Saheb got control in September 1857 to the eventual defeat in May 1858 after the gruesome genocide at Jhansi.

In the letters, the word 'sarkar' refers to the government of Nana Saheb Peshwa. Nana Saheb's government focused on activities that one would expect a government during times of war to engage in. The focus was on managing the war, revenue collection, efficient administrative processes, maintaining law and order, and putting in place a judicial system.

Planning and executing battles was coordinated between different kings and Nana Saheb's government, though the states maintained different identities.[2] These letters are mainly from the areas that were under the jurisdiction of the Nawab of Banda and Nana Saheb. These are the primary areas referred to in the letters; however, information and copies of letters from other kingdoms were also forwarded to Tatya for his reference.

The letters reveal that unlike what is popularly believed, Tatya Tope was clearly responsible for a lot more than fighting battles. He was the Diwan in Nana Saheb's court. Nana Saheb Peshwa was the king and Tatya Tope was both a military commander-in-chief as well as a prime minister. He was responsible for both military as well as civil administration.

Despite being hundreds of miles away, Tatya was in excellent communication with Nana Saheb and other hot spots.

> ...the rebel leader always kept up communications with the Nana and other chiefs in Oude. This was effected by messengers called cossids, who go thirty and forty miles a-day for weeks in succession. The cossids are much employed by merchants; they are accustomed to start on long journeys to places they have not before visited, and pass everywhere without question.[3]

The *qasids* along with the harkaras created an elaborate communication and spy network that was at the core of a distributed government established in the midst of a war.

Some letters were written by Syyed Mohammed Isaakh to Tatya Tope. These are like summary reports or pending issues that varied from battle strategies, law and order and revenue collection. These letters are what one would expect a 'home minister' writing to a 'prime minister'.[4]

There are letters that report the condition of people in areas under the English and the brutality the people were facing at the hands of the English. Stories of extortions and daily hangings from the harkaras were part of the reports as well.[5]

The word 'mutiny' is context sensitive. In the communication of the 'Sarkar' of Nana Saheb, any reference to *baagi* soldiers or *bagawat* was about soldiers who turned against Nana's government.[6]

While some soldiers did 'mutiny' and abandon the army, some simply did not want to fight. In these cases these soldiers were simply paid their salary due and removed from the payroll.[7]

'CREATIVE' REVOLUTION

Savarkar was not privy to these letters and the related information when he concluded that the reason for India's defeat in 1857 was because of the missing 'creative' part of the revolution.

The letters cover some important functions that Nana Saheb's government was administering, which demonstrate that not only was Tatya Tope attemping to 'destroy' the English rule, he had in parallel 'created' a government that would provide an alternative continuity. These functions include administration of civil, financial, personnel, office and military functions. Considering these functions are visible only from a small sampling of letters written during a three-week period, they demonstrate a significant achievement of a civilian administration set-up in the midst of war.

Civil Administration

In the short time that the government of Nana Saheb was established, the existence of the judicial process and methods for enforcing law and order is evident. Due process is visible in addressing crimes from small theft to plunder and extortion. The following are some examples that demonstrate the establishment of the administrative functions. These demonstrate the establishment of courts, legal framework and maintaining law and order.

A legal framework was established that included a process for settling disputes between a petitioner and a defendant. The judgment was then sent to the press for publication.[8] A letter reports the successful prosecution of a hawaldar who was extorting the civilians and involved in looting, who returned the property to the rightful owners.[9] Another refers to a soldier named Mardan Singh, in the second company of an unnamed regiment, responsible for guarding the treasury was found guilty by the court of stealing, and was removed from the army.[10]

Times of war can create chaotic situations, and maintaining law and order during such a period becomes an important function for any government. From soldiers involved in extortion, to local gangsters who were looting households had to be brought to justice. Jodha Singh was one such gangster, who is referred to as a criminal both by the English[11] as well as by the government of Nana Saheb.[12] The identification cards[13] of erring soldiers were confiscated and these soldiers were struck off from the rolls.

Financial Administration

Two areas of financial administration are visible in these letters: revenue collection and accounting and control.

Analysis of the letters that addressed tax collection reveals the existence of an established system, with an established hierarchy and responsibilities. At the local level, there was a civil representative, a military representative and one person who represented Nana Saheb's authority. These personnel in turn reported all matters to Syyed Mohammed Isaakh and Tatya Tope.

Lalpuri Risaldar, who was the head of a cavalry unit, appears in a few letters. The following letter reveals some interesting facets of Tatya's administration:

After our proclamation from last month, we have been successful in encouraging thakurs and other landlords to join our effort. They have assisted us for a couple of jobs. Since they have volunteered to contribute, we should avoid keeping an unduly high tax burden. Pandit Lakshmi Rao, akhbarnawees, is keeping a record of who is participating in these meetings.

Biswas Rao Bhausaheb from Jalaun is demanding a significantly higher rate of taxation (16 annas) than what you are recommending (8 annas). It is important that we manage the relationship with these thakurs and landlords with care. This might encourage others to volunteer as well.

I am including a list of the attendees so that you can make an informed decision. Please advise Bhausaheb to use restraint while managing this delicate relationship. Please reply as soon as possible. If necessary, I can arrange a meeting with these thakurs and other landlords.[14]

This letter reflects the sensitive issue of taxation, hierarchy and the relationship of the people involved. The hierarchy of the people mentioned in the letter from low to high is, sender—Lal Puri (risaldar), local representative—Lakshmi Rao (akhbarnawees)—recorded meeting minutes, government representative Biswasrao Bhausaheb, receipients—Syyed Mohammed Isaakh and Tatya Topé.

Lal Puri is making an argument to lower the rate of taxation, despite the demands of his civilian superior and the representative of the government. This letter displays an organisation, which allowed views that challenged hierarchy when presented with evidence and logic. Lalpuri Risaldar is polite but direct in his communication. Additionally, this letter also displays that there were checks and counterchecks to prevent corruption.

Contrast this with another letter sent the same day, which reveals the English methods of collecting taxes.

Buddu Mahajan, a rich man from Jahanabad was asked for rupees 2 lakhs by the British when he declined he was arrested and hanged.[15]

Many Bundeli chiefs had risked their lives by breaking the Ikrarnamas with the English. As the Proclamation of Freedom indicates, Nana Saheb's government also promised fair taxation to the the people of Bundelkhand. Progressive (tiered) taxation is evident in one of the letters that was proposed by Lal Puri.

All the thakurs and landlords mentioned in the letter are here with me. They have requested clarification on land tax. The table that is considered is Rs 1, Rs 500, Rs 800, Rs 1000. Please advise if this structure is acceptable.

Mahants, chowkidars and others owe Rs 800, Rs 400 plus 8 anna. The rest will be written off. Rs 400 will be taken from the thakurs.

We will finalise the tax rates as per your order. Please reply with the tax rates in a tabular form.[16]

There is evidence of the existence of administrative offices that collected the taxes. Circulars were sent to these offices to enforce processes. In one letter, the tehsildar of Kalpi is apprising the local chief tax officer of new appointees and tax procedures.[17]

Not only were the revenue collection streamlined, the expenditures were also managed with checks and balances. Detailed accounting was required for all expenses. In one such letter, Inayat Ali, a harkara (spy or intelligence agent), sends an account statement that included the salary payments to harkaras and akhbarnaweezs for the period of one month.[18]

The existence of medical staff is also apparent in one letter. This is an example where a group of physicians were drawing more salary than what was authorised. After an inquiry they were forced to return the extra amount.[19] Corruption was managed by creating high incentives to report such acitivies.[20]

Human Resources Administration

A significant amount of personnel management issues were related to the military, but they provide an insight into the administrative policies for human resource management enforced by Tatya Tope. These include processes for recruitment, dismissal, recognition of contribution and payroll administration.

Recruitment

Tatya was enlisting soldiers from local militia groups, irregular armies or fresh recruits as part of his army. In addition some soldiers whose regiments had not participated in the war wanted to join Tatya's army. Processes were established to recruit both types of soldiers.

One letter is seeking Syyed Mohammed Isaakh's permission to enroll, '...soldiers currently with the English at Chilla Tara. They are eager, but are disarmed'.[21] Another letter seeks permission to recruit soldiers who were enrolled with the English but were taking time-off in their villages. Many soldiers stayed on with the English purely because of the paycheck.

> ...about enrolling soldiers who have guns. We will gather 16 soldiers in the next 2-3 days and then send you their details. After looking at the leave chart of the villages around here, it seems that soldiers in (4 + 2 + 10) houses are on leave. These soldiers have guns, cannons and swords. They do not want to go back to work with the English. These soldiers can be enrolled in our army, if you order. They are eager to fight. Once enrolled, we can attack and take the local Engligh treasury. Please advice.[22]

Dismissal

There are examples of dismissals with and without cause. In cases where the dismissal was without cause the salary was paid in full.

> As ordered, Ram Singh Jamadar has been struck-off the role on 22 Jumadassani 1274H. His salary has been paid.[23]

Soldier Mardan Singh, referred earlier; who was found guilty of extortion by the court was fired from the army in a separate letter with orders.[24]

Recognition

Recognition of valour is a significant element for the morale of troops. In one such letter, Subhedar Udhar Singh of Paltan 7, reports the valour of Deena Deen Shukla's to their superior.

> Deena Deen Shukla Nizamat (Brigadier) of the Government showed great courage in this battle. Many soldiers are talking about it here. Splendid.
> We need more like him to be successful. Our success is because of Deena Deen Shukla and his courage. He is worthy of praise and prize.[25]

Another letter recognises the achievements of an officer by his superior:

> To Rana Deen Bhanak Subhedar:
> Congratulations on your successful and timely offensive and victory against the English. I am very pleased by your actions.
> You did whatever a good and courageous soldier would have done…
> It was your planning and foresight that helped us succeed today. No one was disturbed and make sure no one does in the future.[26]

Payroll

Payroll was a significant part of human resources management. Considering that there were periods where the finances were running extremely low. In some cases, soldiers were given back pay for months of service, when finances became available. In some cases, the arrangement was for payment after three months or six months.

The following letters seek clarification for such payments:

> I need clarification about the salary papers that I have received. This is about 420[27] soldiers from Hamirpur, but now in Kalpi. Do they get three monthly or a six monthly salary?[28]

Another sought clarification on the salary structure and process for back pay.[29]

Although finances were running low, the payment of salary was considered a critical part of personnel management. Processes were established to make sure that the heirs of soldiers that had died in combat were paid the balance. The following letter attempts to amend the payment that was made in error:

> Ranjit Singh was a servant of the 8th company of the platoon and order was sent that his heirs will get his salary. The heirs will have to collect it from the office in Kalpi. The heirs however claim that the salary was incorrectly given to Jawahar Singh, soldier of 8th Kate's platoon. You are being ordered to resolve this issue.[30]

Military Administration

Several functions relative to military administration are visible in the letters. These include intelligence, procurement, provisions, troop movement and battle tactics.

The elaborate spy network provided the primary information for Tatya Tope that allowed the many successes in adverse conditions. The akhbarnaweeses and harkaras were the sources who gathered information and passed it on to army officials. A system of information gathering and using it to plan the battles is evident from many letters.[31]

There were established processes to hire harkaras and akhbarnaweeses as well. One letter is a report after the initial screening of the job applicant, including their references.[32]

The English recognising this strength, made attempts to bribe Tatya's spies.[33] The English would attempt to intercept these qasids or messengers as much as they could. This was countered by writing letters with cryptic and coded messages to prevent critical information from falling into enemy hands. These letters are hard to decipher since the context is unknown.[34]

A letter from a harkara reports of his escape from the English by paying a bribe of two rupees. Interestingly, the harkara is requesting reimbursement for that amount.[35]

Procurement

A significant cost of running a war is not only the payroll and provisions, but procurement of ammunition and artillery as well. While systems were not completely in place for the first phase of the war, by late 1857 during the second phase, Tatya had established a fully functioning army with all logistical elements that were required for its operations.

There are several references to letters that are a procurement list for ammunition and food.[36] After the supplies were requisitioned, the supplier would forward copies of the letter to both the person who made the request as well as the person who received the supplies.[37] When the ammunition was received, a receipt was sent to the sender.[38]

Troop Movement and Battle Tactics

The offensive was ordered only after all the relevant parties were present. During January through March, Tatya maintained a mobile central command, with Syyed Mohammed Isaakh as his aide-de-camp. In one such battle, an officer is regularly informed of Syyed Mohammed Isaakh's position.[39] Every movement of the troops was updated to the central command as well as other other troops to allow coordinated movements.[40]

The movements and counter-movement of the English troops were also reported regularly to central command. In one such battle, this allowed the Indian troops to intercept the English in a pass, prior to crossing the ghats.[41]

India's transitory freedom during the few months of 1857 was never recognised by Victorian historians. Later Indian historians, possibly compelled by their beliefs, marginalised India's fleeting freedom and the Indian leaders who fought for it.

Veer Savarkar, who was not privy to these letters, assigned the cause of India's defeat to the missing 'creative' part of the revolution. These letters, although only a small snapshot of the events that were happening, reveal something very important. From the creation of a civil administration that provided justice, maintain law and order to fair taxation, Tatya Tope had demonstrated the 'creative' side of the revolution as he attempted to 'destroy' the oppressive English authority.

If Savarkar was wrong in assessing the cause of India's defeat, why indeed, did India lose the war, if the planning of the war was so meticulous?

Why did India have to wait until 1946 to achieve political freedom?

The answer is in the bloody figure of eight...

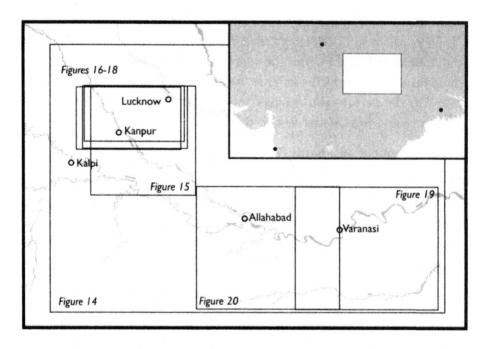

Figure 14a: Locator for Figures 14-20 in the following pages

Chapter 9

THE FIGURE OF EIGHT

Why did India's freedom come late?
The answer is in the ghastly figure of eight

Was it not weapons or perhaps fate?
All mattered little; it was grisly, that figure of eight

Was it not betrayal, or a failure innate?
Those are distractions, it was always the figure of eight

Every move and action he did anticipate
The one thing he didn't, was the bloody figure of eight

PARAMETERS FOR DEFEAT

Tatya Tope's Operation Red Lotus was a success with the liberation of Delhi, Gwalior, Kanpur, Lucknow, and hundreds of other surrounding villages. The advanced planning and the coordination had successfully created a strong position for the Indians.

Most of the regiments had successfully overcome their local English forces and marched to predefined locations. In quick succession, many towns and cities were liberated.

> ## Troop Strengths
>
> The section titled 'Troop Movement Table' in the appendix provides a breakdown of the regiments of the Bengal Army and their participation in the War. Of the 123 regiments of the troops that 'mutinied' at varying times, fifty-four were either destroyed or disbanded. Of the disbanded, a few companies from thirteen regiments were able to reach their destinations. Altogether, about seventy full regiments and thirteen half regiments were actively involved in liberating and defending a free India.
>
> Of these sixty-one were infantry regiments, twenty cavalry and two were artillery regiments. The maximum size of a native infantry regiment was about 1,000. Although, an average strength of an infantry regiment was about 850, a cavalry regiment averaged about 500. Using the information above, one arrives at a total strength of the Bengal army that fought the English at 58,000.
>
> Most narratives place this number at over 200,000, an obvious exaggeration.
>
> The English had 24,500 'European' troops stationed in India. Over a few months additional 75,000 troops were brought in from several locations, bringing the total strength to about 100,000.

If the situation favoured the Indians, the obvious question is why then did India lose this phase of the War?

When the English leadership became aware of the scale of the Indian operation, they had to have wondered about the logistical arrangements of the war. Amongst all the questions the English asked, one question had to be the most important. Who was indeed providing for the Indian troops?

Troop strength, although important, played a secondary role in the War of 1857. Although this chapter discusses the real reason why India lost this phase of the War, the inset provides an analysis of the actual number of troops that fought the English.

Of all the regiments of the Bengal Army, about 58,000 Indian troops were actually able to participate. The English had about 24,500 troops stationed in India.[1] Over the next months, the English brought in over 75,000 soldiers into India, increasing the total strength of 'European' troops to nearly 100,000.[2] In the earlier months, Indians did have a numerical superiority; however, it disappeared as thousands upon thousands of English troops arrived into India.

Much has been written about numerical strengths of the soldiers and the impact on the outcome of the war. Although these numerical advantages changed with time, the Anglo-Indian War of 1857 was less about the numbers of troops, than it was about provisions for the soldiers. It was about logistics and supply lines.

Once the English found the answer to the questions regarding the logistics of Operation Red Lotus, England's reaction was immediate, specific and chilling. The counter-offensive, if it can be called that, was clearly two-pronged. First, was the offensive response, directed towards Indian non-combatants *before* confrontation with Indian soldiers. Second, was a deliberate defensive response, which was perfectly demonstrated by the events at 'Cawnpore'. This chapter discusses the first, the offensive response, or as we call it the 'Figure of Eight' response.

Euphemism is a convenient tactic in narrating military operations for civilian consumption. It gives the narrators the proverbial fig leaf behind which to camouflage horrors, and earn wider social acceptance for their atrocities. English narratives of the period can then be described as displaying mastery in these euphemisms. Innocuous expressions such as the village was 'taken', 'settled', or 'cleared' was a more acceptable way of reporting that, the entire village with its population was burnt and cleared of any human traces.

This offensive policy, targeted hundreds of thousands of Indian civilians including women and children, who were systematically and ruthlessly massacred by the English. However, most historical accounts simply gloss over these dark facts of history or bury them under these euphemisms. Amongst the books that *do* openly acknowledge the killings, most repeat the standard explanation that the massacre of the Indian civilians was a 'deadly retribution' for what happened at 'Cawnpore'. The events at Kanpur, which represented England's deliberate defensive response and the background behind their near mythical regurgitation, are discussed in a separate chapter. However, what is clear is that the English offensive policy had started much *before* the 'Sati chaura' or the 'Bibighar' incident had taken place (both discussed later).

In *Spectre of Violence: The 1857 Kanpur Massacre*, Rudrangshu Mukherjee discusses the barbaric slaughter of Indian villagers. He accurately points out that the English did not only destroy objects that were impersonal but they destroyed homesteads, human shelter and set fire to barns and fields. However, he concludes that by targeting the village 'which is the locus of stories, myths and histories', the English were attempting to 'obliterate a culture'.[3] If the goal was to obliterate a culture why limit themselves to the Grand Trunk road and the Doab region and villages where Indian soldiers would be marching? Was there a method to the systematic slaughter of non-combatants?

The answer is in the travelling chapatis.

There is a direct, yet an invisible, link between these English policies and India's defeat in the War. This link is represented by another euphemism used in many accounts in describing certain villages as 'guilty', which were ordered to be 'cleared'. One of the key English counter measures was the campaign of Brigadier General Havelock and Lieutenant Colonel James Neill who were marching towards Kanpur from Calcutta. Before facing the armies of Nana Saheb and Tatya Tope near Aung, the English created a path of carnage and butchery along the Grand Trunk road. This created a 'zone' that allowed the English to freely send reinforcements as well as maintain a strong supply line for their troops. Havelock and Neill were part of a broader directive, which was part of the English offensive response to the War. This is evident not only in the bloody campaigns of Havelock and Neill, but also in the supporting 'laws' that were created by the English authorities to support these campaigns.

THE INDEFENSIBLE OFFENSIVE—DEATH BY NUMBERS

A possible difference between history's infamous barbaric massacres and those committed by the English in India, particularly in 1857, was that it was executed using numbers: Roman and Indian numerals. Numbers XI, XIV, XVI and '8' each have the blood of hundreds of thousands women, men and children smeared on them. The first three were the numeric identification of the 'laws' that were enacted, which legalised the wholesale yet systematic slaughter of Indians. These 'laws' called for 'the indiscriminate hanging not only of persons of all shades of guilt but also those whose guilt was at the least very doubtful'. 'The perpetrators of the crime showed no regard to who they were slaughtering'. 'The innocent as well as the guilty, *without regard to age or sex*', were 'indiscriminately punished and in some instance sacrificed'.[4]

Act No. XI of 1857 was brought into action on 30 May 1857, when the English recognised that the Indian soldiers had widespread support of the local population. This act applied to anyone accused of 'rebellion or of waging war against the Queen or the Government, or of aiding or abetting therein'.[5] This included soldiers, the private militia who joined hands with the soldiers as well any civilians supporting the soldiers. In a wider sense, it could include the villagers transporting the soldiers on their carts or even the women providing food to soldiers. The punishments included death and forfeiture of all property. If this was not arbitrary enough, the local commissioners were empowered to act alone and were vested with absolute final powers of judgment.

In about a week, on 6 June 1857 another Act was passed. This was Act number XIV of 1857 to make provisions for 'trial and punishment' of people who were 'exciting mutiny or sedition in the Army'. The punishments were the same as Act XI. This act enlarged the power given to the military courts to try *all* persons whether amenable to the articles of war or not, charged with any offence mentioned in the previous Act.[6]

In a commentary on the English rule in India, the *New York Times* wrote: 'Each revolving day echoes the execrations of thousands, aye millions on the authors of those laws, for the misery which they have inflicted on misgoverned and plundered India'.[7]

By late June, the theatre of war had enlarged and many cities were now liberated. England was losing its grip in northern India. Although the English armies (and their Scottish mercenaries) were on a large-scale spree of massacres, the fervour for freedom of the Indian population had not yet diminished. The sham commissions and courts that Acts XI and XIV spawned, were not able to massacre people in large enough numbers to put down the spirit of the civilians. England needed another law to widen the scope and number of executioners, and Act XVI did precisely that.

This enormous power to put people to death and forfeit property was now extended not only to military officers but also to civilian officers and 'trustworthy persons not connected with the Government'. Never had the world ever heard of such arbitrary and convoluted a *law* for such indiscriminate abuse of power. It is uncertain as to what monetary incentives these 'trustworthy persons not connected with the Government' were provided. Were they paid per hanging, or did they have 'quotas' for massacre? Many villages were targeted by these 'trustworthy' persons who perversely called themselves 'volunteers'. Kaye observed, '...volunteer hanging parties went out into the districts and amateur executioners were not wanting to the occasion'.[8]

These new 'laws' gave these cruel and inhuman acts a fig leaf of legitimacy. 'A list of persons tried by the Commissioner appointed at Allahabad under Acts XI and XVI of 1857 showed that anything from rebellion, to stealing, to desertion, to possessing money for which the accused could provide no explanation, was punished by death'.

The question here is: what were the compelling circumstances that, necessitated the mega mass killings that could not be inflicted by the army alone? The two incidents of 'Cawnpore' had not even occurred yet, which could offer them even an excuse of justification. The answer lies in the method. Execution parties were sent out all along the villages where the Indian troops had marched or were possibly planning to arrive to engage the English troops. Neill had marked out specific villages, which had helped the Indian soldiers and could help further reinforcements. As Neill marched toward Kanpur in June, his orders were that 'all the men inhabiting them (the villages marked out) were to be slaughtered'.

A CAMPAIGN OF 'ACORNS' AND NUMERICAL FORMS

This is in reference to two villages on the Grand Trunk road ('guilty' of protecting the grain).

I proceeded with a party of the Fusiliers to the said villages and called upon the principals to appear but they had made their escape and I ordered their houses to be burnt... On arriving at the village named Dobaur I found it deserted and everything carried off with the exception of some grain and small quantity of gun powder and ordered Babur Singh's house and village to be burnt...

Consider some references relative to Havelock and Neill's campaign from Varanasi to Kanpur.

A party of Fusiliers proceeded to another village belonging to the same people [who had plundered a Dak Bungalow] but it was found deserted and I ordered it to be burnt.[9]

An officer in a column moving to Kanpur related to Russell that *'All the villages in his front were burnt* [Emphasis Added]'.[10]

On the morning after the disarmament parade, the first thing he saw from the Mint was a 'row of gallowses [sic].[11]

These executions have been described as 'Colonel Neill's hangings'.[12]

On one occasion, some young boys, who, perhaps, in mere sport had flaunted rebel colours and gone about beating tom-toms, were tried and sentenced to death.[13]

An English officer C.W. Moore writes, that they 'destroyed the village of Goura', upon reaching it.[14]

Witnessing Havelock and Neill's campaign, Bholanath Chandra, an Indian traveller writes: 'Neill loosed his men in the city of Allahabad. Their cannon, torches and cross firing killed hundreds of natives, including old men, women, and children. They caught all men they could lay their hands, porter or pedlar-shopkeeper or artisan, hurrying them through a mock trial and dangle them on the nearest tree'. Nearly six thousand were killed. Neill's execution parties burned all the crops; hanged every man and boy, they could catch; carelessly; purposely killed women and children in their crossfire. Babies were bayonetted and women raped and tortured.[15]

'Rebel corpses,' said Chandra, 'were hanging by twos and threes from branch and sign post all over the town.' Neill did this for three weeks in Allahabad—burning villages and hanging natives, when Havelock finally caught up almost three weeks later.[16] Three weeks of burning houses and hanging natives emptied the pool of Indian labourers Neill would need for his march to Kanpur. Back in Varanasi, the hanging parties continued to make their rounds.

In Varanasi Lieutenant Colonel James Neill hanged hundreds of suspected 'rebels, including a number of boys accused of romping around the city beating drums and flourishing rebel flags'.[17] Over the whole of Sepoy War—there is no darker cloud than that which gathered over Allahabad in this terrible summer. It is on the records of our British Parliament, in papers sent home by the governor-general of India in Council, that 'the aged, women and children are sacrificed, as well as those guilty of rebellion'.[18]

Brigadier General Havelock and Lieutenant Colonel Neill and his 'brave men' took the battle to the Indian civilians. Neill's instructions to Major Sydenham Renaud, his advance guard commander, were specific. All the villages alongside the Grand Trunk road were to be entirely destroyed. 'Certain *guilty* villages were marked out for destruction, and all the men inhabiting them were to be slaughtered. All Sepoys of mutinous regiments not giving a good account of themselves were to be hanged'.[19] On one such occasion on 9 June, weeks before the events in 'Cawnpore':

> One gentleman boasted of the numbers he had finished off quite *'in an artistic manner'*, with mango-trees for gibbets and elephants for drops, the victims of this wild justice being strung up, as though for pastime, *'in the form of a figure of eight'*. [Emphasis added][20]

Major Renaud's advance guard had over seven hundred men.[21] All of Renaud's 'efforts were being exerted to *settle* the country'. The scene of Indian villages as described by Malleson in his *Red Pamphlet* was of 'blackened homesteads, and the bodies hanging by half dozen from trees on the roadside, and nick-named by our soldiers "acorns", afforded ample evidence that Renaud had not been slack in his work'.[22]

One official in a letter to the *Daily News* provided a graphic description of Neill's operations:

> Every native that appeared in sight was shot down without question, and in the morning, Colonel Neill sent out parties of his regiment... and burned all the villages near where the ruins of our bungalows stood, and hung every native they could catch, on the trees that lined the road. Another party of soldiers penetrated into the native city and set fire to it, whilst volley after volley of grape and canister was poured into the fugitives as they fled from their burning houses... and natives we employ are provided with a pass. Any man found without one, is strung up by the neck to the nearest tree.[23]

Neill sent his regiment out into Indian settlements that bordered British cantonments, where they 'burned all the villages' and 'hung every native they could catch'. Another detachment burned down the native quarter 'whilst volley after volley of grape and cannister was poured into the fugitives as they fled from their burning houses'.[24]

Patrick Grant congratulated Neill for providing for 'every possible present circumstances as well as eventualities', and hoped that Renaud would be guided by these same 'admirable instructions, and by them and them only'.[25] 'Our first spring was terrible', William Howard Russel would write of Renaud's advance, 'our claws were indiscriminating'. According to an officer, 'Renauld's executions of Natives were indiscriminate to the last degree'.

Every possible excuse was used to attack villages. 'Men were executed because their faces were turned the wrong way'.[26] All the villages in front of them were burnt when he halted. The idea was to avoid a direct confrontation with the Indian soldiers. The orders to burn down villages also helped keep their men 'exposed as little as possible'. Allahabad was being plundered by 'lawless and reckless' British.[27]

The propaganda associated with the systematic killings was so great that newspapers had become cheerleaders for these murders. *Friend of India*—an English newspaper—had the following to say about the indiscriminate killings on 12 July 1857. Again, we note that this was published before the events at Bibighar. 'We shall drive the rebels before us and leave nothing in our rear, but lines of burning villages and hanging bodies...' A *friend* indeed.

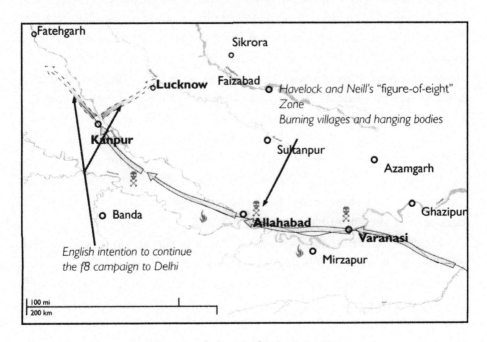

Figure 14: The Figure-of-Eight Campaign

It is preposterous to distance the English from the Scottish murderers, or to present this genocide to be perpetuated by the British. Neither Neill nor Havelock and their men were trigger-happy. They were following directives and laws that were specifically created to facilitate this holocaust unleashed on the Indian civilian population. While the executioners might be Scotsmen or Irishmen, the orders came from their English bosses in Calcutta and London.

The direct but invisible link between these gruesome policies and why the Indians lost these battles is symbolised by the chapatis in Operation Red Lotus. In what was plausibly the biggest strength for the Indians in this War revealed the primary weakness.

Havelock and Neill's campaign achieved some important landmarks for England. They created a 'dead zone', a corridor, between Kanpur all the way to Calcutta on either side of the Grand Trunk alongside the Ganga. This extended into the Doab region between the Ganga and the Yamuna. In military terms, the objective was to create pockets around main towns and cities that the English could use. These 'pockets' were the destroyed villages, possibly in a radius of twenty-thirty miles or more.

We describe this dead zone as the 'figure of eight' or the F8 zone (see Figure 14) in the future. Therefore, if any large body of Indian troops would attempt to arrive at these locations they would need to have well-planned supply columns to march two or three days with food. This would restrict Indian troop movement. The English were able to use this zone to continue bringing in reinforcement and effectively dominate the entire belt between the Ganga and Yamuna. Havelock and Neill were successful breaking the back of the Indian Army by butchering civilian men, women and children in well-defined and selected pockets. Their glorification in English narratives and the strangely quiet response from most Indian historians exposes the dark side of the entire narrative of 1857.

Shockingly, even today, two Indian islands in the Andaman and Nicobar continue to be named after these wanton murderers, Havelock and Neill. A free India should consider reviewing its policy of this implicit glorification of English profligacy during 1857.

BURNT VILLAGES AND STARVING SOLDIERS

One cannot over-emphasise the importance of supply lines while fighting a war. Keeping an army fed is critical for any success. Troop movement in the nineteenth century needed three, or sometimes more, camp followers for every soldier and bullock carts for transportation. In addition, there were elephants that pulled the guns and horses for the cavalry. These animals needed to be fed as well. The feed for the animals was carried by camels.

Operation Red Lotus was designed to use the Indians employed by the English to wage a war against the English. A planned war with an embedded mutiny, per se. Any planning that would include elaborate logistical operations and massive supply lines risked being exposed. The key was the support of the villages for food and transportation. These villages had provided for many regiments of marching soldiers as they passed by their villages. These villages along the Grand Trunk road were 'guilty' of supporting their troops as they waged a war to set their nation free. However, by burning and massacring these 'guilty' villagers, the English were dismantling the implicit supply lines that the Indian army depended upon.

As Havelock marched towards Kanpur, the news of the massacres in Varanasi and Allahabad and all the villages along the Grand Trunk road travelled quickly. By displaying the bodies of the hanged civilians along the trees by the roadside, they wanted to send a message to the civilian population that all the villages along the Grand Trunk road were going to be destroyed. The situation was tense.

On one hand, there was Kanpur that was under Indian control; and a hundred miles away was an army marching towards Kanpur destroying villages and butchering men, women and children along the way.

Shortly after Wheeler's surrender in Kanpur, Nana Saheb had to send some troops to check the advances of Havelock. Havelock was marching at roughly ten miles per day with Major Renaud taking his time in 'clearing' the villages of both people and rations. As news of the impending massacre spread, the population in the villages ahead abandoned their homes and started arriving in Kanpur. The Indian Army depended on these very villagers to provide rations. With abandoned villages, the reach of the Indian soldiers was limited to a day's march form the last few villages around Kanpur that were not abandoned.

'Few Hundred' or a 'Few Thousand?'

Edited Content

Unedited Content

Records of the Intelligence Department of the Government of the North-west Provinces of India During the Mutiny of 1857, Sir Willian Muir, vol. 1. T & T Clark, Edinburgh, p. 463-464.

English reports on their own troop strength shows that the English were either numerically challenged or obfuscating the truth. Records of intelligence departments for example, were clearly 'edited' for content before being released or published. For example, the above record from 12 August 1857, was edited later before it was published.

However, in a rare error, a communication revealing the actual troop strength was published. This shows that what was supposed to be a force of a 'few hundred men' with Neill at Kanpur was in reality 4,000 men. In addition, the troops at Fatehgarh were 8,000. Similarly, Fatehpur was also a stronghold, had a large force. Therefore, the number of troops marching from Allahabad towards Fatehpur, probably exceeded 8,000, not the 1,200 that the English report. This pattern is consistent across many records.

Havelock had succeeded in probably creating a three to four day radius where all the villages were abandoned in fear. This would translate into about a thirty-forty mile 'zone'. In fact, this deadly policy to destroy villages put some pressure on his own army's supply lines. One English officer 'remonstrated with Renauld, on grounds that, if he persisted in his course, he would empty the villages and render it impossible to supply the army with provisions'.[28] In another case, a soldier observed that, 'none of the villages along route were inhabited, the only visible signs of life about them being a few mangy pariah dogs'.[29]

By creating this 'zone', Havelock created an implicit shield for his army. If the Indian infantry did march toward him, they would have needed to travel at least two days without food.

To induce the population of an even larger town, like Fatehpur to leave, Neill gave orders that the entire town 'was to be attacked, and the Pathan quarters destroyed, with all their inhabitants'. In addition, 'all the heads of insurgents, particularly at Futtehpore, (were) to be hanged'.[30]

In early July 1857, Nana Saheb sent an army along the Grand Trunk road from Kanpur to check the advances of Havelock. There are three important considerations about this campaign that have never been discussed in any account, or any narratives presenting the Indian side. First, how far was this column able to travel without any meaningful logistics supporting them, considering that all the villages along the Grand Trunk road were abandoned? The second consideration is, what was the total strength of the forces that Nana Saheb had under his command at Kanpur? The third is, how many troops did the English have in their march towards Kanpur?

The answer to the first question is that Havelock's 'figure of eight' campaign had severely limited the mobility of the Indian infantry. The bulk of the infantry was probably camped only a few miles from Kanpur, where provisions were accessible. However, the provisions were under pressure with the arrival of hundreds of thousands of the 'figure of eight' survivors. It is possible that some elementary supply lines were set up that would have allowed a few platoons to engage the advancing columns of Havelock and Renaud. However, the cavalry was far less dependent on the supply lines, since they were able to travel much longer distances within a day.

WALL OF DEFENCE

In the middle of July, Nana Saheb and Tatya Tope's main priority was to stop the march of Havelock to either Delhi or Lucknow. In a message to his officers of the cavalry, infantry and artillery units Nana wrote:

...the enemy is coming up the river in steamers, and strong defences have consequently been constructed without the town of Cawnpore... you are, therefore, informed that the enemy is opposite the district of Baiswara on this bank of the river. It is very probable that they may attempt to cross the Ganges. You must, for this reason, send some troops into Baiswara country to shut them in on that side...

...should these people not be destroyed, there can be no doubt they will press in to Delhi. Between Cawnpore and Delhi there is no one that could stand against them.

It is also said that the British may cross the Ganges... send troops immediately across the river, at Sheorajpore, to surround and stop the enemy.[31]

The mission was clear; it was to create strong defence north of Kanpur and along the left bank of the Ganga. These were areas unaffected by the F8 campaign.

The situation on 12 July 1857 was as follows: Renaud and his seven hundred men were four miles east of Fatehpur.

Tatya Tope's goal was to create a wall of defence (see Figure 15) beyond Kanpur in the areas where the impact of the F8 campaign was limited, and to reinforce the Awadh side of the Ganga to stop Havelock from marching on to Lucknow.

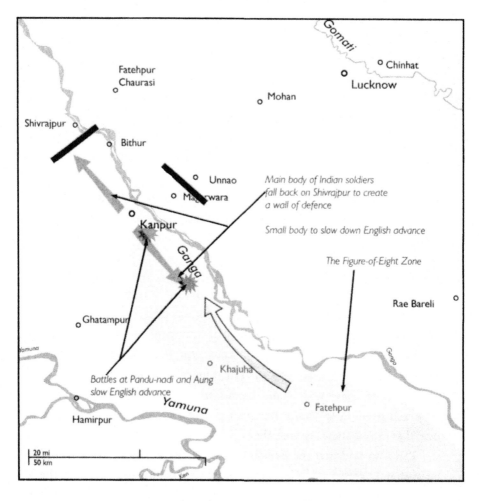

Figure 15: Tatya's Wall of Defence

Three battles were fought in the second week of July in F8 zones. The first was near Fatehpur, second at Pandu-nadi and the third at Aung. Knowing that they were fighting with limited resources, the primary goal was to slow the English advance as the troops strengthened the defences in the 'safe' zone.

Based on the description of the battle of Fatehpur, the Indian attack was primarily a cavalry charge with a possible support of some limited artillery. The cavalry regiment was about 500 men—with the intention of taking on the 700 men in Renaud's column—a task that was manageable. However, Havelock, who was a few miles behind, had managed to march through the night and catch up with Renaud.

Based on the above records, the combined English strength exceeded 6,000. Recognising the asymmetry of the numbers, the Indian cavalry retreated.

The deputy collector of Fatehpur, Hikmat Ulla, had also supported the Indian troops. After taking Fatehpur, Neill's orders were that, 'if the Deputy Collector is taken, hang him and have his head cut off and stuck up on one of the principal buildings of the town'.[32]

While Kanpur was lost on 16 July 1858, the areas north of Kanpur and on the left bank of the Ganga remained strongly under Tatya's control. The battles at Pandu-nadi and Aung, which were facing the brunt of the F8 campaign, were primarily to buy time for creating these defences. Fighting on an equal footing over the next month, many battles were fought across the Ganga and north of Kanpur. In each case, Tatya and his men forced Havelock to retreat.

THE METHOD IN THAT MADNESS—ENGLAND'S QUINTESSENTIAL SOUL

The systematic massacre of Indian civilians raises the question of whether this represented an English reversion to their bloody and violent roots. During the fifteenth and sixteenth centuries, England still carried over the mindset of their dark ages. England *then* was still a primitive society with neither a strong economic basis, nor many products to export, merely thriving on a *vrijbuiter mindset*. This was symbolised by the large-scale plunder, looting on the oceans, especially in the Indian Ocean, and reflected an intrinsic 'buccaneer' mindset of a society that was also thriving on trading slaves across the Atlantic. The behaviour *then* could be explained, if not justified, on the grounds of a primitive society suffering from brutal sectarian violence.

However, by the eighteenth and nineteenth centuries, with the large-scale transfer of wealth from places such as India, Africa and the American subcontinent, England had seen tremendous improvement in their economic and social conditions. England had caught up and surpassed industrial nations such as India and China in manufacturing and had finally become an industrialised country themselves. England had become a country with actual products that they manufactured and traded; it finally considered itself 'enlightened and civilised'. The killings in 1857 do not reflect an English *retrograding,* but these systematic executions of women and children represent a well deliberated and a cold-blooded, 'civilised' policy of a modern and 'enlightened' England.

Many historians have attempted to distance the English from the massacres by suggesting that the killings were actually perpetrated by the 'naked demons' referring to the Scottish Highlanders wearing kilts. Can these systematic executions and display of savagery be simply blamed on the Scottish mercenaries? Certainly, the English historians of that period reflected the mindset of the nineteenth century English society. The English had scant respect for the Scottish or the Irish in general, and found it easier to blame the atrocities on the Highlanders. When it was convenient, the *English* became the *British*. However, when it was not, it was easier to blame the atrocities on these *lesser* Britons, viz., the Scottish soldiers. Nevertheless, were these 'naked demons' not simply following orders given by their English superiors including the likes of Canning?

As mentioned earlier, specific laws calling out for the execution of civilians were enacted in late May and early June of 1857. These laws institutionalised the execution of women and children. *Laws to execute thousands of men, women, and children?* That certainly was more than *just* a savage response. Was it a cynical juxtaposition of England's perceived sense of its civilisation and its barbaric roots? The *New York Times* had an answer. Commenting on the events of 1857, the *New York Times* described the English rule of India as a 'disciplined tyranny'.[33]

The War with India in 1857 demonstrated this paradox and exposed England's quintessential soul.

WITHERED LOTUSES AND BURNT CHAPATIS

Operation Red Lotus from its conception to its deployment was nearly perfect. Most of the regiments in the Bengal Army had been recruited. Their troop movements were systematically planned and their dates for their marches were set with considerations of logistics. The village chiefs were aware of the period they would be expecting these regiments and the women were stocking up with provisions and ready to play host to these travelling guests who were going to set the nation free.

The initial phase of the War was tremendously successful. All the cities targeted by the leaderships were set free. The soldiers were well supplied and most reached their destinations on time. The design was incredibly simple with the villagers providing key logistics. The soldiers were transported by the village men in the bullock carts and the women were the embedded supply lines. There was no need to carry thousands of pounds of grains or need for too many camp followers. The soldiers were agile and could travel much longer distances than the English—who could barely march ten to fifteen miles per day with their elaborate supply lines.

Neither Nana Saheb nor Tatya Tope anticipated that the English would actually directly and specifically target women and civilians and punish them for providing food and transportation for the soldiers. They did not expect young boys celebrating Indian victories to be hanged. No one ever imagined that old men would face the same fate as these young boys. No one expected that villages would be burnt to the ground and the villagers would be shot at as they ran from their homes. India had seen the savagery of the English in the past, where they had targeted merchants, tortured weavers, or brutally punished prisoners. In the many mutinies that had taken place earlier, the death that many soldiers faced was also well known. Indirect civilian casualties during times of war possibly factored in, however, Indian leaders simply did not anticipate the systematic killing and raping women, as a *policy* from the English.

If the Indian leadership was to be blamed for a blunder, it would be in their expectancy of a 'courageous' fight from the English. The English did what they did best. In the two hundred year interaction, the English had raised the level of violence in India up several notches. The Nadir Shahs and the Taimur Lungs were aberrations who appeared, plundered, and then went away. Civilisation had eventually tamed the West and central Asians. The Mughals rulers had become largely Indianised in their views and attempted to rule the land like Indian kings.

However, the introduction of institutionalised, systematic, and sustained looting and plundering accompanied by brutality was new to India. While the Marathas and the Mughals, both had adapted to the higher levels of brutality that was introduced into the methods of control by the English, however, nothing had prepared them for the possibility of the English taking this war to the civilians as a *policy*.

The link between the villages and the soldiers was so strong that when people were massacred and the villages were burned down, the impact was directly on the soldiers. The basis of fighting the war in the first phase was the tight link between the villages and the soldiers. As villages all along the Grand Trunk road were burned down, the soldiers who were depending on these villages starved. An army travels on its stomachs, and these stomachs were empty. The English in their quintessential glory subdued the only people they *could* subdue, and they were the unarmed civilian men, women, and children.

The first phase of the War ended with the defeat of the civilians. The Indian soldiers would eventually regroup and put up a valiant fight for another eighteen months in two additional phases. The civilians were broken, so were the logistics. Although the economic support for the War was diminishing, it was still not over. Tatya Tope, redesigned his campaigns, and led the second and the third phases of this War against these enemies of civilisation.

Chapter 10

DECONSTRUCTING *'CAWNPORE'*

There is 'Kanpur', and then there is 'Cawnpore'. There is more to these variant spellings than the semantics. It is not just the obvious variance created by the phonetic limitations of the Roman script. For the Indians in 1857, it was simply 'Kanpur', a strategic centre liberated by India, twice, during the War. For English historians, however, 'Cawnpore' represents an obsession. To them, the story of Cawnpore plays a dominant part in any narrative. Fictional or not, hundreds of books on the subject dedicate pages upon pages to 'Cawnpore'. Sometimes it is hard to distinguish between what are 'fictional' stories about the 'mutiny' or what are considered 'historical' accounts. What is common to all these narratives is the regurgitation of the mythical interpretations of the events that took place in Kanpur starting in late June and July 1857.

Understanding 'Cawnpore', is important because historians in most accounts have 'explained', and in some cases even 'justified', the large-scale massacre of Indians on the basis of this story of Cawnpore.

Deconstructing 'Cawnpore', has significance *not* for what *has* been written, but for what has *not* been written. Exposing 'Cawnpore' is critical because, hidden behind the plethora of fallacious arguments, is an important truth, which exposes England's perverse tactical response to the War.

SKIRTING VALOUR

The waters of the Ganga shone majestically as they caught the morning sun. Little eddies whipped around the spots where the waters curled around the numerous sandbars that were common in summer. Women rested in the shade of the neem and banyan trees that dotted the shore, as their herd of buffaloes clambered down the slope. The impatient calves raced joyously towards the waters some hundred metres away, while the rest of the herd ambled unhurriedly. In June, the Ganga receded well beyond the steps, where devotees usually washed their feet before entering the Hardeo Temple at its shores. It was one of the loveliest spot on the outskirts of Kanpur, which many an English lady often frequented.

It would have been the picture on any other day...

This timeless tranquility, however, was shattered on that fateful morning of 27 June 1857. Forty requisitioned country boats now dotted the waterfront. The birds were conspicuously restrained, and the bustle of human activity drowned all other familiar sounds. An army of 400 labourers, supervised by a visibly agitated boat contractor, were busy victualling the boats.[1] The morning sun began to unleash its heat. Dust kicked up by footfalls of the crowd that had gathered before daybreak, choked the narrow lanes of the *mohallas*. Crowds swarmed towards the riverfront. All prime spots of shade were the first to go. Much pushing and jostling followed as the edgy crowd got increasingly impatient. Charged moments ticked by.

Meanwhile, in the city, General Wheeler led the evacuees out of their entrenchment in a mixed convoy of elephants, *palkhis* and bullock carts. The motley caravan that stretched for more than half a mile lumbered its way to the banks of the Ganga. Relentless glares, muttered expletives, and even derisive jeers greeted the convoy from the multitudes gathered to watch the spectacle. *Palkhi*-bearers shifted their burden from shoulder to shoulder as the sun beat down on their bare bodies. Inside the palanquin, lay the sick and wounded in their soiled bandages, while others had English women fanning their restless children. Women, who 'in another time would have been returning from their morning rides to breakfast on their verandahs or bathe in their cool and shuttered rooms'.[2]

It was a bizarre sight. English women and children marching alongside deflated soldiers in the middle of a bitter war.

What were women and children doing in the midst of Her Majesty's troops in the first place?

One of the English officers, Mowbray Thomson, who was a witness to these events, later wrote that 'never surely was there such an emaciated, ghostly party of human beings'.[3] Why were women and even children compelled to go through twenty-one torturous nights of bombarding at the entrenchment? Was it for their safety? Would they have been safer at another place? The answers to these questions, which the inmates often asked themselves, lay elsewhere.

FOR WANT OF COURAGE—WHEELER'S SHIELD

The War had started a few weeks before these events. Delhi was liberated on 11 May. English garrisons in different parts of the country were overpowered in quick succession. The victorious Indian soldiers then marched to take up positions in previously identified villages to safeguard important logistic routes in preparation to liberate other key cities.

The English garrison at Kanpur woke up to the news of the liberation only on 14 May 1857, since the telegraph lines were severed by Indians in preparation of the war. Instant panic gripped the cantonment. Mrs Freeman of the American Mission drove to the cantonment to find 'all the ladies in tears and their husbands pale and trembling'.[4] The district collector, Charles Hillersdon, represented the civilian authority and the military authority was represented by the experienced Major General Wheeler.

Kanpur was strategically significant; the River Ganga was navigable downstream to Allahabad, Varanasi and right up to Calcutta. The great Grand Trunk road also ran through the city, serving as an important line of communication for troop movement. To add to its value as a military target, it boasted of a huge ammunition magazine and had a large treasury exceeding ten lakh (one million) rupees.[5]

It was, therefore, only a question of *when*, rather than *if*, Kanpur would face hostilities.

Kanpur's strategic importance could not have been lost on the English military authorities. There were many warning signs that the War was going to expand to Kanpur. On the night of 16 May there was a fire reported in one of the barracks of an infantry line, which was mistaken by the shaken English population, to be the signal for commencement of hostilities. The next morning, a great many English rushed to the ghats to send their families downriver to Calcutta. Amongst them, ironically, was Wheeler's own adjutant, Major Lindsay.[6] On 20 May, Mrs Fraser, who had escaped from Delhi, brought further despondency to the garrison with first-hand information, since all communication with Delhi was cut-off.[7] So widespread was the despondency amongst the English that, even the Queen's birthday on 24 May was not celebrated, fearing that the traditional artillery gun salute would be construed as hostile action. An agitated Lydia Hillersdon, the district collector's wife, commented 'what a humiliating state of things... Governors of the country obliged to shelter ourselves behind guns....'[8] Tension in the English quarters was high since each day brought news of more uprisings. There was news of soldiers from Etawah and Aligarh heading towards Kanpur. An Anglo-Indian wife of a soldier in the 53rd reported of being accosted in the Indian market and told: 'You will none of you come out here much oftener; you will not be alive another week.'[9] Though she reported the incident in Mowbray Thomson's words 'it was thought advisable to discredit the tale'.

The danger was clear, present, and understood that the theatre of war would soon expand to Kanpur. When hostilities are imminent, logic would have demanded that the English forces evacuate the non-combatant population of civilians, women, and children. In fact, Edward William, an English civilian, wanted to do exactly that. 'I made up my mind to send my family to Calcutta, and spoke regarding it to Mr Jacobi, the coach builder; he made mention of it to Major General Wheeler, and was told by him that there was no fear, and was advised not to move his family.'[10]

The moot point here is simple; what really prevented an experienced General Wheeler from following a routine military evacuation procedure?

There are two possible explanations. The first, which most historians suggest, points towards making Major General Wheeler a scapegoat for 'Cawnpore'. That he was blindsided by his 'faith' in his Indian troops who he considered would remain 'loyal'. In various writings, the guise of Wheeler is meticulously built up to fit the image of a 'weak' General with descriptions such as '....the little gray general showed himself everywhere, trotting cheerfully....'[11]

The second and more likely possibility was that General Wheeler was behaving consistently with orders originating out of an EEIC central initiative. In Gwalior, Mrs Coopland writes: *'Our last hope for escape was now cut off, as a telegram arrived from Mr Colvin, the Lieutenant Governor at Agra, to say that the ladies and children were not to be sent into Agra till the mutiny really broke out at Gwalior'*. This policy essentially trapped them. She also aptly analyses: *'When the mutinies first began, if all the ladies and children at the numerous small stations had been instantly sent away to Calcutta or some place of safety before the roads were obstructed, their husbands and fathers would probably have had a better chance to escape. Instead of which, the lives of men, women, and children were sacrificed'*.[12] This policy had its echo in faraway Bihar as well. In fact, the commissioner of Patna was *relieved* from his position for displaying so-called *weakness* for removing non-combatants from his provinces of Muzaffarnagar and Gaya, at the signs of the war spilling over into those territories.[13] These orders sent out to commissioners of different territories, specifically asked them to ensure that families of soldiers and other civilians were not to be relocated at this time. The rationale that was presented for this curious decision was 'to avoid arousing the suspicion of the troops'.

It requires no military genius to deduce that, not unlike Gwalior, Muzaffarnagar and Gaya, Wheeler's 'defensive' tactical response to the war was the use of non-combatants as human shields to protect Her Majesty's men in uniform.

Towards the end of May 1857, Wheeler had his orders from Calcutta that asked him to 'begin immediately to make all preparations for the accommodation of a European force and let it be known'.[14] Preparations that obviously included women and children.

While historians have debated the choice of the location of the entrenchment, the rationale of going into a defensive entrenchment has not been addressed. Wheeler has been criticised by many English officers of making some grave 'errors' and blamed these decisions on Wheeler's supposedly naïve belief in the loyalty of his native soldiers.[15] Clearly, Wheeler's hands were tied, as directives came from elsewhere.

On 21 May, women and children were moved into these barracks and the men stayed in their regimental lines at first, and joined them later. Mowbray Thomson quotes some letters sent out at this time which indicate the hopelessness the entrenched English felt about surviving. It has been indicated that from the time Meerut fell, Wheeler and Lawrence did not share the confidence displayed by government in Calcutta. By late May, Wheeler and his English troops were entrenched, seemingly protected by a decision to use a human shield. A decision that in the words of Mowbray Thomson was in 'want of courage'. A decision that would soon lead to disastrous consequences.

THE MYTHICAL MELODRAMA

By the middle of June, tempers had begun to fray as conditions in the entrenchment deteriorated due to the ravages of war. By this time, Neil and Havelock were well honed in the macabre massacre of the innocent of the F8 campaigan. The population of Kanpur swelled as 'villagers from every direction' poured-in, bringing with them their grief and rage and hope of a safe haven.[16] Besides news of Havelock and Neill's march towards Kanpur there were reports of English sending steamers up the Ganga with troops. On 16 June, there were reports of boats carrying English troops sailing up from Allahabad. True to word, twelve boats loaded with ammunition and commanded by English officers, were seized by Teeka Singh, who was now commanding key Indian operations in Kanpur.[17] Protecting the waterways was as important as guarding the key access roads. Guns were moved into position to secure the waterway at the ghats.

The English defensive tactics to mix the combatants with the women and children had already limited Nana Saheb's options. On 24 June, Nana Saheb threw a lifeline to the inmates enduring their eighteenth day of the siege. Recognising the gravity of the situation, an offer was made to offer safe passage to Allahabad for all the inmates as terms for surrender. A few proud English soldiers, obviously upset at the directive to be shielded amongst non-combatants, complained that 'had there been only men there, I am sure the men would have made a dash for Allahabad, than have thought of surrender'.[18] The mood at the entrenchment turned to that of subdued relief. The women, wondering what they were doing there in the first place, were glad that better sense had prevailed, while the men celebrated their imminent freedom with liberal rations of rum.

On 26 June, the tranquility of nesting birds at Sati Chaura Ghat was somewhat disturbed by the presence of a few gentlemen perched anxiously atop elephants. Nana Saheb had permitted inspection of the getaway boats, and had even sent two elephants and escort sowars. The men were Lieutenants Delafosse and Goad with Captain Turner, deputed by Wheeler.[19] The officers saw forty moored country boats, which would cart them and their tattered ilk away to safety at Allahabad.

Nana Saheb had read the pulse of the people and sensed the tension around his soldiers and the town, and urged the English to make their getaway under the cover of darkness on the night of the 26th. However, for some inexplicable reason, the evacuation had to be postponed till the next morning. So brittle was the psyche at the entrenchment that Nana Saheb deputed three trusted lieutenants, including Brigadier Jwala Prasad, to camp the night with them.[20]

On 27 June 1857, the morning finally arrived as Wheeler's beleaguered troops prepared to trudge the mile to Sati Chaura Ghat. In a gesture that few captors extend, Nana Saheb had permitted each soldier to carry his personal arms and sixty rounds of ammunition. In deference to these conditions, 'the able bodied men packed themselves with all the ammunition that they could carry, till they were walking magazines'.[21] The column of seventeen elephants, seventy to eighty palanquins and about sixteen escort horsemen, made its way through the throngs gathered to see the spectacle.

Grief coupled with rage makes for a potent combination. The combination gets heady when the grief shared is common. In the milling crowds that lined the mile to the ghats were innocent people who had witnessed sights of Havelock's macabre massacres that would wake them, screaming. The Indian soldiers had members of their family slaughtered savagely in their villages just days ago and people had their homes torched. People who had seen blood spill on the streets, where they once played. People who had fled, leaving their dead unattended. These stories were dominating the emotions of the Indian soldiers as they watched the English soldiers marching amongst their women.

At the Hardeo temple, on the steps to the ghat, were seated Nana Saheb's most trusted men—Tatya Tope, Azimullah, Bala Rao and Baba Bhat, overseeing this delicate phase of troop withdrawal. Hundreds of people witnessed Wheeler's elephant wade to the first boat, while his people scrambled into the others.[22] As soon as the last boat was filled, the relieved convoy tried to cast off. An anxious Tatya and others on the shore were probably equally relieved that so far the withdrawal had been uneventful. The evacuation from the entrenchment and embarkation had lasted several hours. With the embarkation completed, the boatmen were called ashore to collect their pay.[23]

'...the native boatmen... all jumped over and waded to the shore. We fired into them immediately, but the majority of them escaped...' wrote Mowbray Thomson, in his book, *The Story of Cawnpore*.[24]

Pandemonium broke over the placid waters at this display of audacity.

The escort horsemen at the water's edge retaliated with return fire and within minutes the situation spun out of control. The repository of patience that the soldiers so far were, overflowed in a torrent of rage, as bullets flew in every direction and the guns boomed. With amazing dexterity English officers jumped out of the burning boats and began to swim towards the boats that were already underway. One such officer was Delafosse, who *'may have been disappointed by the rapidity with which many of his comrades-including Thomson – abandoned the women and children in other boats'.*[25] In the frenzy that ensued, these 'walking magazines', and the Indian soldiers began shooting at each other, as the crowds on the banks collectively gasped. In the smoke and the proverbial 'fog of war', however, innocent lives were also lost. At Nana's behest, the frenzy was brought under control by Tatya Tope.

The 120 women and children survivors were quickly led away, some in palanquins, from the ghats to safety under armed escorts. An aroused crowd followed the unlikely 'prisoners of war' as they were shifted on 3 July 1857, again under armed escorts, to Bibighar. The high compound walls shielded them from an increasingly unsympathetic population. The prisoners, however, were cared for, with only women assigned to enter the Bibighar to provide food and attention.

The reader might recall that, even before 'Cawnpore', village after village along the Grand Trunk road was being tyrannically 'settled' and 'executions of natives were indiscriminate to the last degree'.[26] The stench of putrefying bodies hung heavily in the now empty villages.

While Tatya Tope and Nana Saheb were engaging the advancing English troops, displaced villagers recounted their horrors to the locals at Kanpur. They watched with disbelief as 'every morning, the guards escorted the captive women and children down to the banks of the river while their place was being cleaned'.[27]

Trapped between advancing tyranny and increasing panic, the dark cloud of civilian incredulity was ready to burst. However, did it really burst? The events of 15 July 1857 that have filled thousands of pages remain controversial.

A likely scenario was that the civilian anger did burst on that day. With whatever weapons that they could lay their hands on, including some probably from the guarding sepoys who resisted[28] and with swords, the unidentifiable torrent of anger swept through Bibighar, 'reducing' everything in its path. Within a matter of a few minutes, 'they borrowed from the British and replicated the violence', they had witnessed to their own peoples.[29]

Amaresh Misra presents a controversial, but a very plausible, argument of the events at Bibighar.[30] The chapter titled 'The Great Game (How the British Killed *their* Women and Children)', Misra argues that the English themselves were responsible for the killings of the prisoners at Bibighar once they had captured Kanpur. Once the reader accepts the premise, that English were capable of falling very low, this argument is not as incredulous as it sounds.

Whether it was an Indian civilian retaliation or an act of cold blooded murder by the English, after Bibighar the English became 'British'. The divisions and rivalries between the various British ethnic groups were overridden by a common hatred for the Indians. The lack of motivation amongst the British soldiers to fight against an inspired Indian army was countered with a war cry—'Remember Cawnpore'.

The tragedy at Sati Chaura and later on at Bibighar, though pale in comparison to the barbaric slaughter of Indians preceding these events, has been at the centre of many a narrative about 1857. The melodramatic presentation of the events have been told and retold countless times with the fault laid squarely on the Indians. Some British authors go to the extent of making a grudging acceptance that Sati Chaura 'might have been a pure accident'.[31]

This cacophony of accusations and smokescreens of diversionary analysis cannot hide the truth that the English used their women and children as human shields and as Misra suggests, possibly even slaughtered them.

Although Mowbray Thomson writes that at Sati Chaura, the English shot first, the situation that was created was so fragile that it did not matter who actually did shoot first. The presence of women and children amongst the English soldiers was a situation entirely created by the English. Mowbray Thomson writes in the Preface of his book, *The Story of Cawnpore*, that direct imputation were made in some journals of the 'want of courage' on the parts of the English soldiers.[32] The tragedy cannot be blamed on the Mowbray Thomsons or General Wheelers, who displayed this 'want of courage', because they were simply following orders. It can be blamed only on their bosses in Calcutta who ordered them to do so.

OFFENSIVE DEFENSE

'Cawnpore' not only highlights the reprehensible use of human shields by the English to protect their combatants, it also represents a tool that the English have used to justify their grisly offensive policy. This characterisation, despite its obvious flaws, has been largely unchallenged and promoted by even recent authors.

In the Preface of *Our Bones are Scattered*, Andrew Ward writes about the 'cycle of massacre and retribution' being an imperial rite. He goes on to compare what happened in India in 1857 with Custer's last stand at Little Big Horn and the Zulus at Isandhlwana. At Little Big Horn and Isandhlwana, the 'cycle' started with the 'massacre' of the Europeans (in North America in the first case, and Africa in the second) people followed by their 'retribution'. He compares the killings at these two places with the killings of the English in Kanpur, first at Sati Chaura on 27 June 1857 and then later at Bibighar on 15 July 1857; and concludes that these events at 'Cawnpore led to a terrible vengeance'.

The logic of this argument fails on two simple accounts.

First, the English began their targeted violence against Indian civilians weeks before the events of 'Cawnpore'. In reality, the cycle started with the mass murder of Indian civilians by Havelock and Neill, *followed* by the incidents at 'Cawnpore'. The news of burning villages and slaughter by

Havelock and Neill had reached Kanpur by late June. The population in Kanpur was extremely tense and were looking for a form of a payback. The terrible retribution came in the form of Bibighar. For a well-researched book, Ward's metachronism, hopefully, is an outcome of a genuine error in understanding the sequence of events; else it would simply be another of many disingenuous attempts by historians to muddle the *real* story of 'Cawnpore'.

Second, England's defensive strategy was to use their women and children as human shields, causing unwarranted deaths of the innocent. The events of Sati Chaura represent the manifestation of this deliberate English policy.

The English took the war to the Indian civilians as a means to an end. The hundreds of thousands of Indian non-combatants who paid the price in blood were being punished for enabling Indian soldiers secure freedom. English 'courage' was well displayed in their justifying these massacres, for regurgitating 'Cawnpore' and in hiding their combatants behind the human shields.

This English 'courage' is the *real* highlight of the story of 'Cawnpore'.

Chapter 11

THE UNWITHERED LOTUS

HAVELOCK'S 'RETROGRADE MOVEMENTS'

England's immediate and vicious response to the War in the end proved to be their metier. It was a decisive factor in India's eventual defeat in the War. The English were firmly entrenched in Varanasi, Allahabad, Fatehpur, and along the Grand Trunk road. A thick stench of half-burnt bodies hung heavily in the smoke rising from stretches of burnt villages. The remaining civilian population was deeply anguished at the sight of limp bodies hanging from branches of every tree that lined the Grand Trunk road. The Indian soldiers themselves were hamstrung in their movements without any logistical support. Havelock's 'figure of eight (F8)' campaign was more than simply 'scorched earth', because it targeted the villages and the *villagers*. Accounts of grisly English brutality were carried by surviving travellers in every direction.

Although the English 'successes' in their slaughter of civilian men, women and children and the implicit destruction of the Indian supply lines would eventually win them this War, Tatya Tope, Nana Saheb and their brave soldiers continued their quest to liberate India. Metaphorically, the chapatis had burnt but the red lotuses remained unwithered.

Strategically the bloody F8 campaign had achieved an important milestone for the English. From Calcutta to Varanasi the English had created a massive shield along the Grand Trunk road. This extended into the Doab region between the Ganga and Yamuna between Varanasi and Kanpur, and this effectively cut off Central India from Awadh and Rohailkhand. However, the Doab region north of Kanpur remained in Indian hands. Tatya leveraged this strength in his next manoeuvres.

After losing Kanpur to the English in July 1857, Tatya crossed the Ganga with Nana, Bala Rao, Rao Saheb and others and camped at Fatehpur Chaurasi, north-east of the Ganga, considering different options to prevent Havelock from taking Lucknow.

The reader would recall that Havelock had marched into Kanpur with his 'figure of eight' campaign in the middle of July. The carnage had cost the villagers along the Grand Trunk road their lives, homes and foodstock. However, the wide expanse of the Ganga shielded the population on the other side (the Awadh side) of the river, from this *purposeful* slaughter. Therefore, this relatively unscathed side of the Ganga was adequately prepared in logistics to engage the English. After taking over Kanpur, Havelock had orders to invade Lucknow and had to cross the Ganga in order to carry out the order.

Havelock hesitated.

In fact, he was shrewd enough to hesitate. In his earlier encounters, Havelock had not faced much resistance because of the macabre success the F8 campaign had brought him. The Indian infantry was unable to march for more than a day without provisions. Their only other option was to send the cavalry. The Awadh side of the Ganga was a different story.

The town of Unnao lay on the other side of the Ganga, relatively shielded from the F8 campaign (see Figure 16). Havelock balked at the idea of engaging Tatya Tope at Unnao, possibly because the villages on the Awadh side of the Ganga had not been 'cleared' earlier by Renaud, for Havelock's 'victorious' columns to march in. The next best possibility to absolve him of dithering was the Ganga itself. Havelock devoted innumerable pages in his reports, to the real and present perils of crossing the river during an Indian monsoon. Eventually, Havelock had to follow the orders and set out on this arduous 'passage'.[1] He claimed that the task was 'most difficult on account of the breadth and strength of the stream' and reported without being committal that he hoped to 'complete the passage in two days'.[2]

As we will see in the following pages, the same 'difficult passage' in reverse was overcome in six hours flat by Havelock's columns in their retreat frenzy a few days later!

In the end, the English did win the War. However, some of the English narrators get a little too zealous in their attempt to romanticise the English victory. Their assumption is that the readers are either blinded by their admiration for England, logically challenged, or consistently willing to suspend disbelief. Deconstructing English narratives of 1857 is equivalent to getting a degree in decrypting metaphorical misinterpretations, elaborate euphemisms and numerical exaggerations. For example, Havelock's defeats and the resultant retreats are varyingly described as 'victories' with 'retrograde movements',[3] 'relinquishment of enterprise',[4] 'abandonment of advantages',[5] or 'retracing of steps'.[6]

Numerical exaggerations are even harder to normalise, because of the inconsistency in exaggeration. Consider English estimates on the numerical strength of the Indian forces. Commanding officers like Havelock are cunningly conservative in their exaggeration, but lower ranked officers give the game away. For example, at one of the battles in Unnao, Havelock claims that the Indians 'had come down in force to Busherut-gunge; and that 4,000 infantry and 500 cavalry' were encamped.[7] However, an officer in Havelock's column described the strength as '10,000 strong, with lots of guns, and about 2,000 cavalry'.[8] Typical multiples used by the English to describe the Indian forces vary from two to ten, and their own forces about a half to a tenth, based on the seniority of the perpetrator.

Given that the authors question the objectivity of these narratives, consider some of Havelock's 'retrograde movements' and 'relinquishment of enterprise' from 28 July until 18 August 1857. The situation on 28 July 1857 was as follows: Nana Saheb and Tatya were at Fatehpur Chaurasi, having crossed over the Ganga near Bithur with a total force of about fifteen hundred, with the 1st and the 56th NI.[9] Havelock was in Kanpur and was ordered to invade Lucknow. Havelock was wary of crossing the Ganga 'with so weak a force, into a province filled with a hostile and armed population....'[10]

Despite Havelock's hesitation in crossing the Ganga, his orders were clear. Any further delay would have been disobeying orders. Evetually, when Havelock did cross the Ganga, Tatya, was still in the process of assembling his army in Fatehpur Chaurasi, about fifteen miles northwest of Unnao.

Tatya asked for a regiment of Oudh irregulars to be sent forward from Lucknow to stop Havelock's advance towards Lucknow.[11] There were two possible instructions from Tatya to the Oudh Irregulars; one was to obstruct Havelock's progress for Tatya's army to effect an engagement, and two to contain the damage Havelock could inflict on the surrounding villages and villagers.

There were two battles on 29 July, where the Oudh irregulars, despite being heavily outnumbered were able to force Havelock to retreat. Havelock had miscalculated the resistance the Oudh irregulars offered. In Havelock's words, 'a third of his gun ammunition had been expended in the attack on (Unnao) and (Bashiratganj), and the army had as yet advanced only one-third of its way to Lucknow'.[12]

Havelock simply did not want to go on to Lucknow. He fell back to Magarwara, and attempted to explain his retreat after claiming to be victorious in the battlefield, writing, '...under these circumstances, when asked my opinion as to the probability of at once relieving Lucknow, I decided against it....'[13] Despite his appeal, Havelock's orders remained unchanged. He had to continue his march toward Lucknow and was reinforced with ammunition on the 3 August.[14]

While English narratives suggest that the Indian forces were led by Nana Saheb, it is unlikely in the first week or two of August, since Nana

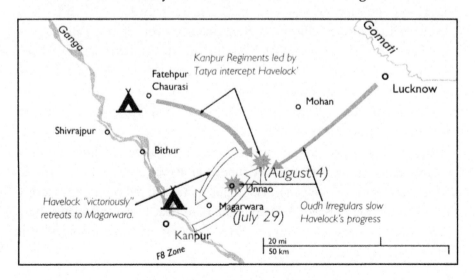

Figure 16: Havelock's 'Retrograde' Movements

Saheb had departed for Lucknow on 2 August, leaving Tatya Tope in charge. Nana Saheb took over command again after Tatya had left for Central India a few weeks later.

On 2 August, Tatya Tope was in charge of the Kanpur NI regiments who had crossed into Awadh, ready to take on Havelock if he attempted to make another advance towards Lucknow.

The objectivity of the events that took place on 4 August 1857, as presented by Marshman in his book on Havelock, as many narratives by the English, is in question. One can speculate what really happened on the battlefield, but at the end of the battle, Havelock made a decision to make a complete retreat and gave up on the idea of marching to Lucknow. If it was indeed a victory for Havelock as his spin doctors, John Marshman and others claim, then, the 'relinquishment of the enterprise for a time', certainly take up many pages of their narrative. Marshman dedicates pages 334-39 to justify the eventual retreat, even before getting to the part of winning this 'victorious battle'. The battle itself though is concisely described in two paragraphs. Marshman dedicates pages 341-44 to Havelock's 'increasing difficulties'.[15] After his 'exemplary victory', Havelock 'retreated' to Magarwara and started doing something very important—writing letters, explaining his 'abandonment, with great grief and reluctance'. He spent the next few days 'writing' more letters to the commander and others, 'explaining' his 'glorious victories' and 'retrograde movements'.

His fellow British officers at Kanpur also wrote letters, not exactly complementary or convinced of his self-claimed victories; General Neill's ADC wrote on 9 August: 'Havelock a second time fallen back on his original position, 3 miles on the other side (of the Ganga)... Reasons for Havelock's retrograde movement *unknown*... Alarm from Havelock's retrograde movement'.[16] [Emphasis added]

Based on information from earlier battles, Tatya Tope had limited battery and the ammunition was in short supply. However, unlike earlier battles, where Havelock's F8 campaign had crippled and starved the Indian troops, this time they were prepared. Despite the odds heavily stacked against him, Tatya Tope, we deduce contrary to English claims, had scored a significant victory over Havelock.

THE 'GREAT RECROSSING'

While this was an important victory for the Indians, Havelock remained camped at Magarwara, on the left bank (the Awadh side) of the Ganga. This was potentially dangerous because he could relaunch his F8 campaign into Awadh. He had already demonstrated English savagery against civilians while in Awadh, including the slaughter of zamindars, claiming that they were killed in battle.[17] The morale of the civilian population was already low. Tatya simply had to push Havelock beyond the Ganga back into Kanpur. He did that successfully in the next battle on 11 August 1857.

After Havelock's defeat (or 'victory' as claimed by Havelock) at the second battle near Unnao, he 'retired to position five miles from the river (at Magarwara) to prevent, (Unnao) and (Bashiratganj) being occupied in the rear'.[18]

It would be fair to assume that Havelock wanted to camp at Magarwara until he got reinforcements so he could make another push towards Lucknow. It would also be logical to assume that Tatya and his army wanted to push Havelock across the Ganga back into Kanpur to prevent them from destroying the civilian population in Awadh.

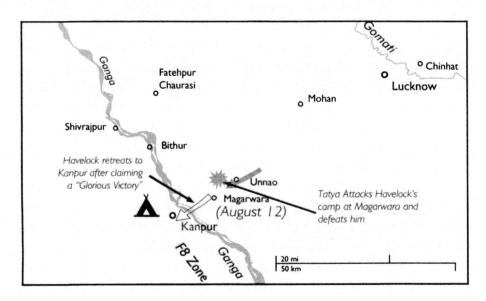

Figure 17: Havelock's Great 'Recrossing'

A battle was fought on 12 August, which, going by the English narratives, the English won 'brilliantly'. In the spirit of the logic of the English narrators, here is the paraphrased interpretation of the many long pages dedicated to this battle, and the English actions thereafter: 'The English troops, in their continued celebration of the victory over Tatya, hurriedly fell back across the Ganga and triumphantly marched backward in to Kanpur!'

The English retreat was so fast that they accomplished the entire task of this 'great' crossing of the Ganga in *less than six hours*.[19] It is worth repeating that three weeks prior, when Havelock had marched into Awadh, the same spin doctors describe that task of a mile-and-half-wide Ganga[20] as nearly insurmountable. However, with Tatya giving him a chase, Havelock's retreat to Kanpur was as fast as lightning! In a display of another euphemism for defeat, an English officer reported in a letter: 'General Havelock decided to *recross* the Ganges; reason not known [emphasis added]'.[21] General Neill himself wrote a letter, rather sarcastically about Havelock's achievements, and questioning why Havelock after all his victories wanted to retreat.[22]

Tatya had succeeded the third time in two weeks in defeating Havelock, and this time, Tatya pushed Havelock all the way back into Kanpur.

'ABANDONMENT OF ADVANTAGES'

On 15 August, Kanpur remained under Neill and Havelock's control. The British had 4,000 troops at Kanpur and 8,000 at Fatehgarh.[23] The English kept the Grand Trunk road towards Fatehpur and Allahabad 'clear' by continuing Havelock's approach towards the civilian population. All the towns in that area continued to be abandoned, the houses, the farms and the granaries burnt down. The English had created a 'dead zone' where only the English could access with their more stable supply lines.

This 'dead zone' for Indians was a safe zone for the English. This included the lower Doab region and the Grand Trunk road corridor until Calcutta, which Havelock had 'cleared'. Havelock's retreat into Kanpur was to continue to be the English strength in this corridor.

However, the northern part of the Grand Trunk road remained free of destruction from Havelock's F8 campaign. Tatya Tope remained camped at Fatehpur-Chaurasi, on the Awadh side of the Ganga, defending Awadh from any further attempts by the English. The 42 NI, stationed at Sagar, had marched into Kalpi on 22 July 1857.[24] After liberating Kalpi, they handed over the administration to Mohammed Isaakh, the local *thanedar*. Mohammed Isaakh would later play an important role as 'Mir Munshi' for the Nana Saheb government and assist Tatya Tope in coordinating his activities. The 42 NI continued their march towards Kanpur to enable Tatya Tope to attempt to maintain control over the districts north of Kanpur. They camped on the northern side of Kanpur along the Grand Trunk road in a town called Shivrajpur, about twenty miles from Kanpur and about ten miles from Bithur. English narratives place the number at 4,000. Therefore, we are uncertain if the multiple used by the English was two, four or ten.

Meanwhile, the Oudh irregulars had remained camped at Unnao, preventing any attempt by the English to march towards Lucknow. The only troops that were available to Tatya were possibly the 56 NI and the newly arrived 42 NI from Sagar via Kalpi. We estimate that the strength of Tatya's army at about 1,600 infantry and some cavalry, which gives us an estimate of the English multiple of two and three.

Havelock recognised that the Indian strength near Fatehpur-Chaurasi was complemented by the presence of Indian troops near Shivrajpur. Havelock decided to expand their position to the areas north of Kanpur.

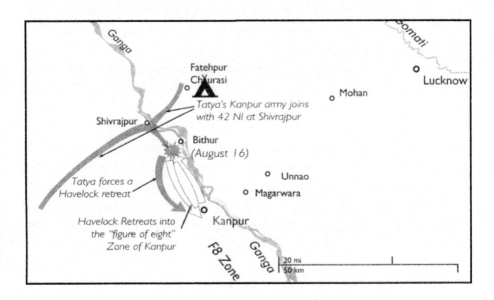

Figure 18: Havelock's 'Victorious' Retreat

152 \ *Tatya Tope's Operation Red Lotus*

The English forces at Kanpur had a full inventory of supplies, with their supply line connected to Fatehpur, Allahabad and all the way to Calcutta. However, the situation was not very favourable for the Indians. Although shielded to some extent, the food situation in the districts north of Kanpur was still tentative. On the news that Havelock had started his march towards Shivrajpur, despite limited supplies, Tatya moved forward towards Bithur to stop Havelock's advance on 16 August 1857. This battle was going to be different from the battles fought on the Awadh side of the Ganga. Despite Havelock's obvious advantages, in the impending battle, Havelock left Kanpur with heavy feet, taking over eight hours to cover the short distance.[25]

The description of the battle in English narratives follows the by now predictable routine of 'exemplary bravery and courage'. The effect of the disrupted supply lines was evident on Tatya's army, as some of his soldiers simply collapsed on the battlefield, exhausted, because they were fighting on empty stomachs.[26] Despite their obvious weakness, Tatya's army had fought bravely.

Who actually did win the battle? Again, all narratives take Havelock's word and hand the victory to the English. However, at the end of this 'courageous' battle that had given Havelock another 'victory', Havelock 'deemed it important to *retrace his steps* without delay'.[27] After this 'victory', Havelock's troops, 'slowly and sadly marched back'.[28] By 18 August 1857, after his so-called victory, Havelock and his men were now 'surrounded at Cawnpore' by the Indian forces.[29]

Technically, Havelock was not surrounded, because the part of the Grand Trunk road south of Kanpur was the F8 zone, largely impenetrable by the Indians.

Did Tatya's army give Havelock a chase as he 'retraced his steps' into Kanpur or did Tatya's army seek 'safety by flight', as Havelock claims?[30] If the Indians did seek 'safety in flight', was there a reason for Havelock to have holed himself and his troops up in Kanpur along with Neill's men?

Consider the first message that Havelock sent out when he retreated to Kanpur. On 21 August at 12.30 pm, Havelock wrote to his commander-in-chief:

I see no alternative but abandoning for a time the advantages I have gained in this part of India and retiring upon Allahabad.[31]

Despite the insistence by Havelock and his spin-doctors, that Havelock returned victorious, we take the liberty to translate these events as another defeat for Havelock. Shivrajpur remained firmly under Indian control.

Around the same time, Havelock received important personal news. In the spirit of his continued 'victories', he was being 'rewarded'. In recognition of his series 'relinquishments of enterprise', 'retracing steps', and 'retrograde movements' against Tatya's army, Havelock was relinquished of his command. Major General Outram was 'appointed to the military command of the Cawnpore and Dinapur divisions'.[32]

COORDINATING THE WAR

Although the areas north of Kanpur were in Tatya's hands, the English continued to control the southern corridor of the Grand Trunk road all the way to Calcutta. The English supplies at Kanpur were strong as an English officer writes: 'European stores are scarce, but wheat is plentiful—so we have nothing to fear, I believe, on their account'.[33] It allowed them to continue to bring in reinforcements that could be used to take Lucknow back from Nana Saheb, who was bravely holding out.

On 20 August, Kanpur was in temporary status quo. Havelock had retreated into the southern parts of Kanpur, holed up and shielded in his F8 zone, and Tatya Tope controlled the areas north of Kanpur, unable to push Havelock back with his current situation in terms of troop strength, ammunition and logistical support. The Indian troops attempted an incredible second assault on the English entrenchment but were not successful.[34]

At this time, although India was structurally and strategically weakened by England's barbarism, the Indians held a temporary upper hand. Delhi remained liberated, so were Lucknow and the districts north of Kanpur. Gwalior was untouched and Central India was largely under Indian control. However, England had achieved a strategic upper hand. They had carved a deadly and nearly impenetrable corridor by destroying the surrounding villages. They had succeeded in breaking the spirit of a large portion of the population by the large-scale and systematic massacres in the name of Acts of XI, XIV and XVI of 1857.

This corridor would be their launching pad to take Awadh, Rohailkhand and Lucknow.

India's military success was largely with local civilian support. Nana Saheb and Tatya recognised that if the population faltered, logistical support and supply lines could vanish. On 25 August, a proclamation was made to the people at Azamgarh, which has been discussed in the Introduction to this book. Nana and Tatya, in the spirit of their hero Mahadji Shinde, wanted to free India from the English tyranny. Learning from Mahadji's pragmatic precedence, they united the people under the name of Bahadur Shah the Mughal.

The authorship of the proclamation remains unknown, primarily because Indian historians have largely ignored it or have never given this manifesto the credit it deserves. The declaration was made by Bahadur Shah's grandson who was closely associated with the Nawab of Awadh. Begum Hazrat Mahal was fully cooperating with Nana Saheb and had handed over the command for Awadh's protection to Nana Saheb.

The proclamation was in Urdu and Hindi and copies of it were circulated in many places.[35] Considering that Nana Saheb was the leader of the War, and in Awadh during the period, we believe that it was Nana Saheb who initiated the declaration. Additionally, it is entirely possible that Tatya Tope, who was mulling the next steps after his success in pushing Havelock back, was consulting with Nana Saheb around 20 August. Raised by a father who understood India's ethos, Tatya was witness to the tragic economic decline, especially after he moved from his birthplace Yeola to Bithoor. It is likely that Tatya Tope could have contributed his thoughts in accurately indicting the rule of the English in this manifesto of freedom.

At this critical juncture of the War, the troop movements of the Indians were coordinated. There was communication with Delhi. As an example, Nana was seeking advice from his counterpart in Delhi (either Bahadur Shah himself or a representative) on the issue of the treatment to the English prisoners.[36] In addition, Kunwar Singh's movement from Bihar was following patterns that seemed to be timed to support Tatya Tope.

This War, as discussed earlier, was *not* merely about the numbers of troops. It was about provisions for the soldiers, logistics and ammunition. In fact, a *few* well-fed troops were far better off than *many* but starving soldiers. Tatya fought this phase with the popular mandate of the villagers. Tatya, like Havelock had lost many men in these intense battles fought in the previous five weeks. Fighting any future battles near the Kanpur area was going to need ammunition, guns and reinforcements.

Meanwhile, there was news of more English reinforcements arriving in Calcutta in the form of James Outram. Outram headed straight for Kanpur and arrived there unopposed by the middle of September. Havelock's F8 zone was paying rich dividends for the English. With established lines of supply and communications, the English were able to maintain an upper hand in this area.

There is no data available on the economic situation of Indians during the War. Guns, rifles and ample ammunition were always critical in battles. The marshy areas near the Ganga where many battles were fought made it difficult to transport the guns that weighed hundreds of pounds. Elephants were better in these swamps, but not horses. Did Tatya have enough elephants? Was there sufficient feed available to keep these massive animals fed and strong? Was there enough money to take care of all the expenses? The answer is in Tatya's next move, when Tatya attempted to counter the impact of the English F8 campaign in the second phase of the war. While the first phase of the war depended on the civilians for logistical needs, Tatya's second phase addressed these critical issues.

Tatya's whereabouts after his victories near Kanpur remain unrecorded, until he arrived in Gwalior by late September 1857. Tatya Tope's arrival in Central India coincided with the establishment of Nana Saheb's government in Bundelkhand with the support of the local chiefs. In all likelihood, Tatya Tope was in Bundelkhand, coordinating the finances and other planning, prior to his arrival in Gwalior.

It was imperative that the English did not get access to the Grand Trunk road north of Kanpur. What is likely to have happened is that Tatya Tope kept most of his existing troops stationed at Shivrajpur to maintain status quo vis-à-vis the English forces at Kanpur, and attempted to dislodge the English from their strongholds and their safe F8 zones. Kanpur at this time had 5,000-6,000 English troops.[37] In addition, the English had strong positions at Fatehpur, Allahabad and Varanasi.

Given the English upper hand in the Doab region, Tatya planned a strategic countermove to strengthen Central India. In what was quickly turning into a game of chess, a set of coordinated events followed in late August and September that led to the creation of a new command centre at Kalpi. These included Tatya's visit to Gwalior, the unexpectedly late 'mutiny' of the 52 NI and 50 NI stationed at Jabalpur and Nagod respectively and the emergence of Kunwar Singh.

A month earlier, just as Havelock was getting ready to reach Kanpur, Kunwar Singh, an eighty-year-old zamindar from Jagdishpur was carrying out 'intimate conversations with the sepoys at Dinapore'.[38] There were three regiments stationed at Dinapur—the 7 NI, 8 NI and the 40 NI. Dinapur is on the outskirts of Patna, in Bihar and Jagdishpur is about twenty miles east of Arrah. Around the end of July, the troops at Dinapur marched towards Arrah. Something important happened the day after Tatya Tope defeated Havelock at Unnao and chased him across the Ganga back into Kanpur. As if on cue, on 5 August, Kunwar Singh proclaimed himself the King of Shahabad.[39] With Kunwar Singh leading them, these three regiments started to march towards the Grand Trunk road. No narrative, English or Indian, has suggested that Kunwar Singh's announcement was coordinated with Tatya Tope's success in chasing Havelock across the Ganga. However, what is well known is that Kunwar Singh eventually joined Tatya Tope's forces in Banda the following month and eventually helped establish the command centre at Kalpi. However, in the following pages, we make a case that Kunwar Singh's movements and actions had a lot to do with Tatya Tope's attempt to reignite the spirit of freedom.

THE OCTOGENARIAN'S CAMPAIGN—THE INVISIBLE SHIELD

For R.C. Majumdar, who for some is India's 'greatest historian', Bahadur Shah was a 'dotard', a senile old man. Majumdar was obviously not very impressed with Bahadur Shah, who 'dared' to rise against the English, when he was supposed to be nothing more than a 'puppet in their hands'. However, Majumdar, despite all his vitriolic reserved for the Indian leaders of 1857, could not have succeeded in labelling Kunwar Singh a 'dotard'. Although he was nearly as old as Bahadur Shah, Kunwar faced the hardship of long marches, crossing rivers, camping with little or no facilities and braving every obstacle, until his death in April 1858. His later campaigns and the victories are worthy of an entire book, however, for the purpose of the current narrative, his early campaign is of significance.

The English strongholds along the Grand Trunk road, especially Varanasi, Allahabad or Mirzapur, were the primary targets for Tatya Tope. Taking either one, would have severely restricted English reinforcements to arrive by the Grand Trunk road. In the end, the Indians never succeeded in uprooting the English from these strongholds. However, Kunwar Singh attempted it twice, but he was blocked by an invisible shield. His abortive marches towards Mirzapur demonstrate the success of the barbaric and overwhelming English response.

Once Kunwar Singh took over the leadership of the three Dinapur regiments, his immediate responsibilities were clear; he had to attempt to liberate one or more of Allahabad, Varanasi and Mirzapur. Allahabad is where the Yamuna merges into the Ganga. Varanasi was on the northern side of the Ganga and Mirzapur was on the southern side. It is important to remind readers that the English had destroyed all villages around these English strongholds, in addition to many villages along the Grand Trunk road. Based on Kunwar Singh's movement, it is clear that his target was Mirzapur.

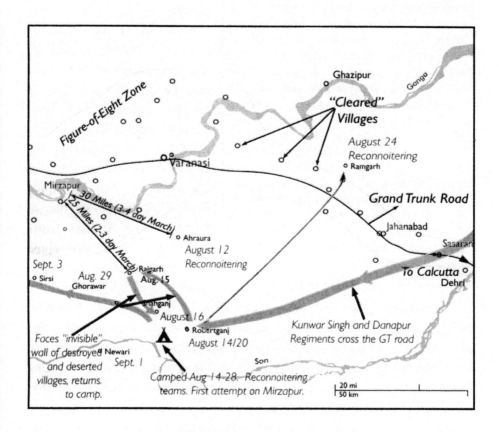

Figure 19: Kunwar Singh's Abortive Attempt—East

Supply Logistics

Consider that the F8 zone was possibly about twenty-thirty miles around each of these towns. A typical infantry regiment could march about eight-ten miles in a day. In preparation for an attack on Mirzapur, in addition to the guns and rifles, Kunwar Singh would need the provisions for the men. Assuming that Kunwar Singh had about 3000 men, according to earlier estimate, he would have needed about 4000-4500 kg of grain per day. Once at Mirzapur, he would have to expect at least two to three days of battle, and have the ability to fall back on an 'uncleared' village. If the enemy remained entrenched, he would need to have a well-established and protected supply line to the areas near Robertganj, where he had set up camp. This would translate into about eight to nine days worth of grain—about 35,000 kg. Assuming a bullock cart could carry 500-700 kg of grain, he would have needed about sixty additional carts or provisions alone. This would be in addition to the hundreds of carts for the men, ammunition, pots-pans, tents and many miscellaneous items, that his troops were already marching with. Some narratives suggest that Kunwar Singh had more than 4,000 men—which would translate into even a more developed planning for supplies. In general, for the Indian soldiers, the villagers would often play host, at least in this phase of the war. Tatya demonstrated a fully developed supply lines in the next phase of the war.

When Kunwar Singh with his three regiments (probably a little more than 2,000 men), in addition to some new recruits, reached the Grand Trunk road, they found a path of carnage and destruction and abandoned villages. Kunwar Singh and a body of men crossed the Grand Trunk road at Sasaram,[40] and set up camp in the area of Robertganj, about forty-five miles south-east of Mirzapur.

Setting up camp along the Grand Trunk road was rendered difficult because of the destruction of villages and the lack of availability of provisions. However, a body of Kunwar Singh's troops stayed back for reconnoitering the Grand Trunk road, nearby areas and block the English supply lines. They had some success when on 13 August some bullock carts were intercepted by people who called themselves 'Baboo Koer Sing Ka Log'.[41]

Kunwar Singh arrived and camped at Robertganj around 14 August. From there he made a first attempt to move into Mirzapur and marched into Rajgarh, which was about twenty-five miles away from Mirzapur. However, he fell back to Shahganj (near Robertganj) without engaging the enemy. In the next three weeks Kunwar Singh simply hovered around Mirzapur, making two abortive attempts, but never made it to Mirzapur. Other than a few small skirmishes, there was no major action. What explains Kunwar Singh's behaviour? Why was Kunwar Singh unable to march into Mirzapur and at least engage the enemy? We argue that this was the result of barbaric English offensive that had created an invisible wall around these towns.

Figures 19 and 20 illustrate the movement of Kunwar Singh's men from about 15 August 15 to 8 September, based on various sources.[42] Around late August, his intentions to attack Mirzapur were clear:

31 August—'...the Dinapore Regiments have approached to attack Mirzapore'.
3 September—Mr Sherring, 'Mirzapore, I am sorry to say, is still in danger on account of the proximity of the rebel rajah, Koor Singh'.[43]

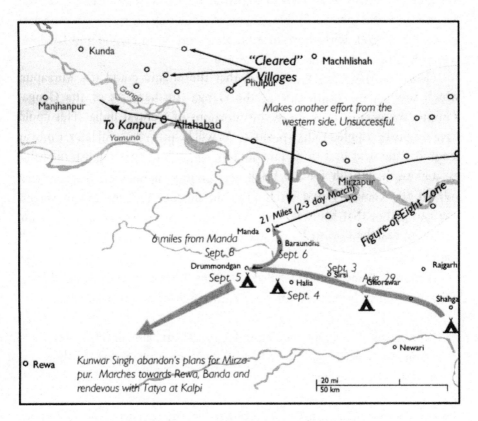

Figure 20: Kunwar Singh's Abortive Attempt—West

However, Kunwar Singh never did attack, despite weeks of hovering around Mirzapur and attempted efforts to make inroads. Kunwar Singh's inability to attack was a direct result of the F8 zone, which presented itself as an invisible wall, practically insurmountable without an elaborate supply line.

Kunwar Singh had to alter his plans, and give up on his attempt to take Mirzapur. An English intelligence message confirms this,

> Koer Singh and the Ramgurh Mutineers are in the backwoods, near Bijeygurh, threatening Mirzapore; but will not dare to attack it.[44]

Kunwar Singh temporarily held off on an offensive. Meanwhile, Tatya Tope was in the process of setting a new command centre at Kalpi and was in Gwalior to receive financial and logistical help towards the goal. Kunwar Singh was working towards this goal by coordinating his movement towards Rewa and Nagod, with those of 50th and 52nd NI in Nagod and Jabalpur, which had near simultaneously 'mutinied'.

However, there remained a risk that the enemy could use Mirzapur, which was on the south side of the Ganga (further east of the Ganga-Yamuna merger) to gain access into portions of Central India. This could have seriously crippled India's position. As will be proved useful later, Kunwar Singh did the next best thing he could do: slow down the English offensive by making it difficult for the English to source supplies on the southern side of the Ganga. Based on English intelligence reports and messages, one can gather that Kunwar Singh was attempting to create a safety zone before he marched on to Rewa and then on to Banda and join forces with Tatya Tope.

Although Kunwar Singh failed in taking Mirzapur, they were able to hurt the English by cutting off their communication with Calcutta.

> Both Electric Telegraph and letter dak to Calcutta are cut off... This is all due to General ___'s wretched conduct in not disarming Dinapore troops. [Name deleted in source][45]

Shortly thereafter, a series of coordinated events occurred in September 1857 (see Figure 21). The 52 NI and 50 NI stationed at Jabalpur and Nagod

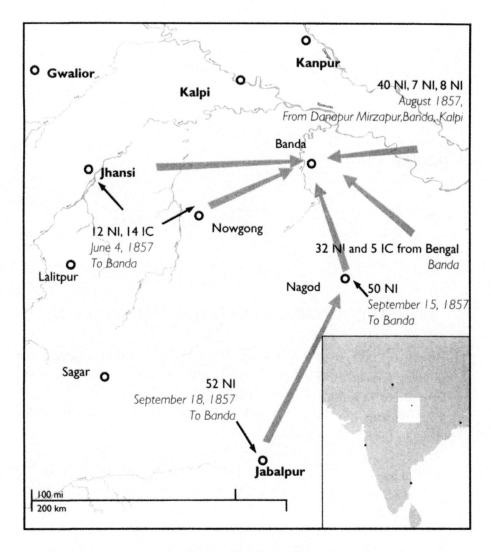

Figure 21: March to Banda

respectively 'mutinied' and marched towards Banda and so did Kunwar Singh. Around the same time, in late September, Tatya Tope went to Gwalior with the intention of using the Gwalior contingent towards the establishment of Kalpi as the new headquarters.

Chapter 12

A NEW WAR—A NEW CAPITAL

OPERATION RED LOTUS—A STRATEGIC REASSESSMENT

In August of 1857, the war in India had shaken the world. England was mobilising tens of thousands of their soldiers in other parts of the world for deployment in India. This needed large amounts of funds.

An American businessman called George Train, who later ran for president, in his book published in 1857, asks:

> England says they are short of funds. Where are the hundreds of millions of silver that have been shipped there, disturbing the currency of the world?[1]

During the summer of 1857, in the months of June and July, the English discreetly withdrew hundreds of millions of dollars of their investments from US banks and trusts, creating a massive liquidity crisis.

On 24 August 1857 the Ohio Life Insurance and Trust Co., in the United States filed for bankruptcy. This failure was the beginning of what is known as the 'panic of 1857', a severe economic crisis that the US faced, and spread into Europe. India was a major supplier of cotton to Britain in this period. The disruption of cotton supply to Britain encouraged the English to look elsewhere for cotton – including the southern colonies of the United States. The panic of 1857, in combination with the dynamics related to cotton trade with Britain, led to the dramatic clash between the northern and the southern colonies of the US.

On 25 August 1857, Bahadur Shah's grandson presented the Proclamation of Freedom that very articulately indicted the English rule. At this time, Lucknow and Delhi were under Indian control. Central India was firmly under Indian control. Most of Awadh was free, so was Central India. Yet, in hindsight, India had already lost the war, and at a strategic level, Tatya Tope's Operation Red Lotus had failed. The failure was not on the battlefield, but it was the victory for England's grisly F8 campaign. It was a victory for England's ability to use human shields to save their men. It was a failure due to Tatya Tope's inability to assess the depths to which the English were capable of falling.

Nonetheless, Tatya Tope and Nana Saheb were determined to continue their effort, inventing new strategies and new approaches. If the end was inevitable, should Tatya Tope, Nana Saheb and others have continued? Was this perseverance justified? We argue later, that despite India's eventual defeat, the war was not fought in vain and Tatya's unfaltering resolution was critical to the survival of India as a nation.

Delhi was under siege and the supplies were diminishing. The soldiers in many parts of Delhi were growing closer to starvation.[2] With the lower Doab, the belt between Ganga and Yamuna, in English control and Delhi faltering, Tatya Tope needed a new approach. Additionally, Kunwar Singh's inability to break past the invisible wall at Mirzapur demonstrated that numerical superiority was no longer a critical factor for victory. A new war was going to need a new approach. The focus had to be on logistics, supply lines, artillery and ammunition. In addition, Tatya was in need of new headquarters.

The events that took place over the next few months reveal a clear shift in Tatya's strategy. Nana Saheb took over the responsibility for holding on to Lucknow and Awadh, and the area north of the Ganga, and Tatya Tope would strengthen the Indian position south of the Yamuna, and help establish the capital at Kalpi.

Consider the situation in Central India. This was a period in warfare when rivers created natural military barriers. One can approximately define Central India as the region south of the Yamuna, east of the Chambal and north of the Narmada. Despite English attempts to disrupt Indian strengths in Bundelkhand, Central India remained under Indian control. Many of the troops based in Central India had liberated their respective cities and had marched on to assist in Delhi or Kanpur. Troops were also concentrated at Gwalior; ready to repel any English counter-offensives in Central India or assist Tatya Tope as needed. Two of the regiments in Gwalior contingents the 6th Gwalior Infantry based in Lalitpur had already fought at Kanpur. However, as Tatya Tope crossed the Ganga into Awadh, he asked these men to join the remaining contingent at Gwalior, and await further instructions. English historians, as expected, claim that they returned saying it was 'madness to face Europeans'.[3]

In addition, at least one regiment of the Gwalior contingent, alongwith some troops from surrounding areas, assembled at Mandsaur. These men were led by Shahzada Feroze Shah, a Delhi prince who had returned from Haj in Mecca. He landed in Surat and led a large and diverse group of men at Mandsaur.[4] They marched via Sardarpur to Dhar[5] and positioned themselves to block any English countermoves from the Deccan. Feroze Shah would attempt to rendezvous with Tatya again in January 1859; however, an important event prevented this from taking place.

In addition to the F8 zone along the Grand Trunk road, Delhi was also facing massive food shortages. Despite Bahadur Shah's attempts to address the issue, many Indian regiments were facing problems of provisions.[6] President of the Board of Control, Mr Vernon Smith's statement in British Parliament, otherwise subjected to criticism for being 'ignorant' was coming true. He had said if 'we could not reduce it (Delhi) by force, we could by famine'.[7] Many letters and diaries written by Indian soldiers in Delhi reveal that Delhi in August was a 'wrecked, semi-derelict and starving city'.[8] In fact, many troops that had marched into Delhi after facing hardships were now considering leaving the city for lack of food.[9] Marching into an area where food was becoming a scarce commodity was hardly a prudent idea. The inevitable fall of Delhi finally occurred in the middle of September. Delhi's fall could not have been prevented by sending the Gwalior contingent. Additionally, this force gathered at Gwalior, Dhar and other locations was a natural deterrent for the English in Central India.

Kunwar Singh and the Dinapur regiments were gathering at Banda before heading towards Kalpi. The Nawab of Banda was fully cooperating with Tatya Tope and was also in touch with the Jiyaji Rao Shinde. On 18 November, Jiyaji Rao sent a letter to the Nawab of Banda:

> You have beaten and driven out the English. This is good news to me. Tell me whoever comes to fight with you and I will give you assistance with my army. I heard from Raja Hinddoput's Hurkara that you are in trouble. Therefore I write to you. I hear that the Rewa Raja has allowed the English to stay with him, at this I am much displeased. I also hear that the Punna Raja has protected the Englsih from Nagode. This is not good. I have not heard of your welfare for sometime. Please write to me. We are alright here. I am ready to assist you. You have done well. I have published your name from this to Delhi.[10]

Historians have argued that the Gwalior contingent sat 'idle' while Delhi fell, apparently on the orders of 'Scindia' who was supposedly loyal to the English, thereby 'betraying' Tatya Tope. All narratives about the 'affairs at Gwalior' and the 'Scindia's betrayal' emerge from the information sent out by Samuel MacPherson, who at that time was the English resident at Gwalior. His intelligence reports are the basis for a highly romanticised story of 'loyalty and betrayal'. 'Scindia's deception' has been weaved by historians to create the foundation of India's eventual defeat in the war. While some facts of the story are accurate, many are not. However, more importantly, the implications and relevance are a complete invention. The logic, objectivity and the pertinence of this story are all questionable. Furthermore, many numerical facts underlying this story are also dubious. The author is of the opinion that, while the 'Scindia betrayal' is not of any direct consequence on the current narrative, an analysis of the events in Gwalior is discussed later.

Kunwar Singh's ineffective campaign to Mirzapur followed by the fall of Delhi signalled a need for a different approach. Tatya Tope's actions in the weeks of October and November reveal a clear shift in strategy.

A NEW CENTRAL COMMAND—HQ KALPI

Kalpi became Tatya Tope's command centre starting September of 1857. It did not suddenly emerge as an important city in the middle of the war; it was part of Operation Red Lotus to begin with. Nana Saheb Peshwa had visited Kalpi in January of 1857, prior to his visits to Lucknow and Delhi.[11] Many months later, when Kalpi was eventually lost to the English in May 1858, elaborate arms manufacturing facilities were discovered. Tatya had also established a 'gun-carriage manufactory [sic], and collected warlike stores of all kinds'.[12]

By the end of September, having taken Delhi and the Doab region, the English began making inroads into Central India. Central India was fast becoming the primary battleground in the war. On the one hand, news of Kunwar Singh's march into Rewa forced the English to stay south of Jabalpur,[13] while on the other hand, Feroze Shah was protecting the Bombay-Delhi corridor.

Tatya was planning to leverage Indian strength in Central India for a strategic counterstrike at Kanpur and support Lucknow. The goal was an attempt to overcome the primary difficulties that the Indians had faced because of the English F8 campaign, in the first phase of the war. The English had neutralised the plan of the Indian soldiers depending on the villages. Grains were becoming expensive in areas outside the F8 zone as well. The economic situation remained critical, and important lessons had been learnt. Depending solely on villages could no longer be an option. There was a need to have fully developed supply lines for future battles. Neill's 4,000 men, Havelock's 1,000-2,000 were well provisioned in Kanpur and could face a long siege if needed. Meanwhile, Lucknow was on the verge of falling into English hands. Saving Lucknow entailed a major offensive. Clearly, this operation was going to need men and money, artillery and ammunition in addition to provisions and planning.

Tatya visited Gwalior sometime in late September, prior to setting up Kalpi as a command centre. As explained earlier, English narratives weave a story of an elaborate plot of betrayal by Jiyaji Rao Shinde. The reality was probably something else. The English make no mention of the 'pragmatic patriot' Baija Bai Shinde; however, she was right there in Gwalior, advising Jiyaji Rao Shinde.[14]

Vishnubhat Godse saw Tatya Tope in person in the bazaar of Gwalior sometime in September of 1857.[15] The following is an account translated from his memoirs.

Tatya Tope arrived with 25 sowars and stayed at the Murar Cantonment. With an additional four platoons from the Sinde's on his side, he sent a message to Sinde [sic] saying, 'I have been here for many days now. We have not touched, nor hurt anyone during our stay and plan to return shortly. However, we request that you provide us with *carts, camels, horses and additional logistics*'. Upon receiving this message, Jayaji Maharaj Sinde and Dinkarrao Rajwade Diwan arrived to meet Tatya Tope in the place where he was camped. This place was about six miles from the city by the river. Shinde and Rajwade proposed that, 'we will provide you all that is needed, provided you leave Gwalior in peace'. Upon reaching this agreement with Tatya, the three of them arrived in Gwalior city for 'paan supari' (supposing to celebrate their agreement). The following day, Sinde provided Tatya with *hundreds of carts, camels, elephants, bullocks, donkeys as well as camp followers*. Other officers in the Sinde army, uncertain as to their actions asked Sinde for advice. Sinde suggested that they should provide Tatya for any army units that he requests. He also requested them to ensure that none of the soldiers takes up arms against us [emphasis added].[16]

The need for carts, camels, elephants, bullocks, donkeys and camp followers signify an important tactical shift. Tatya Tope was redefining the mode of warfare by developing a full-fledged army. Jiyaji Rao, with the implicit support from Baija Bai Shinde, was supporting Tatya in the effort. The elephants would drag the cannons. The bullock carts would transport the soldiers. The camels would carry the supply of grain for the cavalry and artillery horses. Donkeys and bullock carts would transport the provisions. More transportation was needed for transporting the hospital stores, wines, medicines, quilts, beds, pots pans of all sorts and sizes.

The idea was to build a full-fledged army that could fight the English on equal terms. Tatya was building an army that would have a supply column, which could provide sustenance in areas devastated by the English. This would have allowed Tatya to penetrate into the F8 zone, which was devoid of any food, as well as protect the villagers from facing more F8 campaigns. Kalpi, which was on the southern bank of the Yamuna, was going to be supplied by the surrounding areas.

Meanwhile, Kunwar Singh had instructions from Tatya to arrive at Banda. The Nawab of Banda was fully cooperating with Tatya Tope in terms of manpower and money. Kunwar Singh was in Banda on 8 October 1857[17] with about 3,000-4,000 men, including the 7 NI, 50 NI, 40 NI and, parts of the 52 NI had arrived at Kalpi by 19-27 October.[18]

After having arranged all the logistics, Tatya left Gwalior sometime in the middle of October with the main body of the Gwalior contingent.[19] Before going to Kalpi, Tatya had some unfinished business to attend. As the de facto government of Bundelkhand and Central India, local power conflicts now came under the purview of the Nana Saheb's government. Two parties were disputing the control over the management of Jalaun. This dispute was partly triggered by the opportunistic Keshav Rao, who viewed the uncertainty as an advantage. He had taken advantage of the situation when the war started, enlisted some armed men and asserted his power over the area and was in discussion with the English. Meanwhile, Tai Bai, the daughter of a former chief of Gursarai, claimed to be the rightful heir to that area. Part of governance was imparting justice, and Keshav Rao's opportunistic behaviour needed to be addressed. After overcoming

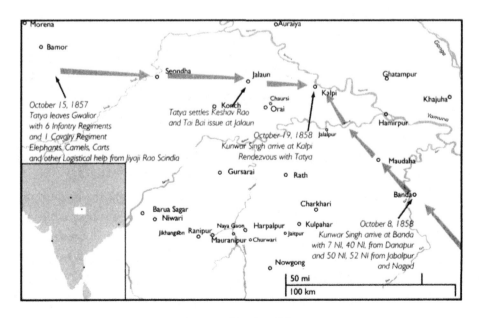

Figure 22: March to Kalpi

some resistance, Keshav Rao was arrested and asked to pay a fine of Rs 3 lakh.[20]

Tatya Tope continued on to Kalpi to rendezvous with Kunwar Singh and Mohammed Isaakh, who helped assist Tatya in various management functions. A bridge over the Yamuna was also planned before Tatya arrived, and the work commenced after Tatya's approval. An expert was brought in from Sikandara named Raja Bhau who commenced the construction.[21]

Foundries for forging cannons, a gun carriage factory, ammunition store and a bridge across the Yamuna were all built in the two months starting late September to late November. Setting up Kalpi as the command centre represented something much more than the headquarters for a war. It was the capital of an India that had tasted freedom again after more than a generation. Kalpi represented the spirit of liberty embodied in the Proclamation of Freedom made at Azamgarh in August of 1857.

Over November and December of 1857, Kalpi was going to play an important role in saving Lucknow from falling into English hands.

BEYOND THE CHESS PLAYERS—LUCKNOW HOLDS OUT

During late 1857, the fates of Kanpur and Lucknow were intertwined. A part of the reason was their proximity to each other, and part of it was the direct involvement of Nana Saheb Peshwa in defending Awadh. With Nana Saheb was Ahmadullah Shah, the de facto general of some regiments in Lucknow, and Azimullah Khan who had witnessed the Sebastopool battle. He had extensively shared his experiences with Nana Saheb and Maulavi Ahmadullah Shah.[22] Monetary support for the war effort came from Begum Hazrat Mahal. Nana Saheb's presence in Awadh was also critical in coordinating the movements of Tatya Tope who was in charge of Central India.

Starting September of 1857, after maintaining a strong army at Kanpur, Neill, Havelock and Outram's next task was to take down Lucknow. This trio's personal bickering, ethnicity, size, shape and other rivalry make for thousands of pages of English narratives. While amusing in their own right, they do not play any significant role in this presentation. Regardless of who was in charge, they continued to follow the English F8 campaign into Lucknow. In November of 1857, the English claimed, 'the road to Cawnpore is now secure to the English who have *seized the grain* and are *burning all villages* along the line [emphasis added]'.[23] While this policy was partly effective, geography did not allow it to be as successful as their F8 campaign. Unlike the Doab region, which was separated by two major rivers, the road to Lucknow was not, thus allowing the villages to revive after the attacks.

From September to November 1857, dozens of battles were hard fought for the control of various parts of Lucknow. The English controlled the Residency and existing buildings prevented a direct line of fire. Artillery ammunition was running low, which added to the difficulty in uprooting the English from their entrenched position.[24] Maulavi Ahmadullah Shah became the face of ground level leadership in these attacks on the English.

Of the various attacks and counter-offensives, Ahmadullah Shah displayed his genius and set up the English for failure in many instances. Ahmadullah Shah personally directed the execution of Neill through a sniper bullet.[25] If anything, a minor retribution for the ruthless massacre, and later torture of thousands of Indian women and children, was achieved through Neill's death. Havelock was killed in November.

After months of fighting, the English were still unable to take Lucknow. After Outram, Havelock and Neill, the English sent Colin Campbell to bring Lucknow down. English troops from around the world were 'pouring by the thousands' into India, primarily for the control of Lucknow and Awadh.[26] In addition to these troops, the English were able to reinforce Lucknow with troops from Delhi, which was now firmly in English hands. The English troops from Delhi, in the words of Malleson, were 'swarthy', and although the guns that came down from Delhi looked 'blackened and service worn', the horses were in 'good condition'.[27]

Estimates of the Indian forces fighting in Lucknow numbering over fifty thousand are highly exaggerated. Part of the exaggeration comes from the familiar 'multiple' of two to ten used elsewhere and part derives from double counting the troops. Part of the exaggeration also comes from the presence of civilian militia and young men who were willing to fight. While these constituted as soldiers, with little or no training they were incapable of taking on the English troops. Some of the troops counted were present in Awadh holding out in other areas, but not deployed in Lucknow.

The key areas of conflict during November were at the Residency and Alambagh. Hundreds of, by now, familiar pages devoted to the 'gallantry' of

English soldiers have been written during their advance towards Lucknow. Very little is written about the situation of the Indian soldiers.

During 1857, the Gomati surrounded Lucknow on three sides. As the English began to exert on the fourth, Lucknow was slowly getting cut off from the rest of Awadh. While the Lucknavi population was supporting the Indian soldiers, the 300,000 civilians who lived in Lucknow were competing with the soldiers for necessities. Prices of food rose and economics of the war became difficult.[28]

Indian soldiers, even court personages, were being forced to go hungry at least once a day. Begum Hazrat Mahal was doing all in her power to provide decent food and pay to the soldiers. Lucknavi tailors were stitching clothing for the new recruits free. There were days when soldiers went without food surviving on 'gram (chick peas) and salt'.[29]

By the middle of November, it was apparent that the fall of Lucknow was imminent. Indians defending Lucknow urgently needed reinforcements and replenishments in large quantities—a task seemingly impossible due to the strong English presence.

TATYA'S KANPUR TRAP—RESCUING LUCKNOW

The game of chess was invented in India more than 2,000 years ago. The infantry, the cavalry and other armies were aptly represented in the little pieces that strategists and kings used to consider moves and countermoves. Chess is a variation of *chaturanga*, which was invented as a strategy game about warfare. The game represented the fundamental principles of warfare, and the rules of the game represented the honour amongst warriors during war.

Munshi Premchand's novel *Shatranj ke Khiladi*, later made as a movie directed by Satyajit Ray is set in Lucknow during 1857. While the two protagonists' obsession with the game presents a dark contrast to the events unfolding at Lucknow, a different kind of chess was being played on the chessboard of India. The English displayed the kind of chess they excelled at, and wanted to play. Destroying villages, civilian men, women, and children was akin to burning up half the chessboard, thereby limiting your opponent's moves. Tatya's countermoves showed his strength in adapting to this burning chessboard. Studying Tatya's moves in the second phase of the war hints at the possibility that he was an excellent chess player, especially while adapting to changing rules.

With Kanpur in English hands, Campbell, Outram's successor, set his eyes on Lucknow, which remained in Indian hands, with Nana Saheb at the helm. After Campbell attacked Lucknow with full force, its fate was hanging on the edge. Tatya Tope, who was coordinating his actions with Nana Saheb, recognised it was critical to reinforce Lucknow with ammunition, artillery and troops. However, Campbell's strong position at Lucknow meant that reinforcing Lucknow would have been impossible. Tatya executed his next move so brilliantly that it not only caught Campbell and other English generals by surprise, but they probably did not know that they had been taken for a ride, until a few days after they claimed their victory on the battlefield.

In the end, the chessboard was burnt and the English claimed victory all over India. However, the battle of Kanpur that was fought in November and December of 1857 was about more than Kanpur. The battle of Kanpur

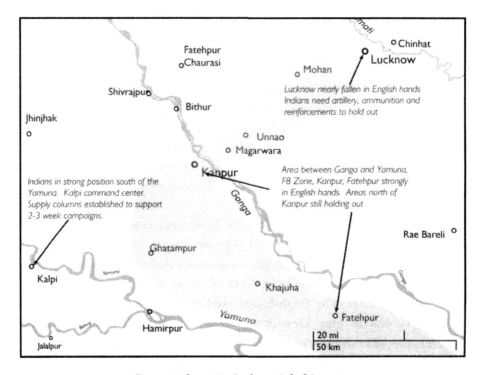

Figure 23: Operation Lucknow Relief Situation

was both, an attempted recapture of Kanpur as well as Operation Lucknow Relief.

Consider the situation in the areas surrounding Kanpur in November 1857. The Grand Trunk road all the way from Kanpur to Calcutta was firmly in English hands. Fatehpur had a strong English presence. Similarly, Kanpur was strongly reinforced now under Wyndham's command.

We do know a little about the logistical situation of the Indian troops defending Lucknow. After nearly four months of holding out, their artillery was battered and ammunition was in short supply. With 'thousands' of English troops pouring into the area, Lucknow, defended by Nana Saheb, was about to fall. Figure 23 summarises the situation in November 1857.

At this time, while Maulavi Ahmadullah Shah under the command of Nana Saheb and Begum Hazrat Mahal, defended Lucknow and Awadh, Tatya Tope was strengthening Central India, south of the Yamuna. Kalpi was ready with foundries for the artillery, a factory for gun carriages and ammunition stores. Tatya with the implicit support of Baija Bai also had the reserve troops. Additionally, after taking control of Central India, Kunwar Singh and the three Dinapur regiments were more useful in Awadh. The goal was to reinforce Lucknow with troops, artillery and ammunition. Given the state of the villages in the area, the belt between Ganga and Yamuna was practically impossible to hold on to for long. Therefore, taking and holding on to Kanpur was not a worthwhile task. However, while seemingly impossible, Lucknow could be reinforced with some ingenuity.

Consider the odds.

Any troop coming from Kalpi needed a supply column, which by now Tatya had developed with the support of Gwalior, in the form of camels, elephants, carts and camp followers. However, the English were strongly entrenched in Fatehpur and Kanpur. Even if Tatya was able to evade the English troops from Kanpur and Fatehpur, and get his troops across the Ganga near Shivrajpur, he would have to eventually face Campbell's full strength near Lucknow. The only possibility of sending reinforcements into Lucknow was to create a diversion attracting a large section of Campbell's forces away from Lucknow.

Starting November, Tatya began a multi-step strike to both capture Kanpur and send relief to Lucknow. His army at this time was the Gwalior contingent with 4 infantry regiments and the 3 Dinapur regiments—7 NI, 8

NI and 40 NI. The idea was to force the English to give up either Kanpur or Lucknow. However, attacking Kanpur was not sufficient, since Fatehpur, which was along the Grand Trunk road, would have come to Kanpur's rescue.

The first step was to block English communication between Kanpur and Fatehpur and keep the English engaged near Fatehpur. Tatya achieved this with the help of Kunwar Singh and his three Dinapur regiments.

With the help of Baija Bai Shinde, Tatya had sufficient supporting infrastructure to maintain long incursions into the F8 zone. Kunwar Singh and his men crossed the Yamuna at Kalpi and started to make inroads towards Fatehpur in early November. The English were drawn out of Fatehpur under Colonel Powell to engage Kunwar Singh's men near Khajuha.[30] Subhedars Bhavani Singh and Shivlal Tiwari distinguished themselves in this battle and

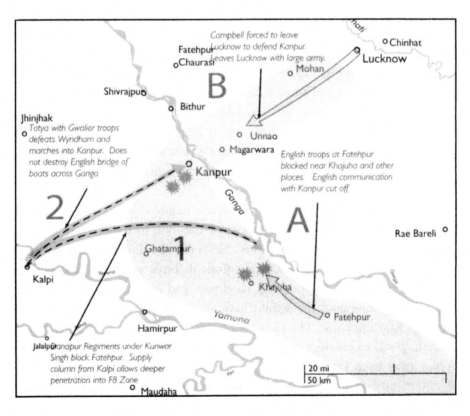

Figure 24: Operation Lucknow Relief—1-2

died.[31] However, the idea was not to take Kanpur, but cut off the lines of communication between Kanpur and Fatehpur.[32] This would force Campbell to make decisions about Kanpur without knowing the full extent of Tatya's troop movement.

Next, Tatya led the Gwalior contingent and marched towards Kanpur. English estimates of the force was about 3,000[33] which seems consistent with the three or possibly four regiments of the Gwalior infantry with him at this time. Tatya left behind a few regiments at Kalpi as his rear guard.[34] As he marched across the Doab, he formed a chain of posts as he advanced.[35] At this time, Kanpur was under the control of Major-General Windham. Two battles took place, first about eight miles from Kanpur on 26 November, and another closer to Kanpur at Nawabganj on 27 November 1857.[36] Tatya's army won both these battles, confirmed by plenty of English narratives. What is relevant is that the English troops were forced to retreat into their entrenchment. The entrenchment was adjacent to the river of boats that the English had built that allowed the troops to re-cross the Ganga. Figure 24 summarises Tatya's actions in late November.

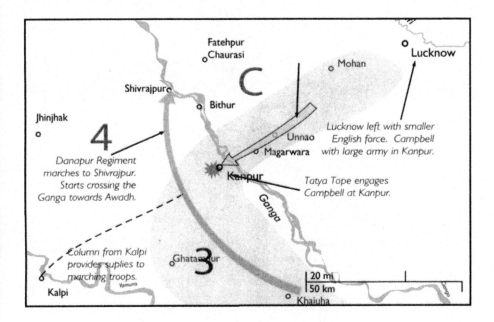

Figure 25: Operation Lucknow Relief—3-4

A few days before Kanpur fell into Tatya's hands, Campbell, who was making a final push into Lucknow received word that Tatya and the Gwalior regiments were marching to Kanpur. On 22 November, he ordered its retreat from the Residency and handed the command to Outram.[37] The retreat was significant and hasty. The English did not have time to carry the guns out of the Residency and the guns were destroyed.[38] Campbell, left Alambag for Kanpur on the 26th with the long convoy and reached Kanpur on the night of the 28 November 1857.[39] A remarkable forty miles in two and a half days. The withdrawal of the British from Lucknow 'gave a fillip to the rebellion' in Lucknow.[40]

From 29 November through 5 December, there was very little action in Kanpur. Windham's entrenchment was adjacent to the ghat portion of the Ganga, which helped the English to cross the river quickly. Tatya's goal was to defend the newly acquired portions of Kanpur as well as send reinforcements to the other side of the Ganga and providing them passage while engaging Campbell in Kanpur. While Tatya and the Gwalior contingent maintained temporary control over Kanpur, the Dinapur regiments were

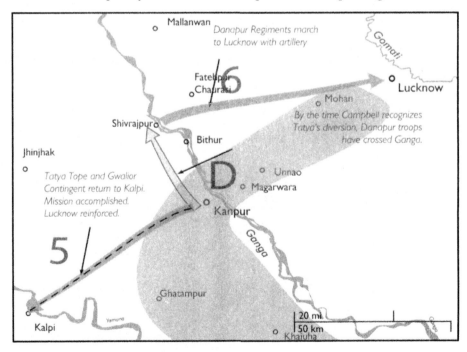

Figure 26: Operation Lucknow Relief—5-6

marching over to Shivrajpur on the northern side of Kanpur ready to make their way on the Awadh side of the Ganga.

On 6 December 1857 a battle was fought between Tatya and Campbell's army. Many pages are dedicated in English narratives to describe the battle. The English narratives claim that Tatya was defeated, and was forced to give up Kanpur. We will never know whether Tatya ever had any intentions of holding on to Kanpur, considering the overwhelming strength the English had in the lower Doab region. Regardless of Tatya's intentions on Kanpur, what is more relevant than the battle itself is the movement of Tatya's troops after the battle. Tatya's army did some 'strange' movements. They split into two sections, apparently 'confused'. Some marched in 'one direction, some in another'.[41] Campbell followed one section of the Indian troops, 'fourteen miles towards Calpee (Kalpi)',[42] while another section marched in a different direction. What Campbell did not realise, that this 'confusion' was deliberate.

Tatya's idea was to split the body of the English troops, so that three-six Indian regiments, whose mission was to reinforce Lucknow, could cross over the Ganga in time. The Gwalior contingent alongwith Tatya Tope returned to Kalpi, which was an Indian stronghold, while the Dinapur regiments marched towards Shivrajpur, at Serai Ghat. On 8 December, Campbell possibly figured out Tatya's game plan and ordered one of his generals (General Hope Grant) to march from Kanpur to Shivrajpur with an estimated army of 2,800 (probably understated).[43]

By the time Grant reached Shivrajpur, most of the Indian army along with the artillery, ammunition and gun carriages had crossed over. He reported that he had 'successfully silenced the guns of the enemy'.[44] That was the best report he could give since the most of the 'enemy's' guns were on the other side of the Ganga.

He also claimed that he had 'captured fifteen guns, including one 18-pounder, eight 9-pounders, three 12-pounder howitzers, two 4-pounder howitzers, and 6-pounder native, with all their stores, carts, wagons, large quantities of ammunition, bullocks, hackeries, etc.' before they could be transported. This claim might be true, since most of the Indian troops had successfully crossed the Ganga, with a large part of the logistical supply having already been transported. An 'enemy' whose goal was to reinforce Lucknow, had succeeded in splitting Campbell's forces and send reinforcement into a precarious Lucknow.

On 11 December, according to English records, seven Indian infantry regiments and a cavalry arrived in Lucknow.[45] On 13 December, three more regiments arrived from Kanpur, making a total of 6,000 men. On 17 December, there were reports of gun carriages arriving as well. Buoyed by the successes and reinforcement, Begum Hazrat Mahal, allocated five lakh rupees to build a wall around the city.[46]

Charles Ball euphemistically acknowledges that 'as the time approached when Lucknow was again destined to revert to the English… the defences of the city had been greatly strengthened and augmented'.[47] Lucknow was incredibly saved with this masterstroke, while Kanpur could not be re-captured. Tatya's Operation Lucknow Relief had succeeded in giving Lucknow a breather, which would allow it to hold out for a few more months.

Chapter 13

NUCLEAR DEFENCE

THE DAGGER'S DEEP THRUST

While Tatya's Kanpur diversion successfully reinforced Lucknow with artillery and ammunition manufactured at Kalpi, and at least four regiments of troops, the number of English troops pouring into India did not stop. Campbell realised that he had been outsmarted and paid with the loss of Lucknow. Tatya had been able to leverage an English weakness in the Doab region of the Ganga and Yamuna, between Kanpur and Farrukhabad. While Lucknow got a breather, the English decided to further consolidate their grip in the Doab.

Campbell moved three columns to 'clear' the villages, thereby restricting the movement of Indian troops. This was the continuation of Neill and Havelock's 'figure-of-eight' campaign that had also destroyed the villages in the southern Doab region. Campbell sent one column towards Kalpi and then along the left bank of the Yamuna to Bewar and Mainpuri. Another started from Delhi on 9 December, and reached Bewar by 3 January. A third column started from Kanpur towards Fategarh and Farrukhabad.[1]

The English now controlled the entire region from Calcutta to Delhi. After this consolidation, the fates of Awadh and Central India were now severed. With Doab coming under English control, Nana Saheb and Begum Hazrat Mahal could no longer depend on support from Tatya Tope. Nana Saheb did make attempts to restore control over these areas.

Campbell's new campaign of 'clearing' villages continued what Havelock and Neill had left unfinished. The F8 dagger was pushed deeper into India's civilian population.

At a strategic level, Tatya had already lost the war, but there were many more battles to be fought ahead. The core of India's defence was going to be Central India. Gwalior remained in Indian hands, with full material and manpower support to Tatya as needed. The façade of a cozy relationship between Jiyaji Rao and the English allowed Tatya to maintain a strong position in Central India. Rani Lakshmi Bai had also postured to be favourable to the English while she was financing Indian troops and providing them logistical support. The Gwalior contingent was under Tatya's command and positioned at Gwalior and Kalpi. Far from sitting 'idle', this contingent was at the core of India's defence.

Tatya's response to Campbell's offensive in the Doab was to shield Bundelkhand from the north. On Tatya's orders, the bridge across the

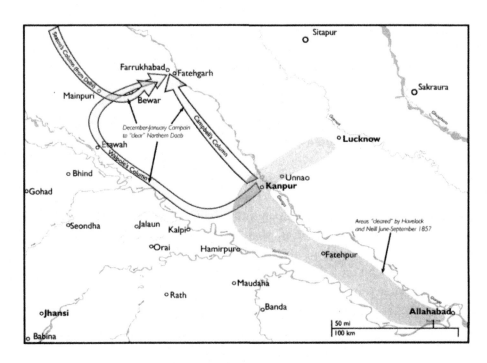

Figure 27: The Ongoing 'F8' Campaign
Campbell's Northern Doab Offensive in December 1857

Yamuna at Kalpi was broken in early January 1858.[2] Additionally all the ferries and the boats across the Yamuna from Jagamanpur to Hamirpur were taken over by Tatya's forces, thereby restricting access to Bundelkhand from the north.[3] In defence of Kalpi, Tatya erected batteries on the ghat of Yamuna and along the Hamirpur road.[4]

Tatya's preparedness in this phase of the war was reasonably strong, although his finances were running low. After getting all the logistical support from Jiyaji Rao Shinde of Gwalior, Tatya had a well-organised army. As would be demonstrated in some battles his army fought systematically. Tatya had hospital doolies[5] and had a large a well-regulated bazaar with abundance of supplies.[6] The following is a description of one of the battles in Bundelkhand that was fought under Tatya's command that demonstrated the improvements:

> They could afford their relief parties; while some fought, others rested; as one set was observed going away, another was seen coming to take their places, even during the continuance of conflict. They had their bugle calls during the last grand assault, and each separate band of matchlock-men was led on and performed their assigned task, under the tuition evidently of some of the smartest sepoys...[7]

By January, of the four targets, Delhi and Kanpur were firmly in English hands. Awadh was cut off from Central India and Lucknow's fate was uncertain. With Kalpi as the operational headquarters, Bundelkhand remained the nucleus of India's defence.

CHHATRASAL'S PRIDE

Bundelkhand lies south of the Yamuna and north of the Vindhya Range. Its gentle slopes are distinguished by a barren hilly terrain. The plains of Bundelkhand are interrupted by three mountain ranges—the Vindhya, Fauna and Bander. A distinguishing feature of the topography of Bundelkhand is isolated hills rising abruptly from a common level. These hills made excellent sites for forts that were the strongholds of local kings. The general slope of the region is towards the northeast, as indicated by the course of the rivers, which traverse or bound the territory, and finally discharge themselves into the Yamuna River.

The main rivers of Bundelkhand are the Pahuj, Betwa, Dhasan, Ken, and Paisuni. The Kali Sindh River, rising in Malwa, marks the western frontier of Bundelkhand. Parallel to this river, but further east, is the course of Betwa and Ken.

While Bundelkhand has a rich cultural history that includes places such as Khajuraho, King Chhatrasal gave Bundelkhand its modern identity. Bundelkhand came under the nominal rule of the Mughals in the early seventeenth century; however, the Bundeli people continued their spirited resistance, until finally they were able to achieve liberation under Chhatrasal. On the outbreak of his rebellion in 1671, Chhatrasal occupied a large province to the south of the Yamuna.[8] During this period, a new pan-Indian power was emerging that was taking on the Europeans along the coast and the Mughals to the north. Chhatrasal was able to forge an alliance with the Marathas and was able to liberate the whole of Bundelkhand. On his death in 1732, he bequeathed one-third of his dominions, including Jalaun and Jhansi, to his Maratha allies.[9] Over the next many decades, the Marathas and the Bundelas kept a spirited resistance against the English.

The Marathas lost parts of Bundelkhand to the British in 1802 after the Second Anglo-Maratha war. After 1802, many of the local rulers were granted *sanads* (leases) by the British, which entitled them to the lands, in return for the rulers signing an *ikrarnama* (written bond of allegiance). This ikrarnama nullified the previous pact the Bundelas had with the Marathas. A political officer attached to the British forces in Bundelkhand supervised British relations with the sanad states. After the Third Anglo-Maratha war, the Marathas under the Bajirao II lost all his rights over Bundelkhand to the British.[10]

Keeping this core of India under their control had proved difficult for the Mughals. The English struggled as well. The Bundelkhand Agency—as the English called it—was headquartered at Banda. In 1818, the headquarters were moved to Kalpi, in 1824 to Hamirpur, and in 1832 back to Banda.[11] The Bundeli chiefs played a critical role in the War of 1857. They became key allies of Nana Saheb and Tatya Tope in the attempt to overthrow English rule.

English offensive in Awadh and Rohailkhand continued through the early months of 1858. More than six months had passed since the war had started and English brutality had brought them closer to victory. The English were handing out rewards and punishment to the fence sitters in an attempt to weaken the popularity of the support that Indian leaders were able to realise. In Central India, including parts of Bundelkhand where Indian military presence was strong, the English attempted to 'buy' support from the local chiefs. The English contacted many chiefs 'urging them [to] employ their troops for the maintenance of British authority'.[12] Most, including the likes of the Nawab of Banda, refused. Ratan Singh, the Raja of Charkhari[13] was one of the few who was not strong enough to resist. On 24 December 1857, he gave an audience to the English political agent in Bundelkhand.[14]

While Tatya eventually had to deal with the Raja of Charkhari with force, Tatya attempted to persuade many other local chiefs to support the Indian leadership to continue the resistance. Bundeli chiefs were encouraged to abandon the ikrarnamas with the English and, reinitiate a pact with the Marathas. Mohammed Isaakh, who was Tatya Tope's assistant while at Kalpi, sent a circular to the chiefs of Bundelkhand, exhorting them to support Nana Saheb Peshwa in this cause of freedom. The following is an excerpt from the circular.

Shrimant Maharajah Peshwa Bahadur (Nana Saheb) has been leading the war against the English at the sacrifice of his every ease, comfort, wealth and property. The purpose of this war is defending the faiths of both the Hindus and the Muslims alike.

Maharaja Nana Saheb has resolved to continue this fight as long as he breathes his last breath. The primary goal of this war is to throw the English out of India, and not to replace the authority of the English with that of his own. After we have successfully overthrown the English, all the respective representatives of the provinces will have the freedom to make their own decisions. The provinces that are presently under English rule, after due consultation, will be distributed amongst the Chiefs that show full cooperation in this effort in defeating the enemy.

I urge you to send troops and guns without loss of any time. My Maharaja warmly hopes that all the chiefs of Bundelkhand will be of one mind to assist him in this task. In the past, the Peshwa rendered assistance to the Chiefs of Bundelkhand and treated them with dignity and honour.

Under these circumstances, it is hoped that you should send troops and guns under the responsibility of a trustworthy person. An early reply as well as any advice is appreciated.

January 2, 1858 – (15th Jumadee Aual, 1274 AH) [15]

Although the momentum was clearly against the Indians, other than exceptions such as the Raja of Charkhari, most other provincial chiefs replied positively. The old pact between the Marathas and the Bundelas was now resurrected under Nana Saheb Peshwa in the early months of 1858.

The villagers, whose overwhelming support to the leaders of the war helped in every way they could. Hugh Rose admitted:

...the villagers did good service to the Rebels by betraying to them our Daks and movements, as well as some carts, drivers, on account of the exhausted state of their cattle, could not keep their place in the Column, or sought water at a distance from the road.[16]

Under Tatya Tope, the Bundeli chiefs and the Bundeli people showed their mettle, their courage and proved once again, that they were Chhatrasal's pride.

CHHABELI'S STAND

Jhansi represented the portion of Bundelkhand where the Marathas collected revenue and performed administrative functions, until their defeat in the Second Anglo-Maratha war.

Rani Lakshmi Bai, who grew up with Nana Saheb, under the guidance of Tatya Tope, played a key role during the war. Tatya, nearly sixteen years older than her, as was not a childhood playmate as many suggest. During the early months of the war, Lakshmibai, like Baija Bai Shinde and Jiyaji Rao of Gwalior, also postured to the English that she was 'loyal' to them, and was 'helpless' as the events of 1857 unfolded. This tactic allowed Jhansi to become an important centre for the Indians. Troops could pass through Jhansi, while the Rani claimed helplessness in communication with the English, but were assured of complete logistical and economic support from the Rani. The funding came through her own treasury, local bankers and even, from the sale of her ornaments.[17] She also established her own mint.[18]

While actively supporting the Indian troops and staying in contact with Tatya Tope and Nana Saheb, Rani Lakshmi Bai sent communiqués to the English asking for help. For example, she sent letters to Major Erskine, the English commissioner at Sagar. In one such letter, she actually asked the English for funds, saying that she had 'run out' and even the local bankers were not lending 'in times like these'.[19]

This posturing worked, Erskine concluded:

> From these it will be seen that by the Ranee's own account she in no way lent assistance to the mutineers and rebels; on the contrary that she herself was plundered and forced to take charge of the District and this agrees with what I hear from other sources.[20]

Lakshmi Bai had the English convinced for many months that the reports of her economic and logistical support to the Indian troops were out of 'helplessness'. While she postured with the English and even asked them for funds, she remained in communication with Nana Saheb, Tatya Tope and the Raja of Banpur, implicitly supporting every move.[21] In August 1857, there were some reports that the Rani had all along actively supported the Indian soldiers. An intelligence message indicated that the Indian soldiers had taken the treasury, 'only at the instigation of the Jhansie Ranee'.[22]

Another English report concluded that the 'Ranee did lend assistance to the mutineers and rebels, and that she gave guns and men'.[23] By the December of 1857, the English had become fully aware of where Lakshmi Bai's loyalty really lay. Tricked by Lakshmi Bai, and outraged at the deception, the English decided to get personal. The English mounted a new offensive for the Rani's head. Hugh Rose's central Indian campaign was in part driven with this intention.

Some historians portray the behaviour of Rani Lakshmi Bai, not as an expression of freedom for India, but as a self-serving rebellion, that was an outcome of England's pension policies. These historians have weaved a narrative that revolves around a statement Lakshmi Bai allegedly made to John Lang, the British Counsel during that period, 'Mera Jhansi nahin dengee'.[24] These narratives consistently downplay the fact that the Indian leadership of the War of 1857, including Lakshmi Bai and Nana Saheb were collaborating during the war, suggesting instead that each of them were simply reacting selfishly and independently out of personal grievances. These historians project the actions of Nana Saheb, the Raja of Banpur, the representatives of Bahadur Shah and the Rani herself as isolated events. However, the following extract from an internal English report directly contradicts these conclusions:

> January 16, 1858
>
> The Nana has a vakeel at Jhansi. The Ranee of Jhansi has a vakeel in the rebel camp at Calpee, and she has made arrangements for the reception of the Nana's family in the fort of Jhansi, which both the Nana and the Banpore Rajah intended to make their last place of refuge. The Rajah of Banpore had engaged a portion of the Gwalior Contingent to go to Saugor, to reinforce his commander there (one Lalla Doolkara), who complained of being hard pressed by the British forces. Some of his own troops, under Sadut Ali and Mahomed Ali Khan, were also sent. The rest, being about 3,000 or 4,000 matchlock men, with two guns, remained at Jhansi, but only about 1,300 were fully armed. The Jhansi Ranee pays the Banpore Rajah 500 rupees per diem. Bukshish Ali, Jail Darogah, had written to say that he was at Allyghur, with the brother-in-law of the King of Delhi, and a large army, on his way to Jhansi, recommending the Ranee to send a nuzzer of 5,000 rupees; she accordingly sent 3,000 rupees. The fortifications of Jhansi are being strengthened. This letter also states that the 'Taee Baee' was in possession of Jaloun, collecting revenue there, of which she is to have one-third, and the Nana the rest.[25]

This report underscores the point, that the various leaders on the Indian side were indeed coordinating their activities, and Jhansi and Rani Lakshmi Bai was very much a part of these activities.

Recognising that the English were beginning a new campaign targeting Central India and Rani Lakshmi Bai, January of 1858 witnessed a fresh resurgence of activity around Jhansi. A few hundred Indian soldiers from various locations started to converge at Jhansi in preparation of a defence.[26] By late January, the Rani had a total of 1,000 soldiers, including some cavalry and ten gunners from the Gwalior contingent at her service.[27] Six new large guns and carriages were manufactured at Jhansi during this period. A few hundred mounds of saltpeter (a critical oxidising component of gun powder) were being brought into the fort.

Lakshmi Bai was working hard in defending Jhansi, not realising that for the English the next battle was more personal. The English goal was not only the capture of the fort of Jhansi, but the real prize was the Rani's head, who had deceived them. This task was handed to Hugh Rose, with added incentives, over which he would later sue his government. Rose's bloody campaign would demonstrate that he was an effective competitor to the genocide perpetrated by Havelock and Neill.

BUNDELKHAND'S WAFFLING WEASEL

In the first few months of 1858, Tatya's battleground was Bundelkhand. In the end, the English did overrun the entire province; however, in the keenly fought months of March and April, Hugh Rose had three primary goals. First, to take Jhansi, second, to take Charkhari and the third was Lakshmi Bai's head. With brilliant tactical manoeuvering, Tatya succeeded in preventing two of Rose's three goals from coming to fruition.

At this stage of the war, Indians were facing financial difficulties.[28] Revenues and tax collection were a key form of support. Realising that the Raja of Charkhari was loyal to the English, Tatya attempted to negotiate with him including payment of taxes. Raja Ratan Singh of Charkhari played along asking for more paperwork and documents with Tatya's signatures, but had no real intentions of cooperating.[29]

Starting early January of 1858, many letters were written to the Raja of Charkhari who had chosen to side with the English. Tatya was attempting to find a way to bring him on the Indian side, and to minimise bloodshed in what would be a 'civil battle'. Unfortunately, all his actions indicated that any delay in acting could weaken Bundelkhand. Tatya had attempted to convince the Raja, but early financial negotiations with Ratan Singh had failed.[30] War with a local chief was inevitable.

This was a battle that Tatya did not desire; yet allowing Ratan Singh's behaviour to stand without any response would have had a devastating effect on the war and would have sent a wrong signal to other 'hesitant hedgers'. To make matters more difficult for Tatya, his troops, comprised companies from different forces, and were reluctant to fight this war against Ratan Singh. Moreover, Tatya's financial situation was getting worse and his army had to go without pay for weeks. Tatya's frustrations show in a letter he wrote to Nana Saheb on 31 January 1858.

> The task of capturing this fort is difficult considering that the place is hilly and I have only a small body of men with me. Unfortunately, the Raja does not wish to be on our side, and he relies on the strength of the English.
>
> The sepoys boast very much now, but in time of difficulty, they might desert us, as they did the day before yesterday. God does whatever is good. Please send the Afghani soldiers as reinforcements, as some of the recruits here have deserted. Additionally, I will also need one hundred pieces of cloth that could provide incentives to our soldiers here. We are also awaiting the karinda and the munitions that I had written to you earlier.[31]

English intelligence reports confirm the situation:

> 30 January—Banda and Hamirpur remained in Indian hands. In Hamirpur a battle was imminent between the Rajah of Chirkari's troops and some of the Gwalior Contingent. The latter however fell out with Tantia Tope, their leader, so the battle was deferred.[32]

This is consistent with Tatya's report that some soldiers had deserted him; the strains of economic hardships were showing. Over the next ten odd months, Tatya's struggle against the English had one common theme—the need for funds to sustain the war momentum.

The battle at Charkhari was important for two reasons, the first reason was to demonstrate strength, and second was to strengthen the finances. The idea was not retribution. In order to minimise losses on both sides, Tatya attempted to convince the officers in the Raja of Charkhari's army to defect. He asked the officers of the Gwalior contingent who were with him to contact the officers at Charkhari directly.[33]

Tatya was a civilian, who over a short period had become the de facto commander-in-chief of the forces. He had assembled an army that had never fought together as a unit before. Some soldiers were from the Gwalior Contingent, some were troops that served the Raja of Banpur and more. Tatya's participatory style of management is visible in another report he made to Nana Saheb on 10 February 1858.

> The troops here at variance with each other. Some say that the fort should be stormed, and others suggest that 'since the Rajah solicits our protection by putting a straw between his teeth', we will not storm the fort. Considering the situation, I shall first attempt to make them unanimous, and then write to you on a course of action.[34]

While Tatya allowed the soldiers to reach a consensus, he also considered disciplinary action against any soldier who he thought might not follow through.[35]

At this time in early February 1858, Nana Saheb still in the northern territories was attempting to take control of the north Doab area that Campbell had 'cleared' in his December campaign. While Tatya was managing the situation in Charkhari, he continued to leverage the Indian strength in Kalpi and towns near the right bank of Yamuna to support Indian attempts to take back lost areas in the Doab region. In the same letter, he wrote to Nana:

> I have learnt whatever you have written regarding Lucknow. As you have stated that our troops will march on Etawah, and that the troops of the Chiefs of Bareilly are coming to Farrukhabad. I will therefore assist their followers in crossing the river at Jagamanpur Ghat. For this, I will depute Niranjan Singh, Rana Mahinder Singh who are here, and Raja Roop Singh with two companies of troops, a gun and Sowars.[36]

Although the impending battle in Charkhari was a distraction, Tatya was able to maintain a mobile central command, and continued to exert an active role in Bundelkhand's defence. Hundreds of letters written in Bundeli and Urdu were all written to and by Tatya in a short two to four week period of

February and March 1858. Tatya's lines of communication were very effective and reveal a strong intelligence network. This unique structure allowed him to be at the battlefront and yet direct operations in other locations.

Tatya sent missives to various officers defending Bundelkhand to prepare for the English onslaught. As waves of English armies started marching into Bundelkhand, the ferries were being guarded to restrict the movement of the English forces across the many rivers.[37] As the siege of the fort of Charkhari was underway, Tatya was directing and checking the progress of the English in other parts. Tatya coordinated the efforts of the armies of the Raja of Shahgarh and Banpur to move towards Tehri where the English had gained strength.[38]

The extract of an English letter demonstrates the success of Tatya's countermoves while still engaged at Charkhari.

February 15, 1858 – Tehri

The insurgents are daily gaining ground and proceeding towards this place. Everyone here is much disheartened on account of the approaching storm which will burst on them, none here can check its progress. We are all in danger.[39]

Tatya played a key role in coordinating the activities of the various Bundeli Chiefs in the defence of Bundelkhand. In a report to Nana Saheb Tatya wrote:

...a letter dated Phalgun, Vadi 9, 1914 (February 7, 1858) received from Jhansi states the English have advanced as far as Chanderi, from which place they are coming in this direction. I have deputed, Raja Bhau of Sikandara. He will sound the disposition of the people therefore. Proper arrangements should be made for the reception of the person that Raja Bhau conducts for this place.

I have sent ten guns under the charge of Vaman Rao Joshi. The carriages for those guns need repair. Please issue the orders for their repairs.[40]

While coordinating various activities across Bundelkhand and assisting Nana Saheb's plans for the Doab, Tatya patiently awaited a breakthrough at Charkhari.

Tatya's patience paid off. After over four weeks of restraint, on 1 March 1858, the town of Charkhari came under Tatya's control. This was largely achieved through negotiations with key officers and civilian administrators of Charkhari, whose loyalties lay with the cause of freedom. The English assistant magistrate, J.H. Carne on duty at Charkhari in his letter dated 4 March, reported the following to the secretary to the governor general:

> The city was taken through the treachery of a Thakoor named Jujhar Singh. He had a large band of men who occupied one of the most important defensive posts. One the approach of their assailants they fled without offering any resistance and are now in the ranks of the enemy. This opening gave the rebels the entry into the city.
>
> Having become masters of this position, they were enabled to make a diversion in favour of another party where attacking its neighboring position, by taking them in the right flank and rear.[41]

The success at Charkhari yielded important material benefits as well. These included elephants, horses with their trappings, carriages, palanquins, conveyances, camels and bullocks, some ordinances and money. This was critical for a campaign struggling with finances.[42]

The defection of the troops loyal to Ratan Singh continued after the town was under Indian control.[43] Even his old servants, men whose ancestors had served his house for two to three generations left him and joined Tatya Tope.[44] Ratan Singh himself was holed up inside the fort. The soldiers, who had not defected, were 'morose, irritable and bluntly declining to fight'. They refused to undertake routine duties of guard and watch. Recognising that he had very little chance for defending himself any further, the Raja was forced to negotiate.[45]

Ratan Singh's 'waffling' was influenced by the English agent who was at Charkhari. Shortly after gaining victory at Charkhari, Tatya wanted to hand over the reigns of Charkhari to a senior officer:

> Come immediately on receiving this; make no delay; you will see all from Punjab Singh's letter. Prevent the agent from communicating with the Rajah.[46]

By the second week of March, the Charkhari affair was settled. The Raja of Charkhari surrendered, and paid three lakh rupees as settlement.[47] Additionally, the treasury that the English were working hard to protect fell into Indian hands. Another letter by an Indian officer summarises the situation:

> The Rewa force is going to Panna and Tatya Tope and the Subadar and all of us are going there. The sepoys are all satisfied; the goras only are the enemies. The Raja of Charkhari affair is settled; he has paid 3 lakhs of rupees and we have besides lakhs worth of treasure of all kinds. The Raja has been deceived by the 'saheb' and by the belief of the advance of an British force.[48]

The 'saheb' that was referred to in the letter was English assistant magistrate, J.H. Carne on duty at Charkhari. Based on the letters that Carne wrote to the English command and to Robert Hamilton, it is unlikely that he intended to deceive Ratan Singh. Apparently, Robert Hamilton did give a direct order to Hugh Rose to relieve Charkhari, just as he had laid siege to Jhansi. As we shall see later, Hugh Rose disobeyed. He did not want the defenders of Jhansi to score a moral victory. Hamilton claims that he took upon himself the responsibility of 'proceeding with the operations against Jhansi'.[49]

Why was Jhansi so important that Hugh Rose disobeyed a direct order from his commander-in-chief? Was it the importance of Jhansi or was it Rani Laksmibai's head? Was there a monetary reward associated with Jhansi that played as an incentive for these two men to battle for the 'credit'?

RIBBONS, REWARDS, RAPE, RAVAGE AND ROSE

In January of 1858, Hugh Rose began his central Indian campaign and the quest for the capture of Rani Lakshmi Bai, the woman who had 'deceived' the English. He continued to follow the English pattern of plunder, pillage and terror, and brought England to the doorstep of victory in Central India. In the repeat of a pattern that was followed in many other places by the English, Rose also made a personal fortune from the looting of Jhansi and other rich provinces of central India.

While Rose was indeed 'successful', after the war ended, England never gave Rose any part of the 'prize money'. While there is no official record of the details of the 'prize money' at stake, Rose did take legal recourse when he was denied his due. Was this 'prize' for delivering Rani Lakshmibai's head—a mission in which Rose could not deliver?

This legal 'quibble' was about getting his share of this prize money, which he claimed was in thousands of pounds. Despite all the 'unofficial' loot from his campaign, he wanted his share of the 'official' booty. Rose, in the true spirit of the vrijbuiters, wanted a bigger piece of the pie. All he had received was a 'medal with a clasp, the thanks of both Houses of Parliament, and the regimental colonelcy of the 45th Foot'. Rose's legal claim was that depriving him of the prize had 'cost' him a 'personal loss' of £30,000.[50] Rose had served England at a young age, earning his first ribbons, while helping England put down the 'Ribbon Outrages', in one of Ireland's long struggle against the English rule.[51]

Regardless of the outcome of the lawsuit, or perhaps because of it, Rose eventually found favour in the English establishment. After the war, he was first promoted to the commander-in-chief of the Bombay Army and later commander-in-chief in India.[52]

However, Rose's *real* competence exceeded these trivialities. His campaign left a trail of brutalities, cruelties, tortures, atrocities, and other inhuman acts against the Indian population. Vishnubhat Godse was a witness to these horrific events at Jhansi.[53] He was also witness to the siege and the war at Jhansi as well. His memoirs present many events at Jhansi that are contrary to what Hugh Rose and others who perpetuate his claims. Godse describes that the English soldiers went house to house looting not only all valuables, but also items such as pots and pans. Hugh Rose justified the plunder saying, 'there was hardly a house in Jhansie which did not contain some article of English plunder'.[54] Suggesting that his soldiers were simply taking back what was looted from the English at the outset of the war!

The 'standard' narrative includes Hugh Rose's march to Jhansi, the siege, followed by the battle with Tatya Tope, where his army of less than 2,000 defeated Tatya's army of 20,000, followed by the Rani's 'escape'. The following chapter deconstructs the myth from the reality of events that took place at Jhansi in late March and early April of 1858 and recollects the horrors that Sir Hugh Rose and Sir Robert Hamilton unleashed on the people of Jhansi after it had fallen into their hands.

Chapter 14

RECONSTRUCTING JHANSI

CHARKHARI, JHANSI AND THE RANI'S HEAD

The three-week period from late March to early April 1858, witnessed a fierce contest between Tatya Tope and Hugh Rose. In this contest, Hugh Rose was attempting to secure three 'prizes' while Tatya Tope attempted to defend and protect them. Two of them were the fortified towns of Charkhari and Jhansi, and the third, was Rani Lakshmibai. It is hard to say what price the English had on the Rani's head, but it must have been high enough for Hugh Rose to disobey a direct order from his commander-in-chief. Of these three, Rose had to settle for only the town of Jhansi. As we analyse later in the chapter, Tatya not only successfully held Charkhari, he also enabled Lakshmibai's successful breakout, right under Rose's nose.

There are major gaps and contradictions even in the English narrative of the events of Jhansi. The source of these gaps is the discrepancies between the reports made by Robert Hamilton and Hugh Rose. T. Rice Holmes, in his book on this subject, attempts to reconcile these gaps.[1] He explains them as caused possibly by lapses in memory of these men, or mistakes in interpretation, or defending accusations of 'inventions' by one man or the other. Additionally there are some numerical inconsistencies between what Hugh Rose claimed and other sources. The numbers aside, the biggest embarrassment to Rose and Hamilton was that Lakshmibai was able to break out of the siege, right under their nose. Considering that the entire idea of a siege is to prevent ingress and egress, Rani's 'egress' with hundreds of *Vilayati* infantry and cavalry² had to have created a major stir amongst the English authorities, which possibly led to the 'legal quibbles', 'lapses in memory', and accusations of 'inventions'. Not only are there inconsistencies between the English narratives, Vishnubhat Godse's account contradicts the English versions significantly. When these accounts are viewed objectively, there are many logical questions that remain unanswered. Few historians have attempted to reconcile these disparities.

After all, if Jhansi was such an open and shut case of victory, why were there lawsuits about non-payment of prize money and accusations flying around about the integrity of these knighted men? The simplest explanation for the failure to reconcile the gaps of the events at Jhansi was the attempt by these men to whitewash the success of Tatya's operation that engineered Rani Lakshmibai's breakout. A breakout that was highly embarrassing considering that both Rose and Hamilton were involved. Tatya was successful in an operation designed to rescue Lakshmibai and protect her from the certainty of a horrifying torture and dishonourable death she would have faced, had she fallen into English hands.

Our analysis also reveals that there are simpler explanations that can reconcile the rather tall claim by Hugh Rose that his army of 2,000 defeated Tatya's army of 25,000. Prior to analysing that battle, and other events at Jhansi, consider the events that took place in and around Jhansi in the middle of March in 1858.

Very little is known about the role of Hamilton at Jhansi, other than that he was in the area³ and his claim that he took upon himself the responsibility of 'proceeding with the operations against Jhansi'.⁴

While the possession of Jhansi was reasonably important, Rani Lakshmibai herself was clearly the prize. Godse's account relates the initial stages of the siege.

An English 'Saheb', (either Rose or Hamilton) arrived about four miles from Jhansi and sent a letter to be delivered to Lakshmibai. The letter asked her to personally come and meet him. She was to arrive with seven other people specified in the letter. She was not to bring anyone else, and arrive without weapons of any kind.⁵

The genocide perpetrated against Indian civilians including innocent women and children, and other 'civilised' behaviour was already on display during the war. For the English the Rani was far from being 'innocent'. Lakshmibai knew better than to surrender herself to the English, so she sent a reply with her ambassadors, maintaining that she did not intend to fight the English. There are three versions of the story of how Hamilton or Rose responded. Godse's version indicates that the 'Saheb' crushed the letter and immediate set out for the plans for the siege. An English newspaper account reported the following of a speech made by an Englishman in London on 11 May 1858.

> The Ranee of Jhansi, an independent sovereign, dispatched two ambassadors to the British camp to negotiate terms of peace. How were they received? They were HANGED [sic].[6]

Hamilton, for obvious reasons, in his own version, refuted these accusations, saying,

> ...the Ranee of Jhansi sent no ambassadors to me or to the Camp or the Central India Field Force; therefore no such persons were hanged.[7]

Obviously, it was Sir Hamilton's story that made the history books.

After Charkhari came into Tatya Tope's hands, his intelligence reported that Hugh Rose, after his troops having taken Chanderi on 17 March, might proceed to Charkhari to wrest it out of Tatya's control.[8] Hugh Rose arrived at a place called Simrawari, halfway between Babina and Jhansi, around 20 March 1858.[9] Robert Hamilton orders for Hugh Rose were to march towards Charkhari, however, Rose disobeyed the order and continued with his siege of Jhansi. With Charkhari secure in Indian hands, Tatya Tope was now free to make the march in the direction of Jhansi.

Jhansi was under siege on 21 March.

BESIEGED

The following is the description of the fort of Jhansi in the words of Hugh Rose:

It stands on an elevated rock, rising out of a plain, and commands the city, and surrounding country; it is built of excellent and most massive masonry. The Fort is difficult to breach, because, composed of granite; its walls vary in thickness from sixteen to twenty feet. The Fort has extensive and elaborate outworks of the same solid construction, with front and flanking embrasures for Artillery fire, and loop-holes, of which, in some places, there were five, tiers, for musketry. Guns placed on the high towers of the Fort commanded the country all around.

The fortress is surrounded by the city of Jhansie on all sides, except the West and part of the South face.

The steepness of the rock protects the West, the fortified city wall with bastions springing from the centre of its South face, running South, and ending in a high mound or mamelon, protects by a flanking fire its South face. The mound was fortified by a strong circular bastion for 6 Guns, round part of which was drawn a ditch 12 feet deep and 15 feet broad of solid masonry. Quantities of men were always at work in the mound.

The city of Jhansie is about 4 1/2 miles in circumference, and is surrounded by a fortified and massive wall, from 8 to 12 feet thick, and varying in height from 18 to 30 feet, with numerous flanking bastions armed as batteries with ordnance, and loop holes, with a banquette for Infantry.[10]

There are six primary roads to Jhansi. To the east was the road to Baragaon that went on towards Kalpi. Another eastward road but south of the Kalpi road was the road towards Barua Sagar, which led towards the eastern towns of Mau Ranipur and Charkhari. The other roads led to Babina to the south, Shivpuri to the west, and Datia and Bhander to the north.

This strong fort of Jhansi was vulnerable only to the south. However, the fortifications of the city were designed in a way to compensate for this vulnerability, and were the strongest to the south. Rose set up his attack force to the south of the city and established seven flying Camps of Cavalry along the primary roads to Jhansi. These camps were meant to prevent anyone from either entering or leaving Jhansi. Hugh Rose describes these Camps of Cavalry in his report as follows:

These Camps detached to the front outposts and videttes (mounted sentinels), which watched and prevented all issue from the city, day and night; each Camp, on any attempt being made to force its line, was to call on the others for help. I gave directions also that the road from the city should be obstructed by trenches and abattis (barriers made out of sharpened trees).[11]

The siege was well planned, elaborate and seemingly unbreakable. The stakes were high with Sir Hamilton and Sir Rose, both wanting to claim the prize on the Rani's head.

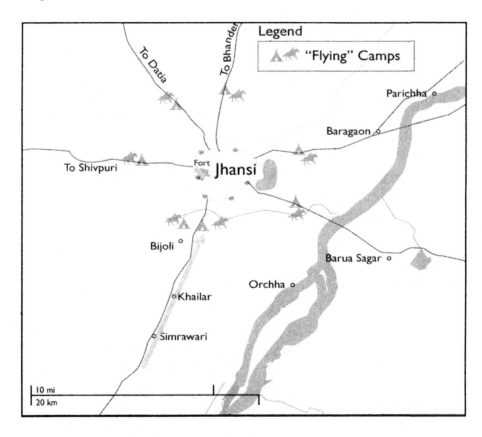

Figure 28: Siege of Jhansi–Situation

Godse was amongst the civilians who were under siege at Jhansi. His narrative is the best description of the siege from an inside vantage point. In the beginning, the English were attempting to identify locations around the fort where they could position their guns. This took two days and many English soldiers were killed in the process.

It started with the English Saheb arriving to the south of Jhansi and setting up camp far away from the fort. That evening I climbed over to the rampart to look. There were thousands of tents all over with many campfires being lit all around. However, there were not too many people to occupy all these tents. Later we noticed that thousands of whites began to appear to the north and to the west. All together, there must have been about 60,000 English soldiers and 30,000-35,000 camp followers.

The following day the English started marching closer to the city. At this point Baisaheb (Lakshmibai) ordered all the gunners to be ready. All the ramparts on the fort were ready for to fire the guns. The English cavalry made an approach to the west. Baisaheb ordered to light up the cannons. A few English were killed in this response. Now the English were making an approach on all sides and our guns were firing on all sides. Many English soldiers were being killed in this firing. This went on for two days, when many more English soldiers were killed.[12]

For the next few days, guns were going off on both sides. Godse's own account reveals a stressful period for the civilians who had taken refuge in the fort. The eight day of the siege was 30 March 1858 and Tatya Tope had arrived and camped at Barua Sagar, three miles from the Betwa River to the east of Jhansi.[13]

THE NUMBERS' GAME

After settling the Charkhari affair, Tatya accompanied by only three regiments of the Gwalior contingent, numbering about 2,000 headed towards Jhansi.[14] On 19 March, he was at Kulpahar[15] and by 25 March at Jaitpur.[16] Tatya Tope intended to march from Jaitpur, camp between Churwari and Naya Gaon (a small village), and then head to Mau Ranipur, which is about 30 miles east of Jhansi.[17] Tatya's primary force during the siege at Charkhari was the Gwalior contingent aided by a local army and militia recruits. This local army was left behind to defend Charkhari.

While camping at Jaitpur, Rao Saheb who was Nana Saheb's nephew came down from Kalpi with some cavalry. The intent of this meeting between Rao Saheb and Tatya is unknown, but he returned to Kalpi shortly afterwards the same route.[18] It is likely that he arrived to reinforce Tatya with logistical and possibly monetary support and the cavalry that Tatya used in a later operation.[19] This cavalry unit was the Afghani soldiers who were referred to as the *Vilayati* army. Vishnubhat Godse's account refers to these Vilayati troops as having served the Rani for a long time.[20] Rani Lakshmibai's personal escort also comprised these Vilayati troops, who considered their primary responsibility as Lakshmibai's protection. Their presence in Kalpi and other locations indicate that the Vilayatis were a contingent that was serving in more than one location, split to support other operations, including Kalpi. Tatya is likely to have asked Kalpi for these units of the Vilayatis as reinforcements to be sent into the fort of Jhansi.

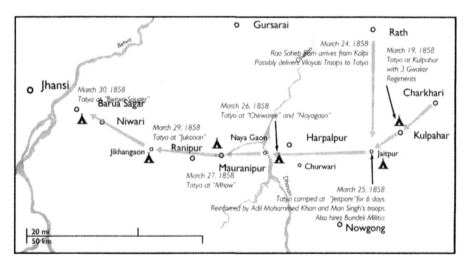

Figure 29: March from Charkhari to Jhansi

These Vilayatis, as we analyse later, would be the key to Rani's breakout from Jhansi.

The actual strength of Tatya's force that arrived at Jhansi has been a matter of debate. There are varying estimates of the strength of Tatya's army that were reported by English intelligence abstracts.[21] Consider the collection of following references:

The killadar of Orchha wrote this morning, that the rebels were reported to have advanced from Burwa Sauger; their number is reported to be about 20,000 men.[22]

The Tantia has under him about 25,000 men, among these there are about 2,000 mutinous sepoys.[23]

...of the 27,000 men that compose this mutinous force, only the sepoys might offer resistance to the British force. The rest are not able to cope with the English.[24]

Vishnubhat Godse, who was present in Jhansi during the siege, placed the number of troops with Tatya at about 15,000.[25]

Tatya had three regiments, 27 guns, about 200 of Banpur Raja's men with another body of men commanded by Rao Sahib, Nana's nephew (the *Vilayati* soldiers).[26]

The most concise report was from Captain Pinkney who concluded that, He (Tatya) was accompanied by the Rajah of Banpore and other leading rebels and his force consisted of 27 guns, 2,000 mutineers, 6,000-7,000 Bundelas and Villayaties, and a large body of Cavalry.[27]

The total strength of the Raja Mardan Singh of Banpur was estimated at about 1,000 and 2 elephants. He arrived at Mau Ranipur on 14 March 1858.[28]

Many mutineers from other broken forces joined them, and Tantia Topee led ten thousand men, with twenty guns, to relieve Jhansi.[29]

From the Urdu and Bundeli letters discovered, the references to a 'bundelu fauz' typically referred to an army of untrained Bundeli militiamen. In what would become a pattern later in the next phase of the war was Tatya's ability to inspire civilians to take up arms. He was able to raise an armed militia in a short time. Tatya Tope was in Kulpahar and Jaitpur for about a week before he moved on. What seems very plausible is that he used that time to enroll the few thousand of militia in his army for his campaign on Jhansi.

There is evidence of Tatya raising such an army prior to the battle of Charkhari. Officer Deena Deen Shukla was decorated for valour in an earlier battle, and was given the authority to help raise an army in a short time. In this attempt, Chattra Singh raised a large army and then made a request for ammunition and trained soldiers possibly to train the new recruits.[30] Tatya's week-long halt in the area, in all likelihood was for the purpose of recruiting and training the local militia.

Tatya's primary trained armies were the three Gwalior infantry regiments numbered at 2,000, the Vilayati and other cavalry units probably numbering about 1,000 and Vilayati infantry, probably numbering around 1,000. This would place his total strength of trained soldiers at about 4,000. In addition, he was accompanied by 6,000 militiamen and later joined by the Raja of Banpur, whose army according to English intelligence reports numbered about 1,000. This places the total strength including trained soldiers and the militia at around 11,000. What would explain the additional 5,000 to 17,000 that were reported? It is possibly that these were exaggerations, or they were likely to be the camp followers or 'less adventurous' militiamen who were willing to be part of the army—who were brand new recruits from Jaitpur or Mau Ranipur, possibly recruited solely for this operation.

Tatya's Army for Jhansi		
Training	Composition	Numerical Estimate
Trained Infantry	Gwalior Contingent	2,000
	Vilayati (Afghani) Regiment	1,000
Cavalry	Vilayati + others	1,000
Untrained Infantry	Bundeli Militia New Recruits	4,000-6,000
Other	Raja of Banpur's Army	1,000
Total Army		9,000-11,000
Camp Followers—(Non-Combatants)		10,000-15,000

Typically, a besieging army would require about two to three times the number of soldiers of the besieged forces to hold a siege and prevent the besieged army from any attempts to sally out. Rose was able to achieve this by creating a strong 'flying Cavalry Camps' with support from the infantry. While the English routinely claim smaller numbers than existed, Rose's army was augmented by the troops of Hamilton. If Tatya had any chance of relieving Jhansi, his relieving force would need to be well trained and stronger than Rose and Hamilton's, in order to be able to relieve Jhansi.

How many troops did Rose and Hamilton really have? English narratives, consistent with a pattern of understating their strengths, place their strength in the low thousands. The only Indian point of view is from Vishnubhat Godse. He writes: 'Altogether the English army totalled about 60,000 with additional 30,000-35,000 camp followers'.[31] Godse's estimate carries some weight considering that he was in Jhansi during the entire period of the siege and after the fall of Jhansi as well. However, as with the English estimates of Indian strength, it is very likely that Godse was also mistaking the camp followers as soldiers. While Godse does provide a separate number for the camp followers, it is significantly lesser than a typical ratio of the soldiers to camp followers that the English army was using. From Godse's account, if we assume that the total English presence, *including camp followers*, was between 60,000-90,000, and assuming that the English had five camp followers for every soldier, then we can calculate the strength of the English army besieging Jhansi at about 10,000-15,000. This number is consistent with the size, scale and the feasibility of the total operation.

Rose + Hamilton's Army at Jhansi		
Type	Vishnubhat Godse's Estimate	Author's Estimate
Infantry + Cavalry	60,000	10,000-15,000
Camp Followers	30,000-35,000	30,000-35,000

The total forces that largely included untrained soldiers and militia, available to Rani Lakshmibai were about 3,000 to 4,000. This included a regiment that was led by Dulaji Singh referred in Godse's account. This also seems consistent with the besieging force that Rose had to hold the siege. Most of this army was defending the city of Jhansi. Additionally Rani Lakshmibai had some Vilayati soldiers by her side, who would have fiercely taken on the enemies if she had to break out, however, they were insufficient in number for what would have been a very difficult operation.

With only four full infantry regiments of trained soldiers numbering 3,000, Tatya was not in any real position to relieve Jhansi. However, he could attempt to assist Rani Lakshmibai to sally-out, by reinforcing her with the toughest and loyal guards. However, reinforcing meant that they had to get past the flying camps to ingress into the fort.

It is likely that by padding his core army with Bundeli militia, Tatya wanted to draw a part of Hugh Rose's army away from Jhansi in advance to allow for an important countermove.

While Tatya would unsuccessfully attempt to relieve Jhansi, an important secondary goal of the operation was to deliver the Afghani Vilayati troops to Rani Lakshmibai and enable her breakout.

'BUNDELI' DECOY, 'VILAYATI' DELIVERY

On 1 April 1858, at around 6.00 am, Tatya's forces started firing the guns near Barua Sagar.[32] Amongst the trained men that Tatya had was the 2,000 or so Gwalior Contingent. The untrained Bundela militia was either a decoy or a second line that would attempt to find a weakness in Rose's lines.

Tatya had positioned his first line, in all likelihood the Gwalior Contingent. With a weak hand in terms of the numerically strong but untrained Bundela's Tatya could not risk placing the Bundela's directly behind the Gwalior Contingent. However, in order to draw Rose's force away from the fort and force a consolidation of some of Rose's flying camps, Tatya arranged his first line to project a massive offensive operation. Many of the eighteen guns captured from Charkhari, were positioned along this line of attack. It was important for Rose to defend what he *perceived* was a massive attack on his front line. Believing that Tatya Tope's primary goal was the relief of Jhansi, Rose moved a large body of his troops in this direction. Rose writes:

> The enemy had taken up an excellent position, a little in rear of a rising ground, which made it difficult to bring an effective fire on him. I ordered my front line of infantry to lie down, the troop of Horse Artillery to take ground diagonally to the right, and enfilade the enemy's left flank... Serious combats occurred between the pursuing Cavalry and the fugitives, who, singly or standing back to back, always took up, like most Indians the best position the ground admitted, and fought with desperation, which I have described on other occasions. One body

wedged themselves so dexterously into the banks of the nullah, that neither musketry nor artillery fire, would destroy them...[33]

As the battle continued, Rose was facing strong resistance, he expected that Tatya's second line was right behind, and if the English did not push forward, the momentum would shift to Tatya's army. Therefore, he ordered his officer and his men to make a charge, which they did, and bayoneted some of the skirmishers on the first line.[34] Buoyed by their early success, but still wary, the English expected to find resistance from Tatya's second line.

However, there was no second line right behind the first.

Surprised and confused, the only explanation for the missing second line that Rose could offer was, 'the second line of rebels, which, by a singular arrangement of the rebel, General Tantia Topee, must have been three miles of his first line'.[35]

Three miles behind! What was Tatya's plan? We infer that Tatya was hoping that his second line, though composed untrained Bundeli militia, would be able to charge through to relieve Jhansi. Whether or not they succeeded, they would serve an important secondary goal, that of being a diversion.

What Tatya had achieved was to draw Rose's army away from Jhansi by positioning a large amount of guns on his front and only line, creating an

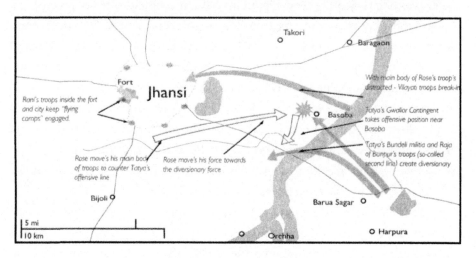

Figure 30: Diversion and Delivery

illusion of a massive offensive, thus forcing Rose's main body in this direction. This first line, occupied the English with a prolonged offensive, while a large body of Tatya's army, comprised the Bundeli militia, was purposefully marching in a different direction. The bravery of Tatya's vanguard, comprised the Gwalior Contingent, is particularly noteworthy, considering that they were fighting knowing well that they had no line of defence to fall back, risking annihilation when the reality was discovered.

Still confused, only after having 'successfully' charged Tatya's first line, and claiming victory, did Rose notice a 'cloud of dust about a mile and half to the right'.[36]

As Tatya's first line fell back, Tatya ordered a second body, the Raja of Banpur's men with the Bundeli militia, to march in a southwestern direction, possibly parallel to the Betwa. This was to divert the English away from his first line, who would have faced certain death. Captain Pinkney described this as 'a very large body of the enemy which had separated from Tatya's main body....' The likely composition of this 'large body' was the Bundeli militiamen that Tatya had recruited along with Raja of Banpur's men.

This was the 'cloud of dust' that Rose had witnessed. Tatya was hoping that this body would be able to make a charge towards the Fort. Expectedly, Rose ordered his 'whole force' to go in 'immediate pursuit....'[37]

While all this action was going on to the east of Jhansi, near Basoba, Jhansi itself was not very quiet. Few historians have attempted to really reconstruct what happened by looking past the fog of misinformation. Few people ask some very pertinent questions, which attempt to reconstruct the events at Jhansi. Allen Copsey, a descendant of a British soldier who fought during the War, has maintained a well-researched website on Rani Lakshmibai; is amongst the few who makes an attempt. He poses a logical question, 'as to why Lakshmibai did not order a sally from the fort and attack the weakened British besiegers?' His explanation is that 'Rose also took the precaution of withdrawing the forces to meet Tope under cover of darkness. The defenders of Jhansi may not have even realised they had gone'.[38]

Many narratives seem to echo similar explanations, but it contradicts Captain Pinkney's account. In his report, he writes: 'during the fight the rebel Garrison of Jhansie manned the walls and kept up rapid fire from all their guns....'[39] Clearly, the Jhansi fort was on top of the situation. Godse also describes that there were eyes in Jhansi who were witnessing the events with interest through telescopes.[40]

While Tatya's primary goal was to relieve Jhansi, it was a difficult one. With that knowledge Tatya had worked towards a secondary goal. The two bodies of troops, though unsuccessful in defeating Rose's force, served as decoys, were engaging the main body of Rose's troops that were drawn away from Jhansi. What is interesting in the narratives is that English intelligence reports the presence of the Vilayati soldiers in Tatya's campaign on Jhansi, who joined him in Jaitpur; there is no mention of these Vilayatis later, except in a passing reference to their presence inside Jhansi, and later at Konch accompanying Lakshmibai.[41]

In addition, Godse mentions in detail of the street fighting and Rani's breakout later, that had great numbers of Vilayatis, over 1,000, fighting the battle. While the Rani did have a small number of Afghani soldiers as bodyguards, they certainly did not number in the thousands and more that Godse describes during her breakout. How did they suddenly appear on the scene inside Jhansi's fort?[42]

We argue that Tatya's Tope's operation, though unsuccessful in the attempt to relieve Jhansi, had successfully spread Rose's forces thin. The Vilayatis had managed to find a weakness and managed to break through Rose's siege, to deliver the Afghani Vilayati soldiers to Rani Lakshmibai. Could Lakshmibai have broken out during the offensive? It would have been possible if the movements inside the forts were coordinated with Tatya Tope, however, the siege had completely cut off communication with the outside. In fact, the constant firing of guns from the fort that Pinkney reports, kept Rose's flying camps occupied, and allowed the Vilayatis to find a point of weak resistance to break in.

After the operation was completed, Tatya's army departed in two bodies—one towards Kalpi and another for Mau-Ranipur.[43] The Gwalior Contingent along with Tatya Tope probably went in the direction of Kalpi, and the Bundeli militia, hired specifically for this campaign, probably returned to their homes near Ranipur and Jaitpur. Though Jhansi remained in Rose's hands, they had assisted Tatya and helped deliver Rani a breakout force.

Tatya's secondary goal was successful, and now the Vilayatis had to demonstrate their mettle to engineer Lakshmibai's breakout from Jhansi.

ROSE'S NOSE AND FORT 'ETCETERA'

Rani Lakshmibai has become an icon of bravery in modern India. Many semi-fictional stories and poems have been written about her courage and bravery. Most of these stories depict her 'escaping' Jhansi on her horse after successfully making a near impossible jump from the Jhansi fort. However, contrary to what you expect from romanticised stories and poems, they actually do disservice to her real heroism. They trivialise the enormity of the task ahead, which was to break out through one of the toughest sieges. A task that was far more risky than jumping off with her horse and her son, and disappearing into the night.[44]

Shortly after the arrival of the Vilayati reinforcements, Rani Lakshmibai continued to defend Jhansi for another day, but the English, true to their competence, were able to breach the walls using human shields.[45] Jhansi was falling, and Lakshmibai had to do what she could to protect herself from the wrath of the English. Tatya Tope had done his job and delivered her the troops who were willing to give their lives for her protection. Two days after Tatya's successful delivery of the Vilayati soldiers, Rani Lakshmibai made a decision to breakout of Jhansi.

It was not going to be easy. On 3 April, a party of 400 soldiers, possibly escorting some important personnel, 'broke out of the town and tried to make off in a northwest direction, but they were followed by Infantry, Cavalry and Artillery, surrounded on a hill and all killed'.[46]

Rose and Hamilton were dead serious when they had proclaimed that no one would leave Jhansi alive.

On the night of 4 April, Lakshmibai decided to break out. Godse writes:

> She emptied her treasury, her personal ornaments, and loaded all that on an elephant, which was in the centre. Accompanied by an army of 1,500 *Vilayati* soldiers, Rani Lakshmibai marched down from the fort and entered the town of Jhansi. This is where she met stiff resistance. In the bloody battle that ensued, 400-500 *Vilayati* soldiers died along with 700-800 English soldiers. Left with about a thousand *Vilayati* soldiers, Lakshmibai broke out of the town.'[47]

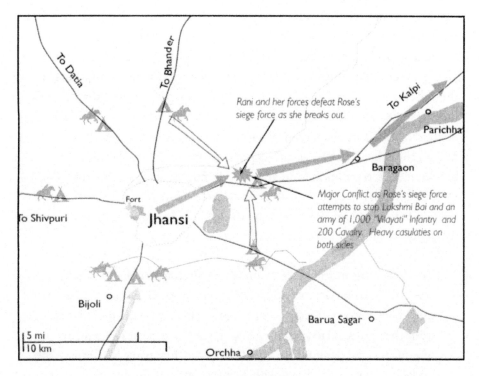

To Datia

To Bhander

To Kalpi

Rani and her forces defeat Rose's siege force as she breaks out.

Parichha

Baragaon

To Shivpuri

Fort

Jhansi

Major Conflict as Rose's siege force attempts to stop Lakshmi Bai and an army of 1,000 "Vilayati" Infantry and 200 Cavalry. Heavy casulaties on both sides

Bijoli

5 mi

10 km

Barua Sagar

Orchha

Figure 31: Break Out!

Knowing well the fate of the 400 who were captured and killed the day before, Lakshmibai and her Afghani escort set out to achieve the impossible. Godse continues:

> Baisaheb (Lakshmibai) was mounted on a white horse, wearing men's clothing, shoes and an armour, weapons and a sword. Her twelve-year-old son was behind her, on the same horse, as she shouted, 'Jai Shankar,' and rode out along with her remaining *Vilayati*, escort of about a thousand Vilayati infantry and about two hundred sowars. As she broke through the English attacking siege force, she and her soldiers killed many English who attempted to stop them. Many soldiers shielding her were killed in the fighting, as she rode towards Kalpi...

Lakshmibai, with her Vilayati escort, had successfully fought and broken out of one of the toughest and bloodiest siege. Manu was saved from a fate that could have been far worse than death.

This news was devastating for Rose and Hamilton, who had staked their reputations on the capture of the Rani.

Godse and Rose's account directly contradict each other. One of the two men either is mistaken, or is prevaricating. Godse is very clear about the description of the battle and Lakshmibai's preparation for it. There is little chance that he was mistaken about Rani's breakout. Could he have deliberately lied in his narrative? Godse had no real motive. However, Rose had all the reason in the world to present this as an escape rather than as a breakout. His reputation, and that of Hamilton, was on the line. The two men simply wrote a version that was convenient.

Predictably, Hugh Rose sought to distance himself from the failure of his army to prevent Lakshmibai's breakout, writing:

> The following morning, a wounded Mahratta retainer of the Ranee was sent in to me from Captain Abbott's Flying Camp. He stated that the Ranee, accompanied by 300 Vilaities and 25 Sowars, fled that night from the fort and that after leaving it, they had been headed back by one of the picquets where the Ranee and her party separated, she herself taking to the right with a few sowars in the direction of her intended flight to Bandiri. The observatory also telegraphed 'Enemy Escaping to the North-East'.[48]

Despite knowing all the details of her so-called 'escape', for obvious reasons the English understated the success of Rani's breakout. Captain Pinkney writes:

> On the night of the 4th the Ranee and a large body of rebels made a dash out of the Fort, but were driven back from the direction, they first took; they then changed their course and got through the picket towards Bhander; they were followed up by Lieutenant Dowker, Madras Army of the Hydrabad Contingent with a small body of Cavalry who inflicted some loss on them, but the Ranee got off although her Fort, etc., were captured.[49]

Pinkney does not acknowledge the battle that Godse describes. A hard-fought battle where hundreds died on both sides. The English only mention the phrase 'driven back...' Pinkney also claims that they 'got through the picket....' Did hundreds of infantrymen and sowars, after 'changing course', just disappear, until they 'got through' the pickets? Did the English soldiers attempt to stop them?

With the main prize gone right from under Rose's nose, for the English, the capture of the Jhansi fort was less gratifying. Rose's version, as expected, does not even acknowledge that she broke out, but simply states that she 'escaped'.

The once indomitable Fort Jhansi, without the *real* prize, had now, in the words of Captain Pinkney become, Fort 'etc....'

BUTCHERS AND SCAVENGERS

Rose's first act after the fall of Jhansi, in the words of Godse was 'Bijyan', meaning genocide.* In the town of Jhansi, all the people that could be caught, from young children to men over eighty were massacred. Women fearing rape started to jump into wells. The English started entering the houses and started demanding money, gold, pearls and jewellry. If a person was spotted, he was tortured and killed. People started leaving behind their possessions in fear or torture or death.[50]

Godse describes the scene at Jhansi after it fell into English hands in detail.

> ...that evening we looked at the town of Jhansi from the rampart. The scene sent shivers down my spine... the entire town had turned into cremation ground. Animals and people wandered the streets for want of water and food. The town was ablaze. The winds carried the flames from one house to the next...'[51]
>
> ...as some people tried to hide in the hay, the English soldiers set it on fire... as the people ran and jumped into the well to escape the bullets, the English chased them to the well... and shot them as their heads bobbed above the water...[52]

---

*Bijyan – 'Bi' – from 'vi' – Sanskrit for without and 'jana' – Sanskrit for people. Devoid of humans.

However, it is the story of Dulaji Singh that reveals the real character of English military commanders. Dulaji Singh was leading a regiment of soldiers who were guarding the town of Jhansi while holding out against the English. After he was arrested, a senior military officer (either Hamilton or Rose) ordered the young children of Dulaji Singh to be brought from his house. These children ranged from ages five to twenty years. After lining them up in front of him, they were ordered to be shot in front of his eyes. Dulaji Singh was then beheaded.[53]

Lower ranked English officers were scarcely better, but to an extent tamed by the Indian soldiers from the Madras army amongst them. Though fighting on the wrong side as mercenaries, their humanity put limits on the atrocities that the English perpetrated. Godse narrates the story of a priest called Agnihotri Baba and his family.

> It was just before sunset and Agnihotri Baba had just finished his 'hom' (prayers that included a fire). As he finished his 'puja' and stepped into the living area of his house, he saw soldiers had entered his house. The two 'white' soldiers went straight into the 'puja room' and saw a couple of straw baskets were covering something. They thought that Agnihotri Baba was hiding some treasure there. They kicked the baskets away and noticed that there were some ashes below. Suspecting that the treasure was buried beneath the ashes, they greedily put their hands inside. It turned out to be the ashes from the 'hom' and the soldiers burnt their hands.
>
> The English soldiers, flaming with anger, killed all the members of the Agnihotri family; total eleven, including women and children.[54]

What to the reader is perhaps a senseless orgy of violence was in fact an important element of the English approach to warfare. These massacres were not 'senseless' from the point of view of the English. Killing civilians was designed to be a lesson for all towns and villages to fall in line. Any implicit or explicit support to the Indian forces was targeted by violence against the civilians with the purpose of cutting of the means of sustenance.

Godse writes about how the English hunted down everyone from temples and dharmshalas and massacred them. In a part of Jhansi called Koshtipur, people were shot and slaughtered as soon as they stepped out of their houses or even dark corners. All the streets had become a cemetery. Far too many women were also shot dead and their bodies scattered on the streets. After the third day, grain was in short supply. Some people had hid it in the drainage and some buried it. People without food were starving.[55]

Rose's report presents a portrayal that is in complete contrast to what Godse writes. Sir Hugh Rose's self-proclaimed integrity and kindness are on full display as he writes about the 'humane' treatment of Indian women. It was not only the soldiers who 'treated with humanity the women and children',[56] but according to Rose, even the heavy English shelling and cannonading during the siege targeted only men. Rose writes, '…besides the damage done to the houses and buildings, the rebels acknowledge to have lost from sixty to seventy *men* a day killed'.[57] Godse writes of very expensive cannon balls that were used by the English during the attack.[58] Rose's explanation gives a possible insight as to why they were expensive. They probably were fitted with futuristic gender-recognising technology to target only men, which obviously added to the costs. Perhaps the historians have it right after all; it had to be technology that enabled the English to win the war, not their brutality.

While these comments about special technology are made in mock humour, the reality was that Indian women indeed were slaughtered. Nevertheless, Rose has an explanation, writing about an Indian man who 'endeavoured to cut his wife to pieces' before killing himself.[59] By Rose's logic, it was neither the English shelling, nor the English soldiers that killed the women of Jhansi, but the Indian men who did it.

According to Rose, not only were English cannonballs and soldiers kind to Indian women, so was Rose himself. Shortly before leaving Jhansi, Rose apparently 'gave orders'[60] to share the grain with the Indian women and children. Rose writes about a scene where his 'troops were seen sharing ration with them'.[61] Juxtaposing Godse's characterisation of Jhansi looking like a cemetery with scattered bodies of women filled with bullets and a starving population, with the picture of humanity that Rose attempts to portray is more like a scene from a horror movie than any plausible image of Jhansi after the genocide that the English had perpetrated.

More than 150 years after the war, Rose's report today stands unchallenged.

Mahasweta Devi, who wrote a dramatised reconstruction of the events at Jhansi, aptly portrays the Jhansi genocide.

> Hugh Rose had a clear definition for success, as he related later. 'After the palace was seized, the rebels started leaving the city. Not a single person was allowed to get out alive, which should speak for the success of the siege. The corpses of rebels filled the forests, gardens and roads around the city'.[62]
>
> Most of the citizens and all of the Queen's soldiers in Jhansi were killed; the streets were left thick with blood slush. Vultures darkened the skies of the city. Hugh Rose had given strict orders not to allow the Indians to perform the last rites for their dead. After 7 April when the entire city was stinking and jackals and vultures roamed greedily in search of decomposed bodies, did he grant permission for the last rites...[63]

This genocide and slaughter of innocent civilians at Jhansi was well recognised by England. The Victoria Cross is the highest British award for exhibiting valour. Seven crosses were awarded at Jhansi. Hugh Rose was knighted by the Queen. Hugh Rose, the butcher of Jhansi, became Sir Hugh Rose. Captain F.W. Pinkney writes about: 'the example made at Jhansie, will, I have no doubt, have an excellent effect in facilitating the tranquillising of Bundelcund'.[64]

TRANQUILISED BUNDELKHAND

The genocide had its desired effect. Bundelkhand was indeed 'tranquilised'. Bundeli resistance was practically broken as news of the inhuman slaughter of the residents of Jhansi spread throughout Bundelkhand and surrounding areas. The cold-blooded slaughter of Dulaji Singh and the Bundeli fighters defending Jhansi had a dampening effect on finding new recruits.

Some of the administrative officers working with Tatya Tope and Rao Saheb attempted to find new recruits from the Deccan. On 11 April 1858, a proclamation was issued to urge the civilians to support the military. With the momentum of the war shifting towards the English, finding new recruits was difficult. Infantry soldiers were paid well, about Rs 12 per month (equivalent to about Rs 4,800 per month in 2008).[65]

We hope that all those who have attained the age of between 16 years and 23 and can use swords will serve as soldiers in the regiments and thereby prosper… Those persons who wish to be appointed are enlisted in the house of Madari Lal Bakht in the vicinity of the Depot.[66]

Fearing death and a fate similar to what many at Jhansi faced, many of the chiefs who had made agreements with Nana Saheb, began to back down. The renewed Maratha-Bundela contract was falling apart. Rao Saheb sent personal letters to Bundeli chiefs as well as made a proclamation to keep them from losing their spirits. The following is an excerpt from a proclamation made on 17 April 1858 to the chiefs in the Kachhwagarh district.

Maharaja Peshwa is pleased to hear that you are ready to take the responsibility of the present undertaking. He recognises that you need a parwana from him as an assurance. His highness has expressed his great satisfaction upon getting this information. You are hereby assured that the more you will display your gallantry, on the present occasion the greater benefit will accrue to you…

…Those who will perform meritorious services will in lieu of them, obtain suitable Jagheers, situations and titles from the Sarkar.[67]

This was an attempt to motivate the chiefs with the promise of future returns. It was a difficult proposition. The finances were running low and motivation alone was not going to build the caps for muskets and carriages for the guns. Another proclamation was made to the zamindars to ask for their monetary support, in return for a promise to reduce their tax burden. There were incentives in the proclamation, but the carrots were backed by some sticks as well. This was a difficult time, when volunteers were not that forthcoming.

Be it known to all the Zamindars, Chiefs, Merchants, Khundsarees (commodity dealers) and Bankers, that whoever amongst the Zamindars shall join me, accompanied by his men with provisions for them and ammunition, will receive credit for the price of those articles in the accounts relative to the revenue of his Zamindaree, and also a remission of the whole of the revenue for two years, and afterwards of 4 annas in the rupee for 8 years; that whoever amongst the Zamindars from a feeling of regard for the English, upon whom the wrath of God has fallen for their evil intention of converting Hindoos and Muslims to Christianity, shall hesitate service to the Sarkar or shall oppose, or deserts it, or shall not procure supplies will be visited with due punishment.

Whoever amongst the bankers shall pay into my treasury one lakh of rupees, will get interest thereon at the rate of 2 per cent until the liquidation of the principal....

The bankers will also obtain from the King, sanad of their good character and sincere attachment to the interest of the Sarkar... That no demand of revenue will be made from the Bankers until debts due to them are liquidated....[68]

Although the incentives were powerful, England's recent offensive and purposeful genocide at Jhansi had a clear effect. Support for the war was running thin. Basic ammunition and logistical elements were becoming difficult. One letter urges the Nawab Bahadur to assist Vaman Rao, a military liaison in charge of finances.

...Vaman Rao, Paymaster, employed at Hamirpur that he stands in need of a small sum of money in order to procure gunpowder and bullets for the sepoys armed with matchlocks, and to construct batteries. I request therefore that you will be good enough to send fifty Rupees, out of the amount received from Hamirpur, to enable him to purchase gun-powder, etc., collect workmen and employ them in erecting batteries.[69]

This letter was for want of Rs 50.

The war was about eleven months old. The early days witnessed civilians, including villagers, zamindars, mukhiyas, mahajans all eagerly supporting the Indian troops. However, as the English started the slaughter, targeting civilians including women and children, the eagerness waned.

Although Tatya had adapted, and had started to provide, economic incentives to motivate people, it had put a strain on the government of Nana Saheb's treasury. Now, even the finances were drying up. A letter from Dhir Singh, an officer, reported:

'The 500 Rupees, which you made a present to Punjab Singh, through Sham Sahai have not yet arrived; take care it reaches us, for we are very much in want of money. He has some 25 men to provide for they are in want and will very soon desert'.[70] The armies fighting with Tatya, including the Gwalior Contingent and the troops belonging to the Nawab of Banda as well as the NI regiments from the Bengal Army had not been paid for months.[71] The treasury at Charkhari had only partly addressed the economic woes. Morale was low.

After perpetrating the genocide at Jhansi, Rose continued his northward march towards Kalpi. Not only were the dispirited Bundeli forces and economics of the war working against the possibility of victory, there was news of another front being opened by General Whitlock marching from the southeast.

At this time, Tatya Tope had the three Gwalior infantry regiments with him, reinforced by parts of the 32, 52 and 56 NI.[72] Most of the Bundeli militia, based on earlier accounts, had retreated. English estimates place the number at 4,000.[73] In addition, the armies of the Raja and Banpur and Shahgarh, which numbered about 1,500-3,000, augmented him.[74]

It is difficult to assess the exact logistical situation at Kalpi. Considering that finances were running low, the manufacturing of ammunition, artillery and more had stopped. Many of the artillery and carriages that were manufactured were damaged, lost or captured.

Meanwhile, the English had consolidated other areas of Bundelkhand. Tatya Tope and Nana Saheb Peshwa's pacts with the Bundeli chiefs were falling apart. With failing logistics and finances, and recognising that the Indian Army was unable to defend Bundelkhand any more; many Bundelkhand chiefs were hesitating in investing more in a losing cause.

Hamilton's report to the governor general makes this observation.

We have relieved the garrison of Saugor, take every fort that offered any resistance... swept the country from Nurbudda to Jumna by the valley of Betwah and opened up communication between Agra and Bombay, and destroyed the compact (pact) between the insurgent Bundelas and the Mahratta party...[75]

Chhatrasal's pact with the Marathas had unravelled after the Second Anglo-Maratha wars, but Tatya Tope resurrected a revised ikrarnama under the name of Nana Saheb Peshwa during the War of 1857. A new pact was agreed upon between the government of Nana Saheb Peshwa and the chiefs of Bundelkhand. The tax revenue was now going to Nana Saheb instead of the English. The chiefs had supported them financially and the villagers had provided help in providing intelligence and logistical support.[76]

The genocide at Jhansi served to dismantle this pact and dampened the spirits of the Bundelas. Hamilton was referring to the destruction of this second pact.

Although Kalpi was the operational headquarters, all the expenses related to the logistics of the war had taken its toll on the finances. Kalpi was set up with 'four foundries and manufactories of cannon' as well as a subterranean magazine.[77] However, with finances running low these factories were no longer relevant. The factories in Kalpi were also manufacturing caps for muskets, however, by April, with shortages of raw material, no one knew what composition they were filled with.[78] When the English took possession of the factories, only four guns were found.[79]

After the fall of Banda, the Nawab retreated to Jalalpur and asked Rao Saheb from Kalpi to help stop Whitlock's advance.[80]

The finance and logistics were collapsing, and Tatya was running low on ammunition and artillery. It was under these circumstances that Tatya

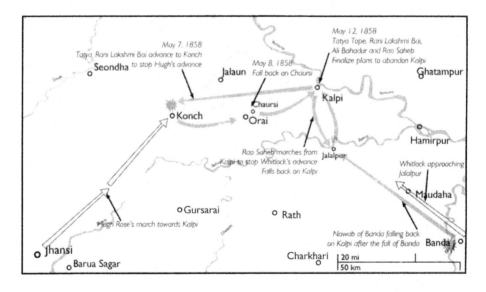

Figure 32: Losing Bundelkhand

Tope and Rani Lakshmibai attempted to stop Hugh Rose at Konch on 7 May 1858.

However, Rose's strength was overwhelming and Tatya's army had to fall back to Chaursi near Orai,[81] and then retreat to Kalpi. Tatya Tope and Rani Lakshmibai were at Kalpi on 12 May 1858, assessing the situation that Kalpi was facing. In March, Lucknow had already fallen into English hands. Running low on capital, ammunition and morale of the Bundeli population, the fall of Kalpi—the headquarters of the war—was now inevitable.

Most people would have capitulated under these circumstances and abandoned their efforts. However, Tatya Tope, Rani Lakshmibai and Rao Saheb did not. Lakshmibai and Rao Saheb attempted to defend Kalpi, while Tatya Tope decided to make a visit to the pragmatic patriot; the only person who could financially help Tatya in keeping the resistance alive. Tatya left Kalpi for Gwalior sometime between 13 and 17 May 1858.[82]

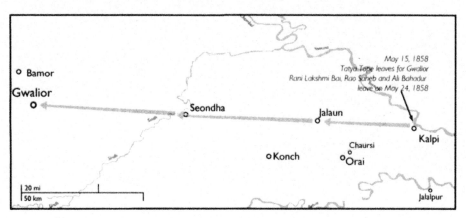

Figure 33: Gwalior to the Rescue

The battle for Kalpi was a relative non-affair. Having learnt the 'lessons' of Jhansi and the genocide of the civilians by Rose, much of the population had already abandoned the city. Tatya Tope was looking ahead to his visit to Gwalior. The Indian troops were also retreating, though a rear guard was left at Kalpi to slow the march of Rose and others to place time for the drama that was to unfold at Gwalior. The Indian troops attacked Rose at Gulauli, outside Kalpi on 22 May 1858. They kept the English engaged for two days, and then unilaterally abandoned the offensive on the night of the 24 May 1858.[83] After his 'success' at Jhansi, and with Bundelkhand tranquilised, Hugh Rose 'advanced on Calpee, there being scarcely any one between him and the empty city...'[84]

Rani Lakshmibai and the troops were heading towards Gwalior, where Tatya was arranging another reversal of fortunes.

Chapter 15

REVERSAL OF FORTUNES

FORMIDABLE IDLENESS

As mentioned before, much of the narrative of 1857 places the cause of India's defeat on the alleged treachery of 'Scindia'. Prior to discussing the events that took place in Kalpi and Gwalior in May and June 1858, it is important to understand the context and accuracy of this alleged betrayal.

Historians have rehashed the young Jiyajirao Shinde's role during 1857, and built the foundation of India's defeat along these lines. Dinkar Rao Rajwade, his diwan, was the adviser to the young king. Consider the following, that we dub as the 'Had Scindia... Hyperbole'. A tale that has been told many times over. The following is a small sampling of an otherwise sea of 'what ifs' about Jiyajirao Scindia's 'betrayal' during the war.

The 'Had Scindia...' Hyperbole	
'Had Sindhia then struck against us—nay, had he even done his best in our behalf, but failed...'	'...the character of the rebellion might have been changed almost beyond the scope of speculation'.[1]
'Had Scindia or Holkar placed themselves at the head of their revolted contingents...'	'...I say, and who dare assert what disasters might have not have occurred?'[2]

'Had Scindia gone over... '	'...Nagpore, the Nizam's country, and southern India must have followed him'.[3]
'Had Scindia taken advantage of our distress to rise in arms against us and summon the Mahrattas everywhere to his standard...'	'...vastly more would have lost their lives, and the Bombay presidency, nay, the whole of India, been put in imminent jeopardy'.[4]
'Had Sindhia, with this army at his command, thrown in his lot with the rebels...'	'...he might, at an early stage of the struggle, have easily marched upon Agra, and have captured the city. Such a disaster would have seriously added to the difficulties with which the British had to contend'.[5]
'...had Dinkar Rao and his master, the young Maharajah Scindia, been less zealous in the opportune help they rendered to the government,...'	'...the British Indian Empire would have had to face almost insurmountable dangers and difficulties, without any strong expectation of sure success'.[6]
'Had Scindia been persuaded by the mutineers to strike against the English...'	'...'the character of the Revolt,' to use the weighty words of an eminent British authority 'might certainly have been changed beyond the scope of speculation'.[7]
'Had Scindia and Holkar not resorted to the treachery on that occasion...'	'...they as well as ourselves (Brahmins) would not have been reduced to this plight'.[8]
'Had Sindhia rebelled...'	'...every Maratha state would have joined them'.[9] 'His loyalty saved India for the British'.
'Had Scindia failed us...'	'...the mutineers from Neemuch, Nuseerabad, and Jhansi, by concentrating at Gwalior, might have rendered that hill-fortress a second Delhi to the British'.[10]

Creativity in speculation is on full display in these 'what ifs...' The real question to ask is what did Scindia have in his possession that could have completely changed the outcome of the war? From all the embellishments above, it would seem that Scindia had some secret weapon that could have destroyed the English rule with its single use.

What could Scindia have done, or *not* done, that would have put the whole of India in jeopardy?

Surendra Nath Sen, who wrote the 'official' history of 1857, writes that the Gwalior Contingent 'whose intervention at different times, decide the fate of Agra, Delhi and Kanpur, sat idle in their lines at Morar (Gwalior Cantonment)'.[11]

Sen is referring to the trained army of seven infantry and two cavalry regiments. This contingent was 'by far the most important force south of the Jumna. This body was, agreeably to treaty, paid by Sindiah, and stationed in his district, but commanded by British officers'.[12]

> Tantia had been to Gwalior in September 1857 to gain the Contingent to the Nana and move it upon Cawnpore. He succeeded. The main body of the Contingent left Gwalior...[13]
>
> In October they marched with six regiments, four batteries, a siege train, and many irregular followers...[14]

If the main body that included six of the seven regiments of the contingent that went with Tatya, it is difficult to understand Sen's assertion that the troops were still 'idle'.

Regardless, after the monsoons ended in Central India, these regiments were active with Tatya in every campaign, as is evident in earlier chapters. They marched thousands of miles, crossing rivers and fighting dozens of battles. In fact, the 6th Gwalior Infantry fought alongside the Kanpur regiments in the early months of the War, as early as June and July of 1857.[15]

Could they have assisted Delhi and Agra, as Sen suggests? Many letters and diaries written by Indian soldiers in Delhi reveal that Delhi in August was a 'wrecked, semi-derelict and starving city'.[16] In fact, many troops that had marched into Delhi after facing hardships were now considering leaving the city for lack of food.[17] Delhi had tens of thousands of soldiers fighting in its defence, competing for food with the civilians. Marching into such an area was hardly prudent. The inevitable fall of Delhi finally occurred in the middle of September. Delhi's fall could not have been prevented by sending the Gwalior Contingent. Moreover, this force concentrated at Gwalior, Dhar and other locations was a natural deterrent for the English to move into Central India. One can argue that *any* army in a defensive position is sitting 'idle'.

Sen and others credit India's defeat to this mythical 'idleness' of the Gwalior Contingent while the rest of India was burning. Not all English 'authorities' concur. Field Marshall Neville Chamberlain's observations directly contradict those of Sen.

> The Gwalior Contingent became a compact force of 10,000 men of all arms... disciplined and trained by English officers. They owed no allegiance to the ruler of the Gwalior State, and, not being a part of the native army, they owned no allegiance to the British Government. During the Mutiny they proved our most *formidable foes*. The lesson is important. [emphasis added][18]

Although, Chamberlain is slightly off on the actual number in the army, which was no more than 8,200, all other facts support Chamberlain's observations.[19] As the previous chapters discuss, the Gwalior Contingent was the most dependable army that Tatya had in his possession. In addition to the Gwalior Contingent, Gwalior did have a secondary army, which remained stationed at Gwalior, largely composed of soldiers, with less training and demonstrable skills. In terms of ability, they were similar to the armies of some of the chiefs of Bundelkhand and the militia that Tatya had recruited. We have argued earlier that in most cases, the battles were not won or lost on numerical superiority, but other important logistical factors. Their strategic relevance to the outcome of the war was insignificant.

In some narratives, the hyperbole exaggerated the numbers.

> It was only thus that he could prevent 16,000 well-disciplined soldiers, with excellent artillery and magazine, from joining the mutiny.[20]

How did the 6,000-8,000-strong Gwalior Contingent become a 10,000-strong compact force that was a 'formidable foe' to 16,000 well-disciplined soldiers who did *not* join the mutiny?

These contradictions emerge from the premise that the English narrative based upon Macpherson's statements, who was the resident at Gwalior is accurate. Although Macpherson was the resident of Gwalior, he moved to Agra at the outset of the war, and simply passed on information based largely on hearsay or second-hand sources. If the premise of the accuracy of Macpherson's statements is rejected, these contradictions cease to exist.

Macpherson took 'credit' for the 'Scindia betrayal', to advance his personal relevance in England's scheme of things. Much of the Gwalior narrative is based on his reports and 'suitable' stories. Subsequently, Macpherson's story was used by historians to weave a narrative as a deliberate camouflage to hide the real causes of India's defeat in the War of 1857. Obviously, the English did not want to take credit for the victory because that would have brought an unwelcome attention on the systematic and deliberate genocide perpetrated against Indian civilians. The logical alternative was to place the weight of India's eventual defeat on India's own shoulders. Indian historians wittingly or unwittingly cooperated in this venture by their reluctance to examine the English narrative closely.

Dinkar Rao Rajwade, the diwan at Gwalior, was indeed 'loyal' to the English. However, neither the inaccurately labelled 'inaction' of Jiyaji Rao Shinde, the alleged 'loyalty' of Dinkar Rao, nor the mythical 'formidable idleness' of the Gwalior Contingent was a determining factor in the outcome of the Anglo-Indian War of 1857.

THE PRAGMATIC PATRIOT

As discussed before, when Tatya left Kalpi, the financial situation as well as the logistics in terms of ammunition and artillery was desperate and Gwalior's help was the only hope. However, Gwalior was supposed to be 'loyal' to the English. Yet, the events that were to take place in Gwalior reversed the course of the war.

At the end of the drama that unfolded in Gwalior, the script of the war was somewhat rewritten. Here is what Major H.W. Norman, a deputy adjutant to the general of the army wrote to the secretary:

...the rebels, who had fled in the most disorderly flight and helpless state from Calpee, were now completely set up with abundance of money, a capital park of Artillery, plenty of material...[21]

How did this drama unfold?

After the battle of Konch, and assessing the situation at Kalpi, Tatya Tope left for Gwalior sometime in the middle of May 1858. Macpherson writes: '...Tantea Topeh—in foresight, resource and influence with individuals and masses, the soul of Nana's cause—went straight from the fight at Koonch, in secrecy, to Gwalior'.[22]

Historians claim that after Tatya left Kalpi, he 'concealed himself in the bazar [sic]'.[23] Some speculate that while Tatya was in Gwalior, he made some kind of a 'grand intrigue against Scindiah's power'.[24]

The reader would recall that Tatya Tope had met Jiyaji Rao Shinde in September of 1857. Vishnubhat Godse, who was in Gwalior at that time, was aware of this meeting. Macpherson and the English narrative on Gwalior, does not acknowledge that the meeting ever took place, although in all likelihood they were aware of this meeting. We know very little of what Tatya Tope did during his visit in May 1858 and what transpired between Baija Bai and Jiyaji Rao's meeting with Tatya Tope. However, there are references to letters and meetings in a later proclamation made by Rao Saheb.

> We have letters from Baiza Baee, Scindia himself encouraged us. Tantea Topeh has visited Gwalior and ascertained all.[25]

Tatya had arrived at Gwalior earlier, and met with Baija Bai and Jiyaji Rao Shinde. Lakshmibai, Rao Saheb and the Nawab of Banda were leading the rest of the Indian Army that had retreated from Kalpi. Their march upto Gwalior was not considered hostile towards Gwalior.

> ...rebels who were in destitute condition had, being still several miles from Gwalior, implored Scindiah's favour and protection in language and with a demeanour the reverse of hostile.[26]

Historians claim that Tatya's 'great intrigue' was with the remaining regiments of the Gwalior Contingent, and that these were like the other regiments who had been fighting with Tatya for nearly a year had *betrayed* their King.

> ...the rebel army had attacked Scindiah at Bahadurpoor, 9 miles from Gwalior; his troops of all Arms, with the exception of a few of his Body Guard, had treacherously gone over, the artillery in mass to the

enemy... the Garrison of the Fort of Gwalior, considered to be one
of the strongest, if the strongest, had after a mock resistance, opened
its gates to the Rebels...[27]

The question is, if it was a betrayal of the troops that Tatya had achieved,
why did they stage a 'mock resistance'? Whom were the soldiers trying to
trick? Why even posture for war? Why array the entire army in a formation,
and only put up a token resistance? Whose benefit was this show for?

One can contrive answers to these questions, but they would be far less
logical than the simplicity that reality offers.

Baija Bai Shinde, we have discussed earlier, was one of the founding
leaders of the war against the English. Nevertheless, she was concerned
about putting the life of her young heir, Jiyaji Rao Shinde, still in his early
twenties, in danger. The reader would recall that Baija Bai Shinde arrived
in Gwalior in 1856 after a gap of several years, which allowed her to be in
the thick of action. She was therefore able to stage-manage covert support
to the war, yet maintain a façade of loyalty to the English.

Tatya Tope's 'intrigue' at Gwalior, was not with the remaining Gwalior
Army, but with Baija Bai herself. However, any projection of voluntary help
would have put Jiyaji Rao's and her own life at risk. This would explain
the need for a mock war. Tatya Tope returned successfully from Gwalior
and had a council meeting with Rao Saheb, the Nawab of Banda and Rani
Lakshmibai at Mahona on 27 May 1858. Mohammed Isaakh, who served
as Tatya Tope's chief coordinator was also present.[28]

The discussion centred on the alternatives after enacting the drama
at Gwalior. Entrenching themselves at Gwalior was not an option. Rani
Lakshmibai suggested wresting Jhansi back and 'moving to Karera, in
Jhansi'.[29] Tatya Tope considered Bundelkhand; however, the consensus
was that, in all probability 'we should find the Bundelas hostile and no
supplies'.[30] The massacre at Jhansi had struck terror and worked wonders
for the English. Therefore, returning to Bundelkhand with the entire army
was also no longer an option.

Tatya's movements after Gwalior as discussed in subsequent chapters,
reveals the ingenuity of the plan that was put into action after the drama
at Gwalior.

Rao Saheb wrote in his letter to Baija Bai:

> I shall halt tomorrow at Gwalior. As it shall be settled after we shall meet, shall it be. What shall be hereafter shall be according to our counsels upon meeting.[31]

One can only guess as to what the 'shall be settled' meant, but the following day, things were indeed 'settled'. The drama that was enacted[32] on the battlefield had the remaining Gwalior Contingent led by Jiyaji Rao Shinde, arrayed against the Gwalior Contingent and other troops that had arrived from Kalpi. Jiyaji Rao gave orders to fire, but his soldiers refused and apparently turned the attack on him.

> ...his Highness himself, after bravely doing his best to make his Troops do their duty, had been forced by the fire of his own Artillery, and the combined attacks of his Troops, and of the Rebel Army, to fly to Agra...[33]

At the end of the mock battle, Gwalior had 'fallen' into the hands of the Indians. The battle claimed some lives; however, it turned out that 'what men whose disappearance or wounds cannot be satisfactorily accounted for' were deemed dead.[34] There was some additional mock resistance at the Palace and the Laskhar area of Gwalior.[35] By 2 June, the drama was over, the 'King' and his Diwan, had 'escaped' to Dholpur heading towards Agra.[36]

At this time, Baija Bai was still in the city of Gwalior near Panniar. The drama was successful with the English believing Jiyaji Rao's story. At this point, Baija Bai herself was considering taking an active role in the war. After Gwalior was officially in Indian hands, Tatya Tope visited her at Panniar requesting her to return to Gwalior.[37]

Baija Bai's covert support to the Indians had its obvious advantage; however, it had also caused consternation amongst the population. Like the English, the population as well as other leaders who were not privy to this covert support, were also under the belief that Gwalior was loyal to the English. Understandably, Baija Bai's overt declaration of support to the Indians could have had a positive effect on the overall morale. Yet, even at this time, there was a possibility that this could have put Jiyaji Rao himself at risk. Baija Bai, much to disheartenment of Rao Saheb, chose not to overtly join the effort. He wrote to her:

> All is well here. Your going from hence was not, to my thinking right. I have already written to you, but have received no answer. This should not be. I am sending this letter through Ramjee Chowley Jamadar.
>
> Do come and take charge of your seat of Government. It is my intention to take Gwalior, only to have a meeting and go on.[38]

For reasons discussed earlier, Baija Bai did not return to Gwalior. She had done her job and supported the war without risking Jiyaji Rao or her own life. Unlike the leonine leaders like Tatya Tope, the role of Baija Bai Shinde had been that of a pragmatic patriot.

Regardless of Baija Bai's decision, it was important to let the people of Gwalior and other areas know that despite the fall of Kalpi, the war was not over and the resistance was still alive. A proclamation was made wherein Nana Saheb was declared the peshwa of Gwalior; Rao Saheb the deputy, and Tatya Tope was declared the diwan.[39]

The treasury at Gwalior was of tremendous value. The Gwalior Contingent which had been fighting with Tatya Tope had not been paid for nearly three months. They were paid three months of pay that was past due, in addition to two months of advance payment, as gratuity. The other troops were also paid handsomely.[40]

Having received tacit support, there was no reason to destroy the authority of Shinde at Gwalior. Rao Saheb reconfirmed nearly all the servants of the Shinde government. While Tatya Tope and a few others were aware that the Shindes had been covertly supportive, their 'escape' from Gwalior had to be addressed.

It was important to reduce the negative impact of Jiyaji Rao's 'flight' from Gwalior. Although Jiyaji Rao had covertly cooperated, overtly he was on the side of the English. It was important to marginalise his importance. It was in this context that Rao Saheb made the following proclamation, slighting Jiyaji Rao.

...we are the Rao and the Peshwa, Scindia is our slipper-bearer. We gave him his kingdom. His army has joined us. We have letters from Baiza Baee, Scindia himself encouraged us. Tantea Topeh has visited Gwalior and ascertained all. He having completed everything, I am for the Lushkar. Would you fight with us?[41]

Insulting Jiyaji Rao was a practical matter to proclaim that the power now was with the Peshwa. The idea was to minimise the fallout of Jiyaji Rao's 'refuge' with the English, and did not necessarily reflect any personal animosity. Other than projecting control, this proclamation reveals that Baija Bai Shinde had actually written letters of support to Tatya Tope, which further corroborates earlier inferences.

The proclamation had its desirable effect. Many local chiefs who had held out against the English were considering surrender after the Jhansi genocide and the fall of Kalpi. However, the events at Gwalior encouraged their defiance against the English. The Raja of Chakarnagar was amongst them. In addition, Ganga Singh encouraged by the events at Gwalior, crossed the Chambal with 1,200 followers and attacked the English customs' offices.[42]

In the letter that Rao Saheb wrote to Baija Bai, there is another matter of interest. He wrote: 'It is my intention to take Gwalior, only to have a meeting and go on'. The key phrase is '...and go on'. The intention was never to 'capture' and 'occupy' Gwalior. This is a critical piece of information which explains some other curious events that were about to transpire in Gwalior in June 1858.

FORT VINCIBLE

The imposing Gwalior Fort is often described as 'Ajeya', meaning invincible. Yet, in a matter of weeks, the fort 'fell' twice. The great kings who had once ruled from its ramparts would have been embarrassed to witness the fort's obvious inability to withstand conquests, capitulating with ease on both occasions.

The first 'fall' of Gwalior was a result of a covert deal between Tatya Tope and Baija Bai Shinde. After 'taking over' Gwalior, the decision was to move away from Bundelkhand and the Gwalior area, with an overall plan to go to the Deccan and attempt to extend the war. There was no reason to be entrenched at Gwalior, especially when the monsoons had not arrived leading to water shortages in the Fort of Gwalior.[43] Moreover, after witnessing the 'punishment' meted out to the residents of Jhansi, for their support to their Rani, Tatya Tope could not have risked 'vijyan' or genocide on the 170,000 population of Gwalior.[44]

Yet, Tatya Tope projected that he intended to entrench his troops at Gwalior for reasons we will see shortly. The English unwittingly complied and ordered many columns from surrounding areas to march into Gwalior. The Brigade from Shivpuri was ordered to march towards Gwalior on 8 June.[45] The English column from Kalpi was at Indurki on 7 June, and it was going to join Rose with other troops.[46] In addition, Riddell's column had arrived at Dholpur on 13 June,[47] and there were reports of an approaching force from Agra.[48]

Much is written about the positioning of Indian troops and the approaching English troops and the battles that were fought in and around Gwalior on 17 and 18 June, when the English claimed to have 'captured' Gwalior. Rao Saheb had clearly written in a letter to Baija Bai that he had no intention to stay put at Gwalior, other than make a 'halt'.[49] With no design of staying at Gwalior or to take over the fort, why would Tatya Tope or others engage the English at Gwalior?

Tatya Tope, as later chapters demonstrate, had a clear post-Gwalior strategy. Being holed up in Gwalior was certainly not the intent. However, despite having other plans, Tatya could have displayed the *intent* to hold Gwalior to draw a large amount of English forces into Gwalior, before he made his next move—a strategy that would work in the future as well.

Rani Lakshmibai's last stand at Gwalior was in support of Tatya's strategy. Tatya Tope, Rani Lakshmibai amassed their troops a short distance from Gwalior at Kotah-ki-Serai, in an area with a chain of low hills and waited for Brigadier Smith to arrive with his large contingent. To oppose Smith, there were six guns mounted on the summit of the hills supported by infantry.[50] Beyond the hills were Tatya's two batteries of six and five guns near the Phulbagh Palace. Rani Lakshmibai was with these batteries. She was 'in the dress of a mounted officer, superintending the movements of the cavalry on the field, and sharing in all the dangers of the struggle'.[51] In the heat of this battle, Rani Lakshmibai was hit by a shot to her side. She was able to ride away in her injured condition, but died from her wounds shortly after.[52] Her body was surrounded by her guard while a pyre was raised.[53] She was cremated nearby. In the day long battle that ensued, Smith lost 85 men, and was forced to retire. Predictably, English euphemisms blame their death on 'hunger, fatigue and sun-stroke'.[54]

Tatya Tope and others had no intention of entrenching themselves at the fort of Gwalior. Expecting a long battle the English had amassed multiple columns of troops around Gwalior, reducing their strengths in surrounding areas. Once the slow moving English troops were positioned at Gwalior, Tatya Tope, Rao Saheb and others made their next move. Although Gwalior Fort fell twice in quick succession, neither of the two times, was there a *real* battle for the fort. Like the spirit of Lakshmibai who died free, Gwalior fort remains 'ajeya'.

RETRIBUTION AND REWARD

The events at Gwalior rekindled the nearly dying flame of liberty. The treasury at Gwalior was about 19 lakh rupees.[55] A large portion of that went in paying the troops, and the balance was used to keep the resistance alive. The remaining body of the Gwalior Contingent had been cleverly dispersed by Jiyaji Rao, which allowed them to join Tatya's army without having to 'betray' their king.

Regardless of what was postured or what was written as the 'Scindia betrayal', Gwalior gave Tatya Tope the remaining army, logistical help and most importantly money. Even if the English narratives conclude that Scindia was loyal to the English; his loyalty did not hurt the cause of freedom. The 'had Scindia hyperbole' is purely a historical diversion in the narrative of 1857.

S.C. Macpherson was the English political agent at Gwalior, whose job was to ensure the 'smooth affairs' of this kingdom. Macpherson takes 'credit' for Jiyaji Rao Shinde's support to the English during the war. Most narratives use Macpherson's own claims as basis for their argument and the unflinching support of Jiyaji Rao during the war of 1857. His own report made on 30 September 1858, despite the obvious spin, reveals that the English had sufficient doubts about Jiyaji Rao's real loyalties. Although, these were never overtly expressed in writing, Macpherson's superiors would have had to be naïve to have ignored them. This was especially true, after

Tatya's success at Gwalior that kept the efforts for liberation alive for many more months.

Macpherson admittedly expresses concern that Jiyaji Rao was not firmly loyal to the English, writing: 'Scindia, meanwhile, had vacillated characteristically between the counsels of the Dewan and those of the party for the rebels'.[56]

We have argued earlier that the Gwalior Contingent never really 'betrayed' their king. It was the king's and Baija Bai's tacit support that allowed them to support Tatya without endangering the young king's life or being disloyal. For many soldiers who were unaware of the intrigue between Tatya Tope and Baija Bai Shinde, it probably was a period of confusion. Therefore, to prevent confusion amongst the soldiers that all the bodies needed to be collected in the same location, Jiyaji Rao brilliantly orchestrated the drama and massed all his troops at Gwalior, which allowed for an easy transition of his troops to Tatya. Macpherson wrote:

Against the Dewan's most earnest entreaties, the Maharaja instead of dispersing half of his troops, at least, over his districts, where the temptation to revolt would be least, and where nearly all have stood faithful, massed his whole force at the Capital, where the emissaries and the contagion of the revolt were strongest.[57]

After the English had taken Gwalior, a portion of the contingent had stayed back with him. Jiyaji Rao could have easily confined them at Gwalior. However, Jiyaji Rao gave orders to disband them, thus giving them the free will to enroll with Tatya Tope. Macpherson obviously was not very impressed. He wrote:

He (Scindia) then most unwisely made public his imprudent resolution to disband on the arrival of our force, all his men from our provinces so depriving them, already hostile to us, of every motive to stand neutral even for a day in deference to Scindia's will.[58]

Did Macpherson suspect that Jiyaji Rao was playing a double game with the English? Macpherson or other English superiors would have had to be naïve to have ignored that possibility.

However, it is logical to assume that the English were hard-boiled in deploying their policy of retribution and reward. While an individual's 'real' behaviour played a role in the English response, the key determining factors for the English were forward looking in terms of 'managing' the situation.

While it would be logical to assume that the rewards went to those who sided with the English, the policy had to be far more dispassionate in its implementation. The English designed the narrative of 1857 as India was slowly reverting in English hands. This narrative benefited from the covertness of the Indian plan for the planned war against the English. Baija Bai Shinde portrayed her son as cozying with the English, while supporting Tatya in every practical way. For the English, once the situation had passed, the unsentimental question to ask was: 'is Retribution or Reward the logical choice in the treatment of Jiyaji Rao and Baija Bai?'

The narrative the English had constructed supported a 'reward' for Gwalior. Retribution against Jiyaji Rao could have unnecessarily fanned the flames that the English had put out in Gwalior and nearby Bundelkhand.

All the English intelligence, largely originating from Macpherson, naturally supported the narrative. Retribution was targeted at someone lower in command. Amarchand Batiya, the chief treasurer, was executed for showing 'all the treasure and other valuables to the rebels'.[59] While in every practical way, Baija Bai Shinde represented the core inspiration for leaders such as Nana Saheb and Tatya Tope, she did not need to be part of that narrative. Her name was simply excluded and Jiyaji Rao Shinde, who had presented the convivial face to the English, was rewarded.

In the English narrative, Jiyaji Rao Shinde was a hero for the English. Therefore, regardless of facts, Indian historians were compelled to vilify him; never attempting to consider that England's rewards and retribution were primarily based on practical considerations and what was known, was not necessarily based on what actually happened.

England's practical approach in determining rewards and retribution cannot be the sole guide for India to determine its heroes and villains.

The main story of Gwalior is neither the alleged 'Scindia' betrayal, nor the mock battles, but that Gwalior reversed India's fortunes and the flame of freedom was again reignited.

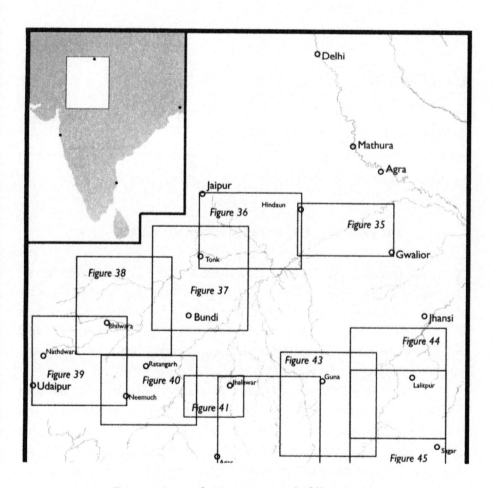

Figure 34: Locator for Figures 35-46 in the following pages

Chapter 16

REIGNITING FREEDOM

TALES OF DOGS, ELEPHANTS AND GUERILLAS

It is more than Tatya Tope's perseverance that is worthy of admiration, it was also his ability to invent and adapt to changing conditions. After the Gwalior episode, Tatya launched the third phase of the war. This was designed to be a preparation for the final phase, which never happened because of a fateful event that took place on 1 January 1859, and is discussed in a later chapter.

This third phase has been described by many historians as Tatya's 'days on the run' and his campaigns have misrepresented Tatya as a 'fugitive'. As the following chapters will demonstrate, Tatya's marches were driven with a clear mission. There were times when Tatya marched through the English defences, defeating them and there were times the English were tailing him. We will also see that the English narratives that portray his movements as purely evasive are nothing more than stories of a tail wagging the dog.

To summarise the events so far, the logistics for Operation Red Lotus, which was the original plan for the war, depended on the villages for the embedded supply lines and transportation. This phase failed, because in response the English unleashed the 'figure-of-eight' campaign.

Tatya adapted. In the second phase, with covert support from Gwalior, he made Kalpi the headquarters, and developed a more elaborate war machine that included transportation logistics, camp followers and purchased grains. All of this was financed with the help of a new pact with the Bundeli people and their chiefs, who directed their revenue to Nana Saheb's government instead of the English. The English responded again. This time they 'tranquilised' Bundelkhand by unleashing the most gruesome genocide on the entire population of Jhansi and other places. The pact with the Bundelas was destroyed, and without revenue, Tatya's campaign ran out of money.

After securing Gwalior and the requisite financing, Tatya decided against entrenching his troops at Gwalior. A part of the reason was that the English now had a strong position in Central India. A second reason was that the population of Gwalior could have faced the same fate as the civilian population of Jhansi.

The English had brought in about 75,000 troops from other places around the world into India and increased their strength to about 100,000 soldiers. These forces were dominant in the areas that had witnessed the most fighting and most of the important cities. At this point, with a much smaller army, any attempt to liberate a city would have been futile. With heavier concentration of armies in a few areas, it would have been impossible to continue the earlier approach. A solution was to spread the English army by opening several more fronts. This could be achieved by reigniting rebellion in areas where the spirit of freedom remained strong, and then draw the English forces into these areas. These English troops would have to be redeployed, thus creating pockets of vulnerability that could be exploited.

Tatya, over the next six months, did exactly that. He demonstrated that the 100,000 English troops that had arrived into India from all over the world, could be dispersed, weakened and then attacked.

Tatya's third phase of the war was in preparation for a fourth phase that would attempt to reconquer the cities. Tatya expanded the resistance into Rajputana, Malwa and Gujarat, and forced the English to spread their forces thin.

At this stage, let us review the cost of the war Tatya was fighting. Assuming an army of about five thousand soldiers, his approximate 'burn' rate for financing the operation was about three lakh rupees per month.[1] The treasury from Gwalior had yielded about 19 lakh rupees. Of that amount, nine lakhs was paid to the Gwalior Contingent for three months' pay due to them and two months of gratuity. Another 7.5 lakh rupees to the other troops including the troops of the Nawab of Banda.[2] The balance of the money from Gwalior would last only for a short while. However, with the English having a clear upper hand, not many local chiefs were keen on overtly displaying support to Tatya, either financially or logistically.

Tatya was in a bind, yet with tenacity, he changed tactics and reignited the spark of freedom that allowed him to grow from strength to strength over the next six months. With an army of over five thousand soldiers in his attempt to spread the resistance, Tatya was going mobile. More familiar with the terrain and the area, Tatya's army had the ability to be far more agile than the English were. He would march into areas and rekindle local insurrections, which would force the English to mobilise their troops.

Despite the popular label, Tatya's warfare was more than 'guerilla'. In some cases, as we present later, Tatya marched with a full-fledged army, complete with all logistical elements that a regular army would have. Tatya's speed of marching varied with circumstances. In areas where Tatya was taking control back, he was reinforced with local troops. These campaigns were about restoration of Indian rule rather than about disrupting English forces. Once his mission in a region was accomplished, Tatya would move on to a different area with a diminished force. This is where he was most vulnerable, and therefore would march at the speed of 'forked lightning'.

He was able to engage the English alternately in regular and guerilla warfare that kept them guessing. He fought most of the battles on his own terms, strengthened by an efficient intelligence and communication networks. When the enemy was in the front, he would raise a supplementary army and march right through them.

The English would often choose to tail Tatya and claim that they were 'chasing' him as he was 'running'. If the English were in a stronger position behind him, Tatya would outpace them. Outflanking the English, however, was not easy. A study of Tatya's routes reveal his ability to outsmart the English even when he was barely a day's march away from strong English forces.

There has been a discussion as to what Tatya Tope's intentions were as he launched the final guerilla-like campaign. Why did he head into Rajputana, Malwa and Gujarat? He did cross the Narmada south towards Deccan, but was his real intention to go south?

While it is possible that Tatya's intention was to inspire the south to rise, there were stronger reasons for Tatya to choose to expand his campaign into Rajputana and Malwa.

England's grip was very strong in northern and southern India. However, in the region that spanned from the Sindhu to Betwa and Narmada to Yamuna, the English only possessed a 'few square miles' of territory directly.[3] The English rule in these areas was only a few decades old. The English government was represented 'by an officer called the Governor-General's agent, in both Malwa and Rajpootana; subordinate to him, a political agent resides at the capital of each of the principal rajahs'.[4] These places in many ways were like Bundelkhand where the resistance against the English was strong, but had subsided after the Jhansi genocide.

The mutinies found most of these princes discontented with the height to which British power had risen, and well-wishers to the revolted sepoys.[5]

'In no other part of India had so much remained of the old dynasties....'[6] These 'old dynasties' were anathema to the English rule, since their resistance was the strongest. Not coincidentally, these 'old dynasties' were also the target of all vitriolic attack by modern historians as well. They echo the English narrative that England was bringing 'civilisation' to India and these 'old dynasties' were resisting it.

Referring to the areas of Rajputana and Malwa's fierce resistance to the English rule; in August 1860, Blackwood's *Edinburgh* Magazine, claimed, 'a quarter of a century was not sufficient to eradicate old habits and traditions and to teach these men to appreciate the advantages of civilisation'.[7] Claims such as these are still not uncommon amongst many 'modern' Indian historians, who view India's defeat as a gateway to 'progress'.

Tatya's rationale to enter Rajputana was based on two goals. First, leverage the region's history of a strong anti-English sentiment amongst the local chiefs. Second, inspire local insurrections, which would force the English to redeploy their troops, thus spreading them then.

Towards his first goal, Tatya 'sent secret emissaries to several of the capitals in Rajpootana'.[8]

Most of the Rajpootana and Malwa chieftans from the first made loud professions of loyalty and attachment to the British. To the rebels they sent secret promises and intelligence, and having thus secured themselves for whichever turn events might take, they passively awaited the result of the arduous struggle going on around them.[9]

Additionally, all the locals rajas had their own independent body of troops in their service with treasury over which they had control.[10] However, while most of these local chiefs were covertly supporting Tatya, they did not want to risk their lives for the cause. This meant that if Tatya needed money and troops, he had to reach a town, where a mock battle would be enacted, and the 'treasury looted'. The troops would disband and then 'join' Tatya.

The English, recognising that such support could be forthcoming publicised a public execution of one such supporter, the Naib Nazim of Badaon, Ahmedullah Khan. He was publicly blown from the mouth of a cannon.[11]

As Tatya began his march through Rajputana, he achieved his second goal, that of inciting local insurrections. As the English mobilised large armies to stop Tatya's advance, local armies rose against the English. From Badoda in Rajputana, to Indurki, and Bhind to Mau Ranipur near Jhansi, the local chief raised armies against the English,[12] forcing the English to fight on several fronts and spread their forces thin.

With covert support from local chiefs, Tatya began his campaign into Rajputana and Malwa. Tatya and his army were constantly on the move, making only 'refuelling' stops for supplies, artillery, ammunition and additional troops; marching literally over 2,000 miles.[13] The civilian population was supportive and many local chiefs pleading 'helplessness' continued to support Tatya's troops; in many cases their armies joining him.

For the next six months, more than half a dozen English columns were attempting to restrict Tatya and his army. Blackwood's *Edinburgh* Magazine commented on the hardships facing the English columns tracking Tatya: 'No troops in the world could endure so much fatigue, sleep so well on the hard ground, or do without sleep at all, and be content with so little food'.

Tatya and his army faced conditions that were far more sustained and severe. The unrelenting march from place to place—facing insurmountable hardships—Tatya's army stuck with him. In the final analysis, India lost the war, but it was Tatya's troops and his own perseverance, as we argue later, allowed India to continue as a nation.

RESILIENCE IN RAJPUTANA

After Gwalior, still high on motivation but low on finances, Tatya and his army headed westward towards Rajputana. After leaving Gwalior, Tatya's army broke up into three columns and regrouped at Sarmathura. Tatya headed the cavalry, Rao Saheb was with the Gwalior infantry and the Nawab of Banda led the remaining army that included foot and mounted elements. They had 'twenty elephants, some *bahelis* (bullock carts) in their possession, but no guns'.[14] In unfamiliar territory, the English already seemed to be outsmarted. Despite having an elaborate spy network, the English were unable to locate Tatya.[15]

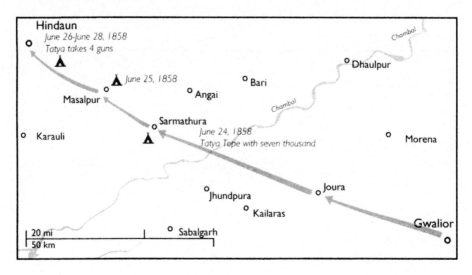

Figure 35: Gwalior to Hindaun
26-29 June 1858

After regrouping in Sarmathura, Tatya and his army headed via Masalpur to Hindaun, evading English troops at Karauli. The march to Hindaun was a success, where they were able to obtain four guns.[16] Figure 35 shows Tatya's march from Gwalior to Hindaun.[17]

The English established their intelligence network to track Tatya's movement, and to anticipate his next target. With a supportive civilian population, Tatya was able to provide disinformation, thus confounding the English. After getting supplies and some limited ammunition in Hindaun, Tatya decided to rendezvous with Feroze Shah who was in the Tonk area. Tatya declared his intention to take on Jaipur that was northwest, thus inviting General Roberts to set up a defensive position outside of Jaipur, instead of continuing his march. The tactic worked as Tatya headed west from Hindaun to Lalsot and announced his intention to march on to Chaksu. However, instead of marching west and north towards Jaipur, he made a sudden turn and headed southwest towards Jhilai, and then reached Tonk four days ahead of General Roberts, and two days ahead of Captain Eden and his advanced guard. Figure 36 shows Tatya's march from Hindaun to Tonk.[18]

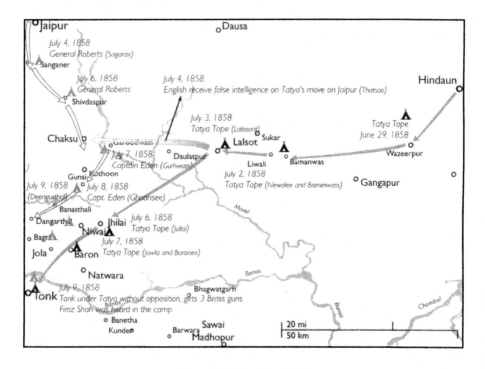

Figure 36: Tatya takes Tonk
29 June–9 July 1858

Part of the English narrative is consistent with the overt behaviour of many local chiefs. The nawab of this area was Vazir Mohammed Khan, who was overtly loyal to the English.[19] Yet, the following events can raise some questions of Mohammed Khan's alleged loyalty to the English.

Tonk under Tatya without opposition where he got three brass guns. Feroze Shah was heard in the camp.[20]

'None of Nawab's men have sided...'[21]

'Nawaub's troops have sided and gone off...'[22]

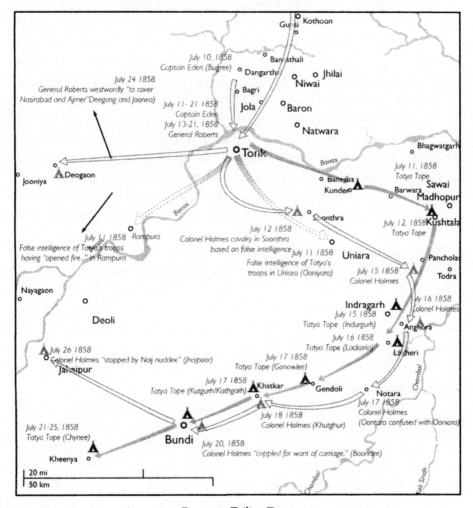

Figure 37: Tailing Tatya
11–25 July 1858

Feroze Shah, who was engaging the English in the west, was already in Tonk, and Vazir Mohammed Khan had failed to provide this key piece of information to the English. Regardless of Mohammed Khan's intentions, Tatya had more reinforcement as he continued to evade the English while gaining strength. Feroze Shah and Tatya, after their meeting in Tonk, established a strategy that would be successfully implemented over the next several months. The idea was to regroup after several months. Their second rendezvous never took place because of a fateful event that took place and is discussed in a later chapter.

By late June, the rivers had begun to rise and crossing them had become a difficult task. The English were counting on this difficulty to be able to catch up with Tatya as he headed out of Tonk.

Heading out shortly before the arrival of the English forces, a diversion was created at Rampur on 11 July, southwest of Tonk that Tatya troops have 'opened fire...' in Rampur and Uniara.[23]

Burnt by bad intelligence thus far, the English decided that they needed a strong mounted unit purely for tailing Tatya Tope. They had assigned this task to Colonel Holmes. Yet, at Tonk the false intelligence created confusion, as Colonel Holmes started marching to Rampur and then changed direction and marched to Soonthra,[24] while Tatya had headed southeast towards Kushtala near Sawai Madhopur, via Kunder and Barwara.[25] Figure 37 shows Tatya's march out of Tonk.

After Kushtala, Tatya made another turn, this time southwest towards Bundi. He reached Bundi on 18 July, via Indragarh, Lakheri, Gendoli and Khatkar.[26]

Colonel Holmes who was 'tailing' Tatya, was claiming that he had 'nearly caught up with Tatya', however, he was unable to take him on because, in his words, he was 'crippled for want of carriage'.[27] We will never know the full import of Holmes' 'crippling'. Was it for 'want of carriage', or, was that a Freudian slip for 'want of courage'.

Like the nawab of Tonk, the Rao of Bundi, Ram Singh, was also overtly 'loyal' to the English. The story as we are told is that 'the Boondee state was indifferent....'[28] and that he had 'more than once displayed a disposition to strike for independence'. Yet, Ram Singh 'was not prepared to link his fortunes with those of Tantia Topi. He shut, therefore, the gates of Bundi in the face of the fugitive'.[29] Additionally, the story goes that Tatya Tope was '...fired upon by the Boondee Chief who refused to give them supplies'.[30]

However, after studying the dates of Tatya's campaign and the locations (see Figure 37) of his camps, it becomes obvious that he definitely made a stop at Bundi. This could only mean that Tatya and his army were 'provided for' at Bundi.

Shortly after Bundi, the English lost all intelligence related to Tatya Tope's movements. Tatya and his troops simply disappeared. 'Tantia was able to change his course without fear of being disturbed by Holmes, for on leaving Bundi he had loudly asserted his intention to continue his course due south, and he counted that information thus disseminated would deceive his pursuers'.[31] What the English described as Tatya's 'loud' announcement probably meant that all the English spies reported on a common destination for Tatya.

Tatya's goal was to leverage the goodwill of the people and the local chiefs, and deliberately spread misinformation about his intentions. Did Ram Singh know Tatya's actual position and not share that information with the English? The intelligence briefs concur; noting that the 'Boondee Chief was very remiss in giving intelligence'.[32] Captain Holmes, who was tracking Tatya, lost him after Bundi.

Holmes kept up a close pursuit from Tonk to Bondee, but did not do more than capture a few stragglers. He was misled, no doubt intentionally, at Boondee, by information that his guns would not get through the Keena (Kheenya) pass, and crossed the hills by another route from Boondee to Jehajpore.[33]

By sending Holmes on a longer route, Ram Singh had covertly helped Tatya without exposing himself to have 'linked his fortunes' with those of Tatya Tope. Misled by intentional disinformation, Colonel Holmes lost track, and went northwest, in the direction of Jahajpur, while Tatya Tope and his army 'marched a few miles southward, then made a sudden detour westward, crossed the Bundi hills by the Kina pass, and made for the fertile country between Nasirabad and Nimach'.[34] Tatya was heading to Bhilwara, which was friendly territory and 'had already been the scene of warlike operations, and the larger towns in which had more than once shown a disposition to favour the rebellion'.[35]

In 1858, Rajputana saw heavy rains, flooding many rivers and rivulets that crisscross the terrain between Bundi and Bhilwara. This made movements slow, both for Tatya and his army as well as Roberts and Holmes. When the rains stopped, the marching resumed.

By 8 August, Tatya was camped at Bhilwara, when General Robert's army was heading south from Sarwar, Chapaneri and had camped at Banera, north of Bhilwara.[36] There was a small skirmish between Tatya and Robert on 10 August.[37]

Nothing decisive came out of the skirmish, where both sides could have claimed victory. Tatya in any case was not interested in staying at Bhilwara,

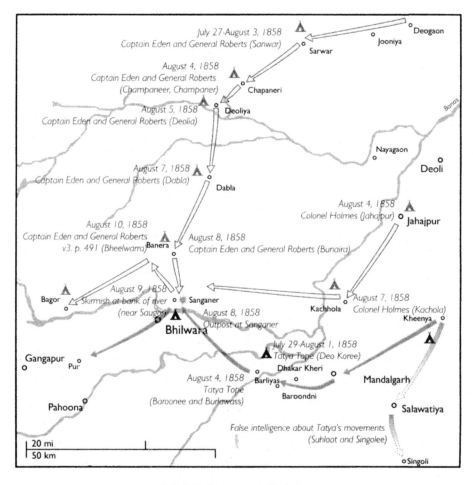

Figure 38: Resistance in Rajputana
27 July–9 August 1858

considering that Holmes'cavalry was a day's march away at Kachhola, east of Bhilwara.

The difficulty in fighting a guerilla war during the 1800s was carrying guns. These had to be pulled by elephants or horses in some cases. This made it extremely difficult in hilly terrain, especially during the rains. The constraint was both money and guns.

By the middle of August 1858, Tatya's movement into Rajputana had forced a massive redeployment of English forces out of Malwa and into Rajputana, and there were renewed insurrections all over.

Raja of Nirwar is in the jungles of kurreyr, in the powree elaka with 3,000 followers no guns. (Narwar is 44 miles south of Gwalior. Karera is midway between Shivpuri and Jhansi. The Raja was Man Singh.)[38]

The Rajah of Barowda (Badoda, in Rajputana) is at Mangrewl (Mangrol) in the Kota border with about 4 thousand followers. He has 3 elephants. No guns.

Bhind, 3 August—A party of rebels has gathered, it is said under the late Jhansee Ranee's brother at Mow near Jhansee, number 3,000.

Koour Dowlut Singh the Indoorkee rebel is at Nachur of that Pergunnah with 1,500 bundookchees, his nephew being at Myla close by with 500 more.[39]

Man Singh and others had taken advantage of the remobilisation of the English troops had launched an attack in Malwa. At this time, Tatya was at Nathdwara. Tatya had succeeded in spreading the English forces thin.

Tatya's 'circular' marches have confounded historians. However, our analysis reveals that Tatya's marches were deliberate and mission oriented. With news about Man Singh and Adhil Muhammed, it was time for Tatya to cross the Chambal and head right back towards Malwa.

MALWA MANOEUVRE

Tatya's march over the next few days was what has been described as a forked lightning. Having accomplished his goal of thinning the massive mobilisation of English troops in Malwa and Bundelkhand, Tatya needed to make a rapid march east. In preparation for this march of 'forked lightning'

Tatya needed to shed some excess weight, which included not only guns but also cooking pots.[40]

After a quick visit to the famous Nathdwara temple on the night of 13 August 1858,[41] Tatya's army exploded towards Malwa. Instead of marching as a group and becoming an easy target to follow, Tatya dispersed his troops in the jungles of Malwa, with a plan to regroup forty miles east near Jat. This movement baffled General Roberts, and he sent his men to tail these dispersed bodies of troops. However, with little familiarity of the jungle, Roberts failed. Despite some casualties at Kothariya and later at Mavli (Baolee) on 14 August 1858, Tatya's troops were able to shake off their pursuers.

Having forced to redeploy a large amount of troops from other areas into Rajputana, Tatya had allowed the local resistance to rise. Tatya's immediate

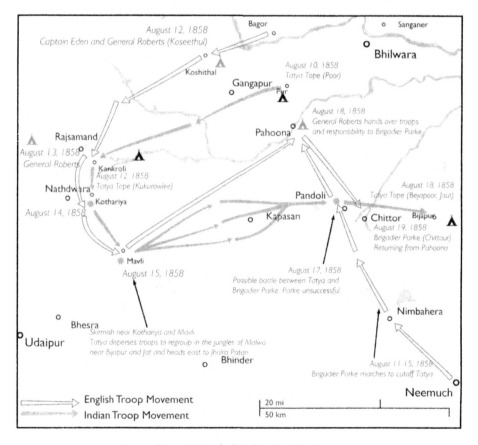

Figure 39: Forked Lightening: Part 1
12–18 August 1858

goals in Rajputana were achieved and Tatya set his eyes on Malwa where Tatya would rendezvous with the armies of Adil Mohammed of Ambawali (near Neemuch), another local chief inspired by Tatya.

Although guns were precious, they considerably slowed down the march. Yet, Tatya could afford to abandon his guns in Rajputana, because Tatya's interim goal was to head east towards Jhalra Patan, where a wealth of artillery, ammunition, and money awaited him.[42] However, Tatya was on a collision course with English reinforcements coming from Neemuch.

Brigadier Parke, who was in charge of the Neemuch detachment was ordered to march north to cut off Tatya before he could reach Bijapur. He set off on 11 August for this task.[43] No conflict is reported in any narrative, though it is highly unlikely that Parke could have avoided crossing paths with Tatya.

An important advantage of authoring history after winning the war is that some 'inconvenient battles' can simply be left out of the narrative. Having control over editorial selection, allows selective recording of events. Going by dates, movement, troop positions, and some laggard actions by Parke at a later date, the authors are of the opinion that Parke's army was handed a strong defeat by a column of Tatya's army, near Pandoli, at the outskirts of Chittor.

With lightning speed, Tatya and his men started marching east, hoping to cross the rising Chambal east of Neemuch. Between 16 and 18 August 1858, Tatya's army had regrouped between Bijapur and Jat.[44] They were in Ratangarh the following day, with elephants and camels.[45]

Tatya's resilience was already having an impact in other parts of Central India. Bundelkhand, once tranquilised by the genocide at Jhansi, was awakening again. Rajputana saw many local chiefs organising local militia against the English. By August, Central and western India saw renewed resistance to the English rule.

The flame of liberty, though flickering, had not yet been extinguished. These reignited rebellions kept the English army occupied, thus creating important diversions. These flare-ups thus reduced the restrictions on Tatya's movements.

At Pahoonah, General Roberts and his tired army handed over the responsibilities to a reluctant Brigadier Parke.[46] Despite Brigadier Parke's

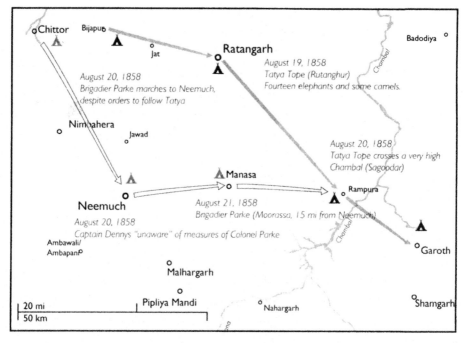

Figure 40: Forked Lightning: Part 2
19–20 August 1858

orders, he did not follow Tatya's tracks but headed straight to Neemuch. After reaching Neemuch, Parke was tardy in acting against Tatya. Apparently, he was 'puzzled' about which action to take. The rains had flooded the Chambal, and a district officer claimed that Tatya would not be able to cross the river, while another claimed that Tatya was resolved. Colonel Parke claimed that he 'had been misled by incorrect information and so missed them'.[47] Meanwhile, Captain Dennys who was stationed at Neemuch, claimed that he was 'unaware' of any measures taken by Parke.[48]

Either way, the appropriate action would have to be to follow Tatya's tracks. Yet, Parke apparently loitered around in the Neemuch area, and then later followed Tatya's tracks claiming he saw a few 'disabled ponies standing on the left bank, and the rebels disappearing among some mango trees in the west horizon'.[49] Tatya was heading east.

Regardless whether Brigadier Parke got cold feet or he was misled, Tatya and his army of about 4,000, had crossed a raging Chambal on 20 August near Rampura, and were heading, unhindered to Jhalra Patan.[50]

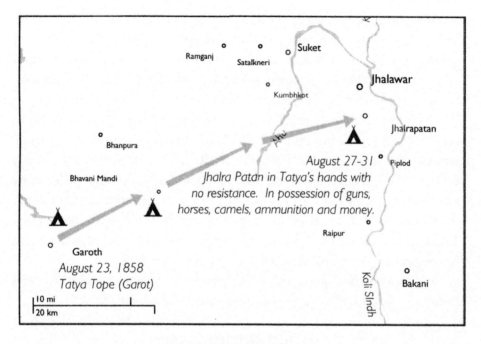

Ramganj   Satalkneri   Suket

Kumbhkot

Jhalawar

Bhanpura

Jhalrapatan

August 27-31   Piplod

Bhavani Mandi

Jhalra Patan in Tatya's hands with no resistance. In possession of guns, horses, camels, ammunition and money.

Raipur

Garoth
*August 23, 1858
Tatya Tope (Garot)*

10 mi
20 km

Kali Sindh

Bakani

*Figure 41: Journey to Jhalra Patan
23–31 August 1858*

On 23 August 1858, Tatya was at Garoth and on the 27th he had reached Jhalra Patan.[51] Jhalra Patan was an important town, not far from the Bombay-Delhi route.

Historically, Malwa had always been a rich part of India; both economically and culturally. During the English rule, however, there was a structural change in Malwa's economy. Unlike other parts of India that suffered due to de-industrialisation, Malwa reinvented itself and 'thrived' as an agrarian economy—an economy that took England's treasury to record highs. A large part of Malwa's revenue to England was from primarily a single product, exported practically to a single country. The product was opium and the destination was China. In 1856, the English had put down a bloody rebellion in China to export 'Patna' and 'Malwa opium'. Chests of opium were 'traded' for massive profits. Revenue from this drug running filled the treasury of many local administrators who in turn fed the English East India Company. It is interesting to note that the origin of the name Neemuch has a drug-stained history. Neemuch's origin is from an English acronym NEMACH (North Eastern Military and Cavalry Headquarters), and was primarily responsible for warehousing the opium that came out of Malwa. This opium was sent under armed escort to the ports of Bombay or Calcutta. It takes no genius to guess the armed escort for this 'precious' cargo was provided by the military.

With little resistance from the Rana of Jhalra Patan, Tatya was able to get a hold of guns, ammunition, bullocks and artillery horses.[52] In addition, was the bounty of 'five lakh rupees',[53] with which Tatya was able to pay up his army and enlist additional troops.[54] The English claim that his army swelled to 8,000 or more, but is likely to be an exaggeration. In addition to the treasury was also a large 'quantity of opium'.[55] The English claimed that Tatya put up the opium for ransom, but more than likely Tatya destroyed it, considering there are no records of its fate afterwards.

With unmatched speed and mobility and, after having rendered General Roberts's efforts futile, Tatya was now east of a high Chambal.

THE TORTOISE TRAP

A study of Tatya's movement reveals that he camped at Jhalra Patan, and the surrounding area for a long time, possibly with the intention of drawing the English forces of Malwa towards him. Meanwhile, Man Singh and Adil Muhammed were strengthening their armies east of the Parvati River. Tatya's march to Rajputana and his lightning march to Malwa had completely caught the English command off-guard. This had forced the English to change their command structure. By the end of August 1858, Major-General Roberts was transferred from Rajputana to Gujarat. Michel, who was heading Malwa, was given the command of both Rajputana and Malwa.[56]

The high waters of the Chambal slowed down English advance and prevented them from being on Tatya's tracks. Nevertheless, they were eager to put an end to this campaign and, Michel was preparing for an offensive to prevent Tatya's movements at all costs.

For this operation, Michel ordered five columns to march upon Jhalra Patan. The first that was ordered from the west was the Neemuch detachment, which had managed to cross the Chambal by the first week of September. It crossed the Chambal on 6 September, reached Garoth on the 7th and was awaiting instructions.[57]

The second was the Mhow column under Colonel Lockhart who had marched from Ujjain on 23 August, and was camped at Susner by 1 September, awaiting Michel's arrival.[58] The third column, under Captain Hope reached Nalkheda by 4 September.[59] The fourth column was under General Michel himself, who had reached Chhapiheda by 4 September 1858.[60] These three columns had marched from the south.

Tatya waited.

The fifth column, under Captain Mayne was ordered to march down from Guna, which is to the northeast. Captain Mayne left Guna in the first week of September and reached Raghogarh on 10 September, Barsat on the 11th and Biaora on the 13th.[61]

Tatya waited.

When these columns arrived in the area south of Jhalra Patan, General Michel's formation was ready. To the west was the Chambal, still running high; to the south and east were Michel and his troops. With this formation, Michel had effectively blocked Tatya from heading either south or east. Tatya's intention was to head east to Sironj, where the army of Adil Mohammed, of Ambawali (near Neemuch) was awaiting him.

Michel's goal was to outflank Tatya and stop his march, giving him the only options of either retreating to the north or face Michel's multipronged attack.

Tatya continued to wait for over a week, before he started his slow march out of Jhalra Patan, barely moving a few miles.

Michel arrived near Chhapiheda on 4 September, stayed there for many days, awaiting reinforcements. Tatya, though in the area, kept his position hidden by cutting off the English lines of communication.[62]

Marching at the speed of a tortoise, after leaving Jhalra Patan on 1 September, Tatya was between Raipur and Soyat by 6 September.[63] He was near Jirapur and Machalpur on 11 September and had reached Rajgarh around 13 September.[64] (see Figure 42). These sixty miles took Tatya an unusually long fifteen days.

Michel and his army had marched to Pachore, southeast of Biaora on 14 September.[65] The English were not keen on action and waited for Tatya to come further south. As Tatya was getting ready for his next move, he wanted to draw out as many English forces away from eastern Malwa as possible.

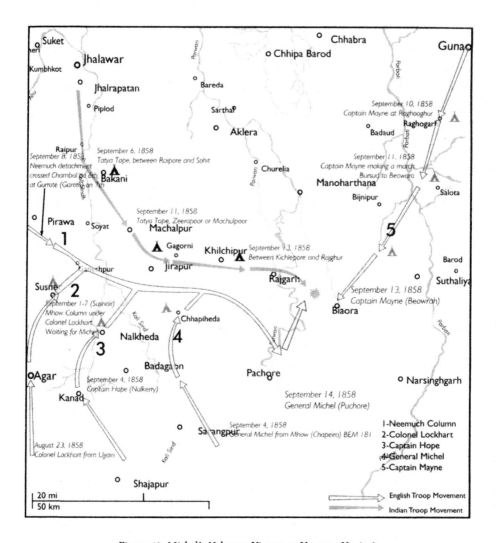

Figure 42: Michel's Valorous Victory or Vacuous Vanity?
31 August–15 September 1858

At the same time, he was in communication with Man Singh, Raja of Narwar and Adil Muhammed from Ambawali, near Neemuch, who would eventually join him.[66]

Tatya continued to march at an unacharacteristically slow pace. Did that mean he wanted to hold out in the region? Tatya was near the walled town of Rajgarh[67]—if he wanted to, he could have entrenched himself in the walled city. The fact that he did not is consistent with his mission that he wanted to head east. After a slow march for over fifteen days, just as the time was right, Tatya made a surprise move.

Tatya lined up all the artillery that he had captured at Jhalra Patan in a full battle formation. His army was ready for a battle that indicated that Tatya wanted to hold out. As the English forces positioned themselves for battle, Tatya's forces marched right through Michel's cordon at lightning speed, without the artillery, completely taking Michel by surprise. Tatya was headed east towards Sironj, where Adil Shah was waiting with several artillery guns. Tatya's resistance was alive, and Michel with a massive army mobilised west of the Parvati River, was stuck. Eastern Malwa was now left only with scattered English forces.

A baffled Michel attempted to stop Tatya's rapid advance, but could not. The only claim that Michel could make was that in the battle that was fought somewhere between Rajgarh and Biaora on 15 September 1858, Tatya 'lost some guns' in the battlefield.

Tatya's goal was to march on to the east and General Michel's orders were to stop him, with five columns under his command. If Tatya did succeed in marching east, logic would dictate that Michel failed in his assigned mission. Michel, fresh with new responsibilities, was ignominiously outwitted by Tatya.

Yet, the propaganda exulted this as a 'victory'. *The Friend of India*, on 23 September 1858 declared:

Tantia Topee appears *at last* to have been defeated...

It appears almost impossible that they should again rally, but Tantia Topee is not yet killed...[68]

However, the 'almost impossible' was a reality as Tatya marched east. The tortoise trap had worked. Local forces now joined Tatya, after Biaora and at Sironj.[69] With men, materials and money, now at his disposal, a reinforced Tatya rallied on.

There were further engagements between Michel and Tatya's forces in the weeks ahead in Jakhlon. In each of these cases, Michel's creativity in describing the battles, is at par with and sometimes exceeds General Havelock's fecundity in imagination.

JAKHLON JUGGERNAUT

Tatya's marches, alternating between lightning speeds and slow movements had thrown the English forces off their rhythm. With Tatya's arrival, Central India had flared up again and local forces were keen on restoring Indian rule. Over the next few weeks, Tatya's mission would be to wrest back towns under English control and hand them to Indian leaders. The towns were along the Malwa-Bundelkhand border, roughly on either side of the Betwa river and had fallen in English hands after the Jhansi genocide.

The English initially celebrated their triumphs at Rajgarh and Biaora. The premature celebrations were aborted, as reality dawned on the English. A telegram from the commissioner of Jabalpur, on 25 September reported:

> Information has been received by me of Tantia Topee being defeated at Beora by General Michel on the 15th instant, but I have since learned (sic) that Tantia's troops having reinforced Adil Mohumed Khan, they (sic), have retaken Seronge and again got some 16 pieces of Artillery.
> ...it is more than probable that this indefatigable rebel will again endeavour to get south and may succeed in doing so...[70]

After the 'action' at Rajgarh and Biaora, Tatya marched to Sironj. Prior to arriving at Sironj, Man Singh's men and possibly Man Singh himself joined Tatya Tope.[71] It is possible that he could have joined Tatya either prior to the action at Biaora or shortly afterwards.

By the end of September, Tatya's position was strong as he set out to restore Indian rule in eastern Malwa. Tatya was marching with supplementary forces of Man Singh and Adil Muhammed, who would hold out these towns after Tatya was finished taking them. Tatya at this time was practically an unstoppable force. Meanwhile, the English were creating a vast cordon of forces to narrow down on Tatya and to put an end to his campaign.

> Roberts was on the west of him; Napier, Smith, and Robertson were on his north; Michel, Hope, and Lockhart, on the south; and Whitlock on the east. Active he assuredly had been; for since the fall of Gwalior he and his mutineers and budmashes had traversed a vast area of the

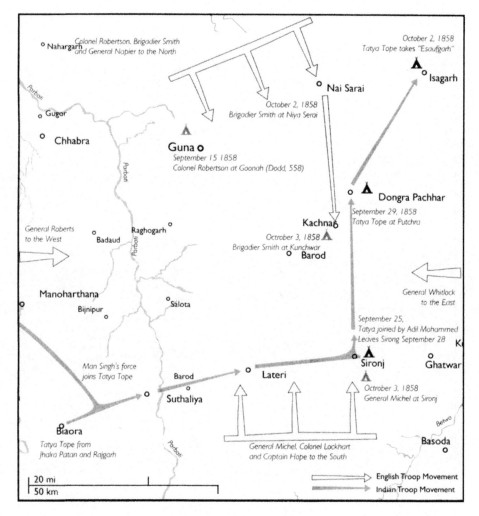

Figure 43: Uncordonable Tatya
15 September–2 October 1858

Rajpoot and Mahratta territories; but he was now within the limits of a cordon, from which there was little chance of his ultimate escape.[72]

On 28 September, Tatya left Sironj and headed towards Isagarh to the north.[73] On 2 October, Isagarh was in Indian hands. Reinforced by Adil Mohammed and Man Singh of Narwar's troops, Tatya's army, according to English estimates had swollen to 15,000.[74] With this army, over the next two weeks, Tatya took control of all the towns on both sides of the Betwa, from Isagarh to Lalitpur.

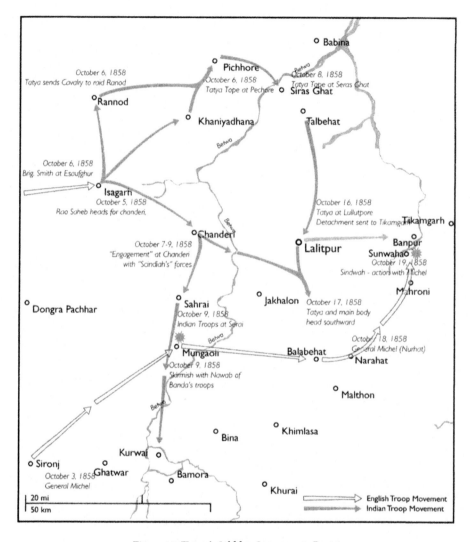

Figure 44: Tatya's Jakhlon Juggernaut: Part 1
3–19 October 1858

Meanwhile, the English forces were reassessing their next move. Colonel Robertson was at Guna,[75] General Michel had moved towards Sagar after the action at Rajgarh/Biaora had now moved upon Sironj after Tatya left. Brigadier Smith was very close to Isagarh, at Nai Sarai, when Tatya captured it, yet he did not move upon Isagarh while Tatya was there![76]

Isagarh was under Jiyaji Rao's Shinde's army. The 'Scindia's Army' was different from the Gwalior Contingent, most of which was fighting alongside Tatya. Some of them had dispersed after Gwalior. Jiyaji Rao's army was supposedly 'loyal' to the English, yet when Tatya Tope reach Isagarh, instead of attacking him they 'fraternised with Tatya Tope'.[77]

Although 'cordoned' by the half dozen approaching English columns by early October 1858, Tatya was still in a strong position.

Maintaining a very strong army, possibly over 15,000, meant higher funding. At this time, all the 'thanas' and the treasuries in these areas were full. Tatya split his forces to raid these English treasuries to keep up with the 'burn rate' for his army.[78] At this time, Tatya Tope and Rao Saheb decided to split their forces as they attempted to re-establish Indian rule in this important area at the border of Malwa and Bundelkhand.[79]

Tatya split his army into three columns. Each of them taking circuitous routes to eventually meet south of Lalitpur. He sent one cavalry regiment to raid the *thana* where the English administrator maintained the treasury, and, establish Indian control. Tatya himself took the longer route via Siras Ghat and Tal Behat and reached Lalitpur by 16 October.[80] Another column under Rao Saheb or the Nawab of Banda went east to Chanderi, where they were apparently 'repelled' by the 'Scindiah troops'.[81]

Rao Saheb was primarily responsible for the safekeeping of the 'mobile treasury'. Rao Saheb, with the treasure, went in the direction of Chanderi.[82] If 'Scindiah' forces had not responded positively to messages sent earlier, would Rao Saheb, with a diminished force, have actually taken the risk to march into hostile territory with the entire treasury? Seems very unlikely.

Tatya marched into Lalitpur without any resistance. The English had abandoned it on the news of Tatya's arrival in the vicinity. After marching into Lalitpur, Tatya probably sent a detachment to the east towards Tikamgarh. This detachment was probably the one that came across General Michel's army on 19 October 1858. Michel's army was marching around in the area 'claiming victories' that in no way impeded the free movement of Indian troops in the area.

Despite being 'cordoned' by the approaching English columns, none of the English forces seemed eager to take Tatya on. In the next three weeks, there were two skirmishes with General Michel. One of these skirmishes has been labelled as a major victory by Michel himself, which was simply repeated and exaggerated by historians without checking facts.

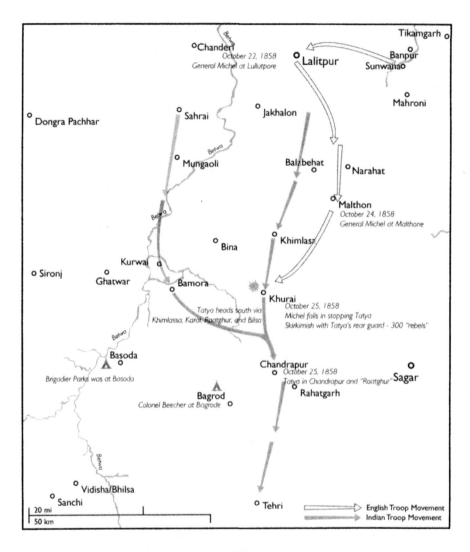

Figure 45-1 Tatya's Jakhlon Juggernaut: Part 2
19–26 October 1858

One of the most severe defeats he (Tatya Tope) received was at Sindwah, on the 19th of October, at the hands of General Michel; another, on the 25th, near Multhone, from the same active general.[83]

One of Tatya's alleged 'severe' defeats of 25 October was near Khurai, as his rear guard was marching south. One telegraphic message reports this as

Michel having intercepted the march of the Rao's army of about 2,000'.[84] Of Tatya's total army, this had to be only one column under Rao, which Michel attacked. Was it really 2,000 strong? Another report refers to this as him having 'succeeded in intercepting about 300 of the rebels....'[85]

Regardless of whether Michel forced a 'severe' defeat on a small column of Tatya's army, or invented a story to avoid further embarrassment; at the end of this encounter, Tatya and his army continued to march down south.[86]

Michel's presence on banks the Betwa, in the jungles of Jakhlon was irrelevant. Brigadier Parke was right at Basoda, watching helplessly, as Tatya's army marched south. Colonel Beecher was at Bagrod, probably hiding during this period. Colonel Liddel's presence to 'guard' Tatya's movement had failed.[87] Tatya, at this time was too strong to be dared by the English. All other English columns that were considering 'cordoning' Tatya in this area, despite tall claims, had failed miserably.

After completely disrupting English command over Malwa, and despite all odds, Tatya had managed to break off and head straight down to Narmada, with his army of about 4,000 to 6,000, including Adil Mohammed.[88] The army of Man Singh stayed back in Malwa to hold on to the newly liberated towns. Tatya's first 'circular' march from Gwalior to the west in Rajputana, and back to the east had rejuvenated the spirit of freedom. Tatya's seemingly circuitous marches, designed with a purpose were thinning the English forces as Tatya ignited new insurrections wherever he marched. While the Christian missionaries celebrated their success in the suppression of 'the procession of the car of Juggernauth (Jagannath), which took place annually at Pooree, in Orissa',[89] Michel was unable to stop Tatya's juggernaut.

General Michel's inability to rein Tatya's movement had a significant impact on the war.

At no time since Tatya's departure from Gwalior, 'or indeed since the fall of Delhi, had the Bombay and Madras Governments felt so seriously alarmed as they did on the receipt of the intelligence that he had got to the south of all the columns in Malwa, and would cross the Narbudda in a few days.'[90]

Tatya crossed the Narmada on 31 October 1858, about forty miles upstream of Hoshangabad and camped in a village called Fatehpur.

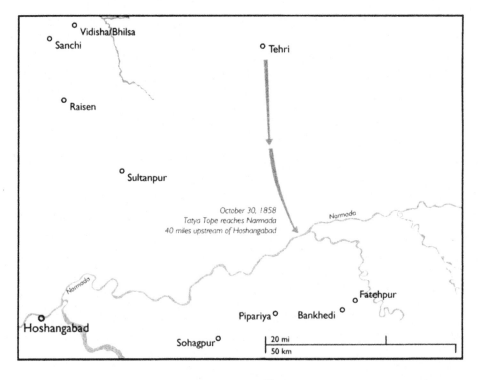

Figure 46: Unstoppable Tatya
27 and 30 October 1858

It was not just the physical act of crossing the Narmada that demonstrated the magnitude of the action. It was a metaphorical statement on the English inability to decisively win the war. It was evident that the soldiers and civilians were determined to support Tatya despite the genocide and terror they had been through.

In the process of hiding their inability to stop Tatya, the English leadership at Calcutta recognised something significant. As soon as the news of Michel's inability to rein in Tatya reached Calcutta by the middle of October, an important and far-reaching decision was made. A decision that was probably in the process of making, as Tatya began gaining momentum after Jhalra Patan.

For Tatya Tope, and India in general, this was going to be a piece of good news wrapped in bad.

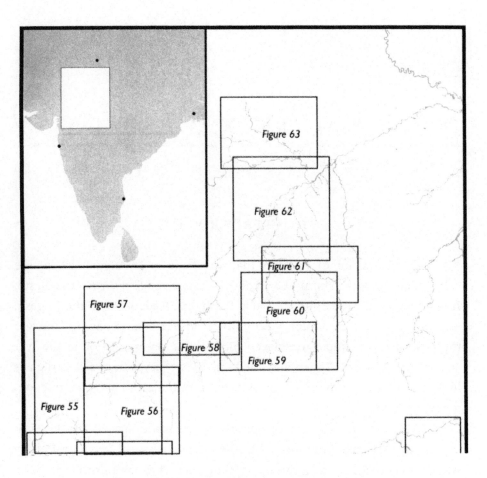

Figure 47: Locator for Figures 48-63 in the following pages

Chapter 17

FRACTIONAL FREEDOM

THE GREAT CROSSING

The Proclamation of Freedom that was made on 25 August 1857 by the Indian leaders fighting the English was in essence a simple manifesto. It was an appeal to the public to help the Indian leaders defeat the English, so that all Indians could enjoy economic and personal freedom. This was the powerful yet simple message, which was a key motivator in the war against the English. A nation's freedom, as we have discussed earlier, is founded upon these three pillars, political, economic and personal freedom for its subjects.

Of the indictments that the proclamation made against the English, the last one resonated the most with the people: personal freedom. Indians wanted freedom from religious oppression from Christian missionaries who were working in concert with the government machinery. Indians wanted freedom from unfair laws that favoured Christians over non-Christians, and they wanted the English to stop overt, or covert, methods of conversion.

Despite the most horrendous attacks on civilians, including women and children, during the war, Indians continued their support to Tatya and others. The support for Tatya was so deep and so widespread that people were risking their lives to uphold the cause of freedom.

England had expected to silence the voices demanding freedom soon after Delhi fell. Yet, Tatya and Nana persevered. Then, England expected to silence India after Bundelkhand was tranquilised with the Jhansi genocide. Yet, Tatya and the flame of freedom remained alive. From late June to October of 1858, Tatya demonstrated that widespread English brutality simply could not extinguish this flame.

It was only after Tatya proved in Malwa that half a dozen English columns were incapable of stopping him, that English leadership recognised that this fire had the potential to spread into other areas and become a wildfire.

England responded with an important concession.

The English made a critical proclamation under the name of their queen.

While the proclamation ran into many pages and conceded on many little things, the most critical concession was the following.

That she (Queen Victoria) would not interfere with the religion of the native, or countenance any favouritism in matters of faith.[1]

This English gave the proclamation widespread importance and was propagated in every town of India—large and small. On 1 November,

the transference of governing power from the East India Company to Queen Victoria was made known throughout the length and breadth of the empire. A royal proclamation was issued, which many regarded as the Magna Charta of native liberty in India. At Calcutta, Bombay, Madras, Lahore, Kurachee, Delhi, Agra Allahabad, Nagpoor, Mysore, Rangoon, and other cities, this proclamation was read with every accompaniment of ceremonial splendor that could give dignity to the occasion in the eyes of the natives; British station, large or small, it was read amid such military honors as each place afforded. It was translated into most of the languages, and many of the dialects of India. It was printed in tens of thousands, and distributed wherever natives were wont most to congregate...[2]

The stranglehold of Christianity, whose foundations in India were laid by Macaulay and unleashed by Bentinck from 1834, was finally removed. The queen implicitly blamed the English East India Company for all the coercive Christian actions, and stripped it of all power and eventually shut it down.

With this, the most exoteric goal of the India's Proclamation of Freedom from 25 August 1858 had been achieved.

Yet, the other goals were nowhere in sight. The English had decided that the only way they could continue the plunder of India, was to allow her people personal freedom. For an old nation such as India, this was devastating in the short term, for a 100 or 200 years; yet in the long term, it would allow India to remain the only living ancient civilisation.

This news was a victory, albeit small, for Tatya. Another goal in the manifesto had been achieved and, for many Indians, this was a significant personal victory. England's deliberate efforts to force dogma on Indians had worked against their rule. By forcing the English to back down, Tatya Tope had lit a small flame, a pilot light.*

It would be this flame, which remained lit for another eighty-seven years, and allowed a fire of freedom to rage again within India.

Eighteenth February 1946 would not have happened if Tatya had not broken through General Robert's columns in Rajputana, and through General Michel's columns in Malwa; and it would not have happened if Tatya had not crossed the Narmada.

THE PARADOX OF PARTIAL LIBERTY

The timing of the queen's proclamation was critical. The proclamation was being worked upon probably for many weeks earlier. However, the English were hopeful that Generals Michel and Robert would be able to stop Tatya. Once Tatya broke through Robert's column in Rajputana, the English were concerned, but when Tatya broke through Michel's columns on 24 October 1858, the English recognised that they had to concede. In all likelihood Calcutta was in contact with London for the weeks leading up to this event. The proclamation was made shortly after Tatya Tope crossed the Narmada. An English historian provides a precise reason:

---

*A pilot light is a small gas flame, which is kept alight in order to serve as an ignition source for a more powerful gas burner.

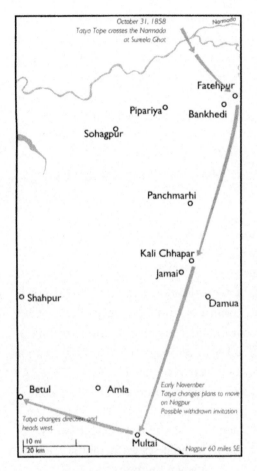

Figure 48: The Great Crossing
31 October–7 November 1858

The queen's proclamation was eminently calculated to withdraw his (Tatya Tope's) misguided followers from him...[3]

There were three categories of people, which the English label as 'misguided followers' who had been the core support for Tatya during the war. First, leaders like Ali Bahadur the Nawab of Banda, who had relentlessly supported Tatya so far, but saw this small victory as sufficient, and therefore an opportunity for truce. Second, the local chiefs who had been covertly supporting Tatya while overtly posturing neutrality or resistance. Third, the villagers who had supported Tatya and his army in providing supplies and critical support. However, the promise of freedom, no matter how small, dampened the spirits of continued revolution.

Tatya too would have been buoyed by this small victory; yet, he would have read more into it. He was in a difficult position.

We analyse the effect Victoria's proclamation had on these three categories of supporters.

Impact of Victoria's Proclamation on the Support of Local Chiefs

Thus far, Indian leaders who had risen against the English had faced brutal punishments, including being blown from a cannon. This proclamation was making a promise of conciliation with the hedgers who had supported Tatya.

As discussed earlier, since leaving Gwalior, Tatya had made 'refuelling' stops in places where his private communication with the local chiefs was encouraging. Similarly, Tatya's movement south was also, likely based on positive encouragement.

> The probabilities are that there were emissaries and agents of the Nana in the city of Nagpore.[4]

In the first two days of crossing the Narmada, Tatya's immediate goal seemed to be Nagpur.

> It was impossible not to suspect that this sudden movement, apparently direct upon Nagpur, had been made by invitation.'[5]

In fact, letters in Hindi and Marathi were found written to ministers in the court of Nagpur. Additionally, communication between Nana Saheb and General Chintaman Bhau, the commander-in-chief of the late Raja of Nagpur's troops, indicated an organised plan on Nagpur.[6] The English took measures to cut off communication between Nagpur and Tatya Tope. All the late Raja's family members and important personnel were arrested.

> Amongst other measures, all the members of the late Rajah's family, and all the other principal and most influential residents of the City were required to encamp within the Residency premises.[7]

Nonetheless, while he was at Multai, Tatya never actually attempted to go to Nagpur. What changed in these few weeks? There are two possibilities. First, in response to Victoria's proclamation, the Bhonsle family could have changed their minds about their invitation to Tatya. Like many others, they were satisfied with the small victory that the war had achieved. A second reason could have been the large-scale arrest of the Bhonsle family. Tatya could have been concerned that the English would use them as hostages. Regardless of the actual reason, Tatya did change direction. Instead of heading south, Tatya decided to head back towards Gujarat and Malwa, to reignite the rebellions started by the Naikdas and the Bhil people in the Panchmahal and the Banswara districts respectively.

While Tatya was heading in the direction of Gujarat, many historians claim that his target was Vadodara, however, that is very unlikely. We have argued that in this phase of the war, Tatya's goals were to reignite the spark of insurrection in wider areas, not to occupy cities. Tatya had recognised that holding on to a major city, with his current strength would not have been possible.

Impact of Victoria's Proclamation on the Support of Villagers

Victoria's proclamation threatened the widespread support Tatya had received from the Indian population, especially the villagers. The villages south of Narmada had witnessed little action and had probably heard about the slaughter of humans unleashed by the English.

With news of approaching armies in their villages, many villagers started abandoning their homes. While the English had more elaborate supply lines, their logistics was not as dependent on support of local villages. However, Tatya's mobility depended largely on local logistic support. Tatya recognised that starving soldiers and guns had the potential to threaten the extent of goodwill he had with the villagers.

To maintain continued support from the villagers, Tatya responded with a proclamation he made under the name of Rao Saheb.

7 November 1858.

Let it be known to all people, to the gentry, the merchants, the shopkeepers, and the military of every city, town and village, that the army bearing the standard of victory, had marched in this direction, only for the destruction of the Christians, not for the spoilation of the resident inhabitants...

Let one know this—that this army, buoyed on the waves of victory, is at enmity with the English, not with the native cultivators of the soil. It has never been the intention of anyone in this force to cause loss to the villagers and residents of the country through which we pass; but it is evident that daily supplies must be had, more especially when an enemy is our front; villages have been looted through the folly of the inhabitants in leaving their homes...

Now this proclamation is put forth, that no villager shall leave his home on the approach of this army, but producing the supplies there may be, receive the fair price of the same. Beyond the current rate, a price shall be fixed. When the proclamation reaches any village, the headman thereof should send a copy of it to the adjacent villages, that fear may be dispelled.[8]

Tatya's urgency in passing on this message was obvious.

Notwithstanding the rapidity with which the movements of Tantia Topee were necessarily made, he found the time and opportunity to distribute the following notifications to the inhabitants of the districts through which he passed.[9]

Although the financial strain on Tatya remained high, with these assurances, Tatya was able to continue the war.

Impact of Victoria's Proclamation on the Support of Tatya's Followers

By conceding some personal freedom, the English wanted to take the wind out of Tatya's sails. The English partially succeeded. Victoria's proclamation had a dampening effect on spirited leaders such as the Nawab of Banda.

The Nawab of Banda has separated from the rebels and is going to General Mitchel's camp en route to Indore. He states that he comes in under Her Majesty the Queen's Proclamation.[10]

On 19 November 1858, the Nawab of Banda surrendered to the English.[11] As anachronistic spectators, nationalistic Indian historians have viewed decisions such as these in black and white, contrasting them with Tatya Tope. While they accurately praise Tatya Tope's perseverance, the role of the Nawab of Banda and others is unjustly diminished and even vilified.

What Tatya was facing was the paradox of marginal liberty. A paradox India faced again on 18 February 1946. Yet, old nations such as India emerge victorious over time.

Without the continued invitation from Nagpur, Tatya decided to head back to Rajputana, where the plan was to combine forces with Feroze Shah. Feroze Shah was continuing his resistance in Rohailkhand during the second half of 1858.

Tatya made an important detour in Gujarat where a local rebellion against the English could use his support.

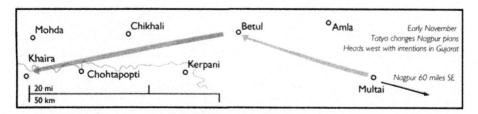

Figure 49: Westward March: Part 1

Tatya had crossed the thick jungles near the Satpura range of mountains and had camped at Multai, when he made the decision not to press towards Nagpur. At Multai, Tatya began his march towards Gujarat, heading west. Tatya's rapid march to the west left the English completely unready for his next moves. Tatya covered over 200 miles in about ten days starting 7 November; first from Betul to Khandwa to Khargone on 19 November.[12] Tatya reached Khargone, near the Grand Trunk road connecting Bombay with Delhi at Julwaniya.

English military commanders accuse Tatya of possibly 'exaggerating his successes' in his communications with Nana. They write:

> Tantia Topee took advantage of the privilege which most generals, especially unsuccessful ones, assume, of depicting the aspect of affairs rather more favourably than they deserved.[13]

While accusing Tatya of exaggeration, almost all English narratives based on reports made by English generals, betray exactly the same 'privilege'—a privilege that has gone unchallenged because of England's eventual victory.

Consider the events between 19 and 23 November 1858. Major Sutherland was posted in Julwania on 19 November. General Hugh Rose, responsible for the genocide at Jhansi, after his transfer to Bombay, had arrived at Sendhwa on 19 November. At this time, Tatya Tope was at Khargone, fifteen miles east of Julwaniya on the Grand Trunk road.[14] Hugh Rose's and Sutherland's mission was to stop Tatya from crossing the Grand Trunk road.

Regardless of what Rose and Sutherland claim, within four days, Tatya Tope not only crossed the Grand Trunk road to be at Rajpur,[15] but also reached the Narmada in a few more days.

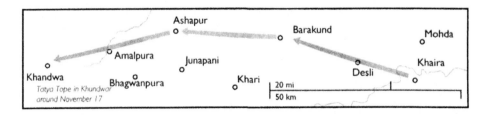

Figure 50: Westward March: Part 2

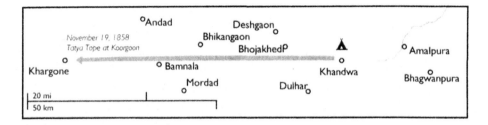

Figure 51: Westward March: Part 3

With General Rose in the area, with obvious orders to stop Tatya Tope and Major Sutherland 'guarding' Julwaniya, there has to be some explanation for their failed mission to stop Tatya Tope. The only reported event is a 'little skirmishing' where Tatya's troops 'fled' and 'the loss on both sides was trifling....'[16]

However, once the place and events are viewed on a map, the lie can be easily nailed. If Tatya's troops did indeed 'flee' the battlefield—they would have had to make some kind of a retreat, not march forward! In reality, Tatya had crossed the Grand Trunk road and marched from Khargone to Rajpur in about three days.

There are only two possible explanations. Either General Rose with Sutherland chose not engage Tatya, fearing defeat, or if they did attempt to stop Tatya, they were indeed defeated. The former seems more likely, since, only a 'trifling loss' is reported. Sir Hugh Rose followed the footsteps of other 'great' English generals as he benefited from the 'privilege which most generals, especially unsuccessful ones assume of depicting the aspect of affairs rather more favourably than they deserved'.

The best that Sutherland could do was to trail Tatya and file a report. He finally 'caught up' with Tatya, 'at sunset' when he 'reached the Nerbudda in time to see the rebel force comfortably encamped on the opposite side'.[17]

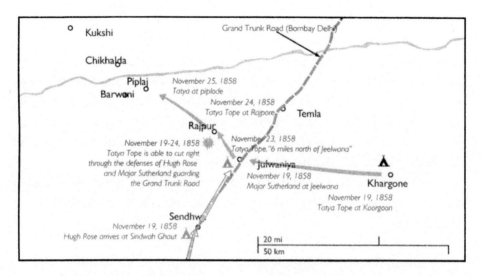

Figure 52: The 'Grand' Crossing
Breaking through the Bombay–Delhi Grand Trunk road—19–26 November 1858

Tatya had managed to cut right through the wall of defence that Hugh Rose and Sutherland had attempted to put on the Grand Trunk road and was now heading towards Gujarat.[18]

There was an obvious asymmetry in the motivation between men like Tatya and Rose. For Tatya and many of his men these long marches, the battles, the river crossings, were for a cause. On the other hand, generals like Hugh Rose were motivated by the loot, the prize money, promotions and knighthoods. They were fully incentivised to portray defeats as victories, losses as gains and invent colourful euphemisms for the more obvious retreats. However, it would be the versions of people like Hugh Rose that would make the history books remain unchallenged, even by Indian historians.

Victoria's proclamation promised personal freedom for Indians. However, this freedom remained incomplete. Politically India remained in chains. While India had gained personal freedom in religion, education remained firmly under state control. Tatya's continued will to fight testifies that he understood this reality. With dampened support from local chiefs, Tatya was a victim to the paradox of incomplete freedom.

BANYAN OR SANDALWOOD?

After deciding not to head south, Tatya headed west towards Gujarat, and as his movement suggests, his immediate target was Chhota Udaipur. Tatya recrossed the Narmada around 26 November 1858, near a town called Piplaj on the left bank and Chikhalda on the right bank. After leaving Chikhalda, Tatya and his army marched through Nanpur, reached Ali Rajpur by 28 November 1858 and Deohati the following day.[19]

When it comes to narrating Tatya's campaigns, almost all English narratives follow a simple four-step pattern of fallacious and deceptive storytelling.

Let us say Tatya's real target was 'A', first the historians would fallaciously claim it was B, which was near 'A'.

Second, once a false target was assigned, historians would minimise the relevance of 'A' and increase the relevance of 'B'.

Third, after Tatya had achieved 'A', claim that Tatya failed at 'B'.

Fourth, declare that the English had achieved in stopping Tatya.

Therefore, in his march toward Gujarat, regardless of what Tatya actually wanted to achieve, historians would claim that Tatya's target was Vadodara, although it was not.

Consider.

Operation Red Lotus had inspired many local rebellions around the country as well. The district of Panchmahal hosts the people who call themselves the Naikas or the Naikdas. Panchmahal has a rich history that dates back many millennia. A traveller in the seventeenth century described this as a place having the best mangoes in the region and sandalwood so plentiful, so as to be used in house building.

Inspired by Operation Red Lotus, the Naikdas or the Naik people of Panchmahal began a rebellion in 1858 against the English under the leadership of Keval Dama and Rupa Gobar. The main areas in their resistance were Chhota Udaipur and Bariya.[20]

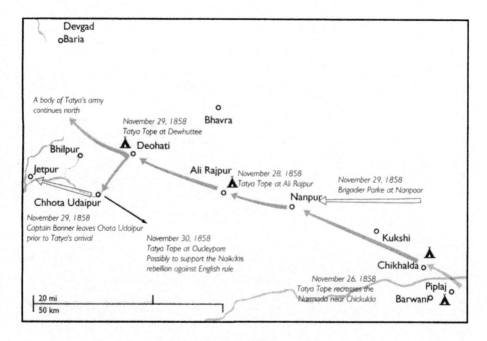

Figure 53: The Great 'Recrossing'
26–30 November 1858

After Gwalior, Tatya had coordinated his efforts with the Bhils in the Bhilwara area, Man Singh and Adil Muhammed in Malwa. As Figure 54 indicates, Tatya's detour from his northerly destination of Rajputana was Chhota Udaipur and Bariya, exactly the same region where the Naikdas people were fighting the English. With support from Tatya, the Naikdas' were able to continue their resistance for a few more months until Keval Dama surrendered on 10 March 1859 and Rupa Gobar on 23 May 1859.[21]

The reported presence of Tatya's army in surrounding towns indicates that Tatya's army split itself into small task forces, to assist the Naikdas in retaking control of these areas.[22] A main body including Tatya Tope and Rao Saheb headed north, and other smaller bodies to Chhota Udaipur and surrounding towns. Chhota Udaipur was under the command of Captain Bonner, who abandoned the place and marched west, prior to the arrival of Tatya's army.[23]

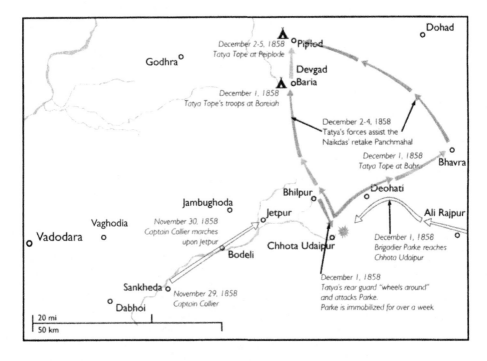

Figure 54: Sandalwood, not Banyan
30 November–4 December 1858

Brigadier Parke, who a few months ago was routed by Tatya in the jungles of Malwa was reassigned to stop Tatya's northward movement at Chhota Udaipur. However, by the time he reached Chhota Udaipur, most of Tatya's army had already left,[24] except possibly the rear guard, which was at the outskirts of Chhota Udaipur. It was possibly this rear guard that in the words of Brigadier Parke, 'wheeled around and fell on his baggage'. Parke's losses were tremendous. 'The loss of equipments and stores, and even carriage cattle was so great that Brigadier Parke was compelled to halt at Chota Oodeypoor until stores and tents, etc., could be sent from this to re-fit his Force'.[25] Parke's apparent 'immobility' was blamed on an irrational panic in his camp followers based on 'infinite exaggeration'.[26]

Despite the mauling received from Tatya's rear guard, Brigadier Parke, in the routine tradition of his colleagues and superiors, claimed victory.

Tatya's army assisted the Naikdas in taking control of many towns around the areas from Jambughoda to Bhavra. Tatya had effectively assisted the Naikdas revive their rebellion against the English.

The Naikras are becoming more troublesome. They attacked on the 12th instant a Company... They plundered the same night a village in the Sokhera Pergunnah and their excesses in the Hallole Pergunnah are reported...[27]

The 'plundering' being referred to was the treasury chests in the administrative offices. The attacks on the English in various locations by Tatya's so-called 'scattered' forces had the English state of affairs in complete disarray.

From 2 to 5 December 1858, Tatya re-grouped his army near Piplode to head towards Banswara, his mission of supporting the cause of the 'turbulent' Naikdas people having been achieved.

Tatya and his forces were in the Piplode area for over three days. The English detachment at nearby Godhra chose not to press forward on Tatya, claiming that they were 'defending' Godhra. In fact, as Tatya's forces started their march northeast towards Banswara via Jhalod, the Godhra detachment reported that Tatya, 'completely changed the whole of his designs. He started at once for the northeast by Jhullode (Jhalod)'. Interestingly, they chose not to follow Tatya's trail either, writing, '...but the pursuit by our troops was delayed by circumstances which have not as yet been enquired into'.[28]

We will never know what reality that euphemistic report was hiding.

English historians claim that Tatya's intentions were upon the important city of Vadodara (Sanskrit for the womb of the banyan tree). They also claim that Brigadier Parke had foiled Tatya's plans by his arrival at Chhota Udaipur in time. However, a body of Tatya's troops had already left Chhota Udaipur even prior to Parke's arrival. Tatya's goals were to reignite the spark of anti-English activities, which were plenty in the Panchmahal district. Tatya's next goal was to march into Banswara district where the Bhils were also causing similar 'turbulences' against the English.

WAG THE DOG

English narratives consistently claim that Tatya was 'on the run' because English forces were giving him a chase, not giving him a moment to breathe. The narratives claim that Tatya was 'running' too fast for them to catch up.

On the surface, the facts are consistent with this claim. Often at times, there was indeed an English army behind Tatya, typically a day or two's march away. Does that automatically mean that Tatya was on the run because the English were chasing him? What about cases where the English troops were ahead of Tatya, and he marched right through them?

The question to ask is, were the English *chasing* Tatya or simply *tailing* him? Tatya's marches were typically driven with a mission in mind. In many cases, such as Malwa and Panchmahal, the missions worked, and sometimes they failed, such as Nagpur, because of circumstances outside the battlefield. From the analysis presented so far, one can conclude that Tatya's marches were on his own terms. Tatya's own proclamation to the villagers requested them to provide for his troops especially when the 'enemy was in front'. He obviously had to factor in the presence of English troops, but the armies behind him were simply tails claiming that they were wagging the dog!

In most cases, Tatya simply left these tails alone, except possibly to teach them a lesson and shake them off, as in the case of Brigadier Parke at Chhota Udaipur. Tatya's rear guard wheeled around and gave Parke a beating that left him stranded in Chhota Udaipur for over a week. While the English claim that Tatya was 'weakened' and his army 'scattered' after Chhota Udaipur, none of the English detachments moved even a mile for over four days while Tatya and his supposedly 'weakened' army were camped in the Piplode area.

Brigadier General R. Shakespear was a political commissioner of Guzerate (Gujarat) and a Resident at Baroda (Vadodara). From his letter to the secretary to the government, it is apparent that the English had an elaborate plan to 'close Tatya Tope's career', in the Banswara area.[29] Based on English strengths, Shakespear drew a triangle that would completely cordon off Tatya. There were detachments no more than one or two day's march away. The Godhra detachment did not move until Tatya had left Piplode, for 'unknown reasons'. Captain Muter in Dohad started his march only on 10 December, and many days after Tatya had left Piplode. The only explanation is that the English forces did not dare to engage Tatya but simply tailed him when they could and claimed that he was 'running'.

If the presence of an army in the rear automatically represents flight, consider that behind Parke was another body of Indian troops about 800 strong.[30] They were headed by a woman and following Tatya's trail. This body of troops had crossed the Narmada and was arriving in Chhota Udaipur.[31] Did Parke leave Chhota Udaipur in a hurry? Can we automatically assume that Parke was 'running away' from them? The point is that the mere presence of an army on your tail cannot be conclusive evidence of 'flight'.

Despite some low points in this long campaign that had exceeded marching over 2,000 miles so far, Tatya was growing from strength to strength, and generating excitement in the places he marched to. His next stop was going to be Banswara, where the Bhil people who had been rebelling against the English were awaiting Tatya's army. Following Banswara was Tatya's planned rendezvous with Feroze Khan who had also continued his resistance in northern India.

Tatya's successes continued to fuel the fires of freedom in areas he had earlier marched. News such as the following started to become more common. Early December,

> ...in central India, a body of rebels to the number of nearly 4,000 had early in December concentrated in vicinity of Nagode, under a chief named Radha Govind, from whence they threatened the garrison at Kirwee, and on December 22, a portion of the force made an attack upon the place...[32]

Tatya's marches largely were on his own terms. Tatya adjusted his destination based on the shifting tactical conditions in the landscape of the war. Tatya was not only skilled in the battlefield; he displayed a mastery of understanding complex linkages and dependencies in warfare, which allowed him to keep the resistance alive for nearly eighteen months so far. Tatya's successes in the third phase were preparing the grounds to launch the fourth and the final phase of the war. However, unfortunately, Tatya or India would never see the fourth phase.

Something dramatic happened on 1 January 1859 that would completely change the course of the war.

Chapter 18

FLICKER

'UNCORDONABLE' TATYA

Ever since the war started in the May of 1857, tens of thousands of English troops poured into India in the early weeks and months that followed. They continued to flow in as Tatya kept the resistance alive. By late 1858, the English had brought over 70,000 troops into India from various locations around the world.

> The Queen's troops in India at the beginning of November, those on the passage from England, and those told off for further shipment, amounted altogether, to a little short of hundred thousand men.[1]

The English had invested millions of pounds into this war simply to mobilise the troops and bring them over to India. Despite this massive strength, why did the English have difficulty in defeating Tatya? The answer was obviously not in Tatya's ability to 'run' according to English claims. What Tatya had achieved in his post-Kalpi campaign was to ignite several local rebellions wherever he marched.

Tatya's trail left behind upheavals and 'turbulences', which the English had to deal with. This forced the English to splinter their enormous army for such operations. While the core troops, including the loyal Gwalior

Contingent was with Tatya, his army would grow and shrink as he marched from town to town. This forced the English to redeploy their troops in maintaining control over these areas.

Despite English claims to the contrary, Tatya's tactics thus far were not to attempt to retake important cities, but primarily to reignite the spirit of revolution that had died after England's gruesome responses in the earlier phases. It is likely that Tatya considered retaking the cities as he became stronger. However, the massive presence of English forces in the strongholds needed a stronger army. Tatya was going to need to combine his efforts with Feroze Shah who had been continuing the war in the north.[2] The target was to rendezvous in Malwa in early January in the belt between Rajgarh and Indragarh.[3]

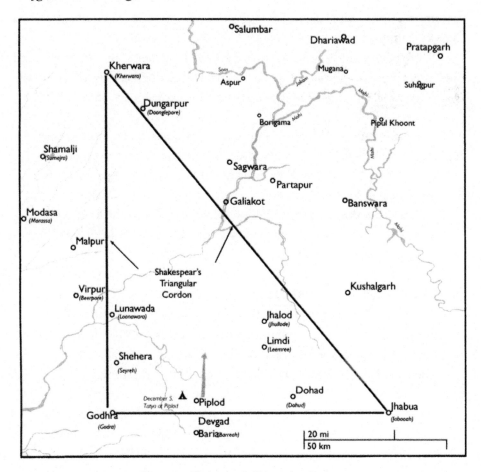

Figure 55: Shakespear's Triangular Cordon

North of Panchmahal is the Banswara district, home to the Bhils. After consolidating his forces that were assisting the Naikdas people regain control over the towns in Panchmahal, Tatya started his march from Piplod towards Banswara on 5 December 1858.

Tatya's arrival in the district reignited the Bhil rebellion in Banswara, a word that literally means 'the land of the forests'.

> ...the passage of the rebels through these districts has caused great disorganisation as might have been expected where so large a part of the population consists of the turbulent classes.[4]

This time the English decided to create a cordon north of Piplod with columns from Godra, Salumbar, Rutlama and Jaora all attempting to end Tatya's campaign.

With plenty of time to restrict Tatya's movement, Brigadier General Shakespear writes about an elaborate plan, described in his letter to the secretary, English government in India. Some excerpts are shown below:

> ...my proceedings will be seen from the enclosures... I am trying to get the Ahmedadbad Detachments advanced from Morassa to Beerpoor and Sameyra and to occupy Loonawarra and Godra from this. (see note[5] for details of thee elaborate geometric descriptions of the triangle.)
>
> ...within this triangle we have Captain Muter with the force which advanced from Godra passing steadily on the enemy's heels, and he was either at or very close to Jallode on the 7th.
>
> In theory, *Tantia Topee must inevitably have closed his career* somewhere between Jallode and Rutlam yesterday or today... their ultimate destruction I consider to be reduced to a certainty. Of course Tantia Topee and ten or twelve mounted men may break through the line but out of the four thousand who invaded Guzerat on the 1st at Oodeypoor, I do not think a hundred men will escape out of the Province...

> Signed R.C. Shakespear,
> Brgr. Genl., Political Commissioner,
> Guzerate and Resident at Baroda[6]

Yet nothing of this sort happened. Shakespear was unable to 'close Tatya's career' with his 'Triangular Cordon'. Over the next two days, Tatya with his full force, crossed Limdi,[7] and Jhalod.[8] The English force from Ratlam known to be of 'great strength' was supposed to have intercepted Tatya at Jhallod. It did not; and no circumstances of their inability to do so are reported.

The Godhra column under Major Muter was in the area and so were Brigadier Parke's troops. Jhalod was where the English were supposed to have completely barricaded Tatya; nonetheless, Tatya marched on. With money always the key to sustaining warfare, Tatya was easily able to attack the administrative offices and take away the treasure chest.[9]

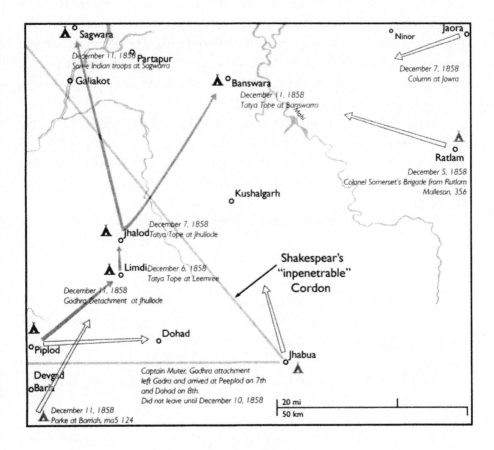

Figure 56: The 'Uncordonable' Tatya
5–11 December 1858

What were Tatya's goals at this time? Again, the English narratives are of little help, since they assign a false target for Tatya, and then claim that they were able to prevent Tatya from achieving it.

As mentioned earlier, Tatya was planning to rendezvous with Feroze Shah in Malwa near the Kota and Indragarh area north of Jhalra Patan. Their goal was to launch the fourth phase of the war, where the cities would be targeted.

In August, Tatya had broken through every English column as he had marched from Rajputana to Malwa. This time around, in the same locations, the English were in a far stronger position. The English estimate Tatya's army to be about 3,000 to 5,000 at this time. Unable to stop Tatya at Banswara the only option the English had was to barricade the three passes, which presented the only path for Tatya to march eastward. The English consolidated their strength near Pratapgarh. Therefore, in order to rendezvous with Feroze Shah, Tatya needed to cut through the barricaded passes and then rapidly march the 100-mile stretch and again penetrate past the Agar area.

Navigating the complicated terrain needed local expertise. Tatya needed assistance to identify passes in the region to face the English in a strong position. To achieve this Tatya would need a supplementary army, reinforcements and guidance of the topography to simply to get past Pratapgarh.

Tatya knew exactly where to get help.

THE PEOPLE OF THE FOREST

Tatya was gathering support from the Banswara area, home to the Bhil people. The Bhils had already been helping Tatya in gaining control of the towns they had taken. The English report states:

> The Bheels are very troublesome here, and have plundered in concert with the rebels.[10]

The Bhil strongholds were in towns that were on the edges of a dense forest tract that looped from Banswara, Salumbar, Gingla, Bhinder, Dariawad, and Pratapgarh as shown in Figure 57.

A body of Tatya's army continued towards Sagwara and a body marched towards Banswara.[11]

Tatya's army regrouped at Aspur on 13 December,[12] marching towards Salumbar whose chief *rawal* was cooperating with Tatya.[13] After a stop at Gingla, Tatya continued marching through the edge of the jungle tract on the invitation of the chief of Bhinder.[14] Tatya continued his march through Dariawad and through thick jungles and emerged near Pipul Khoont.[15]

Despite having half a dozen columns at their disposal, the English were unable to stop Tatya's advance. The English could not even defend Banswara,

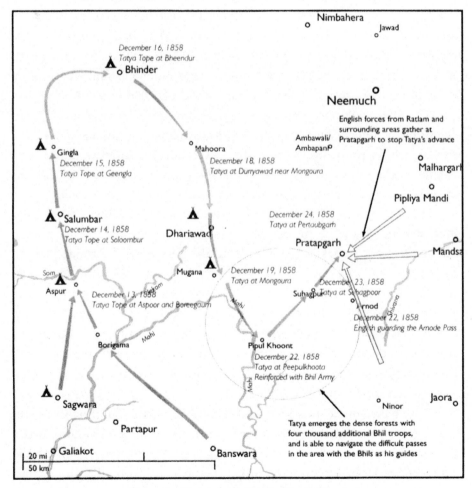

Figure 57: Circumnavigating the 'Jungle Tract'
12–24 December 1858

again claiming to be tardy. With Tatya averaging no more than ten miles per day, the English had plenty of time to plan.

Brigadier General Shakespear had predicted:

> I still think the night of the 9th will see the career of Tatya Tope closed.[16]

Four days later, on 13 December, Tatya was as strong as ever. Was there even a battle fought? Perhaps, courage left the English as it had on many prior occasions where impending battles were inexplicably never fought.

Tatya's one column left Jhalod followed by the other that left Banswara around 12 December. They 'disappeared' near the jungle tract and were reported in the towns mentioned above until Tatya reappeared at Pratapgarh on 24 December. He now had with him a supplementary Bhil army, led by the Bhil chiefs of nearly 4,000, making a total of 8,000 to 9,000.[17]

G.B. Malleson's purely fertile imagination claims that the Bhils far from aiding Tatya, 'followed his track as the vulture follows the wounded hare....'[18] Available facts not only reject Malleson's claim, but Charles Showers (a colonel in the English army who wrote about these events later), who was in Banswara at the period specifically repudiates it in his memoirs.[19]

The Bhil chiefs helped provide more than just the men. With their intimate knowledge of the local terrain, the Bhils helped Tatya navigate the complicated passes in the hills. With the pass west of Arnode blocked by the English, Tatya needed an alternative route. The Bhils navigated the terrain for Tatya to arrive at Pipul Khoont instead of Suhagpur. Tatya's goal at this point was to explode the English forces gathered at Pratapgarh and rapidly march through directly east without allowing the English to consolidate their forces along the way. The target was to rendezvous with Feroze Shah, who was breaking through English defences and marching towards the rendezvous point.

Tatya's first battle was going to be at Pratapgarh. The English forces would have consolidated at Pratapgarh with many of the 'Ratlam' forces, the remaining forces, being re-deployed to quell the resurrection of the Bhil rebellion. It had to be an important battle, considering that the English were aware that Tatya Tope was planning a rendezvous with Feroze Shah. English narratives minimise its importance, and greatly understate their own strength, because Tatya won this battle decisively. More importantly, Tatya had discarded his artillery before entering the jungles, as they would impede movement. Therefore, he would be engaging the enemy without artillery support.

At Pratapgarh, Tatya marched straight at the English army for a direct confrontation. While the battle raged, Tatya's newly acquired supplies, baggage and elephants cleared the passes.[20] Without artillery cover, Tatya's front line had to risk their lives charging the enemy's guns. Tatya won the ensuing battle decisively. The details of this battle are inconsistent among English historians, with Malleson suggesting that Major Rocke was 'baffled'[21] and Colonel Showers countering Malleson's claims.[22]

After defeating the English at Pratapgarh, Tatya and his army marched on to Mandsaur. The English spin on Tatya's victory is self-evident in the different versions of the battle presented in English narratives. Unable to stop Tatya's advance, Colonel Showers wrote: 'Pertabgurh was thus saved'.[23] An English historian has another creative euphemism for this defeat, '...darkness prevented pursuit, and the rebels were allowed to escape unmolested'.[24] The English claimed victory, but found an explanation for their inability to check Tatya's advance. '...and it is probable, if the action had commenced earlier in the day, that few of the enemy would have reached Chumbul'.[25] The fact that this battle generated so much controversy amongst the English suggests that it was a decisive victory for Tatya.

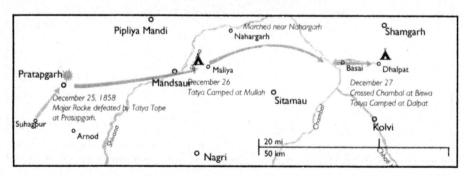

Figure 58: Eastward Ho!: Part 1
25–27 December 1858

Nevertheless, it was more than the 'few' of Tatya's army that reached Chambal. With the help of the Bhil people, Tatya had broken through English defences at Pratapgarh. Having accomplished their mission in successfully helping Tatya get through the pass at Pratapgarh, the Bhil troops returned to Banswara.[26] Tatya marched rapidly from Pratapgarh, camping only at Maliya before crossing the Chambal at Basai. Tatya camped at Dhalpat on 27 December, before marching forward and crossing the Kali Sindh River.[27]

THE LAST MARCH

Tatya was heading into a strong English territory with reinforcements from Agar. The English mobilised multiple columns to engage the arriving army of Tatya Tope. Tatya's target was Indragarh, which was a little more than a 100 miles north of Jirapur. With the news of Tatya's crossing the Chambal, the English mobilised Colonel Benson's column, which was ready, and Brigadier Somerset, who was a day behind them.

After leaving Dhalpat, Tatya quickly marched east, while Colonel Benson's troops attempted to cut off Tatya. At Jirapur, Colonel Benson found Tatya's rear guard. In the small skirmish, Tatya's rear guard lost a few elephants and camels, which were captured by the English.[28]

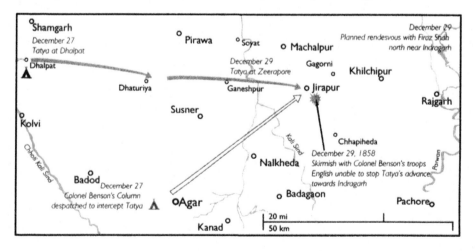

Figure 59: Eastward Ho!: Part 2
27–29 December 1858

Meanwhile, Brigadier Somerset's column, which was right behind Colonel Benson's column, took up the challenge of stopping Tatya's advance towards Indragarh.

While Tatya and his army were at Jirapur, Somerset's column was at Susner, about twenty miles west of Jirapur. They started their march without any baggage or tents, crossed Jirapur and reached Khilchipur by 30 December. They marched another thirty-seven miles via Churelia until they reached Sarthal by late evening on 31 December 1857.[29] As they started marching again around midnight, after four hours they caught up with Tatya's encampment at Chhipa Barod or simply 'Burrode' in English narratives.

Chhipa Barod is part of the Baran district of Malwa in modern day Rajasthan and borders Madhya Pradesh. The many tributaries of the Chambal traverse this naturally rich area.

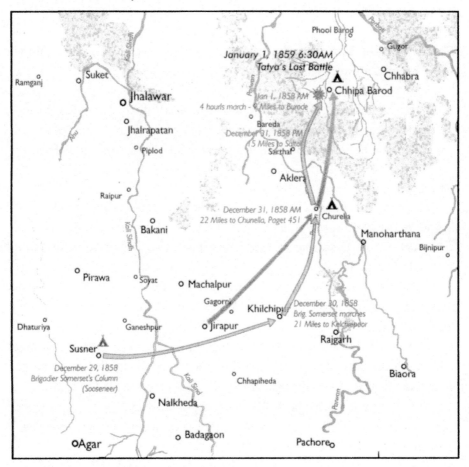

Figure 60: The Last Battle
1 January 1859

At daybreak on 1 January 1859, a battle was fought between Tatya Tope's army and Somerset's column. The following is the description of that battle in the words of Major Paget:

> ...the enemy on the right, however, stood their ground well; and were being led and encouraged by a native, conspicuously dressed in white, and mounted on a handsome white horse.
>
> He waved his sword, and was evidently encouraging them to charge the guns; when, suddenly, a round shot knocked him and his horse over, and several followers rushed out and carried him into their midst.
>
> It was Tantia Topee himself![30]

Shortly after this skirmish, while the English troops were camped at Chhabra they received an important report.

> A report reached us that Tantia Topee was killed... the shot had undoubtedly killed his horse—a very handsome white Arab—but the rider, whether killed or wounded, was quickly carried out of sight.[31]

The lion had fallen.

Contrary to English claims that Tatya was hanged on 18 April 1859, we argue that Tatya Tope was actually killed in the action at Chhipa Barod. A more detailed analysis that attempts to explain this divergence is presented in a subsequent section.

Tatya's death had a significant impact on subsequent events. Consider some of the developments that took place in the three-week period after Tatya's death.

Shortly after the battle at Chhipa Barod, instead of heading straight towards Indragarh, Rao Saheb led the troops to Nahagarh, about twenty miles northwest of Chhipa Barod, where they camped for the night.[32]

On his way to Nahargarh, Rao Saheb quickly dispatched a messeger to Man Singh to meet them at Paron, where they spent the next few days[33] possibly contemplating their next steps.

Given that the Indian troops were retreating, the English could have easily attacked while Rao Saheb and his army who had fought for over a year, were in all likelihood cremating Tatya's body at Paron.

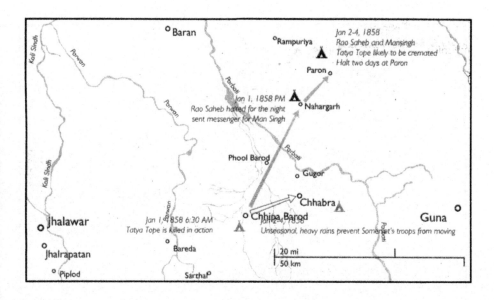

Figure 61: Death and Cremation
1–2 January 1859

However, in a rare occurrence shortly after the battle in Chhipa Barod, there was very heavy unseasonal rain for the next two days.[34] This stranded Somerset's troops at Chhipa Barod, which were marching without tents or shelter, thus giving Rao Saheb and his troops sufficient time to complete the last rites.[35]

On 5 January, they left Paron and headed towards Indragarh. They were near Sheopur around 8 January. It is apparent that Tatya's death had a clear impact on the morale of the leaders and the troops. It also created a divergence in views about the next step to be taken, as is evident in the actions of Man Singh who was accompanying Rao Saheb. After Paron, Man Singh left them for 'unexplained reasons', possibly near Sheopur.[36] It is also plausible that Man Singh considered fighting on in Malwa, as Rao Saheb and Feroze Shah mulled their next steps. Before Tatya's death, the plausible targets were Jaipur and Udaipur.

Rao Saheb's rendezvous with Feroze Shah as planned took place at Indragarh on 9 January, after crossing the Chambal near Lakheri.[37]

The chronology of events from 9 to 21 January as written by the English present some logical inconsistencies. There are two conflicts mentioned. The first battle was apparently at Dausa on 16 January, with Charles Showers.[38] After which, the Indian troops marched north towards Alwar and then west

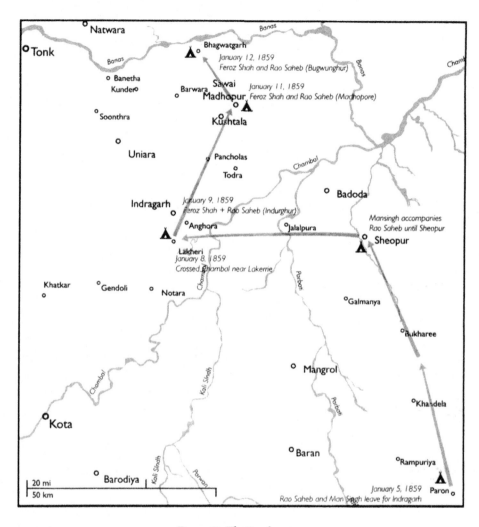

Figure 62: The Rendezvous
5–12 January 1859

to Sikar, where another battle took place. A few days after this battle, 600 men surrendered themselves to the Raja of Bikaner.[39] The surrender of these battle-hardened troops signalled the end of the resistance. The resistance was alive only as long as Tatya was.

The battle at Chhipa Barod was the last that Tatya Tope fought.

Major Paget writes: '...in point of fact, this was the last stand... made by any considerable body of rebels in that part of India'.[40]

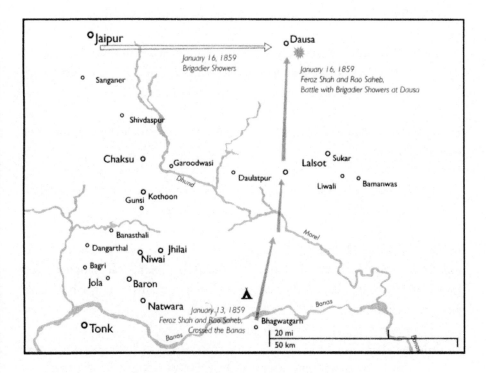

Figure 63: Rao Saheb and Feroze Shah in Rajputana
13–16 January 1859

RESURRECTION

Although Tatya's death signified the end of a substantially organised stand against the English, the spirit of liberty was not dead yet. With the loss of their leader, it is very likely that some soldiers surrendered, and some remained as determined as ever.

One can easily imagine the inspiration that Tatya was to many of his soldiers, who dreamt the same dream that he did. These men stared death in the face day after day, and yet, fought alongside Tatya for the eighteen months of the war. It is possible that they wanted to complete the task that had remained unfinished.

Shortly after the battle of Chhipa Barod, in the 'official' narrative, including Tatya's own purported testimony, Tatya was 'tired of running away'.[41] He then retired in the jungles of Central India. However, there are some strange incidents, which when viewed in the context of Tatya's death on 1 January 1859, corroborate our conclusion.

The English claim that Tatya changed his identity when he 'retired'.

> Tantia Tope who has recently taken to a disguise and assumed the name
> of Ram Singh, has completely disappeared; but it is suspected that he
> was lately near Jhansie, under the name of Jeel Jung.[42]

He apparently changed his name from Ram Singh, to Jeel Jung and then
to Rao Singh.

> Tantia Tope when last heard of was threading the jungles of the
> Chumbul under the assumed name of Rao Sing.[43]

If Tatya was indeed 'hiding' or had 'retired', it is conceivable that he would
indeed take up different identities such as Ram Singh, Rao Singh or Jeel
Jung. However, if Tatya had really retired or gone into hiding what could
explain the following?

> 5 March 1859
> The troublesome and slippery chief (Tatya Tope) was at Seronj
> yesterday, coming down to Rahulgarh. He cut up, on his way, about
> 200 of the Bhopaul troops, by pretending that he had been sent by
> the British to assist them against Tantia Topee, who was at hand; and,
> when among them, cutting them up right and left before they could
> help themselves...[44]

These actions of a man who was 'hiding' or who was 'tired' do not add
up.

What seems likely to have happened is that, Rao Saheb, Feroze Shah and
the few soldiers around him, chose to keep Tatya's death under wraps for
obvious reasons. Could some of Tatya's soldiers, subhedars or other officers,
with names such as Ram Singh, Rao Singh or Jeel Jung, have decided to
carry on Tatya's mission and legacy?

What is very likely is that others with names such as Ram Singh or Jeel
Jung had taken Tatya's identity. Despite the post-war spin presented by the
English, Tatya's name had put fear in the hearts of many an English officer.
This is visible in the many battles that should have happened, but never

took place. It is plausible that Tatya's loyal soldiers attempted to continue his unfinished task.

On 7 April, Major Meade claimed that he had arrested Tatya Tope with the assistance of Man Singh.[45] This so-called 'betrayal' by 'Tatya's trusted friend Man Singh' fills many pages of history books; however, in the current narrative, the discussion is limited to only the relevant facts.

IDENTITY CRISIS

Did this deception actually work? Did the English leadership actually believe that Tatya Tope was alive and had taken on these various identities?

First, consider the possibility that they did believe that Tatya remained alive.

The one reason why Ram Singh, Rao Singh or Jeel Jung could have passed off as Tatya Tope was because very few English had actually seen Tatya, other than those who had close enough encounters during battles. In fact, as far as the English were concerned, Tatya did not emerge on the scene until Nana Saheb and Tatya Tope divided their responsibilities between Awadh and Central India, sometime in the September of 1857.

This confusion in the identity of Tatya starts with John Lang, who had met Nana Saheb at Bithur, and claimed to have met Tatya Tope much before the war.

> ...he was not called Tantia Topee at Bhithoor, but 'Bennie', simply.
> ...and my impression is that Bennie was not a Mahratta, but a member of some obscure family in the Upper Provinces of India, under British rule.[46]

John Lang was writing this in 1861, after Tatya Tope was famous. Despite this, not only did he confuse Tatya with another Indian military leader named 'Baini Madhu',[47] but he was wrong about Tatya's background as well.

Even during the war, there was utter confusion about Tatya's identity.

> ...nobody seemed really to know where the Nana was or who Tatya Topee was...[48]

Not only did they not know who Tatya was, at one point, after Tatya crossed the Narmada, the commissioner of Nagpur made an elaborate and conspiratorial case that Nana Saheb and Tatya Tope was the same person and Rao Saheb was actually Tatya Tope!

> ...I believe the true solution of the evidence which inclined me to think Tatia Tope was in fact the Nana, and of the puzzle which seems generally to exist concerning the Nana, Tatya Tope and the Rao Sahib, may be this, that there are two Nanas—one the adopted son of the Ex-Peishwa Bajee Rao, who is everywhere, but it may be some degree erroneously execrated as the Nana; the other, the son of Ramchunder Punt, the Ex-Peishwa's Soobahdar, who is the so-called Tatia Topee... the Rao Sahib, I believe to be, not the nephew of the Nana, the Ex-Peishwa's adopted son, but the younger brother of the Nana, the son of the Ex-Peishwa's Sobahdar Ramchunder Pant, who now goes by the name of Tatia Topee...[49]

The point in presenting this absurd claim made by the commissioner is that the English were truly unsure who Tatya Tope was. Therefore, his 'reemergence' as Ram Singh, Rao Singh or Jeel Jung could have allowed the myth of his identity to prevail.

Although not completely unlikely, the author rules out this 'conspiracy'.

HANGING A METAPHOR

The second and a more likely possibility was that the English leadership did have their doubts about Major Meade's claim that he had captured Tatya, but played along anyway.

Consider some facts:

Major Paget witnessed the action in which Tatya Tope was killed. Shortly after the battle, their column received the news of his death. A few days later, Major Paget writes about an important meeting that took place in Brigadier Somerset's camp.

On 11th January General Michel and Headquarter Staff arrived, and when the next day Colonel Price, commanding the artillery in this division of the army, with his adjutant Stirling, followed, we wondered what was up. They all believed the report of Tantia Topee's death to be correct.[50]

This meeting was between General Michel, Colonel Price commanding the artillery and his adjutant, specifically, to discuss Tatya's death. However, since Tatya 'reemerged' shortly thereafter, there seemed to be no obvious follow-up of this report. Surely, General Michel had informed Calcutta of this possibility.

After Tatya Tope was allegedly captured, Major Meade's commanding officer from Sironj, Brigadier General Napier, sent a telegraphic message to Calcutta:

> ...unless otherwise instructed I shall proceed to try Tantia Topee by Court-Martial according to the Resident at Indore. There is abundance of evidence obtainable here.
>
> Message from Brigadier General R. Napier, to Major-General W. Mansfield, the Chief-of-Staff, dated Camp Sironj, 11th April, 1859[51]

Calcutta, having doubts about Tatya's identity, responded:

However, the Guna/Indore division hurriedly wrapped a case against the alleged Tatya Tope and reported the following day:

> Tantia Topee was sentenced to death and executed yesterday at Seepree. He was fully identified and acknowledged himself.[52]

To gain credibility for the hanging at Shivpuri, Major Meade and his superiors gave a lot of importance to Tatya's testimony* and his signature.

---

*An analysis of Tatya's alleged testimony was not considered necessary in this narrative, considering that the author is arguing that Tatya had died in battle months before he was supposedly hanged. However, a study of his alleged testimony indicates that it was written by someone who was tailing Tatya, and presenting what was convenient.

If the English did indeed suspect that they were not hanging Tatya, what was their motivation in proceeding with this charade?

Consider Major Meade's personal stake: money. Major Meade and his immediate superiors were laying claim to the prize money in the range of thousands of pounds. For this, they held a mock trial, which was labelled by Charles Showers as a 'pitiful proceeding'.[53]

Did their superiors in Calcutta believe Meade's story?

The answer to this question is surprisingly obvious. Although Tatya had died, Ram Singh, Rao Singh and Jeel Jung had made him a legend. A legend who would continue to threaten the English rule in India even after his demise. A villager from near Jhansi, who asked the author recently, 'whether Tatya Tope had the *vardaan* of invincibility...' was possibly passing on this legend. Therefore, when Calcutta approved this chicanery, they were not hanging a dead man, but they were hanging a legend who had become the metaphor for freedom.

There is another fact that seems too important to be a coincidence, and is worthy of discussion. In an earlier chapter, we discussed that after Tatya's death on 1 January 1859 at Chhipa Barod, Rao Saheb quickly marched on to Paron, and Tatya in all likelihood was cremated at Paron.

Coincidentally, after Major Meade 'negotiated' with Man Singh, the terms of his cooperation, they made a visit to Paron!

If Major Meade, as we argue, was perpetuating this fraud, he needed to ascertain himself that the real Tatya Tope would never ever 'reemerge'. What is likely to have happened is that in the negotiations with Man Singh, Major Meade became aware about the circumstances of Tatya's death. His visit to Paron could have been to ascertain some simple facts. He could have verified Man Singh's claim with the locals. Facts such as, the location of Tatya's cremation. Once Meade was satisfied that Man Singh was telling the truth, he extended the £ 1200 pension for his 'cooperation' in silence. Man Singh became a hero for the English and a villain for the Indians.

What about the story in the family about Tatya's death?

The author recognises that stories in the family can be often myths that are embellished over the generations. Still, embedded within these very stories can be facts that can be relevant in such an analysis.

There is a common thread that runs in the story of the Yeola, Bithur and Vadodra side of Tatya's family. There are two parts to the story, which almost everyone believes with conviction. First, that it was not Tatya that was hanged, and second, that Tatya lived on in disguise as a *sadhu* and visited Yeola, Vadodara and Bithur at varying dates well after he was allegedly hanged.

The first half of the story is consistent with the premise of the present argument. It could not have been Tatya who was hanged in April 1859. However, it is not because Tatya lived on, but because Tatya was already dead. Could Man Singh have communicated with the family and told them the truth? Once induced into the deal of silence, Man Singh, without really having betrayed anyone had become a betrayer for the Indians. Man Singh was indirectly perpetrating a lie in return for his reward, and there was no reason for Man Singh to jeopardise his continuing pension.

The sadhu part of the story in the family could simply have been an explanation based on the firm belief that the English hanged someone else, combined with another fact that Rao Saheb, was indeed disguised as a sadhu right until 1862.

Whom did the English really hang? It could have been Ram Singh, Rao Singh or Jeel Jung, or it could have been an arbitrary victim, that would add to the already long list of English brutality.

While Major Meade walked away with all the credit and money, what about Brigadier Somerset and his columns that had engaged Tatya in his last battle?

Did the English acknowledge Somerset for this 'accomplishment?'

On the contrary, shortly after the battle, Somerset's column was actually disbanded. Major Paget, who was in the artillery section of Somerset's Cavalry column, writes:

...and thus the cavalry column under poor Somerset was broken up. Poor fellow! He died about three years after in England, his death hastened, indeed, I may say, entirely caused, by exposure during this short campaign.[54]

It was probably convenient to disband it.

Notwithstanding the story in the family or the English version of Tatya's death, the author is of the belief that Tatya Tope died around 6.30 am on 1 January 1859.

BEYOND TATYA

After Tatya's death, Nana Saheb continued to fight on in Awadh until he, along with his forces, retreated into the Himalayan hills. Little is known of what happened to Nana Saheb other than rumours of his death. While this book is focused more on Tatya Tope, the key role of Nana Saheb in the planning and in execution cannot be ignored. English historians and their loyal Indian subjects, vilified Nana and the Marxists marginalised him. Nevertheless, without the direct involvement of Nana Saheb the War of 1857 and the fractional freedom that it achieved would not have been possible. Rao Saheb, according to English records, lived on in disguise as a priest and was caught and executed a few years later. Feroze Shah left India and was rumoured to have died in Mecca in 1877.

Historians frequently indulge themselves in the 'what-if' game. The Anglo-Indian War of 1857 is particularly notorious for these what-ifs, all premised on flawed analysis, and a biased and revisionist history.

The author refuses to speculate on what could have happened if Tatya had not died on 1 January 1859. This quest, in the author's opinion, is best left for all the pejorative and 'loyal' academics, who thrive on these what-ifs and assuredly will belittle Tatya's real achievements; or the self-flagellating historians, who can whip up any excuse to implicitly whimper and moan in their narratives.

Tatya's incredible marches in Rajputana, Malwa and the Panchmahal and Banswara districts revived a rebellion. This forced the English to concede personal freedom for Indians.

Although incomplete, it was the flame that Tatya Tope, Nana Saheb and Bahadur Shah and others lit, which would light the fire of freedom and rage again in India exactly eighty-seven years and forty-nine days after Tatya Tope's death. India would soon be breathing the air of freedom.

EPILOGUE

FRESH AIR—PART 2: FREEDOM BEFORE INDEPENDENCE DAY

On a balmy Bombay afternoon, the waves lapping against the hull of the INNS Talwar echoed in the deserted alleyway inside. Radio Operator First Class Mansoor Khan strode purposefully towards the communication room. His fingers expertly turned the dials and switches, as he glanced towards the open porthole. The sudden static from the high power transmitter startled him as it crackled to life.

'*Come in Karachi.. come in...,*' he hissed into the microphone.

Madras, Vishakhapatnam and others, including Aden and Bahrain, had already confirmed, now only Karachi and Chittagong were remaining. It was just a matter of time. He glanced down at the secret message sheet in his hand; there were seventy-eight warships on the list.

'*Karachi... do you copy Karachi...*'

The students listened in a hushed silence as Commander D.N. Joshi (Indian Navy, Retd.) narrated his story of 18 February 1946.

'*Come in Bombay... come in...,*' came the reply, '*this is INNS Hindustan...*'

'*INNS Hindustan? INNS Talwar?*' interrupted one of the children. '*You mean to say INS, short for Indian Naval Ship, right?*'

'*Wait...this was before Independence? It should be HMIS, right?*' exclaimed another proudly.

Commander Joshi, smiled, '*Not bad...but no! On 18 February 1946, for about five days, His Majesty's Indian Ships, HMIS, became the Indian*

National Naval Ships, INNS, borrowing the name from Subhash Chandra Bose's Indian National Army.' Cdr. Joshi declared. *'We will get to other things that happened on 18 February, however, the events of the following day are also interesting...,'* he whispered.

'What happened the next day?' the students asked in unison.

This dramatised 'story' aside. What *did* actually happen on 19 February 1946? Not unlike the historiography of 1857, the magnitude and the significance of the events of Monday, 18 February 1946 have been marginalised in most historical accounts. Let us revisit what is largely forgotten.

MONDAY REMEMBERED

Consider the few years that preceded the events of that fateful Monday. The Indian National Army, under the leadership of Subhash Chandra Bose was making inroads into India through Burma (now Myanmar) starting 1942, with the idea of liberating India from the clutches of the English. Consistent with their 'achievements' in 1857, the English decided to cut off the supplies to Bengal. The transport of rice into Bengal was restricted, in addition to removing the local stock of rice. The idea was to starve the entire region, so that the incoming army would be competing for food with the local population. The English succeeded, and the INA was unable to cross Bengal. This resulted in what is known as the Second Bengal Famine that starved the population of Bengal. Over four million Indians starved to death and the INA was defeated.[1]

After the end of Second World War, there was widespread expectation from Indian leaders who had been 'engaged' with the English, over 'conversations' that hardly went beyond 'autonomy' for many decades. They were expecting that England would be handing over the reins to India, on a 'silver platter'. Months had gone by, and there was no substantive talk of independence. The 'silver platter' was not only empty, but the English were exulting in their post-war euphoria. Adding insult to injury, the English had begun the trials of the INA soldiers who had fought alongside Subhash Chandra Bose.

Independence was nowhere in sight.

Having heard many promises from their pacifist leadership for over twenty years, there was growing impatience amongst the civilians and Indian military personnel in the Air Force, the British Indian Army and the Royal Indian Navy. Railway and postal workers were striking all over India and in Allahabad, a mob of 80,000 stormed ration centres. The ground and maintenance crew in the RAF at Dum-Dum airfield and several other stations 'mutinied'.[2] There was a general atmosphere of restlessness.

In the February of 1946, this impatience boiled over in many places across India. There were protests in Calcutta over the INA trials. There were fourteen trials of INA men resulting in prison sentences. On 11 February 1946, Rashid Ali was sentenced to seven years rigorous imprisonment. Calcutta exploded.[3] There were six days of intense agitations from 11-16 February. The English government attempted to clamp down on the protesters.[4] There were street battles in which eighty-four were killed and 300 injured.[5] At exactly the same time, in Bombay, the Indian ratings of the Royal Indian Navy were expressing their resentment towards English rule. In the second week of February, slogans appeared on the walls of the establishments. 'Quit India', 'Revolt NOW', and 'Kill the English Bastards'.[6] Shortly, the RIAF revolted in an India Pioneer unit in Calcutta and in various centres at Jabalpur.[7]

The air was thick with anticipation.

On Monday, 18 February 1946, the English ensign on the HMIS Talwar was lowered. In a symbol of freedom, the 'Azad Hind' flag of the INA replaced the Union Jack on the mast. The naval leaders also hoisted the flags of the Congress and Muslim League to symbolise that these represented unified actions of Hindu as well as Muslims in the navy. On that day, the Naval personnel changed the name of RIN or the Royal Indian Navy to the Indian National Navy, in the spirit of Bose's Indian National Army.[8] HMIS Talwar became INNS Talwar.

INNS Talwar was so chosen because it was a signals ship, capable of communicating with all the other ships. As soon as the Jai Hind flag was flying on top, other ships were notified. In a short period, seventy-eight other ships and twenty shore establishments from Karachi to Chittagong were under Indian control. These included the WT stations in Aden and Bahrain, a cookery school and two demobilisation centres.[9]

In Karachi, Indians took control of the corvette HMIS Hindustan, and one other ship and three shore establishments. The English response was quick. However, in Bombay, the Indian soldiers that were sent in to suppress the ratings, refused to fire. In the bay, INNS Narbada (erstwhile HMIS Narbada) trained its guns on the Royal Bombay Yacht Club, located just behind the arch of the Gateway of India. Soon the whole city came to a standstill as the civilian population showed its support with strikes, *hartals*, barricades, street battles and the destruction of police stations, post offices and other official buildings, while shopkeepers provided the navy personnel with free food and drink.[10] INNS Talwar, the communications ship at Bombay, became the centre of all negotiations and represented the overwhelming show of strength around all the ports.

An English naval officer, introduced in the prologue of this book, rushed to the top of the RBI building, the tallest in the area to get a bird's eye view of the situation. A sniper bullet originating from one of the ships killed him instantaneously.

Even before the Congress and Muslim League leaders got around to predictably 'condemning' this behaviour, England had already responded. The 'pacifist' voices might have selectively forgotten and even censured India's 'violent' and 'forgettable' history of 1857, but the English knew exactly what the future held for them. The Jai Hind flag was symbolically analogous to the Proclamation of Freedom made on 25 August 1857, but with a military force that was far more powerful.

Could England have retaliated as viciously as it did eighty-eight years earlier, and won this time around as well? Could England have sent their once mighty Air Force to crush the Indians?

However, the real question was, would England, weakened after Second World War, be willing to engage in another bloody war with a highly motivated Indian Navy with support from the other Indian armed forces?

The answer came the following day, loud and clear, from a few thousand miles away.

On 19 February 1946, Pethick-Lawrence in the House of Lords, and Prime Minister Attlee in the House of Commons made a simultaneous announcement. '...that in the view of the paramount importance, not only to India and to the British Commonwealth, but to the peace of the world, His Majesty's Government had decided to send out to India a special mission consisting of three Cabinet ministers to seek, in association with the viceroy.'[11] This mission was to work out the details of India's independence.

REMONSTRATION, EXPROPRIATION AND THE FOURTH COLOUR

The navy ratings were not impressed with that announcement. After all, England in the past had been 'persuaded' by the pacifists to send many 'missions' in the previous decades. None of them had resulted in India's independence. Why would this be any different?

However, the English recognised that the threat this time was real and present, and could spark something much larger. Indian soldiers who had fought for the British Army in the Second World War were witness to the INA trials as well. In stating that India's liberation was necessary for the 'peace of the world', the English implicitly admitted that similar scenes could follow in other parts of the world, where Indian soldiers had fought, from Africa to the Middle East. Therefore, cutting their losses and leaving India was a pragmatic choice that could allow the English to hold on, or control a few of their colonies around the world.[12] However, the leaders of this 'violent' movement were going to need more convincing.

Congress leaders were not only taken by surprise at the coordinated events of the naval ratings that shook the Indian subcontinent, but they had no idea that England had immediately chosen to retreat rather than engage in an all-out war. Obviously, the English had made a decision to withdraw, without even consulting with the Congress leaders. Maulana Azad admitted in his memoirs, *India Wins Freedom*, that he only heard about the English announcement much later that evening, at 9.30 pm, over the radio.[13]

What started as a coordinated event by the naval ratings, with support from the RAF and an eager and rejuvenated INA, was inspiring civilians to join in. There were slogans of 'Jai Hind' all over.

The Congress reaction was swift and the remonstration was immediate.

Jawaharlal Nehru quickly declared himself, 'impressed by the necessity for curbing the wild outburst of violence.'[14] M.K. Gandhi in his speech on 22 February 1946 said that he had followed the events in India with 'painful interest', and scolded the 'members of the navy' for setting a 'bad and unbecoming example for India'.[15] As the popularity and scale of the movement increased, there were slogans announcing India's impending liberation. This was a clear vindication of Bose's approach toward the English. Disturbed by the usage of the INA's war cry, Gandhi said that, 'to shout Jai Hind or any popular slogan was a nail driven into the coffin of Swaraj.'[16]

Muslim League's Jinnah echoed the Congress' sentiments and asked the navy to return to their ships and lay down their arms. Hoisting the Congress and Muslim League flags in addition to the Azad Hind flags, symbolised a unity that superseded the political divisions that were unfolding in India. Hindus and Muslims were united, but Gandhi was distressed. He viewed this combination of Hindus and Muslims for 'violent action' as 'unholy'. In addition to castigating the naval heroes, Gandhi was upset at the civilian leaders who were possibly critical in coordinating these activities with the navy and other armed forces. Who were these civilian leaders of this war? History on this subject is simply missing—for reasons we discuss further; however, Gandhi's speech gives us a hint. Without naming anyone, Gandhi censured the *known and the unknown leaders* of this thoughtless orgy of violence'.[17] Who were the 'known and unknown leaders' that Gandhi was attacking? Did he not want to publicise their names, lest they seize the limelight earned from an 'unholy' and a 'violent' way?

Will they always remain the unnamed heroes who helped set India free?

Will their actions be simply remembered as a 'thoughtless orgy of violence'?

Nevertheless, the events that started on 18 February continued for a few more days. On 21 February, Admiral Godfrey issued his ultimatum 'to surrender or face destruction of the whole navy'.[18] The navy refused. It turned out to be a hollow threat. The impotency of the English rule was self-evident and their rule in India was symbolically over. However, the naval leaders countered with a demand for a more substantial evidence of the English intention to leave India.

The navy representatives agreed to meet with Vallabhbhai Patel. With the press largely gagged, the public at large was not aware of the extent of power the Indian armed forces had over the situation. Not fully trusting Patel, they agreed to back down on the condition, that Sardar Patel made a *public* announcement about the impending freedom. Patel agreed and the naval ratings retreated. They had achieved their goal. Patel gave a speech to the public in Chaupati in Bombay the following day. 'My father-in-law, P.K. Tope was about 23 years old when he was a witness to all these events,' Commander Joshi said. He attended the gathering where he heard Sardar Patel declare that, *'Azadi to ab chand dino ki baat hai'* (Independence is just a few days away).

Despite some hiccups that ensued in the coming months, the English were finally removed from India the following year.

With the mission accomplished, now it was a question of who takes the credit. The 'known and unknown leaders' were never allowed the limelight nor given credit for their sacrifices. In fact, they were castigated for their 'violence'. The INA soldiers were described as people who were 'misguided by a path of violence', the air force personnel and the naval ratings, who had risked their lives, became simply as the 'RAF strikers' and the 'RIN mutineers'.

As expected, the credit for India's liberation was expropriated by the political opportunists, with a helping hand from the English. And Monday, 18 February 1946 was quietly erased from history.

On 15 August 1947, P.K. Tope remembered the sacrifices of Tatya Tope and others during the War of 1857 and the heroes of 1946. As he looked closely at the fluttering Tricolour, he realised that the flag actually had a fourth colour: navy blue. This navy blue colour of the Ashok Chakra metaphorically recognised the events of 18 February 1946. That fateful Monday was never recorded in the annals of history, but the contribution of the navy was forever immortalised in the Indian flag.

Conclusion

HINDSIGHT FORESIGHT

FRUITS, WHIPS AND INDIA'S DEFEAT

Despite enjoying a brief period of freedom during 1857, India's eventual defeat in the War meant it had to wait for another excruciating eighty-eight years before the English were finally removed from India. Yet, the War of 1857 achieved two important results for India.

The first was achieved after Tatya's Great Crossing, which forced the English to concede more personal freedom to Indians. The English backtracked on their overt attempts to force Christianity on the Indian people.

A second, yet important result of the war was the effect of the English propaganda on events at 'Cawnpore' during the War. Written in November 1857, Edward Humphreys' 'Manual of British Government in India', urged the English to 'really colonise India' and to 'raise up a European element in the population....'[1] Regardless of the reality of the events that took place at Satichaura and Bibighar at 'Cawnpore', the English press and popular culture put fear in the hearts and minds of the English people, to make India their home. In a perverse way, the English propaganda to justify their atrocities on Indian civilians, including women and children, worked against the English goal of 'raising the European element in the population', thereby preventing a large-scale settlement of the English in India.[2] This allowed for a seamless transfer of power eighty-eight years later.

To date, the analysis of India's defeat has been articulated by three categories of historians. First, the English historians, who had a transparent Anglo-centric point of view and tended to exaggerate their obvious strengths and India's obvious weaknesses. This continued to be echoed by their loyal Indian followers, the fruits from the Macaulayan tree of education, who not only parroted the Victorian historians' conclusions, but also added their own venom, possibly to seek 'international' recognitions and 'fellowships' in London. By implicitly controlling the purse strings, the English could pay the piper to call the tune.

The second category includes the historians in a free but socialistic India that viewed all history through Marxist lenses. These historians had a predetermined political agenda that in many ways coincided with the predecessors. Their political compulsions forced them to view the Indian leaders of 1857 in dim light and blamed the defeat on a so-called failure, absence, or infighting amongst the leadership. Their pre-determination coincided with earlier narratives, thereby dispensing the need for a more thorough analysis.

A small yet third category of Indians, mostly non-academics, attempted to analyse the history of 1857 for the purpose of contemplation. However, they were unable to extricate honest introspection from self-flagellation. For them, all the roads of original research presented, led to roughly the same conclusions.

As an adviser to Nana Saheb, Tatya was very possibly the main thrust behind Operation Red Lotus. Nana Saheb Peshwa represented the Marathas when he initiated the plan and shook hands with Bahadur Shah, Begum Hazrat Mahal and others as they set out to oust the English from India. Based on the many letters that were addressed to Tatya Tope, it seems that in many cases Tatya Tope was often the proxy for Nana Saheb, making critical decisions, including negotiating revenue collection on Nana's behalf. Tatya's greatness while engaging the English displays not only his tenacity and perseverance in fighting until his death, but his ability to radically alter the strategy of war based on the situation.

In the first phase of Operation Red Lotus as the authors have dubbed it, the economics, the supply lines and the logistics of troop movement was all coordinated with the help of the civil population using the chapati messages, which established the implicit route for the troop movement. This allowed for a rapid deployment of troops to selected locations without setting up elaborate alternate logistics, which could have given the game away.

India's victory came quickly, and exactly as planned. However, Tatya Tope and others made two grave miscalculations. The first, was their failure to consider how low the English could fall. The English, very quickly used their women and children as human shields, where they could, to protect their men. To be fair, however, most British soldiers were following orders, and many of them, in fact, did not actually like this policy. The English leadership put the lives of their civilian population at risk by sending missives directing the creation of this human shield in many locations. Tatya's second miscalculation was that he did not expect the English could be so barbaric as to take the war directly to the Indian non-combatants and wipe out entire villages, including women and children, to such an extent that they did not even leave trees along the Ganga without a dead body hanging from it along the way of their troop movements.

Many attempts have been made to assign causes for India's defeat. These include the issues of technology, such as the telegraph lines and weaponry, the supposed lack of planning and organisation based on the premise that it was either a 'mutiny' or a 'rebellion'. Blame is often placed on a purported lack of unity and cohesion, and infighting amongst Indian leadership is presented as a primary cause for defeat. These are clearly important issues that need to be considered, especially as India looks to 1857 introspectively. However, there are some critical issues, which have been either ignored or sidelined.

In most accounts, the lines of communications are analysed, however, the supply lines are not. The deliberate and systematic use of human shields by the English as a matter of policy is buried under stories of 'scattered bones' and a plethora of fallacious arguments. The genocide perpetrated against the Indian civil population including women and children is projected as a reaction to 'Cawnpore', when in reality it was a deliberate weapon to disrupt the embedded supply lines.

Tatya redefined the parameters of the war and with the pact with the Bundeli chiefs and support from Gwalior created a capital in Kalpi. The genocide at Jhansi destroyed this pact, cutting off all sources of revenue to

Tatya. The criticality of economic issues during the second phase of the war is implicitly recognised but rarely discussed or analysed.

Historians are accurate in blaming the Indian leadership's failure for India's defeat, but for all the wrong reasons. Tatya Tope and others failed to plan properly for England's grisly offensive policies targeting non-combatants, including women and children. They failed to see through England's thin veil of 'civilisation' and they failed to deal with England's 'courageous' defensive policy, when innocent English women and children were used as human shields.

India was defeated because Indian leaders failed to recognise that despite two hundred years of interaction with a five-thousand-year-old civilised nation, the English had never abandoned their 'core competence' that had allowed them to rule India in the first place.

More than a century and a half later, these issues are still relevant. What lessons can a modern and free India take from the War of 1857? Obviously, technology in the modern world remains an important factor. So is organisation, planning and other similar issues of relevance. However, one cannot underestimate the importance of planning for the possible barbarism of a likely or an unlikely enemy, particularly, any country that presents a liberal face, not unlike that of nineteenth century England.

An Indian expert on the Bengal famine chose to view the tragedy that killed four million Indians from 1942 to 1945, as simply 'mismanagement' by the English. Although rice production had not changed significantly during those years, the distribution of rice to rural areas of Bengal dropped dramatically. Did the English government really only make a 'blunder' in Bengal? Was the 'scorched earth' policy only a mistake? Was the removal of rice from the border with Myanmar purely for use somewhere else? Or was it something far more sinister? Could it be a deliberate attempt to cut off all food to the villages in Bengal and thereby destroy the supply lines to the Indian National Army led by Subhash Bose? These are very important questions. Was this expert 'rewarded' with an international award in economics for glossing over facts and for simply slapping the English on the wrists for their 'mismanagement'? The answer to this question goes beyond the scope of this book; however, it is relevant in recognising possible patterns in India's recent defeats, including that of the INA.

312 \ Tatya Tope's Operation Red Lotus

Strategic forecasting and scenario planning that goes beyond the standard military parameters are key to planning any future military engagements. Recognising some hard truths about managing all aspects of war, with any likely or an unlikely enemy is a prerequisite for any introspection, with or without self-flagellation.

Can India break itself from the intellectual chains created by the fruits from the Macaulayan trees or the self-flagellating whip wielders?

THREE STEPS TO FREEDOM

Eighteen months after the events of February 1946, the English were finally removed from India. Those who were clamouring to take credit for India's long awaited liberation marginalised that momentous day of 18 February 1946. Regardless of who was later touted in the carefully crafted narrative of the 'freedom movement', India had finally secured political freedom, a prerequisite for providing economic and personal freedom it its subjects.

Fortunately, they already had a clear roadmap for the future of India without the English. A roadmap created by the leaders of the War of 1857. The Proclamation of Freedom made on 25 August 1857, clearly articulated Indic traditions that manifested themselves in the triad of freedom for its people for thousands of years. The path for the policy makers of a free India was clear. India needed to unshackle the economic and political chains that had prevented its people from enjoying the fruits of their labour. They needed to implement the ideals neatly outlined in the principles presented by India's past leadership to embark on a road of freedom and prosperity.

Unfortunately, the policy makers chose a path that was in complete contradiction to India's history and polity. They chose economic autarky and isolation, and continued variations of the English policy of centralised decision-making that continued to hold India in chains. A goal that was in conflict with the principles laid out in the Proclamation of 1857. Direct and indirect taxation, though reformed, remained high. Contrary to the spirit of the Proclamation, the bureaucracy entrenched themselves even further. Although India had attained political freedom, economic freedom remained a distant goal.

Another key goal of the leaders of 1857 was to liberate India from the tyranny of government policies on religion and education.

Instead of creating laws that were blind to an individual's religious choices, the Constitution of India actually divided people according to their faiths, amplifying their differences and applying different sets of laws to each group. After 1835, following Bentinck's proclamation, English policies of intervention had dismantled India's private and successful educational system. After 1947, Indian policies continued to intervene in education, particularly higher education and continued the monopoly of a foreign language. India's 'personal' freedom though improved remained restricted.

Nevertheless, the biggest opportunity to achieve economic freedom was wasted when trade, commerce, and manufacturing; the primary motivators for the War of 1857, remained under the implicit control of the government.

When the last of the Indian empires fell to the English, India had lost its political freedom. The EEIC's administration was directly or indirectly the final authority. The English used the power of state to attack India's

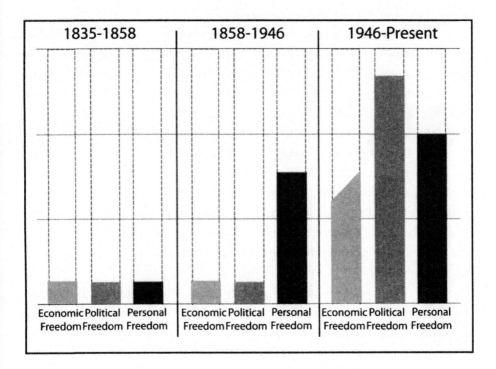

Figure 64: Scoring Freedom

personal and educational freedom after 1830s. India had already lost most of its economic freedom in the preceding decades. On 1 November 1858, England reversed its policies on religion. Overt missionary activities were called off; however, 'education' became a tool of the state to marginalise India's backbone of a private and successful system of education. Tatya and other leaders of the War of 1857 had allowed India to take the first step towards freedom.

India's post-Independence policies were largely a continuation of the English platform relative to personal and economic freedom. These policies were in complete contrast to what the leaders such as Tatya Tope, Nana Saheb and Bahadur Shah had presented in 1857.

The preface argues that historically, India's polity uniquely demonstrated the understanding of the triad of freedom. Western nations have attempted but failed in the creation of a system where these three functions are restricted from misappropriating power.

A 'modern' India went from emulating 'socialism' to emulating 'crony-capitalism', both failed western concepts.

Around 500 BC, this Indic charter survived an assault from one of three sources of power—the priests. The revival period lasted nearly 1,500 years, when parts of India finally lost political freedom. Indic polity faced destruction. Over time the original ideas of this ancient Indic charter were not only lost, they were reversed. Once entrenched, the functional powers that once attacked the charter became its ardent defenders. The letter and the spirit of original Indic polity were destroyed.

However, some aphorisms exist even today that represent the genius of the original guiding principles. For example, the saying, 'Raja bane vyapari, praja bane bhikhari'(If a king became a merchant, the population would become beggars) delivers a simple yet powerful message that recognises the need for the separation of political and economic power as a basis for societal prosperity.

India took the second step towards freedom on 18 February 1946 when political freedom was secured; although the first step remained incomplete. In terms of personal freedom, India needs to create a charter that is blind to people's personal choices.

Bentinck's proclamation had first introduced the *monopoly* of English language in higher education, with the intent to dissociate the elite from the rest. A free India had the opportunity to eliminate this monopoly. Unfortunately, the Indian government continued English policies of an implicit monopoly of the English language of higher education.

While the socialist ideals preached the ideals of opportunities for the masses, the continued elitist policies did exactly the opposite.

There is not a single country in the world, which has successfully forced a foreign language on its people and reaped economic rewards for its masses. Not China nor Taiwan. Not South Korea nor Japan. Not Malaysia nor Thailand. Not England, nor Germany. Not Russia, not France or any European country. The Americans, Canadians and Australians who unleashed genocide against the native populations, and forced a racially segregated society for the longest of times, can hardly be a role model for India.

The *only* countries who have followed policies similar to that of modern India are South American nations where the indigenous languages are *officially* marginalised in favour of European languages. These countries are a showcase of bleak economic divisions and hierarchies that arise from an individual's identification with people of European heritage and language. Is that a role model for India to follow in the new millennium?

Before the domination of English, Spanish was the 'international' language of choice, preceded by Persian. What language could be next? Mandarin? Cantonese? Hebrew? Japanese? Should one of these languages be forced upon India's population next?

The continued state sanctioned monopoly of the English language has created a culture of exclusivity and has limited access to opportunities to the general population. While individuals and institutes should be free to choose any Indian or foreign language of their choice, state patronage of any foreign language, simply represents the continuation of the oppressive ideas within Bentinck's proclamations.

Some 'modern' historians suggest, that in hindsight, India's defeat in 1857 was as a blessing, because the 'old order' represented by the leaders of the war, was supposedly 'regressive' in comparison to the rule of the English. To these historians, the English represented 'change' and the 'old order' represented stagnation. This idea is not only nonsense but also an insult to the concepts of freedom and liberty. It was this 'old order' that made the proclamation of Freedom of 25 August 1857. It was a manifesto that laid out goals of economic and personal freedom and presented ideas that resound even today. These ideas of freedom and liberty and good governance are embodied in Indic traditions, and were clearly presented in that proclamation.

The value of ideas should not be gauged by their novelty or their packaging. Nana Saheb, Tatya Tope, Lakshmibai and others represented this so-called 'old order', fought and died for India's liberty. Vishnubhat Godse met Lakshmibai in a chance encounter while on the road to Kalpi a few weeks after her breakout from Jhansi. In a solemn tone, she gave a precise reason to the priest, for her personal reasons for fighting the war. 'I did not need anything. However, I proudly made it my responsibility to protect our beliefs. That is what motivated me.'[3] Their sacrifice and their perseverance represent these timeless, but yet perpetually fresh ideas. The oldest of them, but perhaps decadent to some, was the idea to defend and fight for your freedom.

Great ideas and traditions do not have expiry dates; they remain new and fresh for eternity. This idea of eternal rejuvenation within Indic thought is aptly represented in these words सनातनो नित्यनूतन:

India should benefit from the wisdom of its ancestors and the message embodied in the proclamation made by its leaders on 25 August 1857. While 1857 and 1946 were two important steps towards freedom, freedom remains incomplete as India continues to face the paradox of fractional freedom. India needs to take a few more steps towards complete freedom.

These additional steps are the key to fulfilling the dreams that Tatya and others dreamt when they sacrificed their lives for the Indian nation. India the *country* lost the war and remained in chains, but India the *nation* was free.

Tatya Tope is not just the grandfather of the Tope family; he is the grandfather of the Indian nation. Completing Tatya's unfinished task is the key to allow the forever nation to remain a nation forever.

Appendix

CHAPTER ZERO
THE REAR-VIEW MIRROR

CENTENNIAL CLUTTER OF ESTEEMED BIASES

As the introduction of this book argues, the historiography of 1857 was challenged for the first time in 1908 by Veer Savarkar. He questioned the motivations of the 'partial and prejudiced' Victorian historians and made a strong case for a significant reassessment of the events of 1857.

Savarkar was pointing out the obvious. The English version of history was predictably Anglo-centric. It would have been naïve to assume that the victors of the War would even attempt to present an unbiased history of the subject.

In 1957, ten years after India's independence, as India observed the centennial year of the War, there was a renewed interest in the historiography of 1857. This was going to be the first time after securing political freedom that Indian historians had an opportunity to reassess the events that took place in 1857.

Logic would have dictated that Indian historians would have attempted to eliminate the biases of the English historians. However, Bentinck's attack on Indic education and the 'reforms' that followed, seemed to have successfully overridden logic. Four generations after 'native' languages were marginalised in favor of English – the English educated and speaking class that Macaulay was proud of, was stupendously successful in defending the English history books written in the nineteenth century. India had secured political freedom, but the intellectuals remained in chains.

Two 'authorative' books on 1857 were published in 1957. The first by S.N. Sen and a second by R.C. Majumdar. They represent the dominant logic that was expressed in 1957, which was not only a continuation of the 'partial and prejudiced' history; it had more venom, considering it was written by Indians. As Marxists ideals took root in India, the biases changed with time. Historians continued to marginalise the leadership of 1857 with the focus more on the 'subaltern' elements of the War. The 'sepoy mutiny' became a 'civil rebellion' but the revisionist elements stayed the same. Savarkar's underlying thesis remained largely ignored.

The following is a short review of the two books written in 1957 by Sen and Majumdar.

OFFICIALLY PEJORATIVE, VENOMOUS AND CLUELESS

S.N. Sen, Eighteen Fifty-Seven, by, 1957

What was considered to be the 'official' history of 1857 was written by Surendra Nath Sen, a former Head of Department of History, Calcutta University and vice-chancellor of Delhi University from 1950 to 1953, in a book titled *Eighteen Fifty-Seven*, published by the Publications Division, Ministry of Information and Broadcasting in 1957.

His conclusions were in line with those of the British historians, that the events of 1857 did not characterise as a nationalist uprising, and ignores evidence suggesting that there was any planning involved in any form but were, at best, an 'inevitable mutiny'.

Sen arbitrarily dismisses pieces of the evidence that indicated some level of leadership or planning in these events. Sen marginalises the proclamation made by Bahadur Shah and copies of which were circulated and posted in many places including Delhi. Sen writes, the proclamation 'purporting to come from the Shah (Bahadur), it is true, was once displayed at the Jami Masjid...' and goes on to suggest instead that 'the paper in question' must have come from an 'individual' or an 'ordinary citizen' instead.[1] He also summarily dismisses the popularity of the proclamation by claiming that, 'it went unnoticed by the general public in Delhi'. We are uncertain what scientific techniques or results of surveys and polls he used to reach this conclusion about the 'popularity' of this proclamation.

The general tone of the narrative is consistent with English accounts. In describing the situations during war, we find Mr. Sen in the 'enemy' camp – sympathising with their day-to-day issues and concerns, distant from the happenings on the 'other' side with Indian soldiers.

He acknowledges that the story of the 'chapatis lend some colour to the theory or prior preparation, propaganda and conspiracy'. However, is quick in dismissing it saying, 'a conspiracy is not conducted through such an unintelligible and uncertain medium of communication'. He goes on to quote Syed Ahmed, knighted by the English Queen, who concluded 'The fact is that even at the present day we do not know what caused the distribution of those chuppaties'.

Sen's conclusions can be succinctly paraphrased to mean, 'because, none of us historians have a clue about the meaning behind these chapati incidents, we are going to ignore this evidence completely'. The incidents of the Red Lotus flowers making rounds of the garrisons have no mention in his conclusions that were officially published by the Indian Ministry of Information and Broadcasting in 1957. Fortunately, after nearly 150 years, we have discovered the planning and the mystery and the meaning behind these chapati and lotus incidents and were presented in preceding chapters.

Perhaps the greatest irony of this book is that it was published in a free India, by the Indian Government, ruled by Indians, but this esteemed Indian historian actually indicates the plausible planning by Indian leaders (which he summarily dismisses) that went into the war of 1857 as a 'conspiracy'.

A conspiracy!

A quick look at the dictionary reveals the following meaning:

con-spir-a-cy [kuhn-spir-uh-see]: an evil, unlawful, treacherous, or surreptitious plan formulated in secret by two or more persons; plot.[2]

Did India in 1957, ten years after it was free, 'officially' consider that any plan to overthrow the English in 1857 was an 'evil, unlawful and a treacherous plan'?

THE MISSING NATION

R.C. Majumdar, The Sepoy Mutiny and the Revolt of 1857, 1957

Ramesh Chandra Majumdar was born in 1888. Not unlike other children who were the product of Macaulay's educational reforms, his skills in the English language combined with due display of loyalty, earned him some important positions during the British rule, including vice-chancellor of Dacca University. The English continued to honour him and made him an honorary fellow of the Asiatic Society of Great Britain and Ireland. He was also an honorary fellow of the Asiatic Societies of Calcutta and Bombay. He was also the vice-president of the International Commission for History of the Scientific and Cultural Development of Mankind set up by UNESCO. Majumdar was certainly a historian admired by the English and the West.

The central thesis of Majumdar's argument can be reduced to one simple question – How can there be a war, if there wasn't even a nation? In Majumdar's opinion that is consistent with western ideas of a nation, India did not even exist as a nation until the twentieth century.

In any case, a War is not necessarily an armed conflict only between nations. It could be between nations, states or any two parties. Eighteen fifty-seven was a war, yet Majumdar and others, use semantics to diminish and dismiss the battle for survival of a civilisation over five thousand years old with a strong self-identity, using misplaced western arguments and ideas.

R.C. Majumdar summarised the events of 1857 as, 'purely a mutiny of the sepoys, joined at a later stage by some discontented elements as well as the riff-raff and other disturbing elements of society'. One would assume that he was implying that the Rani of Jhansi was amongst the 'discontented elements'. Does that make Tatya Topé, Azimullah Khan and others the 'riff-raff'? Or did the 'riff-raff' include the ordinary brave Indians and villagers who supported this war? Surely, the British did not expect the commoners to show exemplary bravery; perhaps, neither do Indian historians such as Majumdar. Perhaps Majumdar and others were dismissing and therefore diminishing various roles, discouraging further study on these areas.

What we describe in this book as the Anglo-Indian War of 1857 signified the coming together of the two greatest Indian empires that existed in the eighteenth century as rivals, the Mughals through Bahadur Shah and the

Marathas through Nana Saheb. Majumdar gets very personal in his criticism of these two men.

Nana Saheb, the adopted son of Bajirao II, was one of the important leaders in the planning and economic support of this war. Majumdar in the footsteps of British historians resorts to name calling, but it is not Nana Saheb's character that he demolishes – but that of his father who adopted him, calling Nana Saheb 'the son of a worthless wicked ex-Peshwa'. Bajirao II died in 1851 and had nothing to do with the events of 1857. We are still uncertain why Majumdar chose to write these words in relation to Nana Saheb. Perhaps he was simply continuing the tradition of English historians in denouncing all the Indian leaders, in any form or fashion, who led the war against the British.

In contrast, we have to assume that Mr Majumdar was generous in his description of Bahadur Shah, calling him only a 'dotard', picking on him for his age and alleged senility and not his ancestry. Majumdar's writings seems to indicate that he was upset that Bahadur Shah, who was supposed to be a 'puppet in the throne', to have actually dared to rise against the British.

You would hardly expect a scholarly historian to resort to name-calling using words like 'wicked', 'worthless' and 'dotard'. While Majumdar's qualifications are not in question his tone betrays a predetermined agenda.

Majumdar's conclusions are consistent with those of the British historians; however, he goes further to suggest that describing these events, as a 'war' would be tantamount to acknowledging that India was ever a 'nation', before 1857. If by Majumdar's definition, 'India' did not exist as a nation or a country, before 1857, we wonder why he did not criticise the English for naming a very important company inaccurately at its inception. Perhaps, if R.C. Majumdar was alive on 31 December 1600, he would have called the English East India Company a name which would have been consistent with his opinion of India before the arrival of the British: 'The English, South Asian Peninsular Collection of Multiple and Disparate Kingdoms, Company' instead.

Born at a time in a nation whose existence he does not acknowledge; ironically, R.C. Majumdar has been called by some as, 'one of the greatest of Indian historians'.

GHOSTS IN THE MACHINE

There are many classifications that exist for fallacious arguments. In the context of history, these classifications become more complex since there are many other factors to consider. Historians, especially relative to 1857 have had a licence to distort. We have attempted to bring order into that chaos of historical equivocations, lies and damned lies (but not statistics). We consider that history is presented on two distinct dimensions, the first that is based on factual presentation and second based on the completeness of the facts and logical rigor. Coherent history is narrated when complete facts are presented in a logical manner.

Based on what and how narratives are presented, we can classify them as Stories, Myths, Noise, and Coherent History, as shown in the figure below. Unlike commonly believed, narrating history is not simply a serialising a sequence of dates and facts. Since the editorial selection of facts can present a distorted view of events – this can be described as 'noise' in history. The argumentative fallacies that fall into this category are omissions, trivialisations and oversimplifications – whereby it is still possible to present only facts – yet still be fallacious.

Similarly, history is different than just narrating a story – where the narrator has the freedom to create characters and events. Inventions and equivocations in history would fall into this quadrant. Neither is history about propagating myths. Where certain ambiguous 'facts' are used to create illogical implications and then indefinitely repeated, until the other historian start believing them to be factual. Often

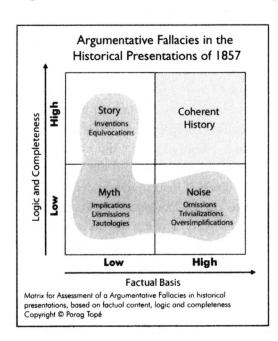

Figure 65: Argumentative Fallacies

important evidence is dismissed to support these 'myths'. History is unique because the writers of history have a significant amount of freedom to narrate events and information based on facts. History can be distorted by presenting only partial facts; which when read would sound factually accurate – but still does not accurate represent the events.

The events of 1857 have been told to us in almost every form. Some are pure inventions. Some stories are only partial presentations of facts. Some stories are regurgitated so often, that they have reached the status of mythological presentation.

Unfortunately, there's a dearth of finding anything that would fall into this category of coherent history. The history of the events of 1857 as presented to us is full of inventions, omissions, trivialisations, dismissions, dutiful yet meaningless repetitions, wrongful implications, equivocations and oversimplifications.

The ability of historians to muddle around these quadrants is dictated by their ability to manipulate the system that defines what is acceptable. Conversely, sometimes even the system allows and encourages distorted mirrors and blurred lenses.

In his book, *The Concept of Mind*, written in 1949, Gilbert Ryle's described the dualism of the mind and body as presented by René Descartes' as 'The ghost in the machine'. In the context of presenting history, we also come across a duality of sorts. The duality of the 'attitude' and the 'aptitude' in presenting history.

The machinery that defines India's history is run by these ghosts of misalignment. We express no opinion about British historians in this context – since they fall into a completely different system, one where the fundamental approach to India is inverted. However, Indian historians – especially when it comes to representation of the events of 1857 are a misaligned lot.

Historians, who claim to have the rigour and knowledge, and the support of the system, unfortunately view India's past with jaundiced and almost colonial eyes. We describe this of history as the 'Pejorative' history. Then there is the bulk of books who simply use derision to demonise Indian heroes and the events – although it is not considered 'rigorous' these books still fill up a large amount of shelf space (the size of which would have made Macaulay proud) associated with the events of 1857. In addition to these, we have many Indian historians who have the right attitude and approach and tend to view the events without the preexisting prejudices displayed by the Pejorative and the Derisive historians. They attempt to filter through the haze of colonial misrepresentation of history, however, are unable to extricate honest introspection from self-flagellation.

Which leaves a big void, where exists the quadrant of plain, unbiased and objective history. The history of 1857, despite the hundreds of voluminous books that have been written about it, is still remains a vacuum.

FACES OF FREEDOM

The War of 1857 was led by leaders such as Nana Saheb, Bahadur Shah and Tatya Tope. We call them the 'leonine leaders'. The 'pragmatic patriots, like Baija Bai Shinde, supported them. Certainly, 1857 had its share of the 'two-timing traitors' as well the 'waffling weasels'. These, we have argued did not have significant impact on the outcome of the War.

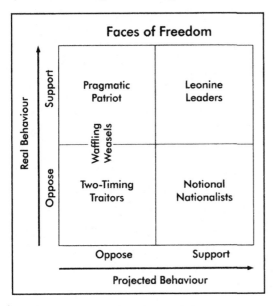

Figure 66: Argumentative Fallacies

However, a fourth category of Indians emerged in the twentieth century who refused to acknowledge that sacrifices of people like Nana Saheb and Tatya Tope were for India, the nation. They attempted to define India through a European lens. They professed to be representing the cause of the Indian nation, but their actions demonstrated otherwise.

By expropriating the credit for India's liberation in the 1940s, they were able to sustain policies that continued to erode India's social fabric and personal freedom. They used the power of the state for the decades after 1947, to redefine and weaken the Indic identity through a rigid framework controlling all areas of academic thought. We call them the 'notional nationalists'. In the decades following India's political liberation, the 'notional nationalists' are resisting the reality of the War of 1857 through a façade of what they described as 'History.'

Savarkar declared a War on 'History' when he challenged the historiography of 1857. His detractors were the English who put obstacles in the way of bringing forth the truth of 1857. These obstacles continue to exist today in varying forms. As India takes additional steps towards freedom, India's history can be liberated only when Savarkar's War on 'History' is won decisively.

TROOP MOVEMENT TABLE

The following table summarises the movements of the Indian troops in the early months of the War. The table includes the name of the regiments, their original location, their role in the war, the date they started their movements and their destination. The table is compiled from various references as provided below.

Legend:

Role Legend:
FP – Fully Participated
PP – Partly Participated
DNP – Did not Participate
DSB – Disbanded
DSA – Disarmed
DST – Destroyed

Reference Legend:

AN – *The Annals of Indian Administration*, Meredith Townsend, 1858, Sept & Dec 1858, Parts IV and V, Serampore, Public Administration
LA – Littell's Living Age, Conducted by E. Littel, Littel, Son and Company, 1857, p.331
AL – Allen's Indian Mail, Register of Intelligence, vol. xv, January-December 1857, Wm. H, Allen and Co., 1857, p.462
V2 – *Freedom Struggle in UP*, Volume II
AH – Major. Agha Humayiun Amin
http://orbat.com/site/history/historical/india/bengalarmy1857.html

GD – *The History of the Indian Revolt and of the Expeditions to Persia, China, and Japan, 1856-7-8*, W. and R. Chambers, 1859, George Dodd, pp.625-28

Regiment	Code	Location	Role	Date -1857	Reference	Marched to
1st Gwalior Cavalry	1 GC	Shivpuri/ Agra	FP		AL	Gwalior
2nd Gwalior Cavalry	2 GC	Agar	FP		AL	Gwalior
1st Gwalior Infantry	1 GI	Neemuch	FP	June 3	AL	Gwalior
1st Gwalior Infantry	1 GI	Etawah	PP		AH	Gwalior
2nd Gwalior Infantry	2 GI	Gwalior	FP		AH	Gwalior
3rd Gwalior Infantry	3 GI	Gwalior/ Shivpuri	FP		AH	Gwalior
4th Gwalior Infantry	4 GI	Guna	FP		AH	Gwalior
5th Gwalior Infantry	5 GI	Agar	FP	July 4	AH	Gwalior
6th Gwalior Infantry	6 GI	Lalitpur	FP	June 6	AH	Kanpur
7th Gwalior Infantry	7 GI	Neemuch	FP	May 28 – June 3	AN, 495	Delhi
1st Irregular Cavalry	1 IC	Multan	DNP		AH	#N/A
10th Irregular Cavalry	10 IC	Unknown	DSB		AH	#N/A
11th Irregular Cavalry	11 IC	Berhampur	FP		AH	Kalpi
12th Irregular Cavalry	12 IC	Sugauli	FP		v2, p. 19	Lucknow
13th Irregular Cavalry	13 IC	Varanasi	PP	June 4	AL, AN, p. 487, 488	Unknown
14th Irregular Cavalry	14 IC	Jhansi-Nowgong	FP		AH	Banda
15th Irregular Cavalry	15 IC	Sultanpur	FP		v2, p. 29	Lucknow
16th Irregular Cavalry	16 IC	Unknown	DSB		AH	#N/A
17th Irregular Cavalry	17 IC	Shamsabad	DSA		AH	#N/A
18th Irregular Cavalry	18 IC	Peshawar	DSA	June 3	LA, 331, AH	#N/A
2nd Irregular Cavalry	2 IC	Gurdaspur	DNP		AH	#N/A
3 rd Irregular Cavalry	3 IC	Sagar	FP		AH	Gwalior
4th Irregular Cavalry	4 IC	Hansi/His-sar	PP	May/June	AN, p. 488	Delhi
5th Irregular Cavalry	5 IC	Rohnee	FP		AH	Banda
6th Irregular Cavalry	6 IC	Jacobabad	DNP		AH	#N/A
7th Irregular Cavalry	7 IC	Peshawar	DSA		AH	#N/A
8th Irregular Cavalry	8 IC	Bareilly	DSB		AH	Delhi

Regiment	Code	Location	Role	Date -1857	Reference	Marched to
9th Irregular Cavalry	9 IC	Hoshiarpur	DST/DSB	May/June	AN, p. 488	#N/A
1st Light Cavalry	1 LC	Mhow	FP	July 1	AN, p. 498	Delhi
2nd Light Cavalry	2 LC	Kanpur	FP	June 4	AN. P. 494	Kanpur
3 rd Light Cavalry	3 LC	Meerut	FP	May 10	LA, 331	Delhi
4th Light Cavalry	4 LC	Ambala	FP		AH	Delhi
5th Light Cavalry	5 LC	Abazai	DSB	May 22, 1861	LA, 331, AH	#N/A
6th Light Cavalry	6 LC	Jalandhar	FP	June 4	AN, p. 498	Delhi
7th Light Cavalry	7 LC	Lucknow	FP	May 31	AL	Lucknow
8th Light Cavalry	8 LC	Lahore	DSB	May 13	AN, p. 482, LA, 331	#N/A
9th Light Cavalry	9 LC	Sialkot	DST		AH	#N/A
10th Light Cavalry	10 LC	Firozpur	FP		AH	Delhi
1st Native Infantry	1 NI	Kanpur	FP	June 4	AN. P. 494	Kanpur
2nd Native Infantry	2 NI	Barrack-pore-Ber-hampur	DSB		AH	#N/A
3rd Native Infantry	3 NI	Phillaur-Ludhiana	FP	June 4	AL	Delhi
4th Native Infantry	4 NI	Nurpur-Kangra	DSB		AH	#N/A
5th Native Infantry	5 NI	Ambala	DST/DSB		AH	#N/A
6th Native Infantry	6 NI	Allahabad	FP	June 6	AN, p. 486	Kanpur
7th Native Infantry	7 NI	Danapur	FP	July 28	vol 4, p. 405	Banda
8th Native Infantry	8 NI	Danapur	FP	July 28, 1859	vol 4, p. 406	Banda
9th Native Infantry	9 NI	Aligarh/Mainpuri	FP	May 23/May 29/June 22	AL, AN. p478, 489, 484	Delhi
10th Native Infantry	10 NI	Fatehgarh	DNP		AH	#N/A
11th Native Infantry	11 NI	Meerut	FP	May 10	LA, 331	Delhi
12th Native Infantry	12 NI	Jhansi-Nowgong	FP	May/June	AN, p. 489, 496	Banda
13th Native Infantry	13 NI	Lucknow	PP		AH	Lucknow
14th Native Infantry	14 NI	Jhelum	DST/PP		AH	#N/A
15th Native Infantry	15 NI	Nasirabad	FP	May 29	AN, 484	Delhi

Regiment	Code	Location	Role	Date -1857	Reference	Marched to
16th Native Infantry	16 NI	Lahore	DST/DSB	May 13	AN, p. 482, LA, 331	#N/A
17th Native Infantry	17 NI	Azamgarh	FP	June 5	AN, p. 479, 497	Lucknow
18th Native Infantry	18 NI	Bareilly	FP		AH	Delhi
19th Native Infantry	19 NI	Berhampur	DSB	April 3	AL	#N/A
20th Native Infantry	20 NI	Meerut	FP	May 10	LA, 331	Delhi
21st Native Infantry	21 NI	Peshawar	DSA	May 22	AL,LA, 331, AH	#N/A
22nd Native Infantry	22 NI	Faizabad	FP	June 8	AH	Lucknow
23rd Native Infantry	23 NI	Mhow	FP	July 1	AN, p. 499	Delhi
24th Native Infantry	24 NI	Peshawar	DSB	May 22, 1858	LA, 331, AH	#N/A
25th Native Infantry	25 NI	Varanasi	DST/DSB		AH	#N/A
26th Native Infantry	26 NI	Lahore	DST/DSB	May 13	AN, p. 482, LA, 331	#N/A
27th Native Infantry	27 NI	Peshawar	DST/DSB	May 22	LA, 331, AH	#N/A
28th Native Infantry	28 NI	Shahja-hanpur	FP	May 31	AH	Delhi
29th Native Infantry	29 NI	Moradabad	FP	May 31	LA, 331	Delhi
30th Native Infantry	30 NI	Nasirabad	FP	May 29	AH	Delhi
31st Native Infantry	31 NI	Sagar	DNP		AH	#N/A
32nd Native Infantry	32 NI	Orrissa	PP		AH	Banda
33rd Native Infantry	33 NI	Hoshiarpur	DSA		AH	#N/A
34th Native Infantry	34 NI	Barrackpur-Chitagong	DSB		AH	#N/A
35th Native Infantry	35 NI	Sialkot-Gujranwala-Jhang	DSB		AH	#N/A
36th Native Infantry	36 NI	Jalandhar	FP	June 4	AN, p. 499, 495	Delhi
37th Native Infantry	37 NI	Varanasi	DSB	June 1857	AN, p. 487, 488	#N/A
38th Native Infantry	38 NI	Delhi	FP	May 11	AL	Delhi
39th Native Infantry	39 NI	Jhelum	DSB		AH	#N/A
40th Native Infantry	40 NI	Danapur	FP	July 28	vol 4, p. 404	Banda
41st Native Infantry	41 NI	Sitapur-Mallanwan	FP	June 3	v2, p. 27	Lucknow

Regiment	Code	Location	Role	Date -1857	Reference	Marched to
42nd Native Infantry	42 NI	Sagar	PP	July 3	AN, p. 498	Delhi
43rd Native Infantry	43 NI	Barrack-pore-Dum Dum	DSB		AH	#N/A
44th Native Infantry	44 NI	Agra	DSB	May 31	AL	#N/A
45th Native Infantry	45 NI	Firozpur	DST/DSB	May 13	LA, 331	Delhi
46th Native Infantry	46 NI	Sialkot	DST/PP		AH	#N/A
47th Native Infantry	47 NI	Mirzapur	DNP		AH	#N/A
48th Native Infantry	48 NI	Lucknow	PP	May 31	AL	Lucknow
49th Native Infantry	49 NI	Lahore	DSB	May 13	AN, p. 482, LA, 331	#N/A
50th Native Infantry	50 NI	Nagod	FP	September 16	GD	Banda
51st Native Infantry	51 NI	Peshawar	DST/DSB	May 22	LA, 331, AH	#N/A
52nd Native Infantry	52 NI	Jabalpur	PP	September 18	GD	Banda
53rd Native Infantry	53 NI	Kanpur	FP	June 4	AN. P. 494	Kanpur
54th Native Infantry	54 NI	Delhi	FP	May 11	AL	Delhi
55th Native Infantry	55 NI	Mardan	DST/PP	May 25	AL, AN. P. 496	#N/A
56th Native Infantry	56 NI	Kanpur	FP	June 4	AN. P. 494	Kanpur
57th Native Infantry	57 NI	Firozpur	DSA	May 13	LA, 331	#N/A
58th Native Infantry	58 NI	Rawalpindi	DSB		AH	#N/A
59th Native Infantry	59 NI	Amritsar	DST/DSB		AH	#N/A
60th Native Infantry	60 NI	Ambala	PP		AH	Delhi
61st Native Infantry	61 NI	Jalandhar	FP	June 4	AN, p. 500	Delhi
62nd Native Infantry	62 NI	Multan	DST		AH	#N/A
63rd Native Infantry	63 NI	Berhampur	DSB		AH	#N/A
64th Native Infantry	64 NI	Abazai	DST/DSB	June 3	LA, 331, AH	#N/A
65th Native Infantry	65 NI	Ghazipur	DSA		AH	#N/A
66th Native Infantry	66 NI	Almora	DNP		AH	#N/A
67th Native Infantry	67 NI	Agra	PP/DSB	May 31	AL	#N/A
68th Native Infantry	68 NI	Bareilly	FP	May 31	AH	Unknown

Regiment	Code	Location	Role	Date -1857	Reference	Marched to
69th Native Infantry	69 NI	Multan	DST		AH	#N/A
70th Native Infantry	70 NI	Berhampur-Calcutta	DSA		AH	#N/A
71st Native Infantry	71 NI	Lucknow	PP	May 31	AL	Lucknow
72nd Native Infantry	72 NI	Neemuch	FP		AN, 495	Delhi
73rd Native Infantry	73 NI	Dacca-Jelpiguri	PP		AH	Unknown
74th Native Infantry	74 NI	Delhi	FP	May 11	AL	Delhi
1st Oudh Irregular Cavalry	1 OIC	Colonel-ganj/Sikrora	FP	June 8	AN, p. 496 (694)	Lucknow
2nd Oudh Irregular Cavalry	2 OIC	Lucknow	FP		AH	Lucknow
3rd Oudh Irregular Cavalry	3 OIC	Pratapgarh/Allahabad	FP		AH	Lucknow
1st Oudh Irregular Inf	1 OII	Colonel-ganj/Sikrora	FP	June 8	AN, p. 496 (694)	Lucknow
10th Oudh Irregular Inf	10 OII	Mallanwan	FP	June 3	v2, p. 27	Lucknow
2nd Oudh Irregular Inf	2 OII	Colonel-ganj/Sikrora	FP	June 8	AN, p. 496 (694)	Lucknow
3rd Oudh Irregular Inf	3 OII	Gonda	FP	June 15	v2, p. 41	Lucknow
4th Oudh Irregular Inf	4 OII	Lucknow	FP		v2, p. 45	Lucknow
5th Oudh Irregular Inf	5 OII	Lucknow	FP		AL	Lucknow
6th Oudh Irregular Inf	6 OII	Faizabad	FP	June 8	AL	Lucknow
7th Oudh Irregular Inf	7 OII	Lucknow	FP	May 31	AL, v2, p. 29	Lucknow
8th Oudh Irregular Inf	8 OII	Sultanpur	FP	June 10	AN, p. 496 (694)	Lucknow
9th Oudh Irregular Inf	9 OII	Faizabad	FP		v2, p. 37	Lucknow
Gwalior Artillery	GA	Neemuch	FP	June 3	AL	Delhi
Gwalior Artillery	GA	Nasirabad	FP	May 29	AL	Delhi
Gwalior Artillery	GA	Neemuch	FP	May 29	AL	Delhi
Hariana Light Infantry	HLI	Hansi	FP		AL	Unknown
Jodhpur Contingent	JC	Erinpura	FP		AL	Unknown

The above list excludes the regiments from the Punjab Infantry and Cavarly, Assam Infantry, Sikh Infantry and the Sylhet Infantry. Some of these troops fought alongside the English.

FAMILY TREE

Descendants of the Tope family are dispersed all over India. We were able to trace several families and created a family tree that shows the linkages.

Family Tree 1

Family Tree 2

(Family Tree 1 and 2 given as pull-outs at the end of book.)

URDU LETTERS

The following are the scans of a few of the Urdu letters that are referred earlier. These represent only a sampling of the many letters that were translated.

Letter 18

From: Lal Puri Risaldar.

To: Syed Mod. Issakh

Dated: 20 Jummadassani 1274H (5 Feb 1858)

After our proclamation from last month, we have been successful in encouraging thakurs and other landlords to join our effort. They have assisted us for a couple of jobs. Since they have volunteered to contribute, we should avoid keeping an unduly high tax burden. Pandit Lakshmi Rao, akhbarnawees, is keeping a record of who is participating in these meetings.

Biswas Rao Bhausaheb from Jalaun is demanding a signif cantly higher rate of taxation (16 annas) than what you are recommending (8 annas). It is important that we manage the relationship with these thakurs and landlords with care. This might encourage others to volunteer as well.

I am including a list of the attendees so that you can make an informed decision. Please advise Bhausaheb to use restraint while managing this delicate relationship. Please reply as soon as possible.

If necessary, I can arrange a meeting with these thakurs and other landlords

Writer: Lakshmi Rao and Sadashiv.

P.S. If necessary, I will reach the ghat with these Thakurs and landlords.

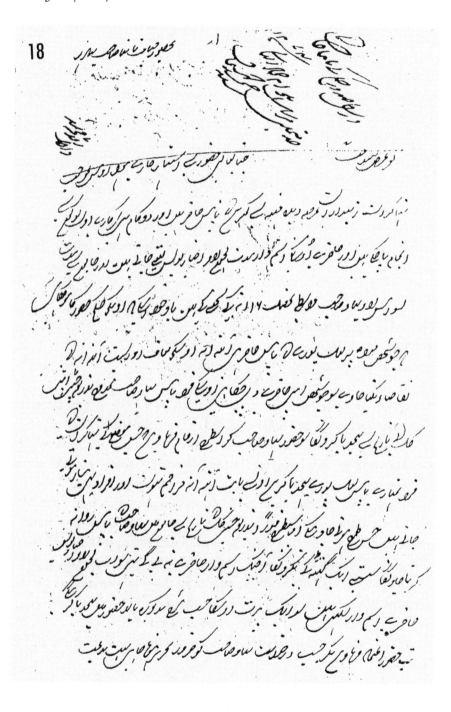

Figure 67: Urdu Letter

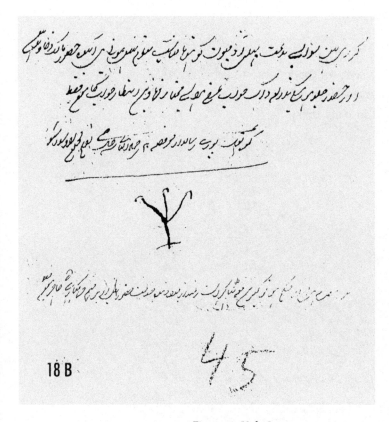

Figure 68: Urdu Letter

Letter 24ª

From: Pandit Gopal Rao Daroga / Jamadar
Place: Pargana, Gujarchalatara
To: Syyed Mohammed. Issakh
Date: 18 Jummadassani 1274H (3-February 1858)

I am writing to you in reference to order of 27 Jummadalaval about enrolling armed soldiers. We will gather 16 soldiers in the next 2-3 days and then send you their details. Looking at the leave chart of the villages around here, it seems that soldiers 2-2, 4-4, 10+10 houses are on leave. These soldiers have guns, cannons and swords. They do not want to go back to work (with the English). The soldiers can be enrolled in our army if you order. They are eager to fight. Once enrolled, we can attack and take the local English treasury. Please advice.

Annotation:

1) Copy to be sent to Tatya Sahib (6-February 1858)
   Date 21 Jummadasani 1274H
2) To be filed in daily diary.

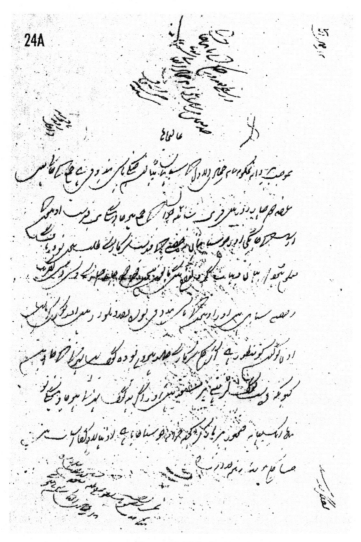

Figure 69: Urdu Letter

Letter 36

Date: 26 January 1858 (10 Jummadassani 1274H)

Received the following amount for the salary of harkaras/akhbarnawees for the month of Jummadalavval 1274H. (December 1857– January 1858)

Rs. 8/ (Rs. 28) – 2 anna 8 paise. Previous amount Re. 1/– and 8 Annas.

Details as follows;

Mir Inayat Ali *akhbarnawees*	
Mutayanna Banda	Rs. 8/–
Sheikh Wajir	Rs. 3
Rasool Baksh	Rs. 1/–, 3 Anna, 4 paise
Main Singh	Rs.1/– 2 Anna, 8 paise
Eshree	Rs.1/–
Kanshi	Rs.1/–
Abdulla	Rs.1/–

The total is Rupees 18. From this amount Rupees 8, 2 anna, 5 pai is due. From this Rupees 5 / 8, 3 paise was spent to buy paper to print daily dairy. Now I have Rupees 7 / 8, 1 paisa, 2 anna is balance with me from the government.

Annotation:

To be filed in office register.
Dated: 12 Jummadassani 1274H.

Letter 37[3]

From:
Place:
To: Syed Mohd Isakh Mir Munshi (Chief Accountant)
Date:

We have received a shocking news from Arybad, that the brave Kunwar Singh Zamindar of Dalube Danda has been hanged by the English.

The English demanded two lakh rupees from Buddu Mahajan, a wealthy person from Jahanabad. When he refsued to comply, he was arrested by the English and hanged.

36

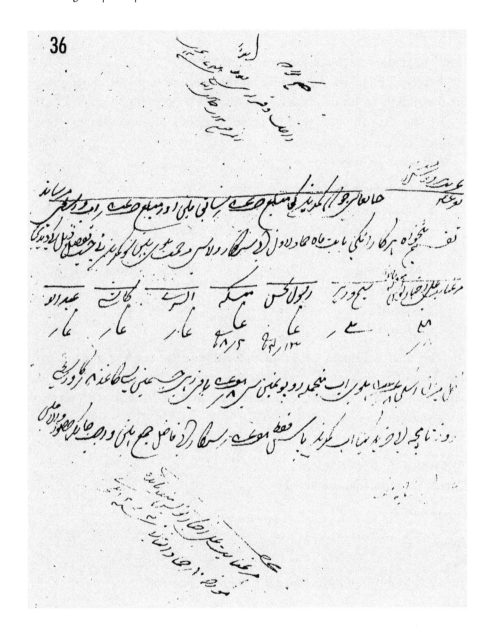

Figure 70: Urdu Letter

The landlords of Chandwara say that they are willing to help our government to take the English treasury in Jarkigadha. This is hidden in a cave and can be taken after defeating the enemy.

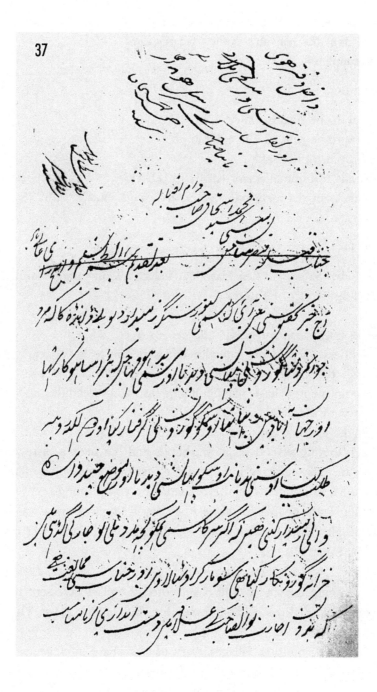

Figure 71: Urdu Letter

As per your advise, we will not attack the English in Nawab Sahib's area without the Nawab's explicit permission.

Incomplete.

Annotations:

1) Copy to be filed in office
2) Copy to be sent to Tatya Sahib
   By: Syed Mohd Isakh
   Dated: 18 Jummadassani 1274H (3 Feb 1858)
3) True copy of original signed by Syed Fazale Ilahi (Syed Fazal Hussain)

Letter 44

From: Fidwi Safdar Ali Beg Hawaldar Paltan 4 Company 5 Camp Brar
Place: Tehsil court of Kurara
To:
Date: 13 Jummadassani 1274H (29 Jan 1858)
His highness Tatya Sahib Bahadur had sent me to be at your service to look after the soldiers and the *tehsil* in the *pargana*. After you confirmed my appointment, I have been fulfilling my responsibilities and currently residing with the *tehsildar*.

For the last few days the tehsil has been disrupted by Jodha Singh. He has been looting several neighbourhoods and has been a disruptive force. Because of these excesses, I am unable to get the cooperation of the people in this area, as hundreds of the residents are complaining.

When I ask people for taxes, they say all their money was taken by Jodha Singh. Thse are the words of the people. I have investigated and confirmed that it is true.

While I was in Sarsi, Jodha Singh came there to loot as well. If we were not there then he would have looted the place. We sent him letters and with help of loyal soldiers forced him out of that place. This took us two days.

These days he loots villages every day. We have intelligence that he is in Holepetha, and others have joined him in the looting. Jodha Singh goes and stays in those villages (that have mutinied against our Government and joined the English). This clearly indicates he is our enemy.

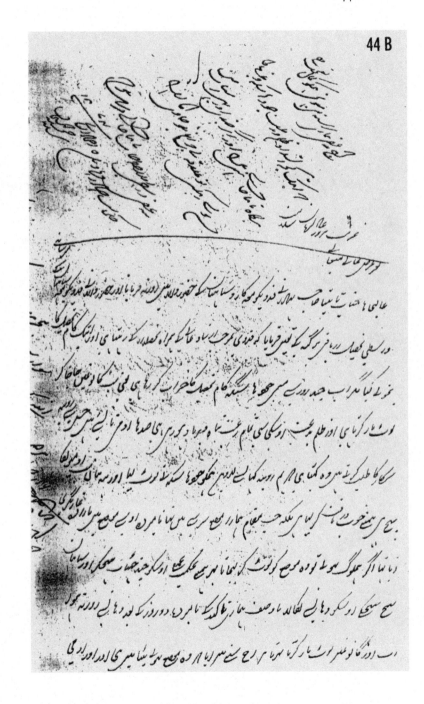

Figure 72: Urdu Letter

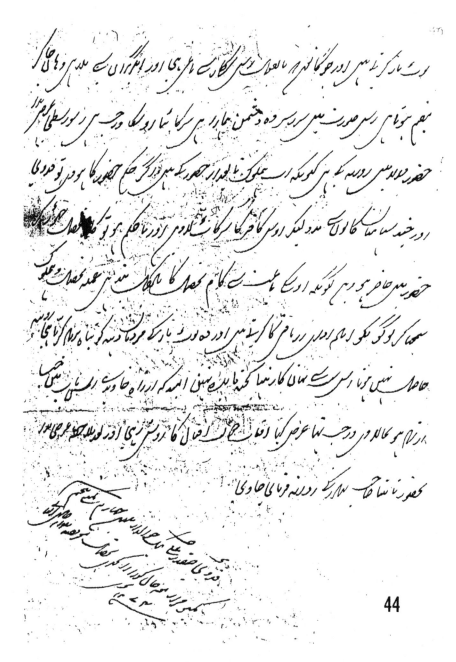

Figure 73: Urdu Letter

This letter is a request to authorise action against Jodha Singh. In my opinion he should be executed.

With your permission, I will be able to accomplish this task, with the help of my soldiers and some locals.

Letter 59

King Chandrama Kunwar Sahib has written that 4 people were followed by a force of 1000 English soldiers. We witnessed this from the ghat. These four people intermingled with the people in Akbarpur. We were unable to stop the English and their wagon with ammunition. Presently, we do not its whereabouts and and have been unsuccessful in tracing it. We have replied to Raja Bhau's letter and sent a letter to Tatya Sahib as well.

Please write as soon as possible. We are expecting you to return here after finishing your job.

Iqbal Peshwa's (Nana Sahib's) transporter Juggal has been killed by mutineers (context sensitive). In this case, there is no other enemy of the nemy but us.

We could not control road to Sangeedra hence the vehicle with ammunition has reached.

Some help arrived for the Sikhs by boat to Itawah. This is dangerous for us and we have to be prepared.

We will return from the battlefield alive if we are careful. Anyone left alive will inform you of the events in the battle.

Letter 60

From: Lalpuri Risaldar staying in Shergadh
21 Jummadassani 1274H. (6 Feb 1858)
To: Syed Mohd. Issak

All the thakurs and landlords mentioned in the letter are present here with me. They have requested clarification on the land taxation. The table that is considered is Rs. 1, Rs. 500, Rs. 800, Rs. 1000. Please advise if this structure is acceptable.

Mahants, chowkidars and others owe Rs. 800, Rs. 400 plus 8 anna. The rest will be written off. Rs. 400 will be taken from the thakurs.

We will finalise the tax rates as per your order. Please reply with the tax rates in a tabular form.

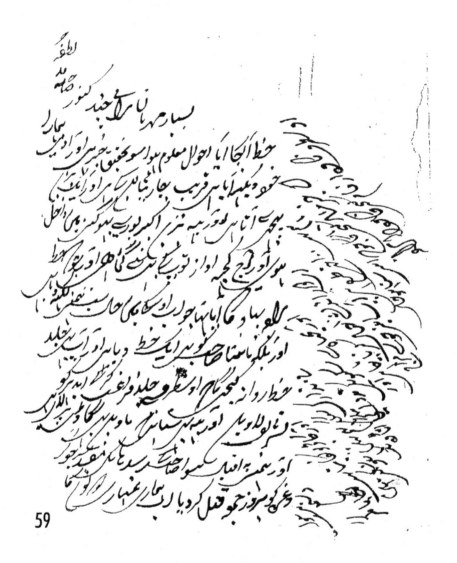

59

Figure 74: Urdu Letter

Next thing – some Thakurs are attached to some other Thakurs and some soldiers are attached to others. How do we deal with this?

The king has sent 2 Zarb cannons 1 with riffling and 1 without. These have been put in action on the ghat. Please send magazines and other material required for the guns. They are in short supply here. This would be useful if the battle starts here.

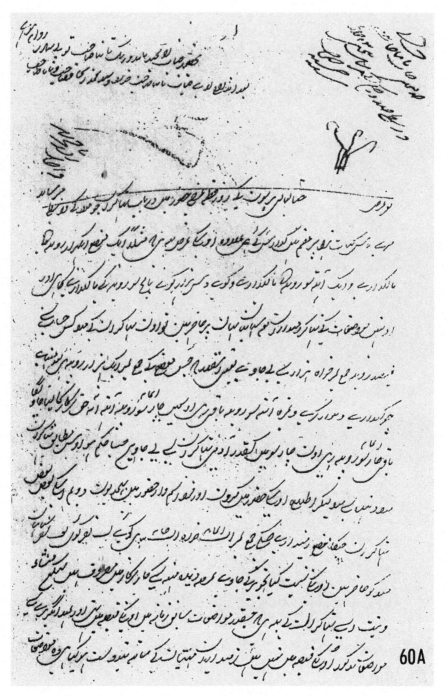

Figure 75: Urdu Letter

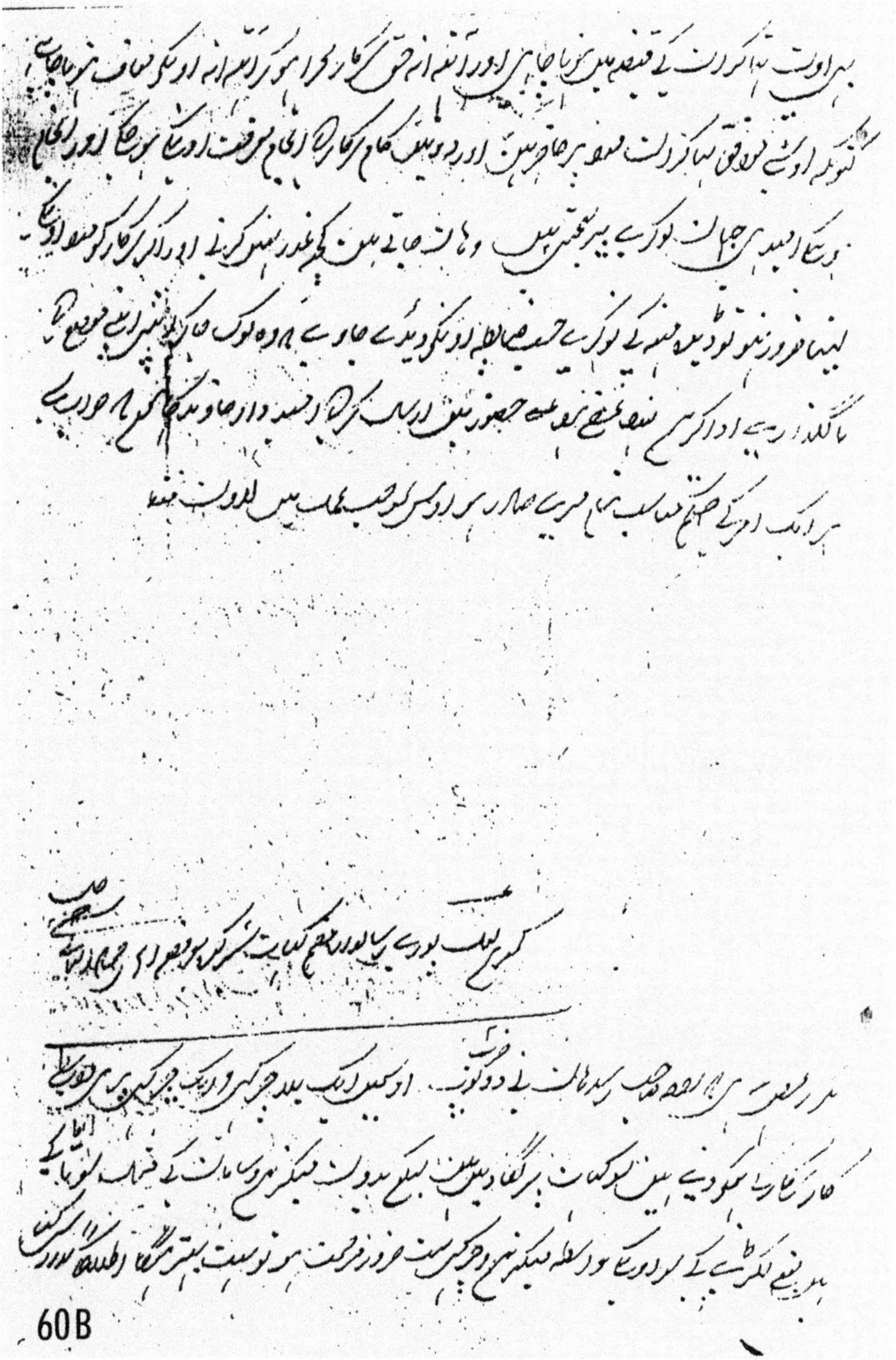

Figure 76: Urdu Letter

Annotation:

1) To Tatya Sahib
   23 Jummadassani 1274H. (8 Feb 1858)
   From: Syed Mohd Issak.
2) Copy to Nawab of Banda, Tatya Sahib Tope, Syed Mohd. Issak and Nana Sahib.
3) Entered in daily dairy.
   Note about the translation
   This area was under Maratha rule till early 19th century. Lalpuri Risaldar is asking Syed Mohd if we should go back to the system of tax collection that existed that time (that is 8 annas) or the system of collecting one Rupee. These people have been useful to us and have not mutinied and joined the English.

No. A

To: Courageous Osri Kamdar

Hope you are well. I have sent you a 18 pin cannon. It does not seem to have reached you. I am now sending you another 18 pin cannon with many magazines. Please consider it important.

19 Jummadasani 1274H

No. B

To: Courageous Rana Din Banak Subedar Bahadur and all officers of Palton Katri.

Hope you are well. You have been ordered to send to company cannons when you send 18 pin cannon from Kalpi. This is important.

19 Jummadasani 1274H.

No. C

To: Udhar Singh

I have understood the situation from your letter. The soldiers and officers, that you have removedfrom the rolls are acceptable to the chief. This was expected and in line with our thinking. Continue this action as required in the future.

20 Jummadasani 1274H

Figure 77: Urdu Letter

Figure 78: Urdu Letter

No. D
To. Rana Deen Bhanak Subedar
I understand that you attacked and killed the English upon your arrival at the destination. I am impressed by your actions. You did whatever a good and courageous soldier would have done.

Our location should not be in the mountains. Were were able to avoid any problems, because of your planning and vision. No one was disturbed so far, and please make sure no one does in the future. God willing the chief will reach their after succeeding in Charkhari.
11 lines not photocopied properly.

No. E

A letter written by Syed Mohd Issakh to Tatya Sahib was sent today. Syed Sahib has also sent forces. The ghats that separate the Yamuna need to be always guarded as per the officers in that area. This is because we don't know in which ghats the English are hiding. Syed Mohd. Issakh has written this to Tatya Sahib so that the English are prevented from getting control of the ghats.

The officers who requested protection of these ghats have changed their mind and sent an order not to make any arrangements. They have sent a copy of this order to me. The officers of Tatya Sahib should not request Syed Mohd. Issakh regarding this. Kindly send me an order not to take action against these officers.

They caught 18 packets of salt and daily rations on those ghats where Nawab of Kadura has a control.

No F

To: Courageous Ram Adharne Singh, Subedar
Hope you are well. Things are fine here. Keep writing me about the situation there.
27 Jummadasani 1274H.

Letters 52A and B

No. 1

To Bahadur Murat Singh, Subedar at Forte Kalpi.

Figure 79: Urdu Letter

Ajit Singh/Ranjit Singh was a servant of the eighth company of the platoon. An order was passed that his heirs will get his salary. The heirs will have to collect it from the office in Kalpi. The heir is claiming that the salary was given to soldier Jawahar Singh of the eight Kate's platoon. You are being ordered to collect the money back from Jawahar Singh.
8 Jummadassani 1274H.

No. 2

Place: Jalalpur Bada
To: Rana Sahib
Ref.: Rana Mahinder Singh Rao, and Ashfaq

Rana Mahinder Sing Rao and Ashfaq were told that they will be leaving shortly, and I am still waiting for their arrival. The battle* will start any time and they have not arrived. I understand that Sheikh Illahi Baksh and his sons are meant to have left this place. However, they actually are still here for the last three days. Sheikh Illahi Baksh tells me that he is going to get to the bottom of this. Please let me know of your well being and who you are keeping via Khan. So that I can look after you.

8 Jummadassani 1274H.

P.S.

Do not engage the enemy yet, as Sheikh Illahi Baksh has been sent with a camel force.

No. 3

Sheikh Illahi Baksh, Thanedar, Sangeedra will be instructed about the salary of the forces when a senior arrives in Kalpi.

No. 4

To Courageous Murat Singh
Unfortunately I did not receive your letter about the condition there. I have been asked to write to you to inform me in writing about all conditions there on regular basis.

25 Jummadassani 1274H.

No. 5

Have not received 18 cannons sent. However (I think) they should reach here tomorrow morning.

25 Jummadassani 1274H.

No. 6

Akhbarnawees **of Banda**

The news that Syed Mohd. Issak was looking for in the newspaper about the condition there has not been received.

25 Jummadassani 1274H.

No. 7

Innayat Ali *Akhbarnawees* of Banda found out the information that Syed Mohd. Issak wanted. Keep sending the information and newspapers that

Syed Mohd. Issak wants without delay and regularly. Keep that in mind.

25 Jummadassani 1274H.

Letter 69

Udhar Singh Subedar Command Officer, Paltan 9
From Mahona
To: Not clear

24 Jummadassani 1274H

Received your letter dated 19 Jummadassani 1274H regarding the Tehsil. I acknowledge that we will not act without the government's order. We will take immediate action, only on the order of Kunwar.

Chhatra Singh has gathered an army of 4000 ready for battle. At this time we urgently need the NAL KA GOLA, 5 Zarb Cannons and 500 soldiers. Please arrange to send them so they reach in the next 2 days either in the morning or in the evening. Please take special notice of this matter.

Received the letter about Bal Gobind Subedar. Many officers of Madhogadh command had gathered and the ordered announce that all the officers will be under Deena Deen Shukla command officers. The following have gathered courage and are with their soldiers and are separate.
1) Bal Gobind
2) Deena Deen Shukla
3) Diljeet Nanak
4) Jakat Singh Sahay
5) Janak Sayee
6) Puran
7) Hari Singh
It will be important to unite them.

As ordered Ram Singh Jamadar has been struck off the role on 22 Jumadassani 1274H. His salary has been paid.

I gathered that 4 camel risaldar and 1 other solder were not home. Their salary will be counted from 17 Rajab 1274H when they gave their attendance.

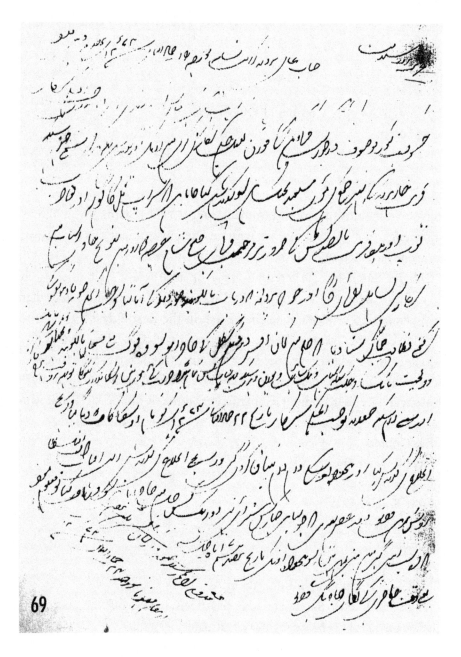

Figure 80: Urdu Letter

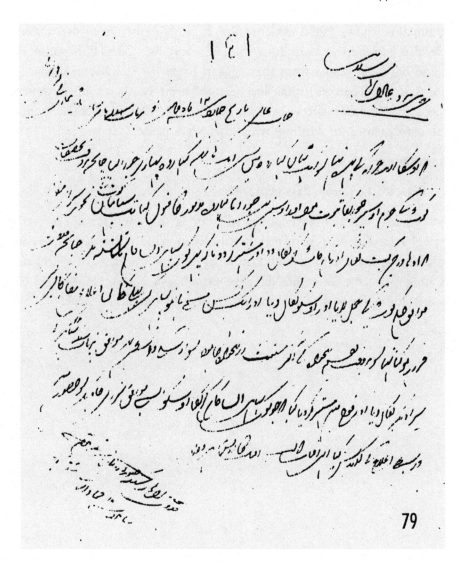

Figure 81: Urdu Letter

Letter 79

To: Someone senior
From: Fidwi Udhar Singh Subedar from Sangeedra

14 Jummadassani 1274H (30 Jan 1858)

Pratap Singh was working in the 2nd company and was responsible for guarding the treasury. A soldier informed us that Pratap Singh went to the mountains, andwe found evidence that he stole money from the treasury. He also admitted to have done so. The court has found him guilty. His name has been erased from the register. Everyone else has been warned not to do so. The court order has been followed. Nanhoo soldiers went to Kalpi and everyone knew that. We have warned the other soldiers about the consequence (of stealing) when they were paid.

Annotation:

1) **filed on 14 Jummadassani 1274H.**

Economics obviously played a key role during the war. The author of the letter has intelligence reports revealing the location of the English treasury and is asking permission for a counterstrike against the English. The permission is sought because an earlier directive from Tatya Tope's Mir Munshi had restricted the soldiers to act without consent of the local Nawab.

ENDNOTES

INTRODUCTION

1. The '...real Tantia Topee is in Bikanair. The Raja of Bikanair has given Tantia Topee 10 sowars and orderlies and there are 5,000 old Bengal Sepoys in the Saloombur jungles. Should occasion offer, some 40,000 men are said to be ready in Sallombur and Bikanair area to be employed during Dusserah...' Maharashtra Archives. Bulletin of the Department of Archives, vol. 9, 10 p.25. Original Source: Compilation No. 36 of Secret and Political Department, vol. 5 of 1863, pp.87–101.
2. Although originally written in Marathi in 1908, it was first published in English, in 1909 in Holland under this title.
3. V.D. Savarkar, *Indian War of Independence, 1857*, pp.98–9, Ram Tirath Bhatia, 1970.
4. Ibid. p.3.
5. Sir John William Kaye, *A History of the Sepoy War in India, 1857–1858*, vol. iii, p.v, W.H. Allen, 1876. 6. The correspondence between Indian leaders was destroyed in two ways. In many cases, secret correspondence was destroyed by the recipients themselves – as the following example demonstrates:
In reference to a letter received from Gwalior to a recipient in Satara which mentioned some events in Gwalior about Baija Bai and others, the witness said:
'...remarked that I would be punished for the publication of such a letter. On hearing this I held the letter to a lamp which was burning before me and burnt it.'
Freedom Struggle in UP, vol. i, p.370, Information Department, Lucknow, Uttar Pradesh, 1957.

In other cases, the English destroyed the evidence, once the narrative of the 'mutiny' was established. For example, the following report indicates the presence of letter written by Indian leaders. Yet this 'box' or its contents are nowhere to be found.

'A box has been found containing most important correspondence belonging to the Ranee of Jhansie which it is said will throw great light on the revolt and its principal authors.'

Freedom struggle in UP, vol. iii, p.386, Information Department, Lucknow, Uttar Pradesh, 1959.

7. V.D. Savarkar, *Indian War of Independence–1857*, p.542, Ram Tirath Bhatia, 1970.

8. Ibid, p.94.

9. China has a long and thriving civilisation that goes back nearly to the third millennium BC. While its traditions date back a long time, Buddhism, a religion *foreign* to China interrupted that continuity in the first millennium AD. The conflicts and the fault lines that were created within China when it first faced a foreign religion exist even today. China had a strong core set of traditions and faiths in existence prior to the advent of Buddhism. Therefore, the assimilation of Buddhism into China was no easy transition and was met with stiff resistance. The Persians have had a similar history. On the other hand, the Jewish people have demonstrated long and unbroken continuity in their faith and their culture. However, the Jewish state itself has had a largely broken existence through the ages, resurfacing again after a long gap, in the twentieth century.

The Southeast Asian countries also faced breaks in their continuity in these core attributes that defined them as nations. Central Asian, West Asian and African nations, which include the great and ancient civilisations of Mesopotamia, Sumeria, Egypt, civilisations of the upper Nile, and others, saw huge upheavals where Islam and in some cases Christianity became not just religious but also major *political* influences. The indigenous people in the Americas, sheltered by distance from outside influences saw the most dramatic collapse in their traditions and faiths, and in some cases even their existence, following the European conquest in the sixteenth century and onwards. Southern European societies, such as, Greeks and the Romans, whose civilisation spans to the first millennium BC, also saw dramatic changes with the advent of Christianity.

In all of these cases, when and where the continuity was broken there was formidable resistance from the people, whether or not the changes were introduced by force; although most were. However, the idea is not to suggest that the changes that were brought on, whether by force or otherwise, were necessarily for the worse, economically or politically. Nevertheless, in fact, these were changes that reshaped the definition of nations. Old nations died and new nations emerged.

10. The battleground with Alexander and the later Greek during the periods of 250 BC and later, were primarily only the western parts of India. India as a political unit was never really threatened by the Greeks. Many western self-proclaimed Indologists and their Indian followers continue to claim that the 'Aryans' were 'foreigners.' While this debate is still ongoing, the 'story' of an 'Aryan Invasion' is no longer considered viable.

11. Ainslee T. Embree, *1857 in India: Mutiny or War of Independence*, p.1, D.C. Heath and Company, Boston, 1963.

12. Hearings of 2 September to 27 October 1913, on 'A bill to provide for the establishment of federal reserve banks, for furnishing an elastic currency, affording means of rediscounting commercial paper, and to establish a more effective supervision of banking in the United States, and for other purposes'.

   In 1913, before the Senate Banking and Currency Committee, Mr Alexander stated: 'But the whole scheme of a Federal Reserve Bank with its commercial-paper basis is an impractical, cumbersome machinery, is simply a cover, to find a way to secure the privilege of issuing money and to evade payment of as much tax upon circulation as possible, and then control the issue and maintain, instead of reduce, interest rates. It is a system that, if inaugurated, will prove to the advantage of the few and the detriment of the people of the United States. It will mean continued shortage of actual money and further extension of credits; for when there is a lack of real money people have to borrow credit to their cost.'

PROLOGUE

1. Based on the recollection of P.K. Tope of the day's events and the story narrated by Manohar, a relative, who worked at the Reserve Bank of India Building, and lived with the family, to P.K. Tope.

2. Sardar Vallabhbhai Patel speaking on 20 February 1946.

3. See family tree in Appendix.

4. Many have suggested that the family name 'Tope' began with Tatya, and that the earlier family name was either Yeolekar, Bhat or Kulkarni. There are two interesting, but logically incomplete stories attributed in this regard.

   The story prevalent in the family was that, when Tatya was a young man, he was awarded a 'topi' or a hat, studded with jewels, after displaying splendid skills in martial arts to Bajirao II. The second story suggests that Tatya, while employed in the Bengal army was in charge of the 'toph khana' – or the artillery department. The words 'topi' or 'toph' changed into 'Tope.'

Tatya indeed was an expert in the martial arts, and apparently, however briefly, he might have joined the Bengal army (although there is no evidence to support this). While Tatya certainly popularised the last name, we can say with conviction, that it is inconceivable that his grandfather's last name was not Tope. Tatya Tope left Yeola as a child; he was no more than eight at that time. Another part of the family, including his cousins stayed behind. If Tatya indeed changed his last name to Tope while in Bithur, it is not very likely for his brothers in Bithur to have changed their last names as well. What is even more unlikely is that his cousins in Yeola to have changed their last names as well, and certainly not because Tatya earned a jewel hat or earned fame while in the artillery. There is another argument that can be made. While the 'jewelled hat' might have earned him some fame, Tatya's real fame was during the War of 1857 and after he martyred his life for the nation. Therefore *if* there was a time, his brothers and cousin did indeed adopt a new last name, it had to be shortly *after* the War. The only problem with this argument is that, after the events of 1857, the English were unleashing their retribution on all and any who were related to the leaders of 1857. It would seem completely unwarranted to take on this risk change their last name to be associated with the person that the English feared and hated it is highly unlikely that Tatya's brothers and cousin would actually take on a completely unwarranted risk and change their 'safer' names such as Kulkarni or Bhat to something that would *invite* retribution.

The fact is that the Tope last name is indeed uncommon. It also is a simple last name that does sound a lot like 'topi' or perhaps even 'toph.' Another fact is that Tatya did indeed make this last name famous. However, because these explanations are logically incomplete to be convincing, we conclude that the Tope last name indeed preceded Tatya.

5. A family photograph was captured on that occasion. Stories about Tatya were also discussed in this family gathering. Kaki telling Baburao Kaka, about Tatya having visited Yeola in the middle of the War. Baburao Kaka talked about Tatya sending messages in Lotuses and receiving them in Chapaties.

Chapter 1
FLICKERING FLAME

1. Gillow, John and Barnard, Nicholas, *Traditional Indian Textiles*, London, Thames & Hudson, 1991.
2. Fujii, Shuichi 1986, *Senshoku no Bunkashi–A History of Dyeing and Weaving*, pp.2/15–2/16, Tokyo, Rikogaku sha.
3. William Bolts, *Considerations on Indian Affairs*, p.194, J. Almon, P. Elmsly and Brotherton and Sewell, London, MDCCLXXII (1772).
4. First, the white bolls were picked from the low plants on which they grow. Then they were ginned—the white hairs separated from the rough seed. Then the hairs were cleaned and carded—brushed so the fibres lie parallel—before being spun into thread.
   The *Economist*, 18 December 2003, Cotton, A great yarn, The thread of life, indeed, and of death, money, music, slavery and ecological disaster.
5. Ibid.
6. Daniel Defoe, *A Plan of the English Commerce*, pp.49–50, Oxford, 1928.
7. Prasannan Parthasarathi, *Rethinking Wages and Competitiveness in the Eighteenth Century: Britain and South India, Past and Present*, p.107, No. 158, February 1998, Oxford University Press.
8. Paul Bairoch, 'International Industrialization Levels from 1750–1980', vol. xi, The Journal of European Economic History, 1982.
9. *History and the Culture of the Indian People*, vol. iii, p.784, Bharatiya Vidya Bhavan, 1991.
10. Rajendra Chola I's conquests included the Malayan peninsula and the capital Kadaram (Kedah).
    C. Mabel Duff, *The Chronology of India*, p.106, Archibald Constable & Co., Westminster, 1899; also, http://en.wikipedia.org/wiki/Rajendra_Chola_I
11. Angus Maddison, The World Economy, Historical Statistics, p.261, Organization for Economic Co-operation, 2003.
12. Dharampal, *The Beautiful Tree – Indigenous Indian Education in the Eighteenth Century*, p.42 and footnote. Biblia Impex, 1983.
13. Ibid, p.23.
14. Most historical analysis suggests that Indians 'stopped' travelling the oceans sometime in the second millennium. What changed in India was that many merchants who participated in the trade were Muslims. This change happened in the same period that India came under Islamic rule. However, the fact remains that India remained a nation that thrived on trade and export regardless of the religion of the merchants.

Notes to pages 11–16

15. *History and the Culture of the Indian People*, vol. iii, p.782, Bharatiya Vidya Bhavan, 1991.
16. Reid, Anthony, *Southeast Asia in the Age of Commerce 1450–1680*, vol.2, p.28, Expansion and Crisis, Yale University Press, 1993.
17. *The Economist*, 23 December 1999, The East India Companies.
18. *History and the Culture of the Indian People*, vol. iii, p.780, Bharatiya Vidya Bhavan, 1991.
19. American Psychological Association (APA): freebooter. (n.d.). Dictionary.com Unabridged (v 1.1). Retrieved 1 January 2007, from Dictionary.com: http://dictionary.reference.com/browse/freebooter.
20. *History and the Culture of the Indian People*, vol. iii, p.783, Bharatiya Vidya Bhavan, 1991.
21. William Foster, *The English Factories in India, 1655-1660*, p. 272, Clarendon Press, Oxford, 1921.
22. *The Economist*, 23 December 1999, The East India Companies.
23. William Bolts, *Considerations on Indian Affairs*, p.59, J. Almon, P. Elmsly and Brotherton and Sewell, London, MDCCLXXII (1772).
24. Iyer, Dr S. Krishna. *Travancore–Dutch Relations*, p.164, Nagercoil: CBH Publications, 1994.
25. Adwitiya Chhatrapati Shri Sambhaji Maharaj, p.235, vol. 1, Anant V. Darwatkar, Shrishambhu Prakashan, Pune, 2007.
26. Ibid, p.237.
27. Ibid.
28. Dr Sadashiv S. Shivade, Daryaraj Kanhoji Angre, pp.4-5, Utkarsha Prakashan, Pune, December 2006.
29. *Encyclopaedic History of Indian Freedom Movement*, p.275, Om Prakash, Anmol Publications, 2002.
30. *A Geographical Account of the Countries Around the Bay of Bengal, 1669–1679*, p.132, Thomas Bowrey, Haklyut Society, 1905.
31. Daryaraj Kanhoji Angre, Dr. Sadashiv S. Shivade, p.44, Utkarsha Prakashan, Pune, December 2006.
32. Robert Orme, official historian of the East India Company in Bombay Gazetteer, vol. I part ii p.89.
33. Roper Lethbridge, *History of India*, p.160, Brown 1879.
34. Daryaraj Kanhoji Angre, Dr. Sadashiv S. Shivade, p.45, Utkarsha Prakashan, Pune, December 2006.
35. A twenty-year period starting 1666 reveals an interesting pattern between Maratha and Mughal military engagements. Shivaji's consolidation of power in the 'Deccan' was largely at the cost of small independent kings who were

once allied to the Mughal Empire. Sambhaji's later 'intrigues' with Aurangzeb shortly before and after the death of Shivaji have been 'frowned' upon by historians as a 'betrayal.' The fact that Aurangzeb's son became a resident at Sambhaji's court is largely ignored by historians.

Chapter 2
PENUMBRA

1. Brooks Adams, *The Law of Civilization and Decay: an Essay on History*, p.308, Macmillan, 1896.
2. Ibid, p.309.
3. Ibid, p.310.
4. Today, the famine of the 1770s is described as the First Bengal Famine. The Second Bengal Famine occurred between 1942 and 1945, when the British cut-off the supply lines of the invading Indian National Army under Subhash Chandra Bose. While this policy was successful in preventing Bose from liberating India; nearly four million civilians perished for lack of food. Under direct British authority rice and other grains were not allowed to be transported to the rural areas where the INA had its strongholds.
5. 7 February 1787, *Speeches of the Late Right Honourable Richard Brinsley Sheridan*. Ed. by A Constitutional Friend, 5 vols. London: Patrick Martin, 1816. 1: 273–96
6. *Social Statics*: abridged and revised; together with The Man Versus the State, p.197, Herbert Spencer, 1892, D. Appleton and Company.
7. *History and the Culture of the Indian People*, vol. iii, p.738, Bharatiya Vidya Bhavan, 1991.
8. Ibid.
9. James Talboys Wheeler, *Early Records of British India: A History of the English Settlements in India*, p.301, Trübner and Company, 1878
10. William Bolts, *Considerations on Indian Affairs*, p.74, J. Almon, P. Elmsly and Brotherton and Sewell, London, MDCCLXXII (1772).
11. *The Economist*, 18 December 2003, Cotton, A great yarn: The thread of life, indeed, and of death, money, music, slavery and ecological disaster.
12. Elaine Shannon Washington (1991-07-01). 'New Kings of Coke'. Times Magazine.
13. World Drug Report – Shared Responsibility, UNODC 2005.
14. Immanuel C.Y. Hsu, *The Rise of Modern China*, pp.169–71, Sixth Edition Oxford University Press, 2000.
15. Price in other years was $590 in 1801, $2,075 in 1821 and $744 in 1835; while a chest of Malwa fetched $400, $1,325 and $602 in the corresponding years.

Notes to pages 22–24

Immanuel C.Y. Hsu, *The Rise of Modern China*, pp.169–71, Sixth Edition, Oxford University Press, 2000.

16. Ibid.

17. *England and China: The Opium Wars, 1839–60, The Opium Trade, Seventh through Nineteenth Centuries*, Philip V. Allingham, contributing editor, Victorian Web; Lakehead University, Thunder Bay, Ontario.
http://www.victorianweb.org/history/empire/opiumwars/opiumwars1.html

18. Incidentally, it was in the late nineteenth and the early twentieth century that a few Indian merchants who were licensed by the English, made handsome profits on opium speculation. Some of them benefited greatly later, from the autarkic and socialistic policies that were enacted after the English were finally evicted after the events of 1946.

19. Thomas George Percival Spear, *Twilight of the Mughuls: Studies in Late Mughul Delhi*, p.38, Cambridge University Press, 1951.

20. Randolf G.S. Cooper, *The Anglo-Maratha Campaigns and the Contest for India: The Struggle for Control of the South Asian Military Economy*, p.1, Cambridge University Press, 2004.

21. Some historians who are willing to acknowledge the Maratha history tend to focus only on the divisions rather than their achievements. Losses are exaggerated and victories marginalised. Stories are abruptly ended to portray grim pictures, rather than follow them to their logical completions. Struggles and rivalries for successions, which are universal are dwelt upon derisively, and presented as causes for weakness, when facts clearly indicate an expanding empire. Political rivalries and struggles for succession have existed in the world from the most ancient times; from the *Mahabharata*, to the Pharaohs of Egypt or all the European countries. China and Japan had their share of political rivalries as well. Great Empires have emerged out of these rivalries, and history shows them as a universal basis for the pursuit of power. However, in the case of Marathas these rivalries, which actually resulted in an empire that controlled nearly three-quarters of modern India is always presented derisively. In addition to the ghosts of misalignment, which dominate the history of 1857, the Maratha history is dominated by ghosts of malignment. The logical and universal rivalries between the various Maratha powers presented by these eminent historians is analysed along lines of division that reflect a modern Maharashtra; faced with degenerated socioeconomic conditions caused by colonial misrule. The rivalries analysed in history books do not portray the economic conditions and the societal integrity that had existed at the peak of the Maratha power. It was this cohesiveness that allowed the Marathas to reach high levels of power during the times when European supremacy was nearly

unchallenged. The miseries of a modern and poor Maharashtra (relative to the eighteenth century and earlier), suffering from a breakdown of social integrity are projected linearly into the past by modern historians. Modern divisions and stratification are assumed to be perpetual rather than dynamic reflections of the economic conditions that existed during various snapshots of time.

22. The authors do not subscribe to the view that Maratha power has to be analysed only along the lines of social stratification of a modern Maharashtra. The Peshwas and the Shindes (and other Maratha strongholds) collectively represent the Maratha power. Too many Macaulayan faithfuls repeat the English tendencies to exaggerate Maratha rivalries and create artificial divisions between the Marathas.

23. 'The Akluj stone demonstrates the use of combined operations with disciplined infantry and two types of cavalry. The defenders of the fort are shown as having launched an attempt to break the siege ring tightening around them. The breakout force featured a vanguard of lancers flanked to the left by tightly packed infantry. This leading line of infantry, with shield and sword, stood shoulder-to-shoulder in formation presenting a shield-wall to the attacking siege force. Behind the line of shields, archers were waiting to unleash their arrows. To thwart this effort the besieging force countered the defenders' cavalry charge with horsemen of its own. As this was being done, the besieging army flanked right, using elephants in echelon to trample and sweep the breakout force's left in an attempt to roll-up the defenders' infantry line. The craftsman who carved the stone chose to freeze in time the screaming agony of a defending infantryman of the line. His open mouth hauntingly depicted as a circular depression and his right leg shown in the process of being crushed beneath an advancing elephant in full stride.'
Randolf G.S. Cooper. *The Anglo-Maratha Campaigns and the Contest for India: The Struggle for Control of the South Asian Military Economy*, p.16, Cambridge University Press, 2004.

24. For example, the Sanskrit word 'Vahini', whose usage is ancient, generically means an 'army'. However, it has a much more specific meaning as defined in dictionaries. A single Vahini consisted of 810 soldiers divided as 81 elephants, 81 chariots, 243 cavalry, and 405 infantry (including archers). Our simple analysis reveals the mathematical simplicity of the Vahini, allowed for various formations that could be driven by tactical needs. The basic unit of a Vahini was made up of 10 soldiers in a 1–1–3–5 formation (1–Elephant, 1–Chariot, 3–Cavalry, 5–Infantry). Each of these units in turn could be arranged in an array of 9x9 units or a triangle with 1, 3, 5, 7, 9, 11, 13, 15 and 17 units or a rhombus. Some arrangements could be made with ranks and without files

and some with ranks and files. The simplicity of the number 81, allowed for complex and useful tactical formations. Multiple regiments allowed more complex formations based on tactical requirements, offensive or defensive needs, terrain, weather, and other considerations.

25. Stephen Peter Rosen, *Societies and Military Power: India and Its Armies*, p.174, Cornell University Press, 1996.
26. Randolf G.S. Cooper, *The Anglo-Maratha Campaigns and the Contest for India: The Struggle for Control of the South Asian Military Economy*, p.143, Cambridge University Press, 2004.
27. http://en.wikipedia.org/w/index.php?title=Beno%C3%AEt_de_Boigne&oldid=83020887

Chapter 3
THE RULE OF DARKNESS

1. Angus Maddison, *The World Economy, Historical Statistics*, p.260, Organization for Economic Cooperation, 2003.
2. The author certainly does not mean to trivialise the hardships faced by the slaves; however, many discussions on the subject have always sidelined the key point that the US economy was more competitive because it was built on the backbone of nearly free labour.
3. While it is impossible to do a 'what if' study to assess India's situation, with and without English 'looting'; we can try to explain this by comparing the per capita GDP growth of India relative to the another Asian country, Japan which had similar economic growth in the period AD 1000–1500. Japan was successfully able to resist the military and therefore economic controls of Britain and other European countries; in other words Japan unlike India, was not 'looted' in the eighteenth and nineteenth centuries. By controlling its indigenous economy, Japan's per capita GDP actually expanded in the period 1500–1820 while India's fell.

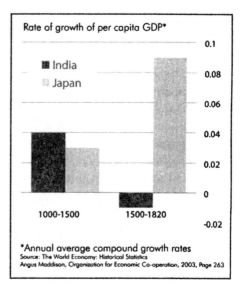

Notes to pages 30–33

4. Sir George Otto Trevelyan *The Life and Letters of Lord Macaulay*, p.2, Longsmans, Green, 1881.
5. Brooks Adams, *The Law of Civilization and Decay: an Essay on History*, p. 309, Macmillan, 1896.
6. Sir George Otto Trevelyan, *The Life and Letters of Lord Macaulay*, p.32, Longsmans, Green, 1881.
7. Ibid.
8. Ibid, pp.329–330.
9. Ibid, p.263.
10. William Isaac Chamberlain *Education in India*, p.36, The Macmillan Co., 1899.
11. Pramatha Náth Bose, K. Paul, *A History of Hindu Civilisation During British Rule*, p.173, vol. iii, Trench, Trübner, 1896.
12. William Isaac Chamberlain, *Education in India*, p.37, The Macmillan co., 1899.
13. Ibid.
14. Ibid.
15. Ibid, p.75.

Philip Hartog, who was the former vice chancellor of the University of Dacca, contested Gandhi's claim. Modern historians have used Hartog's arguments as the basis for conclusions on this subject. The chain of correspondence that ensued between Gandhi and Hartog was an attempt to analyse and interpret the data that was surveyed by the English in Bengal, in the 1830s, after Bentinck's proclamation, rather than the survey in the Madras Presidency in the 1820s by Thomas Munro.

16. Dharampal, *The Beautiful Tree–Indigenous Indian Education in the Eighteenth Century*, p.xi, Biblia Impex, 1983.
17. Ibid, p.41.
18. Ibid, p.14.

Philip Hartog and many later historians have dismissed this assessment by Adam, suggesting that this conservative estimate was an exaggeration!

However, Adam's observations were not isolated or surprising for that period, since many before him had made similar observations, including that of Thomas Munro. That the Indian educational system was strong enough to be considered worth emulating in early nineteenth century, England is sidelined by the English and Indian historians as a policy.

Additionally, it would be bizarre to assume that someone like Adam, who was 'hired' by the EEIC, to *justify* the need for 'educational reform' would want to exaggerate the achievements of the Indian system, the English desired to crush (or 'improve' – if you are on the other side of the argument). Unfortunately, logical reasoning is marginalised in most discussions on this subject. Not unlike the history of 1857, India's English speaking elite are reluctant to admit that the English had any kind of a bias that would have affected the quality of the 'data' presented in Adam's survey.

While Adam's diligence in collecting the data is not in doubt, both his objectivity and attitude are definitely in question. Adam's aggregation of the student population in the schools, in all likelihood presented a floor (a minimum) rather than an average or a ceiling. For example, Adam recognised that some boys were home-schooled, however, a significant number of girls were home-schooled as well, but their literacy rates were ignored. In order to get a better insight, the averages can only be estimations based on the broad observations made by Adam in 1836–8 and by the likes of Thomas Munro and others before him. A pathshala in every village, with high participation from all sections of the socio-economic strata, provided an opportunity for each child to achieve elementary education.

19. Dharampal, *The Beautiful Tree – Indigenous Indian Education in the Eighteenth Century*, p.249, Biblia Impex, 1983.
20. Ibid, p.248.
21. Ibid, p.14.
22. Ibid, p.25.
23. Ibid, p.23.
    The following table summarises the caste-wise participation in the pathshalas in the Madras Presidency.
    Source: Ibid, page numbers as noted.

District	# of Schools	Bramin	Vysea	Soodras	Others	Survey Date	Page
Tinnevelly	607	2016	–	2889	3674	7 November 1822	98–99
Serigapatam	17	38	20	101	62	29 October 1822	96–97
Shahur Gangam	24	10	3	211	96	29 October 1822	96–97
Coimbatore	95	204	60	1049	106	23 November 1822	102–103
Polachy	60	30	9	451	31	23 November 1822	102–103

Sattimungalum	30	73		307	40	23 November 1822	102–103
Cheoor	46	69	16	322	20	23 November 1822	102–103
Parindoora	51	23	4	402		23 November 1822	102–103
Danaiguncottah	24	38	7	220		23 November 1822	102–103
Coligall	24	27	45	202	18	23 November 1822	102–103
Andoor	26	24	8	196		23 November 1822	102–103
Eroad	43	24	2	273		23 November 1822	102–103
Caroor	76	136	39	603	778	23 November 1822	104–105
Pulladeem	79	57	7	720	784	23 November 1822	104–105
Dharapoorand	65	129	16	530	682	23 November 1822	104–105
Kongayund	57	36	14	328	382	23 November 1822	104–105
Checkeragehrry	87	48	42	858	948	23 November 1822	104–105
Total	1411	2982	292	9662	7621		
		14.5%	1.4%	47.0%	37.1%		

These districts show that the 'soodra' and 'other' castes together represented 84% of the student population. College education in the Vedas was dominated by Brahmin students, however, in specialty subjects such as astronomy and medical sciences, there *are examples of a wider variety of backgrounds amongst students. For example, in Malabar, of the 808 students studying astronomy, less than 10% were Brahmin (78. Ibid–p.27). Of 194 students studying medical sciences, only 31 were Brahmins (Ibid–p.28).*

24. Macaulay's Children and the Choo-Choo Salute

To his credit, Macaulay, who wanted to *'create a class of people Indian in blood and color, but English in tastes, morals and opinion,'* was partly successful. Today, this 'class of people,' though influential, remains quite small. Not all who were educated in these 'fine' educational institutes fell for Macaulay's trap. If it were not for the events of 1857, his policies and institutions could have succeeded in their goals. Although Macaulay did not completely succeed, a small percentage of Indians continued to subscribe to the thoughts he intended to propagate.

Long after the English have left, a section of the English speaking Indian elite actually view India's defeat in 1857 in positive light. Some notable historians agree with Sir Jadunath Sarkar's analogy, that the Indian leaders of 1857 were a 'King Cobra', and the War of 1857 was the Cobra's 'last bite' before its head was smashed. Hyperbole aside, some actually, salute the English for bringing 'progress' to an otherwise 'decadent' nation who would have reverted into the hands of the 'old order'.

There are many flaws in this argument – some of them are discussed earlier, however this implicit gratitude to the victor of the war is largely an elitist phenomenon. We label this obeisance as the 'choo choo salute', since it usually starts with thanking the English for introducing the railways to India. Is this gratitude fundamentally valid?

The debate is not whether the railways and other technologies were western innovations, or that they came to India via the English. Nor is there a question about the significance of the railroad and its application to India and the world. However, to be worthy of this *reverence*, the question is, 'was the existence of the English *Regime* in India a *prerequisite* for these innovations such as these to have reached India? 'Was India's military defeat a requirement for these innovations to reach India?

Many believe it does. However, there is a logical fallacy within this argument. India's decadence was not caused by the 'old order', but by a long period of economic decline. India's economy collapsed from being one of the largest to something nearly irrelevant. Should then, the English be thanked for the railways? Consider Japan (Please refer to the figure in notes for Chapter 3).

Despite a series of wars with Europeans in the nineteenth century, the English or the European never directly politically ruled Japan. Does it follow, therefore, that Japan does not have the railways? The answer is obvious. Japan *does* have the railways as well as access to most technological innovations attributed to the west. In that case, what are the prerequisites for any innovation to travel to other locations? While there are many mechanisms in which this can occur, the primary prerequisite is *access to capital* and appropriate preconditions for investments to be channeled toward infrastructure growth.

American and Swiss bankers invested nearly £500 million in the Indian Railways. (Richard Collier, *The Great Indian Mutiny: A Dramatic Account of the Sepoy Rebellion*, p.340, E.P. Dutton and Co., Inc., 1964.) The railways were to make the transportation of opium more efficient and secure. Which it did, and for that, the investors got a great return on their investment.

The question then is whether India would have had the railways if it were *not ruled* by England? Japan as mentioned earlier had similar economic growth as India in the first half of the second millennium. (Actually India's per capita GDP growth was higher than Japan. India also had a stronger export base and range of products that sustained its dominance globally.) In the nineteenth century, Japan had with reasonable success defended itself militarily and therefore economically. Despite English 'gunboat diplomacy' of the 1850s and the resulting restructuring occurred within Japan in the 1860s, most of its domestic policies were set by the Japanese under Emperor Meiji. Japan's domestic economy was large enough to sustain the large capital investments needed in infrastructure projects, such as the railways. Obviously, the Japanese needed western know how and the technology. Of course, the Japanese Emperor could have *invited* the English to *rule* them – hoping that the English would charitably bring the railways. Nevertheless, the Japanese chose a much easier option: *money*. The Japanese hired English engineers to lay the first telegraph line, eighteen miles long in 1869. (Riotaro Kodama, *Railway Transportation in Japan*, p.4, Register Job Rooms, 1898.)

The first railway in Japan opened in 1872. (Riotaro Kodama, *Railway Transportation in Japan*, p.7, Register Job Rooms, 1898.) Technological innovations occurred, as Japan was able to secure the capital needed for the large investments in its infrastructure. Logically, *any* nation with a strong domestic economy and a large export market would have been able to purchase technology not invented on its soil. Innovations travel across boundaries when markets are free. There is always a price associated with any innovation or invention. Considering that India was called as the 'sink' for gold and other precious metals in the centuries preceding the time of the English rule, India, like Japan would have easily qualified to purchase the technology to build the railroad. In fact, the proclamation of freedom made on 25 August 1857 promised an environment where investments in infrastructure would be a priority.

Investment in India in the early 1850s, for many of the American and Swiss investors was thought as a *safe* bet. This was especially since many investors had been burnt in the stock market bubble created by the railroad companies in the US and Britain. In fact, the Great Western Railway was for decades the most admired railway company in Britain, yet anyone who had bought shares at its launch in 1835 (at a fraction of their peak in 1845) and held them until 1913 would have seen an annual return of only 5 per cent. (*The Economist*, 21 September 2000. Survey: The New Economy, Bubble.com, All technological revolutions carry the risks as well as rewards.) Many investors who invested at the peak in 1845 lost their shirt. India, paradoxically, with autocratic financial controls and hundreds of thousands of acres under opium cultivation was actually a 'safe' investment opportunity for many who had the money.

The Anglo-Indian War of 1857 put a damper on *that* irrational exuberance.

25. *The Friend of India*, pp.145-46, 12 February 1857.

Freedom Struggle in UP, p.288, vol. I, Information Department, Lucknow, Uttar Pradesh, 1957.

26. P.C. Joshi, ed. *Rebellion: 1857*, pp.150-59, Bombay: People's Publishing House, 1957.

27. Edward Rupert Humphreys, *Manual of British Government in India*, pp.73-4, Brown, Green and Longmans, London, 1857.

28. Ibid, p.71.

29. '...between them (Muslims) and the Hindus there was, at the first, as little of congeniality or sympathy of any sort, as there is, at present, between either of them and us; and there is no inference more plainly deducible from all the analogies of history, than the certainty that, until we really colonise India, and raise up a European element in the population, we shall be regarded merely as slave-holders and tax-gatherers.'

Edward Rupert Humphreys, *Manual of British Government in India*, p.70, Longman, Brown, Green and Longmans, London, 1857.

30. P.C. Joshi, ed. *Rebellion: 1857*, pp.150-59, Bombay: People's Publishing House, 1957.

31. Prasannan Parthasarathi, *The Transition to a Colonial Economy*, p.139, Cambridge University Press, 2001.

32. Prasannan Parthasarathi, *Rethinking Wages and Competitiveness in the Eighteenth Century: Britain and South India*, p.158, No. 158, February 1998, Oxford University Press.

33. Prasannan Parthasarathi, *The Transition to a Colonial Economy*, p.14, Cambridge University Press 2001.

34. Ibid, p.13.

35. Ibid, p.14.
36. Ibid, p.88.
37. Prasannan Parthasarathi, *Rethinking Wages and Competitiveness in the Eighteenth Century: Britain and South India*, p.97, Past and Present, No. 158, February 1998, Oxford University Press
38. Ibid p.121.

Chapter 4
THE FREEDOM FOUNDATION

1. Biswamoy Pati, *Issues in Modern Indian History*, p.46, Popular Prakashan, 2000.
2. Daulatrao was Tukaji's grandson.
3. Maj. R. Meade, agent to the governor general, Central India, to secretary, Government of India, 8 July 1863, NAI, FDP 'A', 21 August 1863.
4. Edward Balfour, Cyclopædia of India and of eastern and southern Asia, Commercial, Industrial and Scientific: Products of the Mineral, Vegetable and Animal Kingdoms, Useful Arts and Manufactures, 1873, Scottish & Adelphi presses, p. 283.
5. Surendra Nath Roy, *A History of the Native States of India*, p.332, Thacker Spink, 1888.
6. Biswamoy Pati, *Issues in Modern Indian History*, p.46, Ed. Popular Prakashan, 2000.
7. Maj. R. Meade, agent to the governor general, Central India, to secretary, Government of India, 8 July 1863, NAI, FDP 'A', 21 August 1863.
8. Ghatge was apparently murdered by English narrative claim that Ghatge was murdered at the request of his own son-in-law Manaji Phadke. G.S. Sardesai, *New History of the Marathas*, p.322, vol. iii, Phoenix publication 1946-48, Bombay.
9. R. Cavendish, resident, Gwalior, to W.H. Macnaghten, secretary, Government of India, 14 July 1832, NAI, FD Misc., vol. 235.
10. Ibid, 8 June 1832, NAI, FD Misc., vol. 234, pt. i.
11. George Bruce Malleson, *An Historical Sketch of the Native States of India in Subsidiary Alliance with the British Government*, p.161, Longmans, Green, and co., 1875.
12. Biswamoy Pati, *Issues in Modern Indian History*, p.51, Ed. by Biswamoy Pati, Popular Prakashan, 2000.
13. Colonel Fielding to A. Stirling, secretary, Government of India, 18 January 1830, NAI, FDP, 45, 16 April 1830.
14. Biswamoy Pati, *Issues in Modern Indian History*, p.52, Popular Prakashan, 2000.
15. Colonel George Fielding to Lord Bentinck, governor general, 2 February 1830, NAI, FDP 47, 16 April 1830.

16. Ibid.
17. Biswamoy Pati, *Issues in Modern Indian History*, p.53, Popular Prakashan, 2000.
18. Ibid.
19. Capt O. Stubbs, Sindia's Contingent, to Maj. G. Fielding, acting resident, Gwalior, 20 February 1829, NAI, FDP, 50/15 May 1829.
20. The period of his rule is glorified by the English as a period of 'peace' with the English. George Bruce Malleson, *An Historical Sketch of the Native States of India in Subsidiary Alliance with the British Government*, p.161, Longmans, Green, and co., 1875.
21. Ibid p.162.
22. Biswamoy Pati, *Issues in Modern Indian History*, p.58, Popular Prakashan, 2000.
23. Testimony of Sitaram Baba.
24. Ibid.
25. Ibid.
26. Ibid.
27. Ibid.
28. *Freedom Struggle in UP*, vol.III, p.582, Foreign Political Proceedings, Supp: 30 December 1859, Cons. No. 1362. National Archives, New Delhi.
29. Tatya, it seems, did not handle Nana's interactions with the English. However, it was likely that Nana Saheb dealt with the English directly or through another person.
30. Dr. Moti Lal Bhargava, *Architects of Indian Freedom Struggle*, p.11, Deep and Deep Publications, New Delhi, 1981.
31. Allen Copsey very effectively addresses the debate of Lakshmibai's birthdate. http://www.copsey-family.org/~allenc/lakshmibai/qanda.html
    The following is a snapshot of a portion of the website taken in early 2008. Some claim a birthdate of 19 November 1835 which would make her twenty-two at the time of her death. This date seems to stem from Parasnis though I am unaware of his source and this is the date recorded on her memorial in Gwalior. Others believe a date of about 1828 to be more likely, making her about thirty when she was killed.
    Tahmankar, for example, claims she was born in 1827. His reasoning being that she was born in Varanasi, and her family moved from there to Bithur in 1832. He also states that at the time of her marriage which he places in 1842, her father was concerned that she would reach puberty without being married arguing for a later age at marriage. (Just to illustrate the confusion, the cover of Tahmankar's book claims she died when she was twenty-three.)

This date is also supported to an extent by claims that she 'played' with Nana Sahib, Tatya Topi, and Rao Sahib. Since Nana Sahib was born about 1820 and Tatya Topi even earlier in 1814, the later birth date of 1835 would put her 'playmates' into another generation altogether.

More recently (December 2003), I have been able to confirm that she was married in, or about, May 1842. There is an entry in the Jhansi Treasury Accounts held by the British Library which reads: 'To Maharaja Gangadhar Rao to cover the expenses of his marriage ... bill dated 21st May – 40,000 Rs'.

If Lakshmibai had been born in November 1835, she would have been six and a half at this time, early even by standards of the time. Mahasweta Devi for one claims the 1835 date and that she was married when she was eight years old; both of these claims cannot be correct. Further would it have been sensible for a man who had lost one wife, was no longer young and needful of an heir to marry a child and then wait several years before she could bear him a child?

Parasnis, who seems to be the source for the November 1835 date, states that she went with her father to Bithur when she was four years old. As Sinha points out, this move occurred after the death of her father's employer Chimunji Appa and his subsequent employment by Chimunji's brother. This happened in 1832, giving a birth date of 1828.

In John Lang's book, *Wanderings in India*, from which the famous description of the Rani is taken, he mentions that he 'had heard from the vakeel that the Ranee was a very handsome woman of about six or seven and twenty years of age', a description which his own does not contradict. If the Rani had been twenty-six or twenty-seven in 1854 that gives a birth date of 1827/1828. I can think of no reason why Lang or the vakeel should misrepresent the facts.

All in all, a birth date of 1827 or 1828 fits. A birth date of 1835, whatever the source of that date may be, does not and is contradictory.

32. Many narratives indicate that the three 'played' together – which is highly unlikely considering their ages. Surendranath Sen points this out accurately – Dr Surendranath Sen, *Eighteen Fifty Seven*, p.220, The Publications Division, Ministry of Information and Broadcasting, Government of India, 1957.

33. Indumati Sheorey, *National Biography of Tatya Tope*, p.4, National Book Trust, 1973.

34. Ibid.

35. Ibid p.265.

36. माझा प्रवास, **1857** च्या बडाची हकीकत, कै. वे शा. सं. विष्णुभट गोडसे, Maza Pravas, Vishnubhat Godse, Venus Publishers, November 2000, p. 66–67.

Notes to pages 51–59

37. Henry George Keene, *A Servant of 'John Company': Being the Recollections of an Indian Official*, p.161, Thacker, Spink and Co., 1897.
38. Ibid.
39. Amaresh Misra, *Mangal Pandey: The True Story of an Indian Revolutionary*, (dedication page), Rupa and Co., 2005.

Chapter 5
THE PLANNED WAR—PIECES OF THE PUZZLE

1. John William Kaye, *A History of the Sepoy War, 1857–1858*, p.571, vol. I, 1864, W.H. Allen and Co., London, 1864.
2. Ibid, p.570.
3. Edward Rupert Humpreys, *Manual of British Government in India*, p.56, Brown, Green and Longmans, London, 1857.
4. Thomas George Percival Spear, Vincent Arthur Smith, *The Oxford History of India*, p.715, *The History of the Indian Revolt and of the Expeditions to Persia, China, and Japan, 1856–7–8*, p.32, W. and R. Chambers, 1859, George Dodd.
5. R.M. Coopland, *A Lady's Escape from Gwalior, and Life in the Fort of Agra During the Mutinies of 1857*, p.70, Smith, Elder, 1859.
6. *Macmillan's Magazine*, p.9-10, John Morley, Mowbray Morris, David Masson, George Grove.
7. John William Kaye, *A History of the Sepoy War in India, 1857–58*, p.573, vol. i, W.H. Allen and Co., London, 1875.
8. James John McLeod Innes, *Lucknow & Oude in the Mutiny*, p.65, A.D. Innes and Co., 1895
9. http://mainpuri.nic.in/chapter2.htm
10. Justin McCarthy, *A Short History of Our Own Times, from the Accession of Queen Victoria to the General Election of 1880, vol. i*, pp.219. Frederick A. Stokes Company, 1893.
11. George Otto Trevelyan, *The Competition Wallah*, p.335, MacMillan and Co., 1866.
12. *The History of the Indian Revolt and of the Expeditions to Persia, China, and Japan, 1856–7–8*, p.35, W. and R. Chambers, 1859, George Dodd.
13. Benjamin Disraeli (speech by), *Parliamentary Debates*, 3rd Series, pp.440–472, vol. 147, 27 July 1857.
14. 'It was a common occurrence for a man to come to a cantonment with a lotus flower, and give it to the chief native officer of a regiment, the flower was circulated from hand to hand in the regiment... When the lotus came to the last man in the regiment, he disappeared for a time, and took it to the next

military station. This strange process occurred throughout nearly all the military stations where regiments of the Bengal native army were cantoned.'
George Dodd, *The History of the Indian Revolt and of the Expeditions to Persia, China, and Japan, 1856–7–8*, p.36, W. and R. Chambers, 1859.

15. 'I allude to the circumstance of the lotus flower. A man came with a lotus flower, and gave it to the chief soldier of a regiment. It was circulated from hand to hand in the regiment and every man who took it looked at it and passed it on, saying nothing. We must understand that every man who passed it on was acquainted with the plot. When it came to the last soldier of the regiment he disappeared and took it to the next station. The process was gone through in every regiment in Bengal. There was not a regiment, not a station, not an escort among which the lotus flower has not in this way circulated. All these things took place after the annexation of Oude and then the Sepoys were drawn into the vortex of that conspiracy which had been long secretly forming...'
Benjamin Disraeli (speech by) Parliamentary Debates, 3rd Series, pp.440–472, vol. 147, 27 July 1857.

16. Mowbray Thomson, *The Story of Cawnpore*, p.24, R. Bentley, 1859.

17. Edward Rupert Humphreys, p.56, *Manual of British Government in India*, Longman, Brown, Green and Longmans, London, 1857.

18. Pandit Sunderlal, *British Rule in India*, p.276, Popular Prakashan, 1972.

19. S.L. Sharma, M.R. Kumar, *Indian Freedom Struggle Centenary, 1857–1957*, p.13, S.L. Sharma, 1957.

20. Sitaram Baba's testimony.

21. N.K. Nigam, *Delhi in 1857*, p.47, S. Chand, 1957.

22. Maheshwar Dayal, *Rediscovering Delhi: The Story of Shahjahanabad*, p.223, S. Chand Publications, 1975.

23. George Otto Trevelyan, *Cawnpore*, p.59, Macmillan and Co., 1866.

24. George Otto Trevelyan, *The Competition Wallah*, p.337, MacMillan and Co., 1866.

25. 'Ranjit Singh always had the misgiving that perhaps some day the kingdom of the Punjab "would also go red", (*Kisi din to ye bhee lal ho jaega*).' N.M. Khilnani, Nagendra K. Singh, *Panorama of Indian Diplomacy: From Mauryan Epoch to Post-Nehru Era*, p.56, S. Chand, 1981.

26. '...all will become red!'
Gulshan Lall Chopra, *The Panjab as a Sovereign State 1799–1839*, p.48, Vishveshvaranand Vedic Research Institute, 1960.

27. Amaresh Mishra, *Mangal Pandey: The True Story of an Indian Revolutionary*, p.82, Rupa and Company, 2005.

28. Richard Holmes, *Sahib: The British Soldier in India*, pp.121-22, Harper Perennial, London, 2006.

29. It is estimated that the daily caloric intake for an average representative Indian soldier weighing about 60 kg (142 pounds) eating basic food - such as daal and roti (lentils and bread) would be between 1700 and 2000 calories. Let's round this off to 1800 calories. On an active day of duty and during action, the soldier would need about 2400 calories. On a strenuous day, especially during troop movement, a soldier would need about 2800 calories. For the cavalry, an average horse weighing 700–900 pounds will need a minimum, of about 11,000 calories per day. Good quality hay will provide about 800 calories per pound of feed. An average horse should be fed about 2 pounds of hay per 100 pounds of body weight. A horse would also need about 20% more calories during days where the soldiers covered long distances. While it is possible that on an average day, the soldier got some variety of food – but the sake of simplicity in our analysis – we have assumed that most of the calories came from daal and roti. Both daal and wheat flour provide about 350 calories per 100 gm of uncooked source. On a strenuous day, an average soldier would need about 800 grams of daal and wheat flour - making it about equivalent to 1kg of grain equivalent.

Chapter 6
THE PLANNED WAR—LOGICAL INFERENCES

1. Edward Rupert Humphreys, *Manual of British Government in India*, p.56, Longman, Brown, Green and Longmans, London, 1857.

2. Alexander Duff, *The Indian Rebellion, Its Causes and Results*, p.106, Robert Carter & Brothers, 1858.

3. The timing of Rango Bapoji's departure for England is consistent with Sitaram Baba's claim of Baija Bai's Shinde's early involvement in the plan to overthrow the English.

4. Michael Herbert Fisher, *Counterflows to Colonialism: Indian Travellers and Settlers in Britain, 1600–1857*, p.294, Orient Longman, 2004.

5. Andrew Ward, *Our Bones are Scattered, The Cawnpore Massacres and the Indian Mutiny of 1857*, p. 580, note 190, Henry Holt and Company, New York, 1996.

6. This event is narrated in detail in a contemporary book published in 1854. 'During a recent visit to Walton-on-Thames with Azimullah Khan, who is here on a mission from the Peshwa, and who, I may remark is highly talented, and possesses an extensive knowledge of the English language, we attended the service at a church there. Azimullah left his golden slippers at the door, not

presuming to enter a temple with them on. Afterwards they were brought to our pew by the beadle, who said that, if he did not take them, they would be stolen.'
Habeed Risk Allah Effendi, *The Thistle and the Cedar of Lebanon*, p.242, London, James Madden, 1854.

7. Andrew Ward, *Our Bones are Scattered, The Cawnpore Massacres and the Indian Mutiny of 1857*, p.46, Henry Holt and Company, New York, 1996.
8. Ibid, p.43.
9. Ibid, p.48
10. Ibid.
11. W.H. Russel, *My Diary in India*, pp.161-70, vol. 1, London, December 1859.
12. Henry George Keene, *A Servant of 'John Company': Being the Recollections of an Indian Official*, pp.162-63, Thacker, Spink and Co., 1897.
"But of all the evidence on this point the most direct is perhaps that afforded by the letters discovered in the Nana's palace at Bithur. When the place was occupied on 11 December 1857, a quantity of papers were found in the office of the Nana's secretary, a Moslem once well know in England by the name of Azimullah Khan. This fellow, who had begun life in a school established by a benevolent member of the Civil Service, became a table-servant when he grew up, and then promoted himself to the office of 'munshi', or teacher of Hindustani to subalterns desirous of passing an examination in that vernacular.
I have given an account of the contents of these letters elsewhere, and need say no more here than that the writer had a European Assistant, who was murdered before the palace was evacuated. In the handwriting of this man were drafts of letters sent by Azimullah to persons of distinction in Europe; amongst them one addressed to Umar Pasha, the once famous Turkish general. In this communication Azimullah – dating in 1856 – reminded the Pasha that, when they met in the Crimea, His Excellency had mentioned that he would be glad of information as to the condition of India; in pursuance of which he now had the honour to report that the British had sent an expedition to Persia, which was likely to fail, especially when the Persians were aided by a Russian army, as would surely be the case. The writer added that he and the Queen of Oude – who had just returned from an unsuccessful attempt to appeal against the annexation – were engaged in raising the country, and that (please God) the next news would be of the expulsion of the infidels. When one adds, that at the beginning of the year a proclamation in a similar spirit had been torn down from the door of the Jama Musjid – cathedral mosque – of Delhi, it is impossible to doubt the existence of a widespread conspiracy in the interests

of the Moslem revival so persistently dreamed of by the Mohammedans of Hindustan. If it be asked why a Hindu chief like the Nana should have taken an active part in such an intrigue, the simple answer is that the Nana claimed to be Peshwa of the Maratha Confederacy; and that, immediately before the introduction of British supremacy, the Maratha Peshwa had been the titular Viceregent of the Moghul Empire, a post which the Nana would have been glad to fill."

13. Henry George Keene, *A Servant of 'John Company': Being the Recollections of an Indian Official*, p.163, Thacker, Spink and Co., 1897.

14. *Illustrated London News* no. 664, p.54, vol xxiv, 21 January 1854.

15. The number 70,079 is quoted by many as a figure. This was the maximum number, based on full recruitment. Most infantry regiment sizes ranged between 700–1000. A realistic average would be 850 soldiers per Infantry Regiment.

16. Including any Scottish, Irish and other troops but all reporting to their English superiors.

17. The total strength was about a hundred thousand English soldiers in India. George Dodd, *History of the Indian Revolt*, p.611, W and R Chambers, London, 1859.

18. Field Marshal Roberts, *Forty-one Years in India: from Subaltern to Commander-in-chief*, p. 239, Longmans, Green & Co., 1901.

19. Azmi Özcan, Pan-Islamism, Indian Muslims, the Ottomans & Britain (1877-1924), p. 16, ft. 62, Brill, 1997
"It was reported that an agent of Nana Sahib, who was one of the leaders of the insurgents, Azimullah Khan, went to Crimea and Istanbul to get in touch with the Ottomans and most probably to see help. This was also stated in the Mutiny verdict. However, I have been unable to find any Turkish sources relating to this visit. For the information from the English source see, I. H. Qureshi, op. cit., 205; Roberts, *An Eye Witness Account of the Indian Mutiny*, Delhi, 1984 (reprint), 230; Moinul Haq, *The Great Revolution of 1857*, Karachi, 1968, 68."

20. Sitaram Baba's testimony confirms the existence of this line of communication.

21. Field Marshal Roberts, *Forty-one Years in India: from Subaltern to Commander-in-chief*, p. 239, Longmans, Green & Co., 1901

Content of Letters – French	Content of Letters – English Translation
Mon Cher Azimula Khan, Je suis parti de cawnpore le premier du mois et suis arrivé ici ce matin, je partirai ce soir a chandernagor le 7 au matin dans la journée je ferai une visite au gouverneur et le lendemain irai a calcutta, je verrai notre Consul Général. Ecrivez-moi et	My Dear Azimula Khan, I started from Cawnpore the first of the month and arrived here this morning, I will leave this evening for chandernagor. At 7 in the morning, in the course of the day I will make a visit with the governor and the following day at calcutta, I will go
adressez-moi vos lettres, No. 123. Dhurumtollah. Je voudrais que vous puissiez m'envoyer des fonds au moins 5 ou 600 Rs. sans retard, car je ne resterai à Calcutta que le temps necessaire pour tout arranger et le bien arranger. Je suppose 48 heures à Calcutta et deux ou trois jours au plus à Chandernagore, ne perdez pas de temps mais répondez de suite. Pour toutes le principales choses les réponses seraient satisfaisantes, soyez-en assuré. Faites en sorte de me répondre sans délai afin que je ne sois pas retenu à Calcutta. Preséntez mes compliments respectueux. Rappelez-moi an souvenir de Baba Sahib, et croyez moi. Votre bien dévoué A. Lafont Benares, April 4, 1857	see our consul general. Address your letters to me, No 123. Dhurumtollah. I would like that you can send funds to me at least 5 or 600 Rs. without delay, because I will remain at Calcutta only necessary time for all to arrange and to arrange well. I suppose 48 hours at Calcutta and two or three days with more at Chandernagore, do not waste time but answer of continuation. *For all the principal things the answers would be satisfactory, be assured.* Make in kind answer to me without delay so that I would not be retained at Calcutta. Present my respectful compliments. Point out to me year memory of Sahib Baba, and believe me, your devoted good A. Lafont Benares, April 4, 1857
'Mon adresse a Chandernagor,' Care of Mesdames Albert.' 'N.B. Mais ecrivez-moi a Calcutta, car je serai chaque jour la, en chemin de fer, je fais le trajet en 20 minutes. Si vous avez quelque chose de presse a me communiquer vois le pouvez faire par telegraph en Auglais seulement. A. L. Chandernagore April 9, 1857	My address at Chandernagor, 'Care of Ladies Albert.' N.B. But write at Calcutta to me, because I will be each day, in railroad, I make the way in 20 minutes. If you have something of press has to communicate to me see can only do it by telegraph in English. A. L. Chandernagore April 9, 1857

Notes to pages 77–84

Content of Letters – French	Content of Letters – English Translation
Mon Cher Azimula Khan J'ai tout arrange j'apporterai une lettre et elle sera satisfaisante cette lettre me sera donnee le 14 et le 15 je partirai pour Cawnpore. Mes respects a son Altesse. Votre tout devoue A. Lafont 16 April, 1857	My Dear Azimula Khan, *I have everthing arranged and I will bring a letter and it will be satisfactory this letter to me will be given the 14th and the 15th I will leave for Cawnpore. My regards to his Highness.* Your devoted whole A. Lafont 16 April, 1857

22. Field Marshal Roberts, *Forty-one Years in India: from Subaltern to Commander-in-chief*, p.239, Longmans, Green & Co., 1901
23. Charles Henry H. Wright, John Lovering Cooke, *Memoir of John Lovering Cooke, with a Sketch of the Indian Mutiny of 1857-58*, p.32, James Nisbet and Company, London, 1873.
24. Ibid p.32
25. Vol iii p.386
26. Biswamoy Pati, *Issues in Modern Indian History*: p.45, Popular Prakashan, 2000.
27. Ibid p.69
28. Testimony of Sitaram Baba
29. It is important to note here that, while the English filed many things in their archives, this 'incriminating' letter is nowhere to be found. What happened to this 'incriminating' letter?
30. Testimony of Sitaram Baba
31. Ibid
32. Ibid
33. Ibid
34. Ibid
35. Ibid
36. Ibid
37. *The New York Times*, p.71, 1 Februrary 1902.
38. Sitaram Baba's testimony.
39. Sir Willian Muir, *Records of the Intelligence Department of the Government of the North-west Provinces of India During the Mutiny of 1857*, p.454, Sir Willian Muir, vol. 1. T & T Clark, Edinburgh.
40. माझा प्रवास, **1857** च्या बंडाची हकीकत, कै. वे शा. सं. विष्णुभट गोडसे, p.6, Maza Pravas, Vishnubhat Godse, Venus Publishers, November, 2000.

41. Ibid.

42. George Francis Train, *Young America in Wall Street*, pp.198-200, George Francis Train, Sampson Low and Son, London, 1857.

43. *Freedom Struggle in UP*, p.38, vol. iii, Information Department, Lucknow, Uttar Pradesh, 1959.

44. The picture that is portrayed in most history books is that of tens of thousands of soldiers marching helter-skelter, seemingly with no plan or leadership – to be easily vanquished by the English shortly thereafter. The few historians, who do acknowledge that there was some level of planning and leadership, quickly add that the plan was supposed to have a common date but failed to execute because the troops at Meerut blundered and 'mutinied earlier than planned.' Some indicate the date of 31 May and some indicate 22 June, which was the hundred-year anniversary of the Battle of Plassey. They conclude that, '*if only* the soldiers were disciplined and had mutinied on the planned date; the outcome of the war could have been *different.*'

Sitaram Baba confirms the existence of a common date as well. Was there really a common date for when the war was supposed to *start*? Was that common date for the hostilities to 'begin' or a common date for key cities to be 'liberated?' If it was the latter, the goal was a success. Historians suggest that a common date of mutiny in all locations was designed to 'surprise' the English. A logical question to ask is, 'what *specific* goal would have been achieved, if there was indeed a *common* date for the war to *begin*; that was *not* achieved by *staggering* the dates?' The evidence points to the answer '*none.*' The goal of Operation Red Lotus (as will be demonstrated further) was to liberate Delhi, Kanpur and Lucknow; and to that extent, this goal was hugely successful.

In addition to this obvious logic, there are two strong reasons why it could not be a 'common' date for the war to *begin*. First, the logistics would not have allowed for the complicated troop movements to the major cities where the soldiers marched. Some villages who were the primary providers of food and transportation would have been burdened to help multiple regiments during the period. The logistical burden would have been too much for small villages to handle. Second, the dates were staggered in order to allow the troops to position themselves in the correct locations and to restrict the movement of the English troops. The Grant Trunk road and steamers on the Ganga were the primary modes of transportation from Calcutta to Delhi.

To reiterate, the biggest evidence that the staggered dates for the different regiments in different cities were *planned* is the simple fact that *this phase* of the war was indeed *successful*. The cities that were meant to be liberated were free. These included Delhi, Kanpur, Lucknow, Banda and Gwalior. This date was in all likelihood meant to be the date when the Indian soldiers had liberated key Indian cities. Delhi, Gwalior and Bandawere indeed under Indian control. Kanpur and Lucknow were about week away from freedom.

Chapter 7
THE OPERATION

1. John William Kaye, *A History of the Sepoy War, 1857–1858*, p.574, vol. I, W. H. Allen and Co., London, 1875.
2. *Freedom Struggle in UP*, p.30, vol. v, Information Department, Lucknow, Uttar Pradesh, 1960.
3. Ibid p.26.
4. Ibid.
5. Letter by Maj Gen W.H. Hewitt, Commanding Meerut Division to Col C. Chester, adjutant general at Simla No. 395 dated 11 May 1857.
   Freedom Struggle in UP, p.7, vol. v, Information Department, Uttar Pradesh, Lucknow, 1960.
6. The new jail was built near the Suraj Kund pond just outside Meerut. This pond was built by a rich businessman Lawar Jawahar Lal in 1714. Source http://meerut.nic.in
7. Letter by Maj Gen W.H. Hewitt, Commanding Meerut Division to Col C. Chester, adjutant general at Simla No. 395 dated 11 May 1857.
   Freedom Struggle in UP, p.7, vol. v, Information Department, Uttar Pradesh, Lucknow, 1960.
8. Letter by Maj Gen W.H. Hewitt, Commanding Meerut Division to Col C. Chester, adjutant general at Simla No. 395 dated 11 May 1857.
   Freedom Struggle in UP, pp.8-9, vol. v, Information Department, Uttar Pradesh, Lucknow, 1960.
9. Extract from *The Hindoo Patriot* dated 21 May 1857.
   Freedom Struggle in UP, p.25, vol. v, Information Department, Lucknow, Uttar Pradesh, 1960.
10. Ibid p.30.
11. Letter by Maj Gen W.H. Hewitt, Commanding Meerut Division to Col C. Chester, adjutant general at Simla No. 395 dated 11 May 1857.
    Freedom Struggle in UP, pp.8-9, Information Department, Uttar Pradesh, Lucknow, 1960.
12. George Bruce Malleson, *The Mutiny of the Bengal Army: An Historical Narrative*, p.39, Bosworth and Harrison, 1857.
13. Ibid p.40

Notes to pages 94–96

14. Ibid p.41.
15. Andrew Ward, *Our Bones are Scattered, The Cawnpore Massacres and the Indian Mutiny of 1857*, p.107, Henry Holt and Company, New York, 1996.
16. *Freedom Struggle in UP*, p.963, vol. v, Information Department, Uttar Pradesh, Lucknow, 1960.
17. Shahira Naim, *1857 The First Challenge*, *The Tribune*, 10 May 2007, http://www.tribuneindia.com/2007/20070510/1857/main4.htm.
18. Saul David, *The Indian Mutiny*, p.179, Viking, 2002.
19. Faruqui Anjum Taban, *The Coming of Revolt in Awadh: The Evidence of Urdu Newspapers*, Social Scientist, vol. 26 no. 296–99, p.16, January–April 1998.
20. George Bruce Malleson, *The Mutiny of the Bengal Army: An Historical Narrative*, p.81, Bosworth and Harrison, 1857.
21. Maulvi Ahmadullah Shah was born in the royal family of Chinapattam in the southern state of Madras. At birth he was given the name Saiyid Ahmad Ali Khan and, all the training in riding, martial arts, languages and sciences. At a young age, Ahmadullah's coercive prowess appealed to the Nizam of Hyderabad to seek his services in quelling a minor rebellion taking place in his kingdom. The interesting aspect often highlighted is 'his preference for deceptive methods of warfare'. It was just a matter of time before, Ahmadullah was probably spotted for exactly this talent and his services were sought in Agra, Aligarh and Gwalior. Ahmadullah had hit upon a novel plan to mobilise the masses. At Agra, he would hold majalis-i-qawwalis (community singing congregations) that became immensely popular. Through these he influenced the large mass of people gathered, which even prompted British reports 'he is a derwesh only in name, actually he is a prince and, is preparing the masses to wage war against the government.'
S.Z.H. Jafri, *The Profile of a Saintly Rebel–Maulavi Ahmadullah Shah*, Social Scientist, pp.39-41, vol 26, No.1–4, January–April 1998.
At last, conditions were ripe for Ahmadullah's arrival at the seat of action in Lucknow, which was widely reported by the Urdu newspaper *Tilism* of 21 November 1856. The reader would recall that, during this period *Tilism* was also reporting spiralling prices of essential grains and rising unemployment. Ahmadullah's hugely popular majalis-i-qawwalis caught the fancy of the people of Lucknow too. His widespread popularity caused the Englishmen at Lucknow to panic and Ahmadullah was promptly arrested and sent to Faizabad jail citing that he is 'too dangerous a character'. There were reports that at his meetings there was 'distribution of money' and attempts at 'disturbance of peace'. Ibid p.43.
22. *Freedom Struggle in UP*, pp.14, 69, vol. ii, Information Department, Lucknow, Uttar Pradesh, 1958.

Notes to pages 98–101, 104–107

23. George Bruce Malleson, *The Mutiny of the Bengal Army: An Historical Narrative*, p.75, Bosworth and Harrison, 1857.

24. *Freedom Struggle in UP*, p.72, vol. ii, Information Department, Lucknow, Uttar Pradesh, 1958.

25. Ibid p.69.

26. Martin Richard Gubbins, *An Account of the Mutinies in Oudh and of the Siege of the Lucknow Residency*, p.208, Richard Bentley, London, 1858.

27. *Freedom Struggle in UP*, p.65, vol. ii, Information Department, Lucknow, Uttar Pradesh, 1958.

28. Ibid p.65.

29. Saul David, *The Indian Mutiny*, p.225, Viking, 2002.

30. *Freedom Struggle in UP*, p.53, vol. ii, Information Department, Lucknow, Uttar Pradesh, 1958.

31. Martin Richard Gubbins, *An Account of the Mutinies in Oudh and of the Siege of the Lucknow Residency*, p.191, Richard Bentley, London, 1858.

32. *Freedom Struggle in UP*, p.117, vol. ii, Information Department, Lucknow, Uttar Pradesh, 1958.

33. W. and R. Chambers, *The History of the Indian Revolt and of the Expeditions to Persia, China, and Japan, 1856–7–8*, pp.625–28, George Dodd, 1859.

Chapter 8
THE FLAME OF LIBERTY

1. *Freedom Struggle in UP*, p.116, vol. ii, Information Department, Lucknow, Uttar Pradesh, 1958.

2. Letter 51B.

3. Blackwood's *Edinburgh Magazine*, p.188, vol. 88 (538) August 1860.

4. Letters 43, 23 and 66.

5. Letters 30–31, 37, 62 and 96.

6. Letters 8 and 59.

7. Letter 68. We just dismissed that soldier and paid him his due until that date. Bal Gobind Chobe is reported by his officer as not willing to fight. Deena Deen Shukla was the Officer Command Palton 7 of Madhavgadh.

8. Letter 51E. I understand that the accuser (Petitioner) and the Accused (Defendant) are upset. They complaint to Gosai who is an officer with Tatya Sahib, who then informed Vishwas Rao Bhau, Tehsildar of Itawah. It is possible that it is Gosai's doing, therefore send those papers to Vishwas Rao Bhau. Pass a judgement as appropriate. Send the judgement to the press.

Notes to pages 107–109

9. Letter 59b. Your second letter is about Subedar Mardan Singh who terrorised Mahajans and stole there money and belongings. He had returned these items one by one. Now Mardan Singh's behaviour is acceptable and is peaceful. We were told about Mardan Singh in the court. After the court ordered, he returned those things to the government's treasury and to all the Mahajans.

10. Letter 79. Pratap Singh was working in the 2nd company he was guarding the treasury. A solider informed that Pratap Singh went to the mountains. We found evidence that he stole money from the treasury. He also admitted to have done so. The court has found him guilty. His name has been erased from the register. Everyone else has been warned not to do so. The court order was followed.

11. *Freedom Struggle in UP*, p.827, vol. iv, Information Department, Lucknow, Uttar Pradesh, 1959.

12. Letter 44 from Safdar Ali Beg Hawaldar Paltan 4, Company 5, Camp Brar, January 29, 1858. His highness Tatya Sahib Bahadur sent me at your service for work about the Tehsil & the soldiers. You appointed me to look after the soldiers and the work of the Tehsil in the Pargana. I have done the job of the Tehsil well and I am staying with the Tehsildar. However, for the last few days Jodha Singh is disrupting the work of the Tehsil. He goes to all the colonies loots and causes trouble. Because of the excesses my recruits are spoilt 100s of residents are complaining. When I ask people for taxes, they say where they have given the money to him. Jodha Singh has looted us. This is the statement of all the people. I have investigated and found it to be true.

13. An official badge of some kind.

14. Letter 18 dated 6 February 1858 (21 Jummadassani 1274).

15. Letter 37 dated 6 February 1858.

16. Letter 60, dated 6 February 1858.

17. Letter 65, dated 1 March 1858.

18. Letter 36, dated 26 January 1858.
    Date: 26 January 1858 (10 Jummadassani 1274H).
    Received the following amount for the salary of harkaras/akhbarnawees for the month of Jummadalavval 1274H. (December 1857– January 1858).
    Rs. 8/– 2 anna 8 paise. Previous amount Re. 1/– and 8 Annas.
    Details as follows;

Mir Inayat Ali Journalist Mutayanna Banda	Rs. 8/–
Sheikh Wajir	Rs. 3

Notes to pages 109–113

Rasool Baksh	Rs. 1/–, 3 Anna, 4 paise
Main Singh	Rs.1/– 2 Anna, 8 paise
Eshree	Rs.1/–
Kanshi	Rs.1/–
Abdulla	Rs.1/–

The total is Rupees 18. From this amount Rupees 8, 2 anna, 5 pai is due. From this Rupees 5/8, 3 paise was spent to buy paper to print daily dairy. Now I have Rupees 7/8, 1 paisa, 2 anna is balance with me from the government. Annotation:

To be filed in office register.

Dated: 12 Jummadassani 1274H.

19. Letter 53A.
20. Letters 12 and 25.
21. Letter 22.
22. Letter 24A.
23. Letter 69.
24. Letter 39.
25. Letter 68.
26. Letter 54D.
27. Unclear if the number is 420 or 42.
28. Letter 10, dated 4 March 1858 from Gauri Shankar Birgade Major.
29. Letter 10, dated 4 March 1858 from Gauri Shankar Birgade Major.
30. Letter 52A, dated 23 January 1858, to Bahadur Murat Singh, Subhedar at Fort Kalpi.
31. Letters 26, 22, 21, 20, 19, 13, 9, 8, 32, 34, 41, 58, 59 and 61.
32. L–101.
33. Letter 22.
34. Letters 21 and 28.
35. Letter 96.
36. Letter 32, 52E and 57B.
37. Letters 54A, 54B, 56D, 56E and 56F.
38. Letter 64.
39. Letter 56B.

40. Letter 56C.
41. Letter 57A.

Chapter 9
THE FIGURE OF EIGHT

1. 7,000 in the Bengal Army, 11,000 in the Madras Army and 6,500 in the Bombay Army.
2. The total strength was about a hundred thousand English soldiers in India. George Dodd, *History of the Indian Revolt*, p.611, W and R Chambers, London, 1859.
3. Rudrangshu Mukherjee, *Spectre Of Violence, The 1857 Kanpur Massacres*, p. 31, Penguin India 1998.
4. India Office Library and Records – Boards Collection 191546 and 191547, December 1857.
5. On the 4th June an Act No. XI. of 1857 was passed by the Governor General of India in Council providing that all persons owing allegiance to the British Government, who, after the passing of this Act, shall rebel, or wage war against the Queen, or Government of the East India Company, or shall attempt to wage such war, or shall instigate or abet any such rebellion or the waging of such war, or shall conspire so to rebel or wage war, shall be liable, upon conviction to the punishment of death, or to the punishment of transportation for life, or of imprisonment with hard labour for any term not exceeding fourteen years; and shall also forfeit their property and effects of every description: Provided that nothing contained in this Section shall extend to any place subject to Regulation XIV of 1827 of the Bengal Code. All persons who shall knowingly harbour or conceal any person who shall have been guilty of any of the offences mentioned in the preceding Section, shall be liable to imprisonment, with or without hard labour, for any term not exceeding seven years, and shall also be liable to fine. The Act moreover enables the local Governments to issue Commissions for the trial of such persons, or to disarm any class of the population.
   The Annals of Indian Administration, Meredith Townsend, 1858, September and December 1858, Parts IV and V, Serampore, Public Administration, 490.
6. On 6 June an Act No. XIV. of 1857 for making further provision for the trial and punishment of persons who endeavour to excite mutiny and sedition among the forces of the East India Company, and also for the trial of offences against the State, was passed and published, together with the following General Order:

388 / *Tatya Tope's Operation Red Lotus*

Notes to pages 119–122

'In pursuance of Act No. XIV. of 1857 passed this day, the Governor General in Council is pleased to authorize every General Officer Commanding a Division, every Brigadier, and every officer commanding a station, being the senior officer on the spot, to appoint General Courts Martial under the provisions of the said Act, as occasion may require for the trial of any person or persons who may be charged with any offence against the aforesaid Act, or against Act No. XI. of 1857, if such offence require in his judgment, to be punished without delay, and to confirm and carry into effect, immediately or otherwise, any sentence of such Court Martial.'
The Annals of Indian Administration, Meredith Townsend, 1858, September and December 1858, Parts IV and V, Serampore, Public Administration 491.

7. The *New York Times*, p.71, 1 February 1902.
8. John William Kaye, *A History of the Sepoy War in India, 1857–58*, p.236, vol. ii, W.H. Allen, 1870.
9. Rudrangshu Mukherjee, *Spectre Of Violence, The 1857 Kanpur Massacres*, p.30, Penguin India, 1998.
10. William Howard Russell, *My Indian Mutiny Diary*, pp. 281–82, Cassell, 1957.
11. John William Kaye, *A History of the Sepoy War in India, 1857–58*, p.236, vol. ii, W.H. Allen, 1870.
12. Ibid.
13. Ibid.
14. *Freedom Struggle in UP*, p.76, vol. iv, Information Department, Lucknow, Uttar Pradesh, 1959.
15. Of course, Andrew Ward dismisses these as 'rumors.'
Andrew Ward, *Our Bones Are Scattered, The Cawnpore Massacres And The Indian Mutiny of 1857*, p.343, Henry Holt and Company, New York, 1996.
16. Ibid, p.256.
17. Ibid.
18. I.O.L.R, Board's Collection, No. 191547: Revolt of Native Army:C.Chester to C.Beadon, 27 June 1857. Extract of an unofficial letter, from Allahabad, 6 July 1857. Name left blank in original.
Rudrangshu Mukherjee, *Spectre Of Violence, The 1857 Kanpur Massacres*, pp.27-8, Penguin India, 1998.
19. John William Kaye, *A History of the Sepoy War in India, 1857–58*, p.274, Longmans, Green, 1874.
20. John William Kaye, *A History of the Sepoy War in India, 1857–58*, p.236-7, vol.ii, W.H. Allen, 1870.
21. George Bruce Malleson, *The Mutiny of the Bengal Army: An Historical Narrative*, p.144, Bosworth and Harrison, 1857.

22. Ibid.

23. Rudrangshu Mukherjee, *Spectre Of Violence, The 1857 Kanpur Massacres*, pp.28-9, Penguin India, 1998.

24. Robert Montgomery Martin, *The Indian Empire*, p.302, London Printing and Publishing Co., 1858.

25. 'Your instructions to Renaud and Spurgin are admirable, and provide for every possible present circumstances as well as all eventualities, and by them, and them only, Renaud should have been guided.'
John William Kaye, *A History of the Sepoy War in India, 1857–58*, ft. on pp.283-84, vol. ii, W.H. Allen, 1870.

26. John Birmingham, *Anglicania; or, England's Mission to the Celt*, p.162, Thomas Richardson and Son, Dublin, 1863.

27. Robert Montgomery Martin, *The Indian Empire*, p.296, v. 2, The London Printing and Publishing Company, Ltd., 1858.

28. William Howard Russell, *My Diary in India, in the Year 1858-9*, vol. ii, p.402, Routledge, Warne and Routledge, London, 1860 .

29. William Forbes–Mitchell, *Reminiscences of the Great Mutiny 1857–59 including the relief, siege, and capture of Lucknow*, p.26, Macmillan and Co., 1895

30. Rudrangshu Mukherjee, *Spectre Of Violence, The 1857 Kanpur Massacres*, pp.27-8, Penguin India, 1998.

31. *Freedom Struggle in UP*, pp.610-11, vol. iv, Information Department, Lucknow, Uttar Pradesh, 1959.

32. Rudrangshu Mukherjee, *Spectre Of Violence, The 1857 Kanpur Massacres*, pp.27-8, Penguin India, 1998.

33. The complete quote from *The New York Times* was: 'The mutiny marked the end of one of the worst governments that existed. The evil was not with the men, but with the system. For, where you make government an ingenious and disciplined tyranny, the men who carry out the orders are certain to be tyrants'. *The New York Times*, p.71, 1 February 1902.

Chapter 10
DECONSTRUCTING 'CAWNPORE'

1. Andrew Ward, *Our Bones are Scattered, The Cawnpore Massacres and the Indian Mutiny of 1857*, p.305, Henry Holt and Company, New York, 1996.

2. Ibid pp.315-6.

3. Mowbray Thomson, *The Story of Cawnpore*, p. 161, R. Bentley, 1859.

4. Andrew Ward *Our Bones are Scattered, The Cawnpore Massacres and the Indian Mutiny of 1857*, p.209, Henry Holt and Company, New York, 1996.

Notes to pages 135–139

5. G.W. Forrest, *The Indian Mutiny 1857–1858*, p.ii, vol. iii, Appendix A, first published London 1902, reprinted by Low Price Publications, 2000.

6. Andrew Ward, *Our Bones are Scattered, The Cawnpore Massacres and the Indian Mutiny of 1857*, p.111, Henry Holt and Company, New York, 1996.

7. Mowbray Thomson, *The Story of Cawnpore*, p.26, R. Bentley, 1859.

8. *The Times*, p.7, 10 September 1857.

9. Mowbray Thomson, *The Story of Cawnpore*, p.29, R. Bentley, 1859.

10. Deposition of Mr Edward William, Merchant at Cawnpore, taken at Cawnpore under the direction of Lt Col G.W. Williams, commissioner of military police, North Western Provinces in March 1859.
    G.W. Forrest, *The Indian Mutiny 1857–1858*, p.cxiii, vol. iii, Appendix A, first published London 1902, reprinted by Low Price Publications, 2000.

11. Andrew Ward, *Our Bones are Scattered, The Cawnpore Massacres and the Indian Mutiny of 1857*, p.109, Henry Holt and Company, New York, 1996.

12. R.M. Coopland, *A Lady's Escape from Gwalior and Life in the Fort of Agra During the Mutinies of 1857*, p.107-08, Smith, Elder and Co., London, 1859.

13. G.B. Malleson, Kaye's and Malleson's *History of the Indian Mutiny of 1857-8*, vol. iii, pp.76-8, Longmans, Green and Co., London, 1909.

14. Charles Ball, *The History of the Indian Mutiny*, p.300, vol. I, The London Printing and Publishing Company, 1858.

15. 'We were told how, owing to Sir Hugh Wheeler's misplaced belief in the loyalty of the sepoys, with whom he had served for upwards of half a century, and to the confiding old soldier's trust in the friendship of the miscreant Nana, and in the latter's ability to defend him until succor should arrive, he had neglected to take precautionary measures for laying in supplies or for fortifying the two exposed barracks which, for some unaccountable reason, had been chosen as a place of refuge, instead of the easily defensible and well-stored magazine.'
    Field Marshal Roberts, *Forty-one Years in India: from Subaltern to Commander-in-chief*, p.161.

16. Nanak Chand's diary, entry dated 5 June.
    Rudrangshu Mukherjee, *Spectre Of Violence*, The 1857 Kanpur Massacres, p. 54, Penguin India, 1998.

17. W.J. Shepherd, *A Personal Narrative of the Outbreak and Massacre at Cawnpore*, pp. 47-8, R. Craven, London Printing Press, 1879.

18. Mowbray Thomson, *The Story of Cawnpore*, p.150, R. Bentley, 1859.

19. Ibid pp.156-7.

20. Andrew Ward, *Our Bones are Scattered, The Cawnpore Massacres and the Indian Mutiny of 1857*, pp.309-10, Henry Holt and Company, New York, 1996.

21. Mowbray Thomson, *The Story of Cawnpore*, p.161, R. Bentley, 1859.

Notes to pages 140–146

22. Deposition of Khuda Bukhsh, IOLR Board Collection no, 1957, 18, Rudrangshu Mukherjee, *Spectre Of Violence, The 1857 Kanpur Massacres*, p.79, Penguin India, 1998.

23. Andrew Ward, *Our Bones are Scattered, The Cawnpore Massacres and the Indian Mutiny of 1857*, p. 321, Henry Holt and Company, New York, 1996.

24. Mowbray Thomson, *The Story of Cawnpore*, p.166, R. Bentley, 1859.

25. Andrew Ward, *Our Bones are Scattered, The Cawnpore Massacres and the Indian Mutiny of 1857*, p.642 note 215, Henry Holt and Company, New York, 1996.

26. John Birmingham, *Anglicania; or, England's Mission to the Celt*, p.162, Thomas Richardson and Son, Dublin, 1863.

27. माझा प्रवास, **1857** च्या बंडाची हकीकत, कै. वे शा. सं. विष्णुभट गोडस, p.42, Maza Pravas, Vishnubhat Godse, Venus Publishers, November 2000.

28. The soldiers from the 6th NI, apparently, refused to shoot.
    John Harris, *The Indian Mutiny*, p.92, Wordsworth Editions, 2001

29. R Guha, *Elementary Aspects of Peasant Insurgency in Colonial India*, p.75, Delhi, 1983.

30. Amaresh Misra, *War of Civilizations: India AD 1857*, (vol.II), *The Long Revolution*. pp.505-46, Rupa and Co.

31. John Harris, *The Indian Mutiny*, p.80, Wordsworth Editions, 2001.

32. Mowbray Thomson, *The Story of Cawnpore*, p.v, R. Bentley, 1859.

Chapter 11
THE UNWITHERED LOTUS

1. Charles Ball, *The History of the Indian Mutiny*, p.16, vol.II, The London Printing and Publishing Company, 1858.

2. Ibid.

3. Title on the page is RETROGRADE MOVEMENT.
   Charles Ball, *The History of the Indian Mutiny*, p.21, The London Printing and Publishing Company, 1858vol. II.

4. Title on the page is RELINQUESHES THE ENTERPRISE FOR A TIME.
   John Clark Marshman, *Memoirs of Major-General Sir Henry Havelock, K.C.B.*, p.343, Longmans, Green, Reader and Dyer, 1867.

5. *Freedom Struggle in UP*, p.699, vol. iv, Information Department, Uttar Pradesh, Lucknow, 1959.

6. '...he deemed important to retrace his steps without delay.' John Clark Marshman, *Memoirs of Major-General Sir Henry Havelock, K.C.B.*, p.357, Longmans, Green, Reader and Dyer, 1867.

7. Charles Ball, *The History of the Indian Mutiny*, p.22, vol. II, The London Printing and Publishing Company, 1858.

8. Ibid p.24.

9. English references always exaggerate the Indian forces. Based on earlier battles and estimates the number 3,000 indicated by Havelock is an exaggeration. John Clark Marshman, *Memoirs of Major-General Sir Henry Havelock, K.C.B.*, p.329, Longmans, Green, Reader and Dyer, 1867.
   These exaggerations are arbitrary. Havelock reports that the Indian force on 11 August was 4000 infantry and 500 cavalry (Charles Ball, *The History of the Indian Mutiny*, p.22, vol. ii, The London Printing and Publishing Company, 1858). An officer attached to the Allahabad movable column under Havelock reports that the Indians were 10,000 infantry and 2,000 cavalry. (Ibid p.24).

10. John Clark Marshman, Memoirs of Major-General Sir Henry Havelock, K.C.B., p.326, Longmans, Green, Reader and Dyer, 1867.

11. Marshman and Charles Ball refer to these troops as Nana Saheb army. They are technically correct, because Tatya was clearly under Nana Saheb's command, however, Nana Saheb during this period was being welcomed into Lucknow and not directing the troops. Tatya Tope was in charge of the army that had crossed over into Fatehpur-Chaurasi.

12. John Clark Marshman, *Memoirs of Major-General Sir Henry Havelock, K.C.B.*, p.334, Longmans, Green, Reader and Dyer, 1867.

13. Letter from Lt Col Tytler to the commander-in-chief, dated 31 July 1857. Charles Ball, *The History of the Indian Mutiny*, p.20, vol. ii, The London Printing and Publishing Company, 1858.

14. John Clark Marshman, *Memoirs of Major-General Sir Henry Havelock, K.C.B.*, p.337, Longmans, Green, Reader and Dyer, 1867.

15. 'HIS INCREASING DIFFICULTIES' as title for the page. Ibid p. 341.

16. Lt. Gordon ADC to General Neill letter from 9 August 1857. Records of the Intelligence Department of the Government of the North-west Provinces of India During the Mutiny of 1857, Sir Willian Muir, p.457, vol. I. T&T Clark, Edinburgh.

17. Charles Ball, *The History of the Indian Mutiny*, p.21, vol.ii, The London Printing and Publishing Company, 1858.

18. Ibid p.22, vol. II.

19. Ibid p.24.

20. James John McLeod Innes, *The Sepoy Revolt. A Critical Narrative*, p.170, A.D. Innes & Co.

21. Captain Bruce letter to Brigadier Chamberlain. Records of the Intelligence Department of the Government of the North-west Provinces of India During the Mutiny of 1857, p.457, vol. I, Sir Willian Muir, T&T Clark, Edinburgh.

Endnotes \ 393

Notes to pages 151–154

22. 'General Havelock advanced to Lucknow on the 29th ult (sic), thrashed the enemy severely, took 20 guns, but instead of following up, returned to 6 miles off for reinforcements; go on the 5th half battery more, and Company of 84th, started off, *thrashed the enemy* on the 6th in great style and **retired** again. There he remains – more men and guns required... Yesterday the General intimated that he would recross, to prevent the river rising and cutting off our communications with each other. But after sending over everything, even spare ammunition, he suddenly changes his mind, and engaged, *thrashing him* but I have no particulars. On this side we have 4000 and 5 guns at Bithoor, and 8000 and some guns at Futtehgarh.'
    Records of the Intelligence Department of the Government of the North-west Provinces of India During the Mutiny of 1857, p.463, vol. I, Sir Willian Muir, T&T Clark, Edinburgh.
23. Ibid.
24. *Freedom Struggle in UP*, p.99, vol.iii, Information Department, Uttar Pradesh, Lucknow, 1959.
25. John Clark Marshman, *Memoirs of Major-General Sir Henry Havelock, K.C.B.*, p.355, Longmans, Green, Reader and Dyer, 1867.
26. Charles Ball, *The History of the Indian Mutiny*, p.28, vol. ii, The London Printing and Publishing Company, 1858.
27. John Clark Marshman, *Memoirs of Major-General Sir Henry Havelock, K.C.B.*, p.357, Longmans, Green, Reader and Dyer, 1867.
28. Charles Ball, *The History of the Indian Mutiny*, p.27, vol.ii, The London Printing and Publishing Company, 1858.
29. Ibid p.32, vol. ii.
30. Ibid p.26.
31. *Freedom Struggle in UP*, p.699, vol. iv, Information Department, Lucknow, Uttar Pradesh, 1959.
32. Charles Ball, *The History of the Indian Mutiny*, p.32, vol. ii, The London Printing and Publishing Company, 1858.
33. Records of the Intelligence Department of the Government of the North-west Provinces of India During the Mutiny of 1857, p.544, Sir Willian Muir, vol. 1. T&T Clark, Edinburgh.
34. 'The rebels assaulted the work on the 17th, and were driven back with loss.'
    Records of the Intelligence Department of the Government of the North-west Provinces of India During the Mutiny of 1857, Sir Willian Muir, p.544, vol. 1. T&T Clark, Edinburgh.
35. Unfortunately, only an insipid English translation is available.

36. *Freedom Struggle in UP*, p.700, vol. iv, Information Department, Uttar Pradesh, Lucknow, 1959.

37. In a rare case, and possibly by accident, an uncensored communication between Neill and Colonel Cotton was published. Neill writes: 'On this side we have 4000 and 5 guns at Bithoor, and 8000 and some guns at Futtehgurh.' 'This side' refers to the Kanpur side of the Ganga. This note was written when Havelock was on the 'other side' of the Ganga. It is unclear how many troops Havelock commanded. He claims only 1,000. He also claims that Neill had only 300 with him. If 4000 could be downsized to 300 in the narratives, then a reported number 1000 could be easily more. We will have to guess that the number was about 2,000, making the Kanpur strength for the English at a total of about 6,000.

    Records of the Intelligence Department of the Government of the North-west Provinces of India During the Mutiny of 1857, p.463, vol. i, Sir Willian Muir, T&T Clark, Edinburgh.

38. *Freedom Struggle in UP*, p.116, vol.iv, Information Department, Uttar Pradesh, Lucknow, 1959.

39. Ibid p.404, vol. iv.

40. Ibid p.406.

41. Ibid.

42. We have derived the following timeline from various sources and used it to create the map of Kunwar Singh's movement.

    12 August – At Ahraura. 'On August 12, the Danapur regiments plundered the bazaar of Ahraura on the morning of the 12th and marched to Sookrit. On the 14th they camped at Adulgunge Bazar one mile to the west of Robertgunge.' *Freedom Struggle in UP*, p.69, vol. iv.

    13 August – 1 Duffadar and 17 Nujeebs, escorting cars and bullocks from Gya to Benares were stopped at the Poon Poon river at Siris, on the trunk road, east of the soane, by a large body of people armed with swords and lathis, no guns or matchlocks. They claimed to be 'Baboo Koer Sing Ka Log.' *Freedom Struggle in UP*, p.406, vol.iv, Information Department, Lucknow, Uttar Pradesh, 1959.

    14 August – At Robertganj.

    14 August – Kunwar Singh – At Sasaram (iv, 406) Kunwar Singh with the Danapur regiments was at Sasaram on August 14, 1857. Sasaram in on the Grand Trunk road, 65 miles east of Varanasi. All they did in Sasaram was to 'march towards the hill and plundered the thanah and the muskets.' *Freedom Struggle in UP*, p.411, vol.iv, Information Department, Uttar Pradesh, Lucknow, 1959.

16 August – At Shahganj

On 19 and 20 August. Dinapore mutineers passed through the southern pargannahs. An expedition was made against them from Mirzapore, but it was recalled without having any effected and sensible result. This portion has been plundered and harassed by the march through it of Koour Singh and the insurgents and mutineers with him.

22 August – Kunwar Singh at Rohtasgarh (*Freedom Struggle in UP*, p.413, vol.iv, Information Department, Uttar Pradesh, Lucknow, 1959).

24 August – Kunwar Singh's advance guard at Ramgarh (p.414, vol. iv)

26 August – Robertsganj

28 August – Dinapore regiments have crossed tonse. Sheorajpur (30 miles southwest of Allahabad) – Ibid, p.413, vol. iv.

28 August – The advanced body, consisting of 2000 men were at a place called Ghorawa, 30 miles distant, retreated. Rev. M. A. Sherring write 'But even Benares is now said to be in danger of an attack...'. *The Scottish Congregational Magazine*, p.242, A Fullartan & Co., Edinburgh, 1857)

31 August – '...because the Dinapore Regiments have approached to attack Mirzapore.'

1 September – 'Koer Singh and the Ramgurh Mutineers are in the backwoods, near Bijeygurh, threatening Mirzapore; but will not dare to attack it.' Records of the Intelligence Department of the Government of the North-west Provinces of India During the Mutiny of 1857, p.539, vol. I, Sir Willian Muir, T&T Clark, Edinburgh.

3 September – Mr Sherring, Mirzapore, 'I am sorry to say, is still in danger on account of the proximity of the rebel rajah, Koor Singh.'

3 September – 'Dinapore Mutineers began crossing the Jumna at Rajapore, suddenly changed their plans, and marched south on the Tirohan in Banda.' Records of the Intelligence Department of the Government of the North-west Provinces of India During the Mutiny of 1857, p.543, vol.I, Sir Willian Muir, T & T Clark, Edinburgh.

29 August – Ramgarh (Ibid p.404, vol. iv)

29 August – Ghorawal (Ibid p.415)

30 August – Kunwar Singh evacuated Ghorawar (Ibid p.415)

3 September – Kunwar Singh Camped at Sirsaen (Ibid p.415)

4 September – Kunwar Singh camped at 4 miles west of Halia (Ibid p.415)

6 September – recrossed the Belan river camped at Barondha (5 miles southwest of Lalganj (Ibid p.416)

8 September – Kunwar Singh camped at six mile south of Manda (Ibid p.417)

10 September – another body coming from east (Ibid)

12 September – 'quantity of grain belonging belonging to Surnam Singh has been sold off to the parties.' (Ibid p.418)

13 September – Bijaigarh (Ibid)

43. *The Scottish Congregational Magazine*, p.243, A. Fullartan & Co., Edinburgh, 1857.

44. Records of the Intelligence Department of the Government of the North-west Provinces of India During the Mutiny of 1857, p.539, vol. I, Sir Willian Muir, T&T Clark, Edinburgh.

45. Ibid p.464.

Chapter 12
A NEW WAR—A NEW CAPITAL

1. George Francis Train, *Young America in Wall Street*, pp.198-200, Sampson Low and Son, London, 1857.

2. William Dalrymple, *The Last Mughal*, p.292, Alfred A. Knopf, New York, 2007.

3. *The Revolt in Central India, 1857–59*, p.12, Intelligence Branch, Army Head Quarters, India, Simla, 1908.

4. Following compiled from:
    Freedom Struggle in UP, p.154, vol.iii, Information Department, Uttar Pradesh, Lucknow, 1959.
    'A large body of Sindhia's revolted troops...' *The Revolt in Central India, 1857–59*, p.76, Intelligence Branch, Army Head Quarters, India, Simla, 1908.
    English intelligence estimates place the Army gathered at 10,000, including
    3,000–4000 Mewatis (from western Rajasthan)
    500–1000 Afghanis
    400 Makranis (Rajasthan)
    200 Bhils (northern Maharashtra)
    3000 others (including an unknown number of the Gwalior Contingent)
    1000 Cavalry
    Total – 9000–10000.

5. *The Revolt in Central India, 1857–59*, p.76, Intelligence Branch, Army Head Quarters, India, Simla, 1908.

6. Amaresh Misra, *War of Civilizations: India AD 1857, The Long Revolution*, p.848, (vol. ii), Rupa and Co.

7. George Dodd, *The History of the Indian Revolt and of the Expeditions to Persia, China, and Japan, 1856–7–8*, p.221, W. and R. Chambers, 1859.

Notes to pages 164–170

8. William Dalrymple, *The Last Mughal*, p.300, Alfred A. Knopf, New York, 2007.

9. Ibid p. 294.

10. *Freedom Struggle in UP*, p.163, vol. iii, Information Department, Lucknow, Uttar Pradesh, 1959.

11. Ibid pp.377-78, vol. i.

12. Blackwood's *Edinburgh Magazine*, p.173, T. Cadell and W. Davis, 1860, England.

13. *Freedom Struggle in UP*, p.427, vol.iv, Information Department, Lucknow, Uttar Pradesh, 1959.

14. In a deposition by Raghunath Madahv Rao Wankhede, says that Baiza Bai was requested by Jiyaji Rao Shinde to stay in Gwalior once the war started. *Freedom Struggle in UP*, pp.23-4, vol. i.
    Amar Farooqui's essay on Baiza Bai also places her in Gwalior during the period from 1856 until June of 1858.
    Biswamoy Pati, *Issues in Modern Indian History*, p.67, Popular Prakashan, 2000.

15. Vishnubhat Godse says 'in the month of bhadrapad...' Dussehara was on September 29 in 1857, per various English intelligence, which make September 29 as the 10th day of Ashwin, making Bhadrapad end around the 18th of September.

16. माझा प्रवास, **1857** च्या बंडाची हकीकत, कै. वे शा. सं. विष्णुभट गोडसे, p.37, Maza Pravas, Vishnubhat Godse, Venus Publishers, November 2000.

17. *Freedom Struggle in UP*, p.434, vol.iv, Information Department, Lucknow, Uttar Pradesh, 1959.

18. Ibid p.435, vol. iv.

19. Ibid p.409, vol. iii.

20. Ibid pp.86-8 vol. iii, and माझा प्रवास, **1857** च्या बंडाची हकीकत, कै. वे शा. सं. विष्णुभट गोडसे, p.38, Maza Pravas, Vishnubhat Godse, Venus Publishers, November 2000.

21. *Freedom Struggle in UP*, p.776, vol. v, Information Department, Lucknow, Uttar Pradesh, 1960.

22. Amaresh Misra, *War of Civilizations: India AD 1857, The Long Revolution,* (vol. ii), p.1300, Rupa and Co.

23. *Freedom Struggle in UP*, p.252, vol.ii, Information Department, Uttar Pradesh, Lucknow, 1958.

24. *War of Civilizations: India AD 1857, The Long Revolution*, p.1270, vol. ii, Rupa and Co.

25. Ibid pp.1278–81.

26. 'Late arrival of November indeed was a month of unwonted England. stir, of memorable events for India. The troops from England, sent round by the Cape from a fear perhaps well founded touching the perilous heats of the Red Sea, were at length pouring by thousands into Calcutta after a voyage unusually slow.* Their help was needed in many places, but most of them held their way towards Cawnpore, the central starting-point of the next campaign, whose goal was meant to be the conquest of Lucknow.'
    Lionel James Trotter, *The History of the British Empire in India*, 1844 to 1862, p. 244, vol. ii, W.H. Allen & Co., London, 1866.

27. G.B. Malleson, *History of the Indian Mutiny, 1857–1858*, p.166, vol.ii, Longmans, Green and Co., London, 1896.

28. Amaresh Misra, *War of Civilizations: India AD 1857*, Amaresh Misra, *The Long Revolution*, (vol. ii), p.1271, Rupa and Co.

29. Ibid.

30. Futtehpore—A battle was fought between this and Cawnpore on the 1st November, near the village of Kudgwa, between the Dinapore mutineers and a detachment of 500 men, and two 9–pounder guns, under Colonel Powell, her Majesty's 53rd Foot. The enemy had three guns, were in a strong position, and had a numerous force. Their position was carried, two guns captured, and their camp destroyed. Colonel Powell was killed. In consequence of our force being done up by forced marches, it was unable to pursue the enemy, but went into Cawnpore the following day with the wounded. The Banda mutineers appear to have left the Futtehpore district.
    Leone Levi, *Annals of British Legislation*, p.329, vol. v, Smith, Elder & Co., London, 1859.

31. Ibid p.333.

32. When the detachment of which my company formed part, marched through Futtehpore, it was rumoured that the Banda and Dinapore mutineers, joined by large bodies of budmadshes, numbering over ten thousand men, with three batteries of regular artillery, mustering eighteen guns, had crossed the Jumna, and were threatening our communications with Allahabad.
    William Forbes-Mitchell, *Reminiscences of the Great Mutiny, 1857–59*, p.13, MacMillan and Co., 1895, London.

33. Leone Levi, *Annals of British Legislation*, p.332, vol. v, Smith, Elder & Co., London, 1859.

34. McLeod Innes, *Lucknow & Oude in the Mutiny: A Narrative and a Study*, p.261, A.D. Innes and Co., London, 1859.

35. Ibid.

Notes to pages 175–182

36. Leone Levi, *Annals of British Legislation*, p.332, vol.v, Smith, Elder & Co., London, 1859.
37. Ibid p.333.
38. Ibid.
39. Ibid.
40. Amaresh Misra, *War of Civilizations: India AD 1857, Amaresh Misra, The Long Revolution*, (vol. ii), p.1303, Rupa and Co.
41. George Dodd, *The History of the Indian Revolt and of the Expeditions to Persia, China, and Japan, 1856–7–8*, p.380, W. and R. Chambers, 1859.
42. Leone Levi, *Annals of British Legislation*, p.332, vol. v, Smith, Elder & Co., London, 1859.
43. George Dodd, *The History of the Indian Revolt and of the Expeditions to Persia, China, and Japan, 1856–7–8*, p.380, W. and R. Chambers, 1859.
44. Ibid.
45. *Freedom Struggle in UP*, p.258, vol.ii, Information Department, Lucknow, Uttar Pradesh, 1958.
46. Ibid pp.258–9.
47. Charles Ball, *The History of the Indian Mutiny*, p.246, vol.ii, The London Printing and Publishing Company, 1858.

Chapter 13
NUCLEAR DEFENSE

1. McLeod Innes, *Lucknow & Oude in the Mutiny: A Narrative and a Study*, p.265, A.D. Innes and Co., London, 1895.
2. Freedom Struggle in UP, p.218, vol. iii, Information Department, Lucknow, Uttar Pradesh, 1959.
3. Ibid p.215.
4. Ibid p.220.
5. A simple litter used to transport the wounded.
6. *Freedom Struggle in UP*, p.242, vol.iii, Information Department, Lucknow, Uttar Pradesh, Lucknow, 1959.
7. Ibid.
8. *Encyclopedia Britannica*, A Dictionary of Arts, Sciences, Literature and General Information, Eleventh Edition, p.131, vol. xv, New York, Encyclopedia Britannica Company, 1911.
9. Ibid.
10. http://en.wikipedia.org/wiki/Central_India_Agency
11. http://en.wikipedia.org/wiki/Bundelkhand

Notes to pages 183–188

12. Leone Levi, *Annals of British Legislation*, p.334, vol. v, Smith, Elder & Co., London, 1859.

13. Most accounts simply Raja of Charkhari as the Raja of Charkhari, without using his name – Ratan Singh. Charkhari was a sanad states under the Bundelkhand Agency in Central India. *Freedom Struggle in UP*, p.ii, vol.iii, Information Department, Lucknow, Uttar Pradesh, 1959.

14. 24 December 1857 – Banda.—Major Ellis expected the Nawab of Banda to wait on him at Kallinger, but he failed to do so. It is said that both the Nawab and Narain Ram are collecting revenue in different pergunnahs of the Banda district. The district of Humeerpore continues somewhat disturbed. The Political Agent at Bundelcund has called upon the Rajah of Chirkaree, urging him to employ his troops for the maintenance of British authority
Leone Levi, *Annals of British Legislation*, p.334, vol.v, Smith, Elder & Co., London, 1859.

15. *Freedom Struggle in UP*, Information Department, pp.458-9, vol.i, Lucknow, Uttar Pradesh, 1957.

16. Ibid p.387, vol. iii.

17. Ibid p.56, vol. iii.

18. Ibid p.54, vol. iii.

19. Ibid p.67, vol. iii.

20. Ibid p.64, vol. iii.

21. Ibid p.113, vol. iii.

22. Ibid p.61, vol. iii.

23. Ibid p.71, vol. iii.

24. John Lang, *Wanderings in India: And Other Sketches of Life in Hindostan*, p.95, Routledge, Warne & Routledge, New York, 1861.

25. Leone Levi, *Annals of British Legislation*, p.419, vol.v, Smith, Elder & Co., London, 1859.

26. Freedom Struggle in UP, p.217, vol.iii, Information Department, Lucknow, Uttar Pradesh, 1959.

27. Ibid pp.221-2, vol. iii.

28. Ibid p.265, vol. iii.

29. Extract from Bundeli Letter no.8.

30. Ratan Singh's messengers met Tatya and reported that their Raja was offering rupees one lakh. Tatya declined the offer and asked the persons to return. Ibid p.231, vol. iii.

31. *Freedom Struggle in UP*, p.229, vol.iii, Information Department, Lucknow, Uttar Pradesh, 1959.

Notes to pages 188–193

32. Leone Levi, *Annals of British Legislation*, p.423, vol.v, Smith, Elder & Co., London, 1859.
33. *Freedom Struggle in UP*, p.229, vol.iii, Information Department, Lucknow, Uttar Pradesh.
34. Ibid p.266, vol. iii.
35. Tatya wrote to Nana Saheb asking him for a 'Parwana' against Chutta Singh if he chose to disobey any orders. *Freedom Struggle in UP*, p.266, vol.iii, Information Department, Lucknow, Uttar Pradesh, Lucknow, 1959.
36. *Freedom Struggle in UP*, p.265, vol.iii, Information Department, Lucknow, Uttar Pradesh, Lucknow, 1959.
37. Ibid p.260, vol. iii.
38. Ibid p.254, vol. iii.
39. Ibid pp.254-5, vol. iii.
40. Ibid p.264, vol. iii.
41. Ibid p.242, vol. iii.
42. The English 'loss' that was reported by the Assistant Magistrate in his report for rupees. Ibid p.241, vol. iii.
43. Ibid p.242, vol. iii.
44. Ibid p.243, vol. iii.
45. Ibid pp.244-5, vol. iii.
46. Ibid p.239, vol. iii.
47. All the guns were taken from the fort and the Ratan Singh was asked to join the efforts. Ibid p.288, vol. iii.
48. Ibid p.286, vol. iii.
49. Ibid p.297-9, vol. iii.
50. *Encyclopaedia Britannica*, 1911, Online Version
    http://www.1911encyclopedia.org/Hugh_Henry_Rose_Strathnairn
51. *Encyclopaedia Britannica*, 1911, Online Version
    http://www.1911encyclopedia.org/Hugh_Henry_Rose_Strathnairn
52. http://en.wikipedia.org/wiki/Hugh_Rose,_1st_Baron_Strathnairn
53. माझा प्रवास, **1857** च्या बंडाची हकीकत, कै. वे शा. सं. विष्णुभट गोडसे, Maza Pravas, Vishnubhat Godse, Venus Publishers, November 2000, p. 92–99
54. G.W. Forrest, *The Indian Mutiny 1857–1858*, p.43, vol.iv, first published London 1912, reprinted by Low Price Publications 2003.

Chapter 14
RECONSTRUCTING JHANSI

1. T. Rice Holmes, *A History of the Indian Mutiny*, p.622, Appendix Q, Macmillan and Co., London, 1904.
2. G.W. Forrest, *The Indian Mutiny 1857–1858*, p.49, vol.iv, first published London 1912, reprinted by Low Price Publications 2003.
3. Hamilton arrived at Talbahat on 14 March 1858; *Freedom Struggle in UP*, p.293, vol iii.
4. Freedom struggle in UP, pp.297-9, vol.iii, Information Department, Lucknow, Uttar Pradesh, Lucknow, 1959.
5. माझा प्रवास, 1857 च्या बंडाची हकीकत, कै. वे शा. सं. विष्णुभट गोडसे,, pp.81-2, Maza Pravas, Vishnubhat Godse, Venus Publishers, November 2000.
6. *Freedom Struggle in UP*, p.83, vol.iii, Information Department, Lucknow, Uttar Pradesh, Lucknow, 1959.
7. Ibid p.83, vol. iii.
8. Ibid p.vi, vol. iii.
9. G.W. Forrest, *The Indian Mutiny 1857–1858*, p.40, vol.iv, first published London 1912, reprinted by Low Price Publications 2003.
10. Ibid pp.40-1, vol.iv.
11. Ibid p.41, vol.iv.
12. माझा प्रवास, 1857 च्या बंडाची हकीकत, कै. वे शा. सं. विष्णुभट गोडसे, p.87, Maza Pravas, Vishnubhat Godse, Venus Publishers, November 2000.
13. *Freedom Struggle in UP*, p.310, vol.iii, Information Department, Lucknow, Uttar Pradesh, Lucknow, 1959.
14. After Charkhari the armies under Tatya Tope, the Rajas of Banpur and Shahgarh were focused on two targets Jhansi and Tehri. It is difficult to estimate exactly which forces went in what directions. The following excerpt from an English intelligence report provides some idea:
    It is reported that the insurgents left Chirkharee and expected at Goorsaray (Gur Sarai) on the 20th. This news is correct; about 800 foot-men from the force of the Marhattas (one regiment of the Gwalior contingents) have reached Bijeygurh. Kummod Singh reports from Oorcha that the Chiefs of Banpoor, and Nurwur have gone to Chirkaree to persuade the insurgents to attack Tehree...
    ...the insurgents after taking 18 guns, and six lac of Rupees and some troops from the Chirkaree Chief have come to-day to Kool Pahar (Kulpahar) thence they intend to proceed to Jaitpoor and Nayagong. From this is uncertain where they will go. Some say they will go to Jhansi, others give out they they will

move on Tehree. Shahghur Chief as well as the son of the Banpur Chief have joined the rebels. *Freedom Struggle in UP*, p.294-5, vol iii.

15. Ibid p.294, vol. iii.
16. Ibid p.305, vol. iii.
17. Ibid.
18. Ibid.
19. This is supported by an English intelligence report that says that 'these Chiefs (supporting Tatya) have very little ammunition, but Tantia and the sepoys at Kalpee have an abundance.'; p.306, vol iii.
20. माझा प्रवास, 1857 च्या बंडाची हकीकत, कै. वे शा. सं. विष्णुभट गोडसे, p.90, Maza Pravas, Vishnubhat Godse, Venus Publishers, November, 2000.
21. Considering that all the areas east of Jhansi were now controlled by Indians the English lines of communication were probably disrupted, it is possible that Hugh Rose might not have had detailed information from these reports.
22. Freedom Struggle in UP, p.306, vol.iii, Information Department, Lucknow, Uttar Pradesh, 1959.
23. Ibid p.305, vol. iii.
24. Ibid p.306, vol. iii.
25. माझा प्रवास, 1857 च्या बंडाची हकीकत, कै. वे शा. सं. विष्णुभट गोडसे, p.87, Maza Pravas, Vishnubhat Godse, Venus Publishers, November, 2000.
26. *Freedom Struggle in UP*, p.307, vol.iii, Information Department, Uttar Pradesh, Lucknow, 1959.
27. Ibid p.322, vol.iii.
28. Ibid p.289, vol.iii.
29. Blackwood's *Edinburgh Magazine*, p.173, vol. 88 (538) August 1860.
30. Urdu Letter 69, dated 9 February 1858.
31. माझा प्रवास, 1857 च्या बंडाची हकीकत, कै. वे शा. सं. विष्णुभट गोडसे, p.83, Maza Pravas, Vishnubhat Godse, Venus Publishers, November, 2000.
32. *Freedom Struggle in UP*, p.322, vol.iii, Information Department, Lucknow, Uttar Pradesh, 1959.
33. Ibid p.312, vol.iii.
34. Ibid.
35. Ibid.
36. Ibid.
37. Ibid.
38. http://www.copsey-family.org/~allenc/lakshmibai/mutiny.html (Section – The Siege of Jhansi)
39. Freedom Struggle in UP, p.323, vol.iii, Information Department, Lucknow, Uttar Pradesh, 1959.

40. माझा प्रवास, 1857 च्या बंडाची हकीकत, कै. वे शा. सं. विष्णुभट गोडसे, p.87, Maza Pravas, Vishnubhat Godse, Venus Publishers, November, 2000.

41. *Freedom Struggle in UP*, p.320, vol.iii, Information Department, Lucknow, Uttar Pradesh, 1959.

42. Godse refers to the Vilayati's as Rani's security force. Hugh Rose refers to a Hamilton report of the presence of Vilayati's inside the fort's defenses, and lumps them with Bundelas in a highly exaggerated figure. G.W. Forrest, *The Indian Mutiny 1857–1858*, p.42, vol.iv, first published London 1912, reprinted by Low Price Publications 2003.

43. *Freedom Struggle in UP*, p.323, vol.iii, Information Department, Lucknow, Uttar Pradesh, 1959.

44. In the narrative of Lakshmibai's heroism, her 'escape,' was achieved by a jump that she made with her horse from the wall of the fort. Only the western walls, which coincide with the city walls, would allow direct access outside the city. However, the wall is too high for any horse to survive a jump. Additionally, even if a horse had miraculous survived the jump, the south and the west is where Rose had maintained a strong presence. It would have been suicide to head in that direction.

    Though historically inaccurate, the arrival of Tatya Tope's army and her 'jump' is poetically presented in this Marathi verse.

    उत्तरेस धुरळा दिसतो आशेनी राणी पाहे
    तात्या टोपे आले का उत्कंठा लागुन् राहे
    तो तात्या आले आले आनंद गडातुन माये
    टोप्यानी टोपीवाले समशेरी वरती धरिले
    फेकला तटावरूनी घोडा...

    The following is a rough translation...

    Rani looked to the north hoping to see a dust storm from an approaching army... Has Tatya Tope arrived? She asked eagerly... she was elated, when she received the news of his approach. While, Tatya was engaging the English... She jumped with her horse from the rampart of the fort...

    Although Kalpi was the operational headquarters, Tatya Tope and his army came arrived from the east, not north.

45. माझा प्रवास, 1857 च्या बंडाची हकीकत, कै. वे शा. सं. विष्णुभट गोडसे, p.90, Maza Pravas, Vishnubhat Godse, Venus Publishers, November 2000.

    Godse describes the scene as follows:

    'The English got the Indian workers and camp followers to carry stacks of wet grass and deliver it to the mound. These were then stacked up and used by the English to climb over the wall'.

Notes to pages 208–214

By using Indian workers, they put the defenders in Jhansi in a difficult position of shooting at their own people.

46. *Freedom Struggle in UP*, p.324, vol.iii, Information Department, Lucknow, Uttar Pradesh, 1959.

47. माझा प्रवास, 1857 च्या बंडाची हकीकत, कै. वे शा. सं. विष्णुभट गोडसे, p.95, Maza Pravas, Vishnubhat Godse, Venus Publishers, November, 2000.

48. G.W. Forrest, *The Indian Mutiny 1857–1858*, p.49, vol.iv, first published London 1912, reprinted by Low Price Publications, 2003.

49. Letter from Captain F.W. Pinkney, superintendent of Jhansi, to W. Muir, secretary to the government of the N.W.P., April 7, 1858 – Vol iii, p. 324

50. माझा प्रवास, 1857 च्या बंडाची हकीकत, कै. वे शा. सं. विष्णुभट गोडसे, pp.90-2, Maza Pravas, Vishnubhat Godse, Venus Publishers, November, 2000.

51. माझा प्रवास, 1857 च्या बंडाची हकीकत, कै. वे शा. सं. विष्णुभट गोडसे,pp.97-8, Maza Pravas, Vishnubhat Godse, Venus Publishers, November, 2000.

52. माझा प्रवास, 1857 च्या बंडाची हकीकत, कै. वे शा. सं. विष्णुभट गोडसे, p.99-100, Maza Pravas, Vishnubhat Godse, Venus Publishers, November, 2000.

53. माझा प्रवास, 1857 च्या बंडाची हकीकत, कै. वे शा. सं. विष्णुभट गोडसे, pp.92-4, Maza Pravas, Vishnubhat Godse, Venus Publishers, November, 2000.

54. माझा प्रवास, 1857 च्या बंडाची हकीकत, कै. वे शा. सं. विष्णुभट गोडसे, p.100, Maza Pravas, Vishnubhat Godse, Venus Publishers, November, 2000.

55. माझा प्रवास, 1857 च्या बंडाची हकीकत, कै. वे शा. सं. विष्णुभट गोडसे, pp.101-2, Maza Pravas, Vishnubhat Godse, Venus Publishers, November, 2000.

56. G.W. Forrest, *The Indian Mutiny 1857–1858*, p.52, vol.iv, first published London 1912, reprinted by Low Price Publications, 2003.

57. *Freedom Struggle in UP*, p.330, vol.iii, Information Department, Lucknow, Uttar Pradesh, 1959.

58. माझा प्रवास, 1857 च्या बंडाची हकीकत, कै. वे शा. सं. विष्णुभट गोडसे, p.84, Maza Pravas, Vishnubhat Godse, Venus Publishers, November, 2000.

59. G.W. Forrest, *The Indian Mutiny 1857-1858*, p.48, vol.iv, first published London 1912, reprinted by Low Price Publications, 2003.

60. Ibid p.52, vol.iv.

61. Ibid.

62. Mahasweta Devi, *The Queen of Jhansi*, p.185.

63. Ibid p.189.

64. Letter from Captain F.W. Pinkney, superintendent of Jhansi, to W. Muir, secretary to the government of the N.W.P, April 7, 1858 – *Freedom Struggle in UP*, p.322, vol.iii, Information Department, Lucknow, Uttar Pradesh, 1959.

Notes to pages 214–222

65. We arrive at this figure using the price of gold as a measure of inflation. Gold was about Rs. 30/tola in 1858. In 2007–2008 it average about Rs. 12,000.tola, which makes the inflation factor about 400.

66. *Freedom Struggle in UP*, p.356, vol.iii, Information Department, Lucknow, Uttar Pradesh, 1959.

67. Ibid p.359, vol.iii.

68. Ibid pp.360-1, vol. iii.

69. Ibid p.362, vol. iii.

70. Ibid p.376, vol. iii.

71. Ibid p.414, vol. iii.

72. Ibid p.370, vol. iii.

73. Ibid p.369, vol. iii.

74. Again, English estimates of 3,000 are exaggerated, considered earlier accounts placed them at about 1,000. Ibid p.369, vol. iii.

75. Ibid p.382, vol. iii.

76. Ibid p.387, vol. iii.

77. Ibid p.385, vol. iii.

78. Ibid p.360, vol. iii.

79. One 18–pounder, one brass 8–inch mortar and two brass 9–pounder guns were found; p.385, vol. Iii.

80. Ibid p.444, vol.iii.

81. Either Chaursi or Chaurasi Gumbuz, ibid p.372, vol. iii.

82. Ibid p.378, vol. iii.

83. Ibid p.446, vol. iii.

84. Ibid.

Chapter 15
REVERSAL OF FORTUNES

1. Samuel Charters Macpherson, *Memorials of Service in India*, p.322, John Murray, 1865.

2. John Malcolm Forbes Ludlow, *British India*, pp.253-4, Macmillan, 1858.

3. Samuel Charters Macpherson, *Memorials of Service in India*, p.342, John Murray, 1865.

4. Ed. by William Haig Miller, *The Leisure Hour*, p.378, James Macaulay, William Stevens, 1876.

5. C.H. Forbes-Lindsay, Charles Harcourt Ainslie Forbes-Lindsay, *India, Past and Present*, p.171, John C. Winston, 1903.

6. Mukund Wamanrao Burway, *Life of the Honourable Rajah, Sir Dinkar Rao: K.C.S.I., Musheer-i-khas Muntazim Bahadur*, p.66, Tatva-Vivechaka, Bombay, 1907.

Notes to pages 222–228

7. Ibid p.85.

8. Elie Kedourie, p.415, *Nationalism In Asia And Africa*, Routledge, 1971.

9. Sailendranath Sen, *History: Modern India*, p.96, New Age, 2003.

10. Exact quote: 'If Scindia had failed us...'
   George Dodd, *The History of the Indian Revolt and of the Expeditions to Persia, China, and Japan, 1856–7–8*, p.188, W. and R. Chambers, 1859.

11. S.N. Sen, *Eighteen Fifty-Seven*, p.291, New Delhi, 1957.

12. Blackwood's *Edinburgh Magazine*, p.173, vol. 88 (538) August 1860.

13. Ibid p.409, vol iii.

14. Ibid p.173, vol. 88 (538) August 1860.

15. *The Revolt in Central India, 1857–59*, p.12, Intelligence Branch, Army Head Quarters, India, Simla, 1908.

16. William Dalrymple, *The Last Mughal*, p.300, Alfred A. Knopf, New York, 2007.

17. Ibid p.294.

18. G.W. Forrest, *Life of Field-Marshal Sir Neville Chamberlain*, p.172, William Blackwood and Sons, Edinburgh, 1909.

19. Assuming about 800–1000 men per Infantry regiment and 400–600 men per Cavalry regiment the total strength was about – 6,000–8,200.

20. Robert Chambers, Thomas Thomson, A Biographical Dictionary of Eminent Scotsmen, p.84, *Blackie and Son*, 1870, Scotland.

21. G.W. Forrest, *The Indian Mutiny 1857–1858*, p.131, vol. iv, first published London 1912, reprinted by Low Price Publications 2003.

22. *Freedom Struggle in UP*, p.444, vol.iii, Information Department, Uttar Pradesh, Lucknow, 1959.

23. Ibid p.409, vol. iii.

24. G.W. Forrest, *The Indian Mutiny 1857–1858*, p.130, vol.iv, first published London 1912, reprinted by Low Price Publications, 2003.

25. Rao Saheb's declaration at Gwalior, June 1858. Dr. Moti Lal Bhargava, *Architects of Indian Freedom Struggle*, p.91, Deep and Deep Publications, New Delhi, 1981.

26. G.W. Forrest, *The Indian Mutiny 1857–1858*, p.130, vol.iv, first published London 1912, reprinted by Low Price Publications, 2003.

27. Ibid.

28. Freedom Struggle in UP, p.447, vol.iii, Information Department, Lucknow, Uttar Pradesh, 1959.

29. Ibid.

30. Ibid.

31. Ibid p.449, vol. iii.

Notes to pages 228–232

32. 'Whilst far out of range and sight of the rebels, Scindia's Artillery halted and roared. Then it ceased firing and advanced. The rebels were on the move, and it is said, drew back in alarm at the great show of attack. But the Rao and Topeh implored them to make the experiment of a charge. They threw forward Infantry which skirmished up to Scindia's front; and then a Troop of the 5th Irregulars rode, first towards Scindia's centre and then to his left, the two point at which the men of our provinces were massed. After a brief mock-fight Scindia's troops fraternized with the rebels.' Ibid p.454, vol.iii.

33. G. . Forrest, *The Indian Mutiny 1857-1858*, p.130, vol.iv, first published London, 1912, reprinted by Low Price Publications 2003.

34. *Freedom Struggle in UP*, p.454, vol.iii, Information Department, Lucknow, Uttar Pradesh, 1959.

35. Ibid p.416, vol. iii.

36. Ibid p.413, vol. iii.

37. Ibid p.416, vol. iii.

38. Ibid p.414, vol. iii.

39. Ibid p.416, vol. iii.

40. Ibid p.414, vol. iii.

41. Rao Saheb's declaration at Gwalior, June 1858. Dr. Moti Lal Bhargava, *Architects of Indian Freedom Struggle*, p.91, Deep and Deep Publications, New Delhi, 1981.

42. Freedom Struggle in UP, p.421, vol.iii, Information Department, Lucknow, Uttar Pradesh, 1959.

43. Ibid p.418, vol.iii.

44. Ibid p.424, vol.iii.

45. Ibid p.426, vol.iii.

46. Ibid.

47. Ibid p.429, vol. iii.

48. Ibid p.426, vol.iii.

49. 'In your country I have found no supplies. Here have I found none. Our trouble is thence, great. I shall halt tomorrow at Gwalior. As it shall be settled after we shall meet, so shall it be. What shall be, hereafter, shall be according to our council upon meeting.' Ibid p.449, vol.iii.

50. Ibid p.462, vol. iii.

51. Charles Ball, The History of the Indian Mutiny, p.352, vol.II, The London Printing and Publishing Company, 1858.

52. *Freedom Struggle in UP*, p.462, vol.iii, Information Department, Lucknow, Uttar Pradesh, 1959.

Notes to pages 232–239

53. Charles Ball, *The History of the Indian Mutiny*, p.352, vol.II, The London Printing and Publishing Company, 1858.
54. *Freedom Struggle in UP*, p.426, vol.iii, Information Department, Lucknow, Uttar Pradesh, 1959.
55. Ibid p.459, vol.iii.
56. Ibid p.450, vol. iii.
57. Ibid p.452, vol. iii.
58. Ibid.
59. Ibid p.442, vol. iii.

Chapter 16
REIGNITING FREEDOM

1. Wheat/Rice – Rs.3.75/maund (approximated from pages 5 and 19 for wheat and rice –
   http://www.nuffield.ox.ac.uk/users/studer/files/India and the Grea Divergence.pdf
   1 Maund = 37.5 kg approximately – Rs. 0.10/kg
   Assume 1 kg grain per person/day – Rs. 3/month
   Assume other food per persom/day – Rs 2/month
   Assume 1:1 camp followers
   Assume 15% cavalry
   Cavalry payroll – Rs 30/month
   Infantry payroll – Rs. 12/month (History of the Indian mutiny, 1857–(1859), vol. iii, G.B. Malleson, W.H. Allen, 1880, London, p. 327)
   Camp follower payroll – Rs 5/month
   Per 1000 troops rate
   Payroll – 850*12 + 150*30 + 1000 * 5 = approx. Rs. 20,000
   Food – 2000 * 5 = Rs. 10,000
   Transportation and other logistics– Rs. 15,000
   Military logistics, ammunition – Rs. 15,000
   Total – burn rate for 1,000 soldiers – Rs. 60,000 per month
2. *Freedom Struggle in UP*, p.459, vol.iii, Information Department, Lucknow, Uttar Pradesh, 1959.
3. Blackwood's *Edinburgh Magazine*, p.174, vol. 88 (538) August 1860.
4. Ibid.
5. Ibid.
6. Ibid.
7. Ibid.

Notes to pages 239–243

8. Blackwood's *Edinburgh Magazine*, p.175, vol. 88 (538) August 1860.
9. Ibid p.174.
10. Ibid p.175.
11. *Freedom Struggle in UP*, Information Department, Lucknow, Uttar Pradesh, 1959.
12. Ibid pp.487-8, vol. iii.
13. The reference below claims three thousand miles. However, as a later chapter discusses Tatya's campaign came to an end earlier than the standard narrative.
    Blackwood's *Edinburgh Magazine*, p.172, vol. 88 (538) August 1860.
14. Freedom struggle in UP, p.471, vol.iii, Information Department, Lucknow, Uttar Pradesh, 1959.
15. The extent of confusion in the English camp is evident from the spies that reported him to be at Sarmathura, yet the English maps and correspondences were unable to locate the place. Turned out that without standardized spelling and an inability to pronounce the names of villages, the town was spelled varyingly as 'Sree Muttree, Seer Muttree, Sree Muttra and Sir Muttree.'
    One of the daily English bulletins that were sent out notes that 'the maps of Dholpoor and Kerowlee are apt to mislead. The tract of which Sree Muttra is the centre was formerly a part of Kerowlee, but it was transferred to Dholpur some years back.' Ibid p.471, vol.iii.
16. Ibid pp.473-4, vol.iii.
17. 24 June 1858, Tatya Tope with seven thousand, at (Sreee Muttree, Sree Muttra, Sir Muttree); ibid pp.471-2, vol.iii.
    25 June 1858; pp.471-3, vol.iii, (Muchulpoor, Muchilpore, Muchalpore)
    26 June–28 June 1858, Taken 4 guns; ibid pp.473-4, vol. iii, (Hindown).
18. 2 July 1858, Newalee and Barninwass; ibid p.475, vol. iii, p 475; 3 July 1858, Lalsoont; ibid p.475, vol.iii; 7 July 1858, Captain Eden at Gurhwass; ibid p.478, vol.iii; 4 July 1858, English receive false intelligene on Tatya's move on Jaipur (Thatsoo); ibid, p.476, vol.iii; 4 July 1858, General Roberts at Sagarair, ibid; 6 July 1858, General Roberts, ibid, p.477, vol.iii; 8 July 1858, Captain Eden at Ghoonsee, ibid p.478, vol.iii; 9 July 1858, Captain Eden at Deengurthal, ibid p.479, vol.iii; 10 July 1858, Captain Eden, ibid p.481, vol.iii; 6 July 1858, Tatya Tope at Jullai, ibid p.478, vol.iii; 11 July 1858, Captain Eden at Tonk, ibid p.482, vol.iii; 13 July 1858, General Roberts at Tonk, ibid p.482, vol.iii.
19. G.B. Malleson, *History of the Indian Mutiny, 1857–1859*, p.319, vol.iii, W.H. Allen & Co, London, 1880.
20. *Freedom Struggle in UP*, p.479, vol.iii, Information Department, Lucknow, Uttar Pradesh, 1959.

Notes to pages 243–249

21. Ibid.
22. Ibid p.481, vol.iii.
23. Ibid.
24. Ibid p.482, vol.iii.
25. 11 July 1858, at Junder Barwara; p.482, vol.iii; 12 July 1858 at Kushtala.
26. 15 July 1858, p.483, vol.iii; (Indurgurh); 16 July 1858, ibid, (Lackaria); 17 July 1858, ibid, (Gonowlee); 17 July 1858, ibid, p.484, vol.iii, (Kutgurh/Kathgarh).
27. *Freedom Struggle in UP*, p.485, vol.iii, Information Department, Lucknow, Uttar Pradesh, 1959.
28. Ibid p.484, vol. iii.
29. G.B. Malleson, *History of the Indian Mutiny, 1857–1859*, p.320, vol.iii, W.H. Allen & Co, London, 1880.
30. *Freedom Struggle in UP*, p.485, vol.iii, Information Department, Lucknow, Uttar Pradesh, 1959.
31. G.B.Malleson, *History of the Indian Mutiny, 1857–1859*, p.320, vol.iii, W.H. Allen & Co, London, 1880.
32. *Freedom Struggle in UP*, p.485, vol.iii, Information Department, Lucknow, Uttar Pradesh, 1959.
33. Blackwood's *Edinburgh Magazine*, p.175, vol. 88 (538) August 1860.
34. G.B. Malleson, *History of the Indian Mutiny, 1857–1859*, p.320, vol.iii, W.H. Allen & Co, London, 1880.
35. Ibid.
36. *Freedom Struggle in UP*, p.490, vol.iii, (Bunaira), Information Department, Lucknow, Uttar Pradesh, 1959.
37. Ibid.
38. Goerge W. Forrest, *A History of the Indian Mutiny, 1857–58*, p.578, Asian Educational Services, 2006.
39. *Freedom struggle in UP*, pp.487-8, vol.iii, Information Department, Lucknow, Uttar Pradesh, 1959.
40. Blackwood's *Edinburgh Magazine*, .p.178, vol. 88 (538) August 1860.
41. Ibid.
42. *Freedom Struggle in UP*, pp.491-3, vol.iii, Information Department, Lucknow, Uttar Pradesh, 1959.
43. George Dodd, *The History of the Indian Revolt*, p.557, London, W and R Chambers, 1859.
44. *Freedom Struggle in UP*, p.491, vol.iii, Information Department, Lucknow, Uttar Pradesh, 1959.
45. Rutnaghur, Fourteen elephants and some camels; ibid, p.493, vol.iii,
46. Blackwood's *Edinburgh Magazine*, p.179, vol. 88 (538) August 1860.

Notes to pages 249–257

47. *Freedom Struggle in UP*, p.493, vol.iii, Information Department, Lucknow, Uttar Pradesh, 1959.
48. Ibid.
49. Blackwood's *Edinburgh Magazine*, p.180, vol. 88 (538) August 1860.
50. Near Sagoodar. George W. Forrest, *A History of the Indian Mutiny, 1857–58*, p.585, Asian Educational Services, 2006.
51. Garot, *Freedom Struggle in UP*, p.493, vol.iii, Information Department, Lucknow, Uttar Pradesh, 1959.
52. Blackwood's *Edinburgh Magazine*, p.181, vol. 88 (538) August 1860.
53. *Freedom Struggle in UP*, p.494, vol.iii, Information Department, Lucknow, Uttar Pradesh, 1959.
54. Blackwood's *Edinburgh Magazine*, p.181, vol. 88 (538) August 1860.
55. *Freedom Struggle in UP*, p.494, vol.iii, Information Department, Lucknow, Uttar Pradesh, 1959.
56. G.B. Malleson, *History of the Indian Mutiny, 1857–1859*, p.328, vol.iii, W.H. Allen & Co, London, 1880.
57. Gurrote, *Freedom Struggle in UP*, pp.497-8, vol.iii, Information Department, Lucknow, Uttar Pradesh, 1959.
58. Ougein, *Freedom Struggle in UP*, p.493, vol.iii, Information Department, Lucknow, Uttar Pradesh, 1959; Susnair, ibid, p.499, vol.iii.
59. Nalkerry, Blackwood's *Edinburgh Magazine*, p.181, vol. 88 (538) August 1860.
60. Chapeira, ibid.
61. Raghooghur, Bursud, Beowara, Beowrah; *Freedom Struggle in UP*, pp.497-9, vol. iii, Information Department, Lucknow, Uttar Pradesh, 1959.
62. Ibid p.497, vol. iii.
63. Raipore and Sohit; ibid.
64. Kichlepore and Rajghur; ibid, p.499, vol.iii.
65. Ibid, p.499, vol. iii.
66. George Dodd, *History of the Indian Revolt*, p.558, W and R Chambers, London, 1859.
67. G.B. Malleson, *History of the Indian Mutiny, 1857–1859*, p.329, vol.iii, W.H. Allen & Co, London, 1880.
68. *The Friend of India*, 'The Insurrection', p.893, 23 September 1858.
69. *Freedom Struggle in UP*, p.509, vol.iii, Information Department, Lucknow, Uttar Pradesh, 1959.
70. Ibid p.501, vol.iii.
71. George Dodd, *History of the Indian Revolt*, p.558, W and R Chambers, London, 1859.
72. Ibid.

Notes to pages 257–261

73. 29 September at Putchraj/Putchai, Esaufgarh/Eesaghur; *Freedom Struggle in UP*, p.509, vol.iii, Information Department, Lucknow, Uttar Pradesh, 1959.

74. Ibid.

75. George Dodd, *History of the Indian Revolt*,p.558, W and R Chambers, London, 1859.

76. Brigadier Smith at Niya Serai, General Michel at Sironj or Moghal Serai; *Freedom Struggle in UP*, p.508, vol.iii, Information Department, Lucknow, Uttar Pradesh, 1959.

77. Ibid.

78. For example, from Isagarh, Tatya sent a regiment of Cavalry to march north to Rannod (misspelt as Kanode) to 'plunder' the English treasury; ibid, p.509, vol.iii.

79. Shortly after taking Isagarh, Tatya divided his forces in either two or three. Many narratives are inconsistent about the movements of these newly divided columns. These columns were led by Tatya, Rao Saheb and the Nawab of Banda, to march the forces down both sides of Betwa. Our research indicates that Tatya went northeast towards Tal Behat while Rao Saheb went east towards Chanderi and the Nawab of Banda continued south. What is clear is that Michel's so called encounters and 'victory's' over Tatya were not relevant to Tatya's eventual march.

80. 6 October 1858, 800 Sowars gone to plunder Kanode; *Freedom Struggle in UP*, p.510, vol.iii, Information Department, Lucknow, Uttar Pradesh, 1959; 6 October 1858, Tatya Tope at, Pechore, ibid, p.510, vol.iii; 8 October 1858, Tatya Tope at Siras ghat, ibid, p.511, vol.iii.

81. 5 October 1858, Rao Saheb with most treasure left for Chanderi; 7-9 October 1858, attacked for 3 days then beaten off on the ninth...; 9 October 1858, at Serai, ibid, p.510, vol.iii.

82. There is conflicting information on how exactly the troops were split between Tatya, Rao Saheb and the Nawab of Banda. General Michel's false claims to excuse his inability to stop Tatya make decoding the events even more difficult.

83. George Dodd, *History of the Indian Revolt*, p.611, W and R Chambers, London, 1859.

84. *Freedom Struggle in UP*, p.518, vol.iii, Information Department, Lucknow, Uttar Pradesh, 1959.

85. Ibid p.517, vol.iii.

86. The following information amongst other was used in reconstructing the troop movements.

24 October 1858, General Michel at Malthone (estimated based on telegram date of 27 October), *Freedom Struggle in UP*, p.518, vol.iii, Information Department, Lucknow, Uttar Pradesh, 1959.

Tatya travelled south via Khimlassa, Karai, Roatghur, and Bilsa; ibid, p.517, vol. iii; 22 October 1858, G. Michel at Lullutpore, Blackwood's *Edinburgh Magazine*, p.183, vol. 88 (538) August 1860.

87. *Freedom Struggle in UP*, p.519, vol.iii, Information Department, Lucknow, Uttar Pradesh, 1959.

88. Charles Ball, *The History of the Indian Mutiny*, p.515, vol.II, The London Printing and Publishing Company, 1858.

89. Edward Rupert Humphreys, *Manual of British Government in India*, p.75, Longman, Brown, Green and Longmans, London, 1857.

90. Blackwood's *Edinburgh Magazine*, p.184, vol.88 (538) August 1860.

Chapter 17
FRACTIONAL FREEDOM

1. George Dodd, *History of the Indian Revolt*, p.612, W and R Chambers, London, 1859.

2. Ibid p.611–2.

3. Ibid p.611.

4. *Freedom Struggle in UP*, p.528, vol.iii, Information Department, Lucknow, Uttar Pradesh, 1959.

5. Ibid pp.525-6, vol.iii.

6. Ibid pp.528-9, vol.iii.

7. Ibid p.536, vol.iii.

8. Ibid, p.522, vol.iii.

9. Note in the original reference; ibid.

10. Ibid p.524, vol.iii.

11. Ibid p.546, vol.iii.

12. Kurgoon, Blackwood's *Edinburgh Magazine*, p.186, vol.88 (538) August 1860.

13. Ibid p.188.

14. Ibid p.186.

15. Ibid pp.185–186.

16. Ibid pp.185–187.

17. Ibid pp.185–186.

18. Tatya Tope in Khundwar, around 17 November 1858; *Freedom struggle in UP*, p.521, vol.iii, Information Department, Lucknow, Uttar Pradesh, 1959.

Notes to pages 274–282

Tatya Tope at Chickulda Maharashtra Archives, Bulletin of the Department of Archives, p.75, No. 5.

Main body of rebels at Piplode; ibid, p.521, vol.iii; 23 November, Tatya Tope, '6 miles north of Jeelwana', 24 November 1858, Tatya Tope at Rajpore; Blackwood's *Edinburgh Magazine*, p.186, vol. 88 (538) August 1860.

19. 28 November 1858, contribution of Rs. 5000 at Ali Rajpore; at Dewhuttee on 29 November, Maharashtra Archives, Bulletin of the Department of Archives, p.78, No. 5.

20. Ibid p.79; footnote.

21. Ibid.

22. 2-5 December 1858; Tatya Tope at Peiplode; *Freedom Struggle in UP*, p.540, vol.iii, Information Department, Lucknow, Uttar Pradesh, 1959; 1 December 1858, Tatya Tope at Bareiah; ibid, p.539, vol.iii; 1 December 1858, Tatya Tope at Babra; p.549, vol.iii.

23. Maharashtra Archives, Bulletin of the Department of Archives, p.79, No.5.

24. Item #13. Maharashtra Archives, Bulletin of the Department of Archives, p.111, No.5.

25. *Freedom Struggle in UP*, p.539, vol.iii, Information Department, Lucknow, Uttar Pradesh, 1959.

26. Blackwood's *Edinburgh Magazine*, pp.185-7, vol. 88 (538) August 1860.

27. Maharashtra Archives, Bulletin of the Department of Archives, p.114-5, No.5.
28. *Freedom Struggle in UP*, p.540, vol.iii, Information Department, Lucknow, Uttar Pradesh, 1959.

29. Maharashtra Archives, Bulletin of the Department of Archives, p.110, No.5.

30. Ibid, p.122, No.5.

31. Ibid, pp.126-7, No.5.

32. Charles Ball, *The History of the Indian Mutiny*, p.558, vol.ii, The London Printing and Publishing Company, 1858.

Chapter 18
FLICKER

1. George Dodd, *History of the Indian Revolt*, p.611, W and R Chambers, London, 1859.

2. G.B. Malleson, *History of the Indian Mutiny, 1857–1859*, p.359, vol.iii, W.H. Allen & Co, London, 1880.

3. Ibid, p.365, vol. iii.

4. Maharashtra Archives, Bulletin of the Department of Archives, p.125, No.5.

5. A straight line drawn from Godra to Kheirwara to Godra nearly intersects

all the places named and completely cuts of flight of the rebels to the West, while the Edur force supports all the posts mentioned on this line.

A line drawn from Godra to direct east as far as Jabbooa, cuts off the retrograde movement of the Rebels to the South. On this line we have Barrea, Dohud and Jabbooa all occupied with that brilliant officer Brigadier Parke ar Barrea this day.

For the other side of that triangle from Kheirwara to Jabbooa, I depend on the Malwa Troops. We know them to have been in great strength at Rutlam on the 5th and I trust they have advanced so far by this day as to almost have reached Jallode.

We know the enemy beyond a doubt plundered Limree on the 6th and was expected by the Jallode Thanadar to reach his post the next day...

6. Maharashtra Archives, Bulletin of the Department of Archives, p.109-111, No.5.

7. 6 December 1858, Tatya Tope at Leemree, Maharashtra Archives, Bulletin of the Department of Archives, p.125, No.5.

8. 7 December 1858, Tatya Tope at Jhullode, Maharashtra Archives, Bulletin of the Department of Archives, p.126, No.5.
    11 December 1858, English Godhra Detachment at Jhullode; *Freedom Struggle in UP*, p.541, vol.iii, Information Department, Lucknow, Uttar Pradesh, 1959. Captain Muter, Godhra attachment, left Godra and arrived at Peeplod on 7th and Dohad on 8th. By that time they had already 'plundered' Jhalod. Maharashtra Archives, Bulletin of the Department of Archives, pp.124-5, No.5; 10 December 1858, Captain Muter left Dahod.

9. Maharashtra Archives, Bulletin of the Department of Archives, p.126, No.5.

10. Ibid, p.117, No.5.

11. 11 December 1858, Tatya Tope at Banswarra; *Freedom Struggle in UP*, p.542, vol.iii, Information Department, Lucknow, Uttar Pradesh, 1959; at Sagwarra Maharashtra Archives, Bulletin of the Department of Archives, p.125, No.5.

12. 13 December 1858, Tatya Tope at Aspoor and Boreegaum, (incorrectly written as Aspeer and Boxigaum in the reference) heading towards Saloombeer on the, invitation of the Rawul of Solumbeer. Maharashtra Archives, Bulletin of the Department of Archives, p.108, No.5.

13. 'The threatening attitude assumed by the Chief of Saloombra, in concert with Bheendur, on the strength of the rebel force being encamped at his capital...'
    Charles Lionel Showers, *A Missing Chapter of the Indian Mutiny*, p.138, Longmans, Green, 1888.

Notes to pages 285–288

'Soloombar – Here Tantia obtained some supplies, of which he was greatly in need...'

G.B. Malleson, *History of the Indian Mutiny, 1857–1859*, p.356, vol.iii, W.H. Allen & Co, London, 1880.

14. 'Turning off at Geengla, he moved north-east on Bheendur.'; Charles Lionel Showers, *A Missing Chapter of the Indian Mutiny*, p.139, Longmans, Green, 1888.

15. 18 December near Durryawad, 20 December, left Mongoura for Peepulkhoota. Moved north to Sohagpur and finding the pass open marched on Pertaubgarh on the 24th; *Freedom Struggle in UP*, p.552, vol.iii, Information Department, Lucknow, Uttar Pradesh, 1959.

16. Maharashtra Archives, Bulletin of the Department of Archives, p.103, No.5.

17. 'I received intelligence that Tantia, with his whole force, then about 5000 strong, and accompanied by some 4000 Bheels under the Bheel Chiefs, who had given him refuge in their jungles, and had shown him the Pertabgurh Pass.' Charles Lionel Showers, *A Missing Chapter of the Indian Mutiny*, pp.14-1, Longmans, Green, 1888.

18. G.B. Malleson, *History of the Indian Mutiny, 1857–1859*, p.355, vol.iii, W.H. Allen & Co, London, 1880.

19. Footnote on p.143. Colonel Showers, rejects Malleson's claims about the Bhils being 'vultures,' but displays a rather competitive imagination himself, when he speculates that Tatya Tope had 'bribed the Bhils' for support. Charles Lionel Showers, *A Missing Chapter of the Indian Mutiny*, Longmans, Green, 1888.

20. G.B. Malleson, *History of the Indian Mutiny, 1857–1859*, p.357, vol.iii, W.H. Allen & Co, London, 1880.

21. Ibid.

22. Charles Lionel Showers, A Missing Chapter of the Indian Mutiny, p.143, (footnote), Longmans, Green, 1888.

23. Ibid p.142.

24. Charles Ball, The History of the Indian Mutiny, p.558, vol.ii, The London Printing and Publishing Company, 1858.

25. Ibid.

26. Blackwood's *Edinburgh Magazine*, p.189, vol. 88 (538) August 1860.

27. 26 December 1858, Tatya camped at Mullah, Freedom struggle in UP, Information Department, Uttar Pradesh, Lucknow, 1959, vol. iii, p. 552
December 26, 1858 '...marched upon Narghur.' Charles Ball, *The History of the Indian Mutiny*, p.558, vol.ii, The London Printing and Publishing Company; 1858
27 December 1858, crossed Chambal at Biswa, ibid. Tatya Camped at Dalpat,

Notes to pages 288–291

    Freedom Struggle in UP, p.553, vol.ii, Information Department, Lucknow, Uttar Pradesh, 1959.

28. *Freedom Struggle in UP*, p.553, vol.ii, Information Department, Lucknow, Uttar Pradesh, 1959.

29. Georgiana Theodosia Fitzmoor-Halsey Paget, Major Paget, *Camp and Cantonment: A Journal of Life in India in 1857–1859*, pp.450-1, Appendix, Longman, Green, Longman, Roberts, & Green, 1865.

30. Camp and Cantonment: A Journal of Life in India in 1857–1859, Mrs. Leopold Paget, Longman, Green, Longman, Roberts, & Green, 1865, Appendix Titled: A Short Narrative of the Pursuit of the Rebels in Central India, Major Leopold Grimston Paget, p. 453–4.

31. Camp and Cantonment: A Journal of Life in India in 1857–1859, Mrs. Leopold Paget, Longman, Green, Longman, Roberts, & Green, 1865, Appendix Titled: A Short Narrative of the Pursuit of the Rebels in Central India, Major Leopold Grimston Paget, pp. 456–7.

32. G.B. Malleson, *History of the Indian Mutiny, 1857–1859*, p.358, vol.iii, W.H. Allen & Co, London, 1880.

33. 'Somerset started at once, and marching seventy miles in forty-eight hours, came upon Tantia at Barod. After an action fought in the usual Tantia Topi style, the rebels fled to Nahargarh in the Kota territory. Here Tantia was fired at by the Kiladar. Moving out of range, he halted for the night. Rao Sahib then sent a messenger to summon Man Singh, who had appointed to meet him at this place. On Man Singh's arrival, the rebels moved to Paron, where they halted two days. They then pushed northwards towards Indragarh. On reaching the banks of the Chambal, Man Singh, for some unexplained reason, left them. On the 13th of January they reached Indragarh, where Firoz Shah, with his bodyguard and the 12th irregulars, met them.' Ibid, pp.358-9.

34. Main monsoon season July-September. October through December is the post-monsoon showers. Rarely heavy rains.

35. 'We halted three days at Burode, and heavy rain setting in, added greatly to our discomfort, being without tents or shelter of any kind. On January 4th we changed our ground to a place called Chubra, about ten miles off, where we remained till the 9th...'
Camp and Cantonment: A Journal of Life in India in 1857–1859, Mrs. Leopold Paget, Longman, Green, Longman, Roberts, & Green, 1865, Appendix Titled: A Short Narrative of the Pursuit of the Rebels in Central India, Major Leopold Grimston Paget, p. 457.

36. In the narrative that was presented by the English, both Man Singh and Tatya left Rao Saheb at separate times. Tatya Tope, apparently was 'tired' and left

Notes to pages 291–297

Rao Saheb near Sheopur. In all likelihood, it was Man Singh. G.B. Malleson, *History of the Indian Mutiny, 1857–1859*, p.358, vol.iii, W.H. Allen & Co, London, 1880.

37. Crossed Chambal near Lakerrie. With Firoz Shah at Indurghur. Ibid, pp.572-3, vol.ii.

38. Feroz Shah and Rao Saheb, on 11 January 1859 at Madhopore, 12 January 1859 at Bugwunghur, and on 13 January 1859, crossed the Banas; ibid, p.573, vol.ii.

39. Ibid, p.367, vol.iii.

40. Camp and Cantonment: A Journal of Life in India in 1857–1859, Mrs. Leopold Paget, Longman, Green, Longman, Roberts, & Green, 1865, Appendix Titled: A Short Narrative of the Pursuit of the Rebels in Central India, Major Leopold Grimston Paget, p. 456–467.

41. G.B. Malleson, *History of the Indian Mutiny, 1857–1859*, p.368, vol.iii, W.H. Allen & Co, London, 1880.

42. Charles Ball, *The History of the Indian Mutiny*, p.584, vol.ii, The London Printing and Publishing Company, 1858.

43. Ibid, p.593, vol.ii.

44. Ibid, p.583, vol.ii.

45. *Freedom Struggle in UP*, pp.561-3, vol.iii, Information Department, Lucknow, Uttar Pradesh, 1959.

46. John Lang, *Wanderings in India: And Other Sketches of Life in Hindostan*, p.411, Routledge, Warne & Routledge, New York, 1861.

47. Beni Madho or 'Bainie Madhoo' as his name was spelt by the English was in charge of a large body of troops that fought under Nana Saheb in Awadh. As Tatya crossed the Narmada, they continued to fight until they retreated into Nepal. The following are some references about 'Bainie' whose identity Lang confused with that of Tatya Tope. Charles Ball, *The History of the Indian Mutiny*, p.554, vol.ii, The London Printing and Publishing Company; 1858
Nelson Examiner and New Zealand Chronicle, p.2, vol. XVIII, Issue 40, 18 May 1859; Caleb Wright and J. A. Brainerd, *Historic Incidents and Life in India*, p.266, J.A. Brainerd, 1863.

48. *Freedom Struggle in UP*, p.530, vol.iii, Information Department, Lucknow, Uttar Pradesh, 1959.

49. Freedom Struggle in UP, pp.530-1, vol.iii, Information Department, Lucknow, Uttar Pradesh, 1959.

50. Camp and Cantonment: A Journal of Life in India in 1857–1859, Mrs Leopold Paget, Longman, Green, Longman, Roberts, & Green, 1865, Appendix Titled: A Short Narrative of the Pursuit of the Rebels in Central India, Major Leopold Grimston Paget, pp. 457-8.

420 / Tatya Tope's Operation Red Lotus

51. *Freedom Struggle in UP*, p.566, vol.iii, Information Department, Lucknow, Uttar Pradesh, 1959.

52. Ibid, p.567, vol.iii.

53. Charles Lionel Showers, *A Missing Chapter of the Indian Mutiny*, p.149-50, Longmans, Green, 1888.

54. Camp and Cantonment: A Journal of Life in India in 1857–1859, Mrs. Leopold Paget, Longman, Green, Longman, Roberts, & Green, 1865, Appendix Titled: A Short Narrative of the Pursuit of the Rebels in Central India, Major Leopold Grimston Paget, p.467.

EPILOGUE

1. The First Bengal famine was in 1778 when the English had newly conquered Bengal. The causes of the second Bengal famine have largely been attributed to English apathy. In the hundreds of pages of 'research' an Indian expert on the Bengal Famine chooses the fault English 'mismanagement' rather than a deliberate action to cut-off supplies to the region, on behalf of the English.

2. Anthony Read, David Fisher, *The Proudest Day: India's Long Road to Independence*, p.367–68, W.W. Norton & Company, 1998.

3. Ibid.

4. Asok Mitra, *Towards Independence, 1940–1947: Memoirs of an Indian Civil Servant*, pp.183-4, Popular Prakashan, 1991.

5. Anthony Read, David Fisher, *The Proudest Day: India's Long Road to Independence*, p.367–68, W.W. Norton & Company, 1998.

6. Ibid pp.368–369.

7. Ibid p.368.

8. Ibid pp.368–369.

9. Ibid.

10. Ibid.

11. Ed. Nicholas Mansergh, Penderal Moon, *Transfer of Power*, 1942-7, Vol vi, p.1010–1011, UBS Publishers, 1976.

12. Here is an example of how Indian soldiers inspired other in Africa. Geoffrey Aduamah was a soldier from Ghana who fought alongside Indians in World War II and was interviewed on American TV, PBS. He was greatly influenced by the Indian soldiers who were fighting in Africa during World War II. Q: During the Second World War, you fought alongside Indian soldiers. Did you have conversations about independence? What inspiration did you draw? Aduamah: Well, the Indians were very, very political. They were very political.

Notes to pages 306–316

We had conversations with some of them. Some actually didn't like fighting on the side of the British. But one particular matter happened in Durban when we were going to East Africa. We stopped at Durban – it is a big port in west South Africa and there was a big camp of all Commonwealth troops camped in there. They were taking them by ship to their destinations so we saw the Indian troops and also Indians resident in South Africa. Then we had conversation(s) with them, especially those Indians in South Africa. They said they thought we are coming to help them fight the whites. They said, 'Why are (you) fighting for Britain?' We say we are fighting for white freedom. So they ask us, 'Are you yourself free?' We say no. So they said, 'Fight for your freedom first. ' As I said, this had a very big impression on Gold Coasters, me especially. It had a big impression on me. I am fighting against somebody I don't know and the person who is using me to fight is the person who is oppressing me. So it had a big influence on me. We should fight for our freedom first from Britain before we fight for any other freedom.

http://www.pbs.org/wgbh/peoplescentury/episodes/freedomnow/aduamahtranscript.html

13. MaulanaAbul Kalam Azad, *India Wins Freedom*, p.145, Orient Longman, 1998. Maulana writes the date as 17 February, but it is obviously a mistake, since the announcement was on 19 February and not 17.

14. Anthony Read, David Fisher, *The Proudest Day: India's Long Road to Independence*, pp.368-9, W.W. Norton & Company, 1998.

15. Sardar Vallabhbhai Patel, ed. Pran Nath Chopra, *The Collected works of Sardar Vallabhbhai Patel*, Gandhi's statement dated 22 February 1946 on the RIN Disturbances, pp.188-9, Konark Publishers, 1997.

16. Ibid.

17. Ibid.

18. O.P. Ralhan, *Encyclopaedia of Political Parties*, p.580, Anmol Publications Pvt.. Ltd., 2002.

CONCLUSION

1. Edward Rupert Humphreys, *Manual of British Government in India*, p.70, Longman, Brown, Green and Longmans, London, 1857.

2. Ibid.

3. माझा प्रवास, 1857 च्या बंडाची हकीकत, कै. वे. शा. सं. विष्णुभट गोडसे, p.110, Maza Pravas, Vishnubhat Godse, Venus Publishers, November, 2000.

APPENDIX

1. S.N. Sen, *Eighteen Fifity Seven*, p.403.
2. American Psychological Association (APA):
conspiracy. (n.d.). Dictionary.com Unabridged (v 1.1). Retrieved 23 December 2006, from Dictionary.com website: http://dictionary.reference.com/browse/conspiracy
Modern Language Association (MLA):
'conspiracy.' Dictionary.com Unabridged (v 1.1). Random House, Inc. 23 December 2006. <Dictionary.com http://dictionary.reference.com/browse/conspiracy>
Chicago Manual Style (CMS):
conspiracy. Dictionary.com. Dictionary.com Unabridged (v 1.1). Random House, Inc. http://dictionary.reference.com/browse/conspiracy (accessed: 23 December 2006)

INDEX

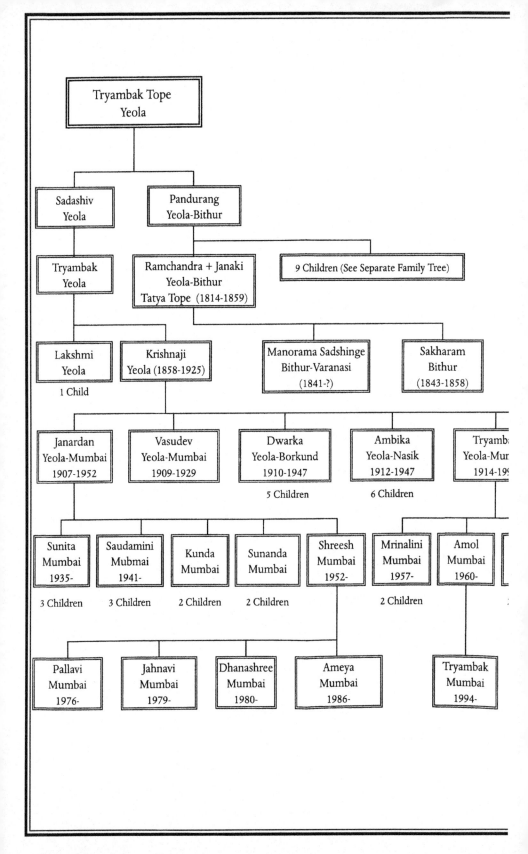

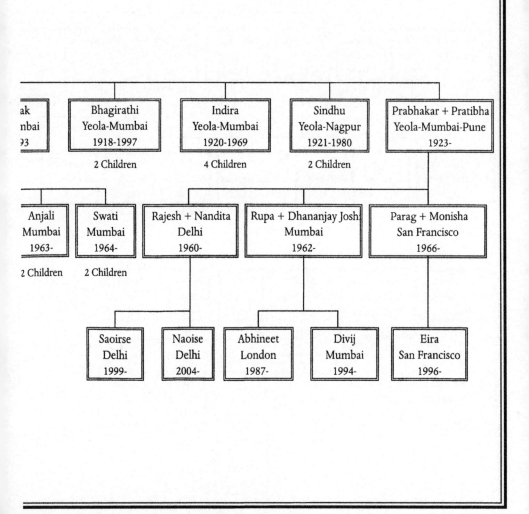

...ak ...mbai ...93	Bhagirathi Yeola-Mumbai 1918-1997	Indira Yeola-Mumbai 1920-1969	Sindhu Yeola-Nagpur 1921-1980	Prabhakar + Pratibha Yeola-Mumbai-Pune 1923-
	2 Children	4 Children	2 Children	

Anjali Mumbai 1963-	Swati Mumbai 1964-	Rajesh + Nandita Delhi 1960-	Rupa + Dhananjay Joshi Mumbai 1962-	Parag + Monisha San Francisco 1966-
2 Children	2 Children			

Saoirse Delhi 1999-	Naoise Delhi 2004-	Abhineet London 1987-	Divij Mumbai 1994-	Eira San Francisco 1996-

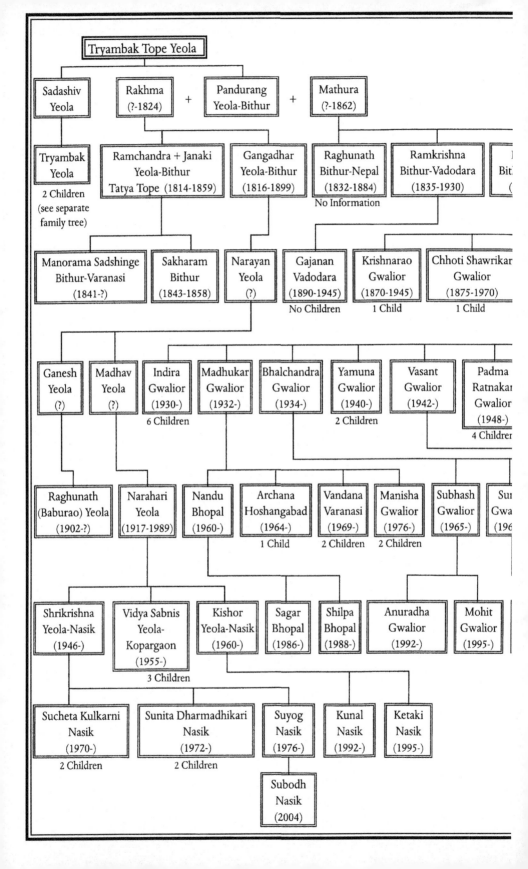

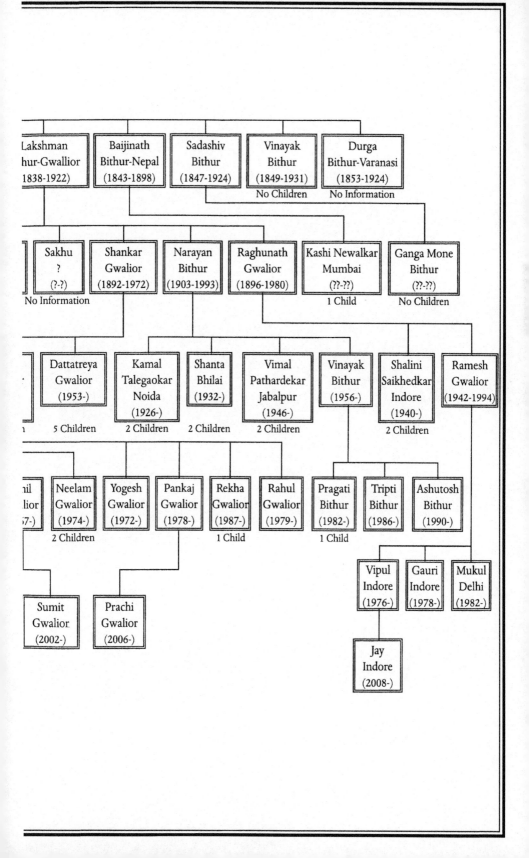